COMPENSATION FOR INDUSTRIAL INJURY

For My Parents
And To The Memory Of
My Grandfathers And Their
Experience of Industrial Injury

COMPENSATION FOR INDUSTRIAL INJURY

A guide to the revised scheme of
benefits for work accidents and diseases

by

RICHARD LEWIS

Faculty of Law
University College, Cardiff

PROFESSIONAL BOOKS LIMITED
1987

Published in 1987 by
Professional Books Limited,
Milton Trading Estate, Abingdon, Oxon.
I.S.B.N. 0 86205 214 9

Printed and bound in Great Britain
by Billing & Sons Limited, Worcester

OUTLINE OF CONTENTS

PREFACE

It is now almost forty years since responsibility for the administration of industrial injuries compensation lay in private hands. Largely run by insurance companies it then provided a meal ticket for certain lawyers. Litigation was so frequent that a new edition of Willis on *Workmen's Compensation* was published almost every year. The final edition was its 37th and contained 1200 closely printed pages offering a detailed analysis of the right to payment. The National Insurance (Industrial Injuries) Act 1946 replaced this privately administered system with a new scheme of benefits run by the state. This marked the end of both Willis and the extensive involvement of lawyers with this form of compensation. In part this was because the Act changed the usual forum for disputes: appeals are no longer heard by judges in the county courts, but are adjudicated by tribunals in which lay people participate. For a variety of reasons representation by lawyers before these tribunals has been rare. Although the absence of lawyers initially may have helped to avoid the excessive technicality and litigiousness which were features of the old system, it has also resulted in less investigation and writing upon the rules governing benefit. These failings have continued in spite of the rules becoming increasingly complex. They provide a further reason for suggesting, as did the Minister of Social Security recently, that compensation for industrial injury has become "something of a backwater".

In spite of the failure to explore fully the legal basis of the modern industrial scheme, it has remained a major source of compensation for injury. In many respects it is even more important than common law damages: the £400 million it pays out in benefit each year exceeds the total damages awarded by the tort system for all accidents causing personal injury, whether or not they are related to work. The stark contrast between the voluminous legal literature upon these common law claims on the one hand, and the almost entirely neglected area of industrial injuries benefit on the other, provided a major incentive for this book to be written. The rules are equally important and, if anything, even more complex. Because they have not been thoroughly examined for over forty years workers and their claims advisers, whether trade union officials, solicitors, or welfare rights workers, are in need of a detailed guide to these benefits. Officials of the DHSS, tribunal members and others concerned with the administration of the scheme may similarly welcome such assistance. The main aim of the book is to meet these needs.

There are two particular features of the book which may be mentioned here. It is one of the first publications to consider the Social Security Act 1986 which made major changes to the benefits system. Among these reforms, the book concentrates upon, firstly, the revision of the procedures governing the adjudication of all social security claims, and secondly, the changes specifically made to the benefits for industrial injury. The industrial scheme has received its most radical overhaul since it was established by the 1946 Act. The Government's belated decision to implement in its 1986 Act proposals which it had put forward five years earlier in its White Paper on the scheme, in effect, caused a second edition of this book to be written before there was a chance to send what would have been the first edition to the printers.

The other feature of the book which should be noted in this introduction is that it attempts to be as comprehensive an account of the scheme as is possible within the space available. In particular it refers to all the cases reported since the modern scheme began provided that they continue to be relevant to the present system. These cases include Commissioners' decisions from Northern Ireland, a jurisdiction sometimes overlooked in writings upon social security law. Reference is also made to many unreported cases although these are mostly confined to decisions made in the past ten years. The books aims to be up to date to the beginning of 1987. This means that the latest British Commissioner's decision considered is *R(I)1/86*, the latest Northern Ireland case is *R 12/84 (II)*, and the latest unreported case is *CI 67/85* (unreported).

Finally I must collectively thank many people who have advised and assisted me in writing this book. They have made my task so much easier and rewarding. This is more than any ritual acknowledgement of help: without these contributions this book would have assumed a different character. In particular, in so far as I have been able to describe how the scheme operates in practice I am indebted to a number of trade unionists, welfare workers, tribunal members and DHSS officials. Several of the latter were also helpful in providing unpublished statistical information. I could conclude simply by stating that it would be invidious for me to single out any particular person or group. However, one exception must be made: I owe the greatest debt to my wife Siân. It was her advice which enabled me to avoid errors in both the style and content of the manuscript. In particular her special skills were brought to bear upon the medical and forensic aspects of the scheme. Her final influence is less easily defined but much more important: this book reflects the love and support contained in our relationship.

THE CONTENTS OF EACH CHAPTER

TABLE OF CASES

TABLE OF REPORTED BRITISH COMMISSIONERS' DECISIONS

TABLE OF REPORTED NORTHERN IRELAND COMMISSIONERS' DECISIONS

TABLE OF UNREPORTED COMMISSIONERS' DECISIONS

TABLE OF STATUTES

TABLE OF STATUTORY INSTRUMENTS

LIST OF ABBREVIATIONS

Statutes

SSA   Social Security Act 1975 except where 1986 is added to refer to the Act of that year.

SSHBA   Social Security and Housing Benefits Act 1982

Regulations

Adj. Regs.   Social Security (Adjudication) Regulations 1984 (S.I. No. 451)

Benefit Regs.   Social Security (General Benefit) Regulations 1982 (S.I. No. 1408)

C P Regs.   Social Security (Claims and Payments) Regulations 1979 (S.I. No. 628)

P D Regs.   Social Security (Industrial Injuries) (Prescribed Diseases) Regulations 1985 (S.I. No. 967)

Book, Reports and Papers

Consultation paper   DHSS, *Industrial Injuries Scheme Consultation Paper* (1985)

Discussion document   DHSS, *Industrial Injuries Compensation A Discussion Document* (1980)

DHSS medical handbook   DHSS, *Industrial Injuries Handbook for Adjudicating Medical Authorities* (3rd ed. 1986)

White paper   *Reform of the Industrial Injuries Scheme* (Cmnd. 8402, 1981)

Pearson Commission   *Report of the Royal Commission on Civil Liability and Compensation for Personal Injury* (3 vols. Cmnd. 7054, 1978)

Willis   *Workmen's Compensation* (37th ed. 1945)

Other

AMA   Adjudicating Medical Authority

AO   Adjudication Officer

DHSS   Department of Health and Social Security

IIAC   Industrial Injuries Advisory Council

MAT   Medical Appeal Tribunal

REA   Reduced Earnings Allowance (formally special hardship allowance)

SSAT   Social Security Appeal Tribunal

Statutory authorities	AO, SSAT or Social Security Commissioner in determining questions other than either (1) medical questions reserved for an AMA, or (2) a question reserved for the Secretary of State
(T)	Decision of a tribunal of Commissioners
TUC	Trades Union Congress

CHAPTER 1

INTRODUCTION TO THE INDUSTRIAL SCHEME

1. AN OUTLINE OF THE SCHEME

The structure of this book broadly falls into three parts. It considers, first, the basic conditions of entitlement under the industrial injuries scheme; second, the nature of the benefits it offers; and finally, so as to adopt the chronological order, the claim for benefit, adjudication upon it, and the amount of payment that may result. This division is maintained in the brief outline which follows. Its purpose is to provide a bird's-eye view of the scheme, and to indicate the contents of succeeding chapters.

(1) Conditions of entitlement

Each day of their working lives 21 million people are covered by the industrial injuries scheme in that, if they were to suffer a work accident or disease, the scheme could provide them with compensation. For many it would be their most important source of income. People are covered by the scheme from their first day at work. They do not have to qualify, as they do for other benefits, by paying a minimum number of national insurance contributions. However, they must be "employed earners", and this excludes from the scheme the two and a half million self-employed (chapter 2).

The scheme covers only those injuries which occur after 4 July 1948. Earlier accidents or diseases are still governed by the workmen's compensation legislation (chapter 11). Injuries within the modern scheme fall into one of two groups. A claimant must suffer:

either (*a*) from "a personal injury caused . . . by accident arising out of and in the course of his employment" (chapter 3);

or (*b*) from a "prescribed disease", meaning that it must appear on a legislative list specifying certain medical conditions as risks for particular occupations (chapter 4).

A final basic condition of entitlement is that as a result of the injury the claimant suffers from a "loss of physical or mental faculty" causing him to be medically assessed as having some degree of disablement. The assessment is made by comparing the claimant to a person of the same age and sex who is of normal health. The difference is expressed as a percentage and this constitutes the degree of disablement. Although the medical authorities are given a great deal of discretion in making this assessment, the legislation offers suggestions as to the percentages to be applied for certain disabilities, especially for anatomical losses (chapter 5).

WHICH INDUSTRIAL INJURIES BENEFIT TO CLAIM
BEFORE THE 1986 ACT COMES INTO FORCE?

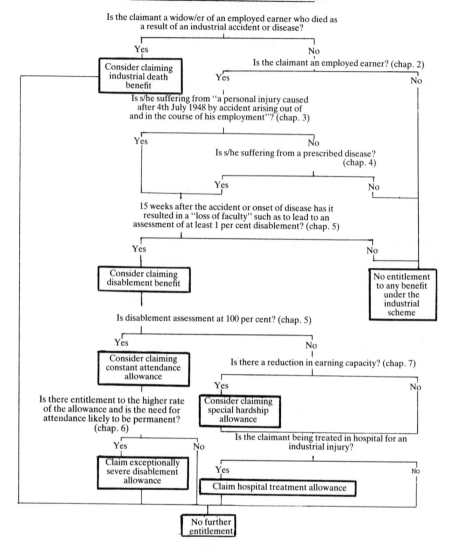

Is the claimant a widow/er of an employed earner who died as a result of an industrial accident or disease?

Yes — Consider claiming industrial death benefit

No — Is the claimant an employed earner? (chap. 2)

Yes — Is s/he suffering from "a personal injury caused after 4th July 1948 by accident arising out of and in the course of his employment"? (chap. 3)

No

Yes

No — Is s/he suffering from a prescribed disease? (chap. 4)

Yes

No

15 weeks after the accident or onset of disease has it resulted in a "loss of faculty" such as to lead to an assessment of at least 1 per cent disablement? (chap. 5)

Yes — Consider claiming disablement benefit

No — No entitlement to any benefit under the industrial scheme

Is disablement assessment at 100 per cent? (chap. 5)

Yes — Consider claiming constant attendance allowance

No — Is there a reduction in earning capacity? (chap. 7)

Is there entitlement to the higher rate of the allowance and is the need for attendance likely to be permanent? (chap. 6)

Yes — Consider claiming special hardship allowance

No

Yes — Claim exceptionally severe disablement allowance

No

Is the claimant being treated in hospital for an industrial injury?

Yes — Claim hospital treatment allowance

No

No further entitlement

There is no entitlement to any benefit unless disablement is assessed as at least 1 per cent. In the case of a disablement pension an assessment of 14 per cent is usually required, and for its two supplements, 100 per cent. The disablement need not be permanent but it must continue for some time because there is no entitlement to benefit for the first 15 weeks following the accident or onset of the prescribed disease.

(2) The benefits

The scheme's two main benefits compensate, firstly, for the physical or

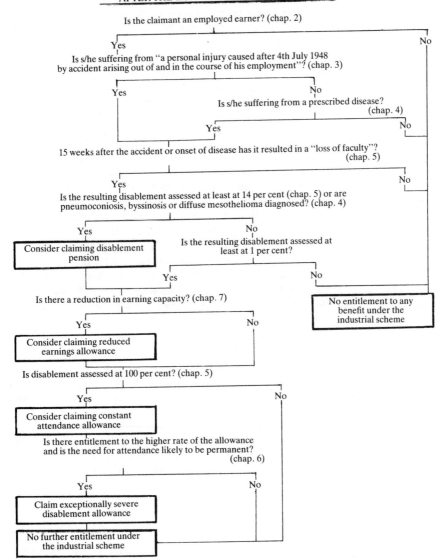

WHICH INDUSTRIAL INJURIES BENEFIT TO CLAIM
AFTER THE 1986 ACT COMES INTO FORCE?

Is the claimant an employed earner? (chap. 2)

Yes — No

Is s/he suffering from "a personal injury caused after 4th July 1948
by accident arising out of and in the course of his employment"? (chap. 3)

Yes — No

Is s/he suffering from a prescribed disease?
(chap. 4)

Yes — No

15 weeks after the accident or onset of disease has it resulted in a "loss of faculty"?
(chap. 5)

Yes — No

Is the resulting disablement assessed at least at 14 per cent (chap. 5) or are
pneumoconiosis, byssinosis or diffuse mesothelioma diagnosed? (chap. 4)

Yes — No

Consider claiming disablement
pension

Is the resulting disablement assessed at
least at 1 per cent?

Yes — No

Is there a reduction in earning capacity? (chap. 7)

No entitlement to any
benefit under the
industrial scheme

Yes — No

Consider claiming reduced
earnings allowance

Is disablement assessed at 100 per cent? (chap. 5)

Yes — No

Consider claiming constant
attendance allowance

Is there entitlement to the higher rate of the allowance
and is the need for attendance likely to be permanent?
(chap. 6)

Yes — No

Claim exceptionally severe
disablement allowance

No further entitlement under
the industrial scheme

mental disablement caused by the industrial injury, and secondly, for the
reduced earning capacity resulting from that disablement (chapters 6 and
7). The focus is upon injury to person and then injury to pocket. The value
of the benefits provided by the scheme can be relatively high. Not only are
they tax-free but they are usually paid in addition to any others available
under the main national insurance scheme. The benefits for disablement
and reduced earnings are not treated as overlapping with any others
because the main scheme does not provide any equivalent to them. This
means that those injured in the course of their job can obtain payments for
losses which otherwise would go unrecognised by the remainder of social

security. This places them in a better financial position than, for example, victims of road traffic accidents, or those who suffer injury at home, or on the sports field. As the example on p. 15 shows, the extra benefit provided by the industrial scheme can more than double the value of the payments made by the social security system.

The benefits have been radically altered by the SSA 1986. This Act withdrew certain allowances and generally made it harder to obtain others. The changes are being made in stages, but most are expected to have taken effect by April 1987. Until the relevant changes are made entitlement continues under the old law. Although this book concentrates upon the new scheme the old law may remain of importance for a short while, and readers may better understand the recent reforms by reference to the previous law. The two flow charts on pp. 2–3 therefore indicate the main questions relevant to a claim for benefit respectively before, and after, the Act is fully in force. The difference between them indicates where the main changes have been made. These changes are further explored in chapter 6.

Following the changes made in 1986 there are now two main industrial injuries benefits. One of these may be increased by the addition of up to two more allowances. They are the first four listed in the table on p. 5, which illustrates their relative importance in the past, and gives their current rates. In particular it should be noted that the two main benefits – for disablement and reduced earnings – constitute 99 per cent of the scheme's total expenditure. In outline the benefits are as follows:

(a) Disablement pension

This compensates for the effects of work injury upon the body or mind, irrespective of whether the claimant is capable of returning to work or whether his earnings are reduced (chapter 6). Except where pneumo-coniosis, byssinosis or diffuse mesothelioma are diagnosed, entitlement only arises if the claimant is medically assessed as at least 14 per cent disabled. The rate of the pension is directly proportionate to the percentage of disablement assessed. Payment continues for as long as the disablement lasts, and this may be for the claimants's lifetime.

(b) Reduced earnings allowance

This was known until the SSA 1986 as special hardship allowance. It compensates for loss of earning capacity where the claimant's injury is such as to make him incapable of following not only his regular occupation, but also any other suitable employment which offers equivalent pay (chapter 7). Entitlement depends upon finding a reduction in the claimant's gross earnings after the accident compared with what he was receiving before. However, the amount of the allowance is subject to a maximum which, in practice, prevents 90 per cent of recipients from obtaining their full wage loss. To be entitled to the allowance a claimant must be assessed as at least 1 per cent disabled. But it is not necessary, as it usually is in the case of a disablement pension, for there to be disablement of at least 14 per cent. However, apart from this one major difference, a claimant must satisfy all the other conditions of entitlement to a disablement pension in order to obtain a reduced earnings allowance.

Relative Cost, Rates And Number of Beneficiaries For Each Benefit
(Italics indicates that it was withdrawn by the SSA 1986)

Benefit or Supplement	Number of Beneficiaries 1981–82	Cost £ million 1978–79	Weekly rate from 6th April 1987 £ p
Disablement benefit			maximum
– pension	189,000	95	64–50
			maximum lump sum
– gratuity	*134,000*	*31.5*	*4,200–00*
Reduced earnings allowance (formerly special hardship allowance)			
– with pension	71,000 ⎫	87	maximum
– with gratuity	73,000 ⎭		25–80
Constant attendance allowance		2	
– Part-time			a sum reason-
(1) Half rate	390		able in the
(2) Intermediate			circumstances
with EDSA	430		38–70
without EDSA	60		
– Full-time			
(3) Normal maximum	1,080		25–80
(4) Exceptional			51–60
with ESDA	400		
without ESDA	10		
Exceptionally severe disable-ment allowance (ESDA)	830	0.65	25–80
Hospital treatment allowance	*100*	*0.2*	*64–50*
Unemployability supplement	*300*	*not known*	*39–50* (plus increases for age and dependants)

Figures on costs and all those for constant attendance are derived from the DHSS Discussion Document (1980). The remainder are from DHSS *Social Security Statistics 1985* (see appendix A, tables 1, 7 and 8). The years are the last ones for which complete figures are available, but the total cost of these benefits almost doubled from £216 million in 1978-79 to £410 million in 1985-86. The SSA 1986 is expected to achieve savings of up to £50 million a year. Benefit rates are examined in full in chapter 10. Figures on benefit in the case of death have been excluded. Although there were over 38,000 such pensions and allowances in payment 1981-82, they added only £3 million to the industrial preference.

(c) Constant attendance and exceptionally severe disablement allowances

These are paid as supplements to those entitled to a 100 per cent disablement pension who need to be cared for constantly. For those in receipt of the higher rate of constant attendance allowance who are likely to need such attendance permanently the exceptionally severe allowance can be obtained (chapter 6).

(d) Benefits withdrawn by the SSA 1986

These were for hospital in-patient treatment, unemployability and for death, when payments were made to widows and other dependants. The benefits are to be drawn from a date yet to be stated and are briefly discussed in chapter 6.

(3) Claims adjudication and payments

Separate claims are required for each of the benefits or supplements. To avoid benefit being lost claims should be made within three months of the conditions of entitlement being satisfied. Generally this means that a claim should be made at the latest within six months of the accident or onset of the disease. However, "good cause" may excuse a late claim and can justify backdated payments (chapter 8).

Adjudication upon industrial injuries benefit is similar to that for the remainder of social security, although there are some special features. The cases are more likely to involve difficult issues of fact or law and as a result have given rise to a disproportionate number of appeals. Medical issues are also far more prominent, with MATs hearing five times as many cases as SSATs. The tiers of adjudication following a claim are given in the diagram which follows. It can be seen that after an initial decision from an AO or AMA an appeal lies to an appeal tribunal. A further appeal then lies to a Social Security Commissioner and, very occasionally, cases may be appealed to the High Court (chapter 9).

If a claim is successful payment takes the form of a weekly pension. There was power to award lump sums in cases of minor disablement but, in

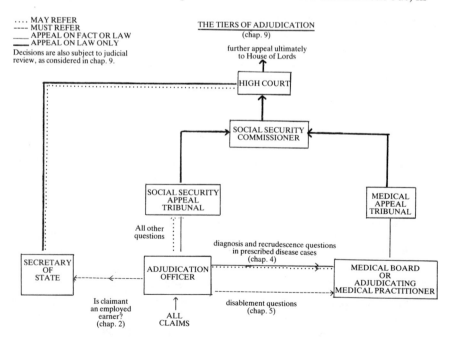

effect, this was abolished by the SSA 1986. The amount of the pension depends upon the degree of disablement and the amount of lost earnings. It is annually uprated (chapter 10).

2. THE IMPORTANCE OF THE INDUSTRIAL SCHEME

This section continues to provide an introduction to the scheme by combining several of its main features under one general heading dealing with the scheme's importance. There are a variety of indicators or approaches which could be used to measure importance. For example, an instrumental approach could be adopted. This would ask simply how much money the scheme distributes and to how many beneficiaries. A comparison could then be made with other sources of compensation. This is done in (4) below where the industrial scheme is compared to other areas of social security and, more particularly, to claims for common law damages. This approach gives little indication of the historical importance of the scheme, or of the recent changes which have taken place. These are considered in (1) below where the developments which led to the SSA 1986 are outlined. The scheme began as a "pioneer of social security" and is still viewed as a model which could be extended to compensate for disablement caused other than by work. Its symbolic importance is therefore wider than simply the amount of money it presently distributes. The historical approach is continued in (2) below with a critique of why Beveridge thought work injuries sufficiently important to merit a separate system of compensation.

In (3) below a departure is made from the historical and instrumental approaches to assessing importance. Instead the scheme is examined from the perspective of those involved in its administration and adjudication. Claims for industrial benefit are generally viewed by such people as more important than others in social security. The cases are more complicated and require a greater level of expertise, nearly all of them involving medical adjudication. They produce more difficult issues of fact or law, a higher number of appeals and additional administrative cost. This section therefore examines the disproportionate importance of industrial injury cases within social security adjudication.

Next, as already mentioned, in (4) below the present value of the scheme is assessed not only by looking at the amount of benefit distributed to individual claimants, but also by examining the scheme's total expenditure. Finally in (5) below these figures are placed in another historical context: an account is given of the fall in importance of many aspects of the scheme since 1966. Its decline in recent years has become less marked. Nevertheless it will continue as a result of the reforms made by the SSA 1986, although the cuts made by the Act may not be as severe as some may have feared. Despite this story of decline there are other indications that the scheme will continue to be a focal point in social security provision. For example, the health and safety statistics indicate that the serious injury rate is no longer falling, whilst certain medical opinion suggests that an increasing connection is to be found between work and ill health. According to some, an epidemic of work-related disablement is about to be uncovered, and this could lead to attention being focussed upon the industrial scheme. Whatever the merit of such a thesis, one conclusion which can be drawn is that the industrial scheme has occupied an importance out of proportion to its number of beneficiaries, and that, for a variety of reasons, it will continue to do so.

(1) The changing face of the "pioneer of social security"

The origin of the present industrial scheme lies in the Workmen's Compensation Act of 1897. This Act imposed a duty on employers to make payments to the victims of industrial accidents irrespective of whether the injuries were caused by anyone's negligence. Employers were left to arrange their own insurance to pay the cost of claims. This is one of the earliest examples of the state being involved in the provision of welfare, and this was recognised by Beveridge[1] when he described workmen's compensation as the "pioneer of social security". The basic structure for this compensation lasted over 50 years until the State took full responsibility for the industrial scheme in 1948. The new model of compensation was based on various compromises upon Beveridge's recommendations, but it involved radically different provision. The Workmen's Compensation Acts were replaced by the National Insurance (Industrial Injuries) Act 1946. Today the legislative basis for the industrial scheme is no longer found in an Act exclusively devoted to it. Instead it is contained in the Social Security Act 1975 which establishes a framework of entitlement to most social security benefits. In particular the Act integrates the administration of the national insurance and industrial injury schemes so that, for example, there are no longer separate systems of funding. Despite such amalgamation there remains a separate chapter of the Act devoted to industrial injury, for it can still be seen in many ways as a distinct feature of welfare provision.

Until 1982 the structure of the industrial scheme had changed little since 1948. It is true, for example, that in 1953 the scheme was extended to cover all forms of minor disablement however transitory, and in 1966 the exceptionally severe disablement allowance was introduced. But otherwise the pattern of benefits and entitlement to them had remained much the same: injury benefit was available for short term incapacity for work, disablement benefit for longer term loss of faculty and reduction of earnings, and death benefit was available for widows. Radical changes have since taken place and now only disablement benefit remains.

These changes have been made in the wake of several reports on the system. The Royal Commission on Civil Liability and Compensation for Personal Injury chaired by Lord Pearson reported in 1978 (Cmnd. 7054). It generally approved of the industrial injuries scheme and, subject to a few exceptions, recommended only minor reforms. The report ranged over a wide area of social security and the law of tort but it has been almost entirely ignored by Government. However, it did prompt a further review of the industrial scheme. This time it was carried out by the DHSS itself and a Discussion Document was published in 1980. This was followed in 1981 by a Government White Paper (Cmnd. 8402). Last minute changes to the SSHBA 1982 led to the abolition of injury benefit, but otherwise the

---

[1]   Social Insurance and Allied Services: report by Sir William Beveridge (Cmd. 6404, 1942).

White Paper proposals seemed to have been forgotten. However, some of them were revived when a further consultation paper was issued at Christmas 1985. Despite strong opposition, the proposals came to fruition – although again as a last minute change – in the SSA 1986. Industrial death benefit was withdrawn and substantial changes made to disablement benefit.

The withdrawal of injury and death benefit was an abrupt change to the structure of the scheme, leaving it only to provide for disablement and reduced earnings. However, these were always the scheme's main benefits. They had steadily grown in importance so that by 1979 they constituted 94 per cent of the industrial preference. (This is the amount of extra benefit obtained via the industrial scheme compared to that which would otherwise be available from social security.) Following the SSA 1986 these benefits now constitute the entire preference. The scheme has thus been simplified but, in effect, the changes have re-emphasised that its distinguishing features are the benefits for disablement and reduced earnings.

The debate which gave rise to these changes again put forward the idea that the industrial scheme might have a wider role. It has been seen as a model which can be extended to compensate for disablement caused beyond the confines of work. Thus the Pearson Commission recommended that a no-fault road accident scheme be set up along the lines of that for industrial injury. In addition the severe disablement allowance introduced in 1984 uses the principles for assessing industrial disablement in order to establish its own threshold of entitlement. Again a former Chief Social Security Commissioner has stated: "I can see no insuperable difficulty about adapting the industrial injury scheme as administered by the statutory authorities to cover all or part of the area now covered by common law claims . . .".[2] One leading commentator sees this as "the most practical and desirable direction of movement".[3]

In partly defending the industrial preference in 1986 the IIAC accepted that:

> ". . . disabled people as a whole – whatever the cause of their disability – have special needs which deserve greater recognition. But it is in our view wrong to attempt to achieve this by a redistribution of resources from the industrially disabled to other groups of disabled people. We adhere to the view. . . that the only acceptable reason for, and method of, abolishing the industrial preference would be by extending industrial injuries-type benefits to all disabled people."[4]

The industrial scheme therefore has not been the "pioneer of social security" only in a historical sense. It continues to lead the way. Despite the cuts made in 1986 it is still seen by some as a basis for future development, and as setting the pace for other social security benefits. However, whether the preference it offers should be confined to victims of industrial injury has been called into question. This fundamental issue is considered in more detail under the next heading.

---

[2] Sir Robert Micklethwait, *The National Insurance Commissioners* (1976) p. 140.
[3] P. S. Atiyah, *Accidents, Compensation and the Law* (3rd ed. 1980) p. 625.
[4] IIAC response of 14th February 1986 to the Minister of Social Security's invitation for reactions to the Consultation Paper.

(2) The justifications for preferential benefit for industrial injury

The industrial preference is the difference between the amount of benefit which is available for an industrial injury and that which otherwise would be provided by the main national insurance scheme. As in the examples at p. 15, the industrial scheme can more than double the value of the social security benefits that would otherwise be paid. Whether this advantage given to one relatively small group of disabled people can be justified is open to question. Beveridge's view was that "a complete solution is to be found only in a completely unified scheme for disability without demarcation by the cause of disability". However, he identified three arguments of principle which "on balance" persuaded him that it was right to treat work injury cases separately. These three principles were:

(a) that many industries vital to the community were dangerous and it was desirable that those working in them should have special protection;

(b) that those disabled at work were acting under orders;

(c) that only if special provision were made could an employer's liability at common law be restricted to the results of his negligence.

Each of these arguments can be criticised and, as recognised by the Pearson Commission, they at least "carry a good deal less weight now". In so far as the argument in (a) is based upon providing an economic incentive to do dangerous work, research has shown that, although payment before a risk is taken and irrespective of whether injury occurs (i.e. 'danger-money') may be effective, payment only after an accident has happened is something people prefer not to think about. In any event, the argument cannot provide a justification for a separate scheme for all work injuries – even those caused by "safe" jobs. With regard to (b) it is difficult to show that risks arising from acts at work are any less voluntary than those involved in driving a car or using a product at home. The DHSS acknowledged in its Discussion Document that working under orders is a less forceful argument nowadays than it was 30 years ago with regard to all the professions except perhaps the police and the armed forces. Beveridge's final argument in (c) has been overtaken by events. The number of successful tort claims for work injury has increased rather than decreased, and the liability of an employer now extends far beyond what Beveridge may have viewed as the limits of moral responsibility. Retaining the industrial injuries scheme has not therefore reduced liability at common law to coincide with an employer's "true culpability". It is now usually accepted that Beveridge's justifications for the industrial scheme are relatively weak.

Many now believe that, whatever the historical position, there can be no good reason today for maintaining the distinction. The conclusion of the International Labour Organisation is that the distinction between work and other accidents is becoming increasingly anomalous and traditional practice is the main obstacle to change. Organisations representing the disabled have argued for an alternative approach to compensation which would emphasise the needs of disabled people and base benefit upon the severity of disablement rather than its cause. They seek to replace the labyrinthine maze of welfare benefits presently facing the disabled with a comprehensive allowance. To afford this it may be necessary to transfer resources from those with minor short-term injuries to those more seriously affected who comprise the longer-term disabled. Whatever the details of such a plan – costed by Government in 1986 at over £3,000 million – the preferential benefit offered by the industrial scheme is thought to hinder a broader-based approach. However, such an approach would not attract the support of the trade union movement if it were to involve a levelling down of benefits. Fearing this result the TUC has argued in favour of retaining special treatment for industrial injuries. For its part the Government has adopted policies which enable it to face both ways: on the one hand in the Ministerial foreword to the Discussion Document it makes a commitment to continue the preference, but in the White Paper it also pledges "to develop, as resources permit, a coherent system of benefit for disability regardless of cause". Over the years the industrial preference has survived, as the Discussion Document recognises, not solely because of Beveridge's three principles but with the help of "powerful practical and political arguments". These arguments were the basis for the DHSS forecast that the industrial scheme will continue to offer separate treatment for the foreseeable future, whether or not it is justifiable that benefit be confined to work injuries.

(3) Administrative costs and special aspects of adjudication

Making a decision upon a claim for industrial injuries benefit is usually more complicated than in the case of other benefits. This accounts not only for its greater administrative expense but also for its disproportionate importance within welfare provision. In its Discussion Document in 1980 the DHSS estimated that the scheme employed the full-time equivalent of 2,000 of its 87,000 social security staff. (The abolition of injury benefit in 1982 was expected to reduce this by 300.) The staff work in the 451 local offices where claims may be made. In 1978-79 the proportion of administrative costs to benefit expenditure was 13.3 per cent[5] compared to only 4.4 per cent for the main national insurance scheme. This reflects the fact that it is more difficult to process industrial injury claims. They usually involve more than routine clerical tasks because they require more questions to be answered and details to be checked than, for example, an application for a retirement pension. Despite this, the administrative costs are very much lower than those of the tort system. The cost of paying damages for personal injury was estimated by the Pearson Commission to be 45 per cent of the total expenditure on the system. The contrast with the industrial scheme is then a striking one. Whereas it costs 85 pence to put each £1 of tort damages into an accident victim's pocket, it costs only 13 pence to do the same via the industrial injuries scheme.

Despite being cheaper than tort the industrial scheme is still more expensive than the rest of social security. There are three particular features of its administration and adjudication which add to its complexity and cost, and in doing so they enhance its importance. The first is that medical authorities are much more likely to be involved. Experts are

---

[5]   Discussion Document p. 1. Similar figures were given for disablement benefit alone in Northern Ireland when the DHSS provided otherwise unpublished statistics for J.C. Brown, *The Disability Income System* (1984) p. 84.

required to make decisions in areas which are often the subject of new research and ever-increasing knowledge. To perform this task in 1983-84 there were 1,026 doctors appointed as adjudicating medical authorities. Their work is not confined to new claims for there is often a continuing need for medical assessments long after the payment of benefit is first made: although there were 119,000 new claims for disablement benefit in 1985, there were 184,000 medical examinations carried out in connection with the scheme. Even among the experts there is need for special expertise. Adjudication upon certain industrial diseases can only be made by 27 specially qualified doctors. They carried out a further 12,000 examinations in 1985. The scheme's emphasis upon medical matters is also reflected in the number of cases disposed of that year by appeal tribunals. The 24 regional MATs decided 8,656 cases – five times as many decisions on industrial injury as were dealt with by all 330 SSATs combined.

A second distinguishing feature of industrial injury cases is that they attract a disproportionate number of appeals. The scheme is seen as more important because of the higher level of adjudication often involved. About 20 per cent of medical decisions refusing benefit are appealed to a MAT.[6] These were so numerous in the scheme's early years that they occupied as many pages of their separate series of reports as all the other social security cases combined. As late as 1974 it was estimated that, whereas the industrial scheme accounted for one in three of all Commissioners' decisions and one in six of all national insurance local tribunal decisions, it comprised only one in eighteen of all decisions made by an insurance officer.[7] Industrial injury appeals no longer take up such a high proportion of Commissioners' time. Although in 1985 they disposed of 350 cases on disablement benefit this represented only 11 per cent of their total workload for that year.[8] Nevertheless this number is substantial, and it can still be said that the rate of appeal to Commissioners in industrial cases is disproportionate to the number of claims made.

A third feature of industrial injuries adjudication is that, if there is an appeal, the decision is more likely than in other benefits to be in favour of the claimant. Both MATs and SSATs find for the claimant in about 40 per cent of disablement benefit cases. This contrasts with success rates of, for example, 25 per cent for sickness benefit, 20 per cent for attendance allowance and only 10 per cent in child benefit appeals. Both the high number of appeals and the success of claimants on appeal can be attributed to several common factors. First, there is the considerable financial gain that may result if a claim is successful. This provides an incentive to seek an authoritative decision and organise an effective case. Secondly, such a claim is more likely to give rise to difficult issues of fact and law upon which an AO or AMA may easily make a mistake. Thirdly, there is a greater likelihood of a claimant being encouraged to appeal and being represented at the hearing. In over 60 per cent of cases a claimant receives such assistance. Usually it is given by an experienced trade union official, but it may also be given by a welfare rights worker, or a lawyer arranged by the

---

6   This figure is based upon the Pearson Commission vol. 2 table 22 which reveals that 80 per cent of AMA decisions are in favour of the claimant.

7   Lewis and Latta, "Trade Union Legal Services" (1974) 12 *B. J. Ind. Rel.* 56 at p. 59.

8   These figures were supplied to the author in May 1986 by the Office of the Chief Social Security Commissioner.

union. Finally, a claimant is more likely to be present at the SSAT hearing itself, for 80 per cent of them attend whereas only half of those claiming other benefits do so. Attendance is encouraged by those acting on behalf of claimants. The presence of both the claimant and an experienced adviser is seen to add importance to the claim. It can result in a more legalistic and adversarial approach and, from one perspective, a more equal contest with the DHSS. Perhaps influenced by all these reasons a law professor and chairman of an appeal tribunal concluded that industrial injury cases "are commonly regarded as the most important".[9]

(4) Expenditure upon benefit and its value to individual claimants

A further guide to the importance of a scheme of compensation lies in comparing it to others with regard to the amount of money each distributes and their number of beneficiaries. The industrial injuries scheme is compared here not so much with other sources of social security payable in such eventualities as unemployment or sickness, but with common law damages for industrial injury because these are paid as direct compensation for the accident itself. The discussion falls into two parts. First the value of the industrial scheme taken as a whole is examined, and then the position of an individual beneficiary is considered.

(a) *The value of the industrial scheme compared to the tort system*

In 1984-85 the expenditure upon disablement benefit amounted to £389 million and was a quarter of that for unemployment benefit and a fifth of that for invalidity benefit.[10] There were 119,000 new claims but there were almost three times as many people actually receiving disablement benefit for they included not only 186,000 pensioners but also the 122,000 people who received the lump sum gratuity[11] which could at that time be awarded. Despite the decline in the importance of the scheme traced in section (5) below, the payments still exceeded the total damages claimed at common law whether for accidents at work or elsewhere.[12] By confining attention only to those injured at work, it could be said that the industrial scheme compensated three times as many people a year as the common law.[13] However, this picture changed if only the annual number of new beneficiaries compensated by each scheme was considered. Then only a few more obtained benefit than were awarded damages. This is because the figures for disablement pensions include all those in receipt of payment in the one year even if their injury occurred many years earlier, whereas there is no such accumulation for past years in the figures for the once and for all payments made by the common law.

---

[9]   H. Street, *Justice in the Welfare State* (1975) p. 18.
[10] DHSS, *Social Security Statistics 1986*, table 44.04. Expenditure rose to £410 million on disablement benefit in 1985-86. H.C. Written Answer, Vol. 102, col. 431, 24 July 1986.
[11] DHSS, *Social Security Statistics 1986*, table 50.04.
[12] In 1977 according to the Pearson Commission, vol. 1, paras. 44 and 772, the value of tort compensation for all accidents was £202 million, whereas for industrial injuries alone it was only £70 million. This contrasts with the £250 million then being spent on the industrial scheme.
[13] This is based upon the Pearson Commission's estimate, vol. 2 para. 168, that some payment of common law damages was made to 90,000 people in 1973.

The relative importance of the schemes has been changed considerably by the SSA 1986. Its effects are traced in (5)(*b*) below. It can be estimated that the annual number of new beneficiaries under the industrial scheme will fall to only a quarter of those compensated by the common law. The effect upon the scheme's annual expenditure will be much less, although by 1989 it is expected to fall by about £50 million a year. This represents a cut of around 10 per cent. Despite this, the annual payments for all beneficiaries under the scheme will still exceed by far the amount of damages awarded each year to victims of work injuries.

(*b*) *The value to an individual of industrial benefit compared to damages*

The value of industrial injury benefit to an individual can be considerable even when compared to common law damages. It is commonly believed that damages are worth far more than social security benefits but, in fact, especially in the longer term, this is often not the case. In 1977 the average award of damages to a person injured at work was £900.[14] This was equivalent to the value for two years of a 40 per cent disablement pension or the maximum reduced earnings allowance (which is paid to 90 per cent of recipients). Of course the systems of compensation are not mutually exclusive; a claim for benefit can be made in addition to bringing an action for damages. However, the purpose here is to emphasise the potentially high value of an industrial injuries award.

Two examples are given in (*c*) below of the high value of industrial injury benefits when compared to those available to accident victims under the main national insurance scheme. If the difference between the weekly incomes over a period of years is capitalised, it shows that the additional benefit provided by the industrial scheme is as high as that associated with general damages at common law. There are two particular reasons for this: firstly, the industrial benefit is tax free, whereas the beneficiary of award of damages must pay tax on the income which arises from the lump sum; and secondly, the benefit is directly protected against inflation in prices whereas the damages award is not. In fact, the disablement pension has exceeded the rise in prices and has kept pace with wages. Since 1948 the rate for 100 per cent disablement has continued to represent about a third of the average earnings of a male manual worker. In 40 years it rose from its original rate of £2.25 a week to £63.50. It is certain that anyone who first received payment in the early years of the scheme and is still doing so has obtained a great deal more than the value of any damages award which might have been made.

A specific example can be taken in order to make a direct comparison between the two systems of compensation. For the loss of a hand the leading text on the assessment of damages[15] suggests that a sum of between £31,000 and £39,000 would be paid at December 1982 prices. Under the industrial injuries scheme this injury would result in the claimant being assessed as 60 per cent disabled and it would then have attracted a pension of £32.16 a week. To calculate the capital value of this pension a realistic approach may be adopted, taking into account current market yields on investments and the rate of inflation. These factors are currently ignored by the courts. If an allowance is made for 5 per cent

---

[14]   Pearson Commission, vol. 2 para. 169.
[15]   Kemp and Kemp, *The Quantum of Damages* vol. 2 para. 9-711.

inflation, the industrial scheme would pay out more than the maximum suggested by the damages textbook to any male worker aged younger than 43 when he lost his hand.[16] This is why the leading textbook on accident compensation states that:

"... it seems clear that industrial injury benefits are as valuable as common law damages whenever long-term incapacity is in question."[17]

(c) *The value to an individual of industrial benefit compared to other social security*

The two examples below compare the benefits available for an industrial injury with those provided by the main social security scheme in the case of other accidents. An estimate is also made of the capitalised value of the difference in benefit. The first example involves extreme injury. As such, it is highly untypical because less than 400 of the 186,000 disablement pensioners are in receipt of an exceptionally severe disablement allowance. However, the example takes no account of entitlement to reduced earnings allowance, although this is featured in the second example. Even if this allowance is ignored, the first example illustrates that, for exactly the same disablement, the industrial scheme can pay out more than twice the benefit otherwise available from social security.

Example 1 – Benefits for a single person who is incapable of work and is assessed at 100 per cent disabled.

Benefit	For industrial injury £ p	For non-industrial injury £ p
Invalidity pension	39.50	39.50
Invalidity allowance	8.30	8.30
100% disablement pension	64.50	nil
Constant attendance allowance at exceptional rate	51.60	nil
Attendance allowance	nil	31.60
Exceptionally severe disablement allowance	25.80	nil
Mobility allowance	22.10	22.10
Total	211.80	102.50

[16] This is based on taking account of the current yields available in the market on fixed interest securities and explicitly allowing for further inflation. The sum is as follows. The current discounting rate is 9¼ per cent and the corresponding rate, net of tax, is 6½ per cent per annum. Allowing for 5 per cent inflation the net interest rate is 1½ per cent. The annual income from the industrial scheme is £1,672. This needs to be multiplied by 23.3 to arrive at the maximum tort award for the injury of £39,000. This multiplier is reached at age 43 according to the *Actuarial Tables For Personal Injury and Fatal Accident Cases* (1984). By contrast a court would ignore inflation and adopt a gross discounting rate of 4½ per cent as suggested by Lord Diplock in *Mallett* v *McMonagle* [1970] AC 166. The corresponding net rate of interest, allowing for basic rate tax, is 3¼ per cent per annum. The multiplier would then be reached at 28 years old.

[17] P. S. Atiyah *op.cit.* p. 395, similarly R. Micklethwait *op.cit.* p. 5.

There is a need for attendance day and night, and this is likely to be permanent. The rates apply for the year beginning 6th April 1987.

The weekly value of the preference is £109.30. The capitalised value of this preference can be calculated as £144,300 for a 39-year-old and £197,200 for a 21-year-old.[18] On the same basis the capitalised value of the entire benefit in this case of industrial injury is £279,700 for the 39-year-old and £382,000 for the 21-year-old.

Example 2 – Income for the victim of an accident which causes a leg to be amputated below the knee leaving a four inch stump. The injured person is unable to return to the previous employment but is able to carry out lower paid work. The fall in earnings is from £160 to £130 a week gross. The calculation of net wages is made after deducting tax and national insurance contributions. The rates apply for the year beginning April 6 1987.

Income	For industrial injury £ p	For non-industrial injury £ p	Before accident £ p
Net wages	93.62	93.62	112.22
50% disablement pension	32.65	nil	nil
Maximum reduced earnings allowance	25.80	nil	nil
Total	151.67	93.62	112.22

The weekly value of industrial preference is £58.05. On the same basis as the calculation made in the above example, for a 39-year-old person the capitalised value of the preference is £76,600, and for a 21-year-old it is £104,700.

(5) The fall and potential rise in importance of the scheme

(a) *The decline in claims and payments since 1966*

For the first half of its existence the industrial scheme grew rapidly but has since experienced a sharp decline. In its first 16 years the number of claims increased almost every year rising from 69,000 in 1949 to a peak of 214,000 in 1965. They have since fallen by half. The decline is illustrated in the table on p. 17 which reveals that most of the relevant statistics have fallen by about a third since 1966. This was caused by a decline in the rate of injuries brought about by a reduction of the numbers in employment, especially in the more dangerous industries such as coal-mining, shipbuilding and steel making. For the decade after 1976, although the Pearson Commission forecast that the scope for a similar reduction in work injuries would be much reduced,[19] the benefit figures continue to show a decline. In addition to a fall in the number of claims and medical examinations, there has been a substantial decrease in new pensions. However, the scheme's accumulation of pensions for injuries in past years

---

[18]   This is based upon the criteria referred to in note 16, and again allowing for 5 per cent inflation. The Diplock formula used by the courts arrives at a multiplier of 19.3 for the 39-year-old and the capital value is then £113,200.

[19]   Vol. 2 para. 161.

means that, as yet, the number for all those receiving payment has hardly fallen at all.

Several of the figures can argue against the scheme being seen as in decline in all respects since 1976. For example, there has been less of a fall in the number of cases heard by SSATs and MATs, although in the case of the latter this may partly be attributed to a change in jurisdiction. Reduced earnings allowances have actually increased. Like disablement pensions they may accumulate within the scheme as the years pass. However, they have gradually become more important so that a higher proportion of disablement pensioners now obtain them than ever before. Finally, the table reveals that the total expenditure upon disablement benefit, including reduced earnings allowance, continues to increase. This reflects not only inflation but also the favourable treatment given to the industrial scheme when benefits are uprated. The value of industrial benefits when compared

The Decline In Claims For Disablement Benefit In Britain 1966–82
Source: various DHSS tables in *Social Security Statistics 1986* and figures supplied directly to the author by the DHSS

	1966	1976 (%age change) from 1966)	1982 (%age change from 1976)	Latest statistics (published in 1986) relating to various years
Benefit claims	210,000	143,000 (−32)	115,000 (−13)	*119,000*
Medical examinations	366,000	244,000 (−33)	192,000 (−15)	*184,000*
Cases to SSATs	3,153	2,138 (−32)	2,149 (0)	*1,766*
Cases to MATs	20,572	11,470 (−45)	10,662 (−8)	*8,656*
Pensions beginning	31,000	19,000 (−39)	12,000 (−29)	12,000
Gratuities beginning	258,000	174,000 (−33)	134,000 (−15)	122,000
Total pensions in payment	202,000	202,000 (0)	189,000 (−6)	186,000
Total reduced earnings allowances in payment	137,000	145,000 (+6)	144,000 (0)	145,000
£ Annual expenditure on disablement benefit including reduced earnings allowance	49,562	144,609 (+192)	314,776 (+343)	*381,203*

to sickness and unemployment benefit has increased by a quarter since 1966.[20]

(b) The effect of the SSA 1986

The SSA 1986 makes the most radical changes to the industrial scheme since it was established. It will lead to a further fall in the benefit figures, some of which will be very substantially reduced. The Act will make the scheme less important especially for minor disablement, but its decline may not be as great as some, including the TUC, have feared.

The main reform is that as from October 1986 the payment of a lump sum gratuity for disablement below 20 per cent has been withdrawn. The Act achieves this by making two changes: first, it withdraws disablement benefit for those assessed at less than 14 per cent disabled, and second, it awards a pension at the 20 per cent rate to those assessed at between 14 and 19 per cent. It may seem that the change will reduce the number of new awards of benefit by 90 per cent for there were only 12,000 pensions awarded as against 122,000 gratuities in 1983 (appendix A, table 8). For accidents there were only 7,000 initial assessments leading to a pension compared to 56,000 leading to a gratuity. However, the reduction is not quite as severe as these figures may imply, and there will not be a commensurate decline in the scheme's importance in certain other respects.

One reason for this is that the reduction in new claims caused by the withdrawal of disablement benefit will be offset by the fact that reduced earnings allowance can continue to be paid even for disablement below 14 per cent. In addition, for the first time 3,500 people a year now qualify for a pension[21] despite being assessed at 14 to 19 per cent and below the previous threshold. They increase the annual number of new disablement pensioners by about a third. Payment may continue for as long as the disablement lasts so that, over the years, these new pensioners will accumulate within the scheme and increase the total number of beneficiaries.

The effect of the change upon other aspects of the scheme will vary. A substantial fall can be expected in both the number of claims made and the number of medical examinations carried out. However, the decline in the number of cases taken to appeal will be less because these have been disproportionately concerned either with reduced earnings allowance, or with more serious injuries, and these are not affected by the changes to disablement benefit. By 1989 expenditure upon the scheme is expected to fall by about £50 million a year,[22] representing a cut of less than 10 per cent. This is largely achieved by withdrawing disablement benefit for less serious injuries, but it also includes the withdrawal of death benefit and hospital treatment allowance, and the freezing of reduced earnings allowance on retirement from work. Against these savings must be balanced the increase in expenditure caused by the new cover for accidents abroad, the removal of the ceiling on payment when disablement benefit is combined with reduced earnings, and the new award of pensions to all

---

[20] DHSS, *Social Security Statistics 1986*, table 46.04.
[21] H.C. Deb., Standing Committee B, col. 1819, 29 April 1986.
[22] *Ibid*, col. 1825.

those assessed at 14 to 19 per cent disabled. The emphasis is upon leaving the scheme to compensate for the more serious injuries.

(c) The relationship of safety and benefit statistics

Most people do not realise how likely they are to make use of the industrial injury scheme. They grossly underestimate the number of serious work accidents which occur.[23] Studies which collect such statistics on health and safety at work may also reflect the importance of the compensation scheme and the potential use that may be made of it. For example, according to the Pearson Commission work accidents account for the deaths of 1,300 people a year, but they also cause 720,000 injuries. Most of these injuries are not serious because within three months, 95 per cent of people have returned to work.[24] However, a few will be left with some degree of disablement and these are the potential beneficiaries of the industrial scheme.

The statistics collected by the Health and Safety Executive similarly ought to bear some relationship to the industrial scheme. However, the basis upon which they are compiled has changed several times recently, and the factors which affect them – such as under-reporting[25] – are often quite different to those for figures on benefit. The result is that any comparison is fraught with difficulty. For example, between 1981-84 the figures[26] indicated that there was an end to the decline in the rate of injury. In the past this decline must have contributed to the reduction in claims for benefit. However, the end to the decline, as shown in the safety statistics, is not reflected in those for the industrial scheme which, in the table on p. 17, continue to show a fall after 1982. The safety statistics also reveal that, although the overall rate of injury remained stable, there was a 24 per cent rise in manufacturing injuries and a 40 per cent rise in the construction industry between 1981-84.[27] The lack of congruence between the safety and benefit statistics casts doubt upon whether this apparent change of emphasis in the incidence of injury is reflected in claims for disablement benefit in those particular industries.

(d) A forecast that the scheme will increase in importance

There is a final argument which suggests that, far from declining or merely retaining its present importance, the industrial scheme will become of increasing significance. This is because the extent that ill health and disablement are caused by work is only now being recognized. The argument depends less upon a forecast of increasing incidence of injury but instead looks at the progress being made in medical research. The increase in understanding of the nature and cause of disease has been such as to give rise to the suggestion that an epidemic of man-made disease and especially

---

[23] P. Prescott-Clarke, *Public Attitudes Towards Industrial Work-Related and Other Risks* (1982) p. 38.

[24] Vol. 2 pp. 45 and 47.

[25] The Health and Safety Executive in *Health and Safety Statistics 1977* estimated that the failure to report was as high as 75 per cent for offices and shops, 50 per cent for the construction industry and 27 per cent for manufacturing.

[26] The major injury rate remained at around 61 per 100,000 workers, with total injuries around 12,700. See the Health and Safety Executive *Statistics 1981-82*, table 1.1B and HSC *Report 1984-85*, table 1.

[27] See Nichols, "Industrial Injuries in British Manufacturing in the 1980's" (1986) 34 *Sociological Rev.* 290.

work-related disablement is about to be uncovered.[28] The present recipients of benefit for disease are widely recognized as representing only "the tip of the iceberg of occupational ill health generally."[29] The Pearson Commission found that "illnesses believed [by the sufferers] to have arisen at work and not at present prescribed may be in the order of five times as numerous as those which are".[30] With rapid technological changes and the introduction into the workplace at an increasing rate of new chemicals, new productive processes and new forms of stress associated with such factors as heat, vibration and noise, there has been all too little evaluation of the impact of the changes upon the health of employees. One study in the USA has suggested the position is so serious that the probable incidence of occupational disease was 28.4 per 100 workers. In only 3 per cent of these illnesses was compensation obtained.[31]

The recognition of some forms of cancer as occupational in origin illustrates this under-estimation of occupational disease. One study cites three different reports appearing in the years 1976 to 1978, each estimating a higher percentage of cancers due to occupational causes than the previous one.[32] The final report states that:

> ". . . there is nothing in the gross cancer statistics which is inconsistent with the hypothesis that up to 20-40 per cent of all cancers are (or will be in the next several decades) attributable to occupational disease."[33]

Even if a much more conservative figure is taken of 1-5 per cent of recent cancer deaths being caused by exposure to hazards in the workplace, if this estimate is applied to the average annual figure for 1974-78 for all cancer deaths in Britain of 140,000 it would yield an annual estimate of between 1,400 and 7,000 deaths from industrially caused cancer. This compares with roughly 100 death benefits which were paid out each year for industrial cancer by the DHSS. This particular example therefore illustrates the gross under-compensation of victims of occupational disease. It can be repeated with other recent studies examining the causes of heart disease, for example, or hearing loss, or mental illness or respiratory disorders.

If this analysis of the causes of ill health proves to be correct the result will be to increase the pressure upon the industrial scheme, perhaps

---

[28] See e.g. Ison, "The Dimensions Of Industrial Disease" (1978) 118 *Can. Med. Ass. J.* 200, and the note "Occupational Health Risks and the Worker's Right to Know" (1981) 90 *Yale L. J.* 1782. Traumatic injury has been over-emphasized as a basis for compensation compared to the potentially very large amount of man-made disease. See J. Stapleton, *Disease and the Compensation Debate* (1986).

[29] Morgan and Davies, "The Costs of Occupational Accidents and Disease in Great Britain" (1981) 89 *Employment Gazette* 477. See also N. A. Ashford, *Crisis in the Workplace: Occupational Disease and Injury* (1976), pp. 92-96.

[30] Vol. 2 para. 420.

[31] See D. Disher, G. Kleinman and F. Foster, *Pilot Study for Development of Occupational Disease Surveillance Method* (1975). Similarly, after completing a detailed review of the literature see P. S. Barth and H. A. Hunt, *Workers' Compensation and Work Related Diseases* (1980), p. 255, and US Dept. of Labor *An Interim Report to Congress on Occupational Diseases* (1980).

[32] A. W. Le Serve *et al.*, *Chemicals, Work and Cancer* (1980), p. 33.

[33] ›The National Cancer Research Institute and National Institute of Environmental Health Sciences, *Estimates of the Fraction of Cancer Incidence in the US Attributable to Occupational Factors* (1978). In Britain one of the higher estimates is that 12 per cent of cancer may be occupationally related. See Fox and Adelstein, "Occupational Mortality: Work or Way of Life?" (1978) 32 *J. Epid. & Comm. Health* 73.

causing it to expand its coverage. The recent admission of claims for occupational deafness and vibration white finger may thus be the harbingers of more radical change. If many more diseases are admitted for a wider range of occupations it could lead to further questioning of whether the industrial preference can be justified, especially if the causal connections reflected in the scheme are less obvious to the layman. However, it may be that there will be only a limited change in entitlement and the exclusive nature of the industrial scheme will be retained. This has been achieved recently by prescribing diseases such as deafness and vibration white finger only subject to severe limits; by abandoning proposals to admit an open proof system for industrial disease, as discussed at p. 131; and by refusing disablement benefit for assessments below 14 per cent. Although the numbers obtaining benefit may not increase, it is likely that more attention will be paid to the boundaries of the industrial scheme. In that respect benefit for disablement and reduced earnings will continue to be a focal point in social security provision.

3. USING THE RELEVANT SOURCES OF SOCIAL SECURITY LAW

(1) Sources

(a) Legislation

The origins of the legislation establishing the industrial injury scheme lie in the Workmen's Compensation Acts which date from 1897. These were replaced when the State took over from private insurers the responsibility for running the scheme following the National Insurance (Industrial Injuries) Act 1946. However, several features of the earlier legislation have been retained so that certain words and phrases have been subject to interpretation by courts throughout this century. The 1946 Act itself was changed and eventually replaced by a new Act as part of the continuing process of consolidation of social security law. Consolidation attempts to clarify and make it easier to use the various piecemeal additions to the legislation by bringing them together under the framework of a single Act. The present structure for the industrial scheme derives from chapters IV and V of the Social Security Act 1975. Industrial injury no longer gives its name to a separate Act but instead has been incorporated into the remainder of the legislation dealing with social security.

The statutes enacted by Parliament are supplemented by a mass of subordinate legislation which is made following the delegation to the Secretary of State of a limited power to make law. The statutory instruments made as a result often do more than merely flesh out the general principles contained in the main Act. Amongst their complex and detailed provisions may be found important principles affecting the basic operation of the industrial scheme. This subordinate legislation again often relates to the social security system as a whole, and titles to the various instruments may not specifically note that they deal with the industrial scheme. By SSA s. 141 the Secretary of State must refer drafts of regulations relating only to industrial injury to an advisory body, the Industrial Injuries Advisory Council, for its consideration and advice.

However, this can be avoided if the Secretary of State thinks the matter too urgent or the Council agrees to the procedure being bypassed.

(b) Caselaw

In seeking benefit a claimant may appeal from the decision of an adjudication officer to a tribunal and then to a Social Security Commissioner. The case may even be taken to the High Court. These Commisioner and court decisions focus upon areas where the legislation is silent, contradictory or otherwise uncertain. Since 1948 there have been over 75,000 Commissioners' decisions on all aspects of social security benefit, but only 2,600 of these have been considered important enough to be reported in a printed form by HM Stationery Office. About a quarter of these decisions deal with the industrial injury scheme and of these only about 20 have been appealed as far as the High Court. These industrial decisions are supplemented by the several thousand cases decided under the Workmen's Compensation Acts. Although these judicial decisions are at least 40 years old they can still be relevant to the interpretation of similar phrases used in the present compensation scheme. Taken together these various industrial injury cases constitute the body of precedent from which principles are applied by analogy to determine the outcome of present day claims.

(2) Guides to finding the primary sources

The references given below begin with the primary sources, that is, they indicate where the legislation and cases which have interpreted it may be found without them being abbreviated or adorned by editorial comment. Interpretation of the law by textbook writers and commentators are secondary sources. Although a full list of such references is not given here, a note is made of the public information available from the DHSS. Although local DHSS offices are supposed to have copies of (*a*), (*b*), (*c*) and (*e*) below for consultation by claimants and their advisers, in practice they may be difficult to obtain. Local tribunals should also have them to hand together with (*d*) which may also be consulted with the others at a law or other large library. The Lord Chancellor's department is conducting a review to discover whether access to the reports of social security decisions can be improved.

(*a*) HM Stationery Office, *The Law Relating to Social Security and Child Benefit* (1976). These four volumes contain all the statutes and regulations relating to industrial injury as well as most of those for social security in general. The volumes adopt a loose-leaf format and are regularly updated by supplements. Editorial notes indicate only the origin of amendments made. The work is often referred to simply by the colour of its cover and is known as "the brown book". HMSO and the DHSS hope that in the future this material, together with (*c*) below, will be available on an electronic data base so as to provide easier access to the up to date version.

(*b*) HM Stationery Office, *Reported Decisions of the Commissioner under the Social Security and National Insurance (Industrial Injuries) Acts*. Commissioners' decisions on the industrial scheme for the period 1948-76 are contained in seven volumes bound in dark blue. They are sometimes known as "the blue books" to distinguish them from "the red books" which contain the reports of Commissioners' decisions on other areas of social security. Since 1976 individual industrial injury decisions have been separately published by HMSO. They have also been incorporated in "the red books", each volume containing the reports for a three or four year period. If a case reaches the High Court the modern practice is to include the judgments as an appendix to the report of the Commissioner's decision. This means that the judgments appear in the HMSO publication as well as in the commercially published general law reports covering High Court cases.

Decisions from Northern Ireland are separately published. The industrial injury decisions are to be found together with the other social security cases in *Report Decisions of the Umpire under the Family Allowances, National Insurance and Industrial Injuries Acts (Northern Ireland)*. This covers the period 1948-61. Later decisions of the Northern Ireland Commissioner on the industrial scheme have been individually published.

Although unreported cases are not published by HMSO, copies of a case in the past have been obtainable from the Commissioners' offices or from the regional offices of the DHSS where assistance may be sought from the information officer. (For addresses see appendix C.) However, at the time of writing it is clear that claimants and their representatives do not share the same access to unreported cases as the DHSS, which is party to every case. The Lord Chancellor's office is investigating the matter and has issued a discussion document favouring equal access to decisions and making various suggestions for making decisions more widely available.

(*c*) D. Neligan, *Social Security Case Law – Digest of Commissioners' Decisions* (1979, HMSO). In two volumes this loose-leaf work by a former Commissioner classifies and briefly summarises those reported Commissioners' decisions of current relevance. However, it is not comprehensive.

(*d*) A.I. Ogus and E.M. Barendt, *The Law of Social Security* (2nd ed. 1982, Butterworths Ltd.). This textbook is one in which the DHSS has taken a special interest and given its support. Chapter 8 deals with the industrial scheme.

(*e*) *DHSS Leaflets* – General guidance as to the wide variety of benefits available as well as a list of other leaflets and sources of advice and information is given in leaflet FB. 2 "Which Benefit?" Leaflets dealing with the various aspects of industrial injury benefit are:

FB. 15	Injured at work: A guide to the industrial injuries benefit scheme
NI. 2	Prescribed industrial diseases
NI. 3	Pneumoconiosis and byssinosis
NI.207	Occupational deafness
NI. 6	Disablement benefit and increases
WS. 1	Supplements to workmen's compensation
PN. 1	The pneumoconiosis, byssinosis and miscellaneous diseases benefit scheme
NI.237	Occupational asthma

Industrial injuries leaflets dealing with medical matters are:

ND. 1	Notes on occupational deafness

NI.226   Pneumoconiosis and related occupational diseases: notes on diagnosis and claims for industrial injuries scheme benefits

NI.238   Clinical notes on occupational asthma

These leaflets are available free of charge from local social security offices or from the DHSS, PO Box 21, Stanmore, Middlesex, although for the pneumoconiosis guide ND. 226 it is better to apply to the DHSS, Norcross, Blackpool. The leaflets may also be consulted at public libraries and post offices. The leaflets indicate the DHSS's attitude to the social security scheme. Each contains the warning that they give general guidance only and should not be treated as a complete and authoritative statement of the law.

The DHSS also produce the following booklets relevant to the industrial scheme. They may be bought from HM Stationery Office:

Notes On the Diagnosis of Occupational Diseases (revised ed. 1983)
Industrial Injuries Handbook For Adjudicating Medical Authorities (3rd ed. 1986, loose-leaf)
Social Security Appeal Tribunals: A Guide To Procedure (1985)

(3) The reporting and citation of Commissioners' decisions

It is important to understand the way in which cases are reported and cited in order to use the references in this book and the system of precedent applied by tribunals. Methods have varied over the years and what follows is a summary of the main features.

(a) Reporting

Of the 75,000 Commissioners' decisions made since 1948 only about 2,600 have been reported in the sense that they have been published by HM Stationery Office. Most of these decisions have been thought to deal with a point of law of some importance in contrast to the unpublished cases which often deal with factual issues of relevance only to the particular claimants involved.

The decision whether to report a case is made by the Chief Commissioner. In October 1982 he issued a practice direction describing how the decision is taken. If any Commissioner thinks a decision worth reporting it is marked with a star (for ease of circulation) and comment is sought from other Commissioners. Representations that a decision should be reported may also be made by the parties to that case, including welfare organisations. However, whereas the DHSS have access to and make representations on all starred decisions, welfare organisations generally only have access to those decisions in which they were a party. Influenced by these comments the Chief Commissioner's decision to report depends upon whether the case involves an issue of legal principle, contributes to the orderly development of the law and commands the assent of the majority of Commissioners. The decisions in cases which are to be reported are sent to the office of the Chief Adjudication Officer where suitable headnotes are drafted. These are then sent for approval to the DHSS legal office and to the Commissioner whose decision it is. The headnote does not constitute part of the decision and carries no authority.

Reporting has been officially controlled in this way in order to avoid creating a large and unwieldy system of precedent. That was one of the defects of workmen's compensation where decisions proliferated such that one writer described them as "a veritable jungle of case law, through which neither light nor warmth could penetrate".[34] However, the present controls have not gone without criticism. A number of important decisions have not been reported. In recent times there has been a sharp fall in the number of published cases in spite of the increasing complexity of the law relating to the industrial scheme. However, following changes made in 1982 the Chief Commissioner expected the revised reporting arrangements to lead to an increase in the number of reported decisions. At present, even including those from Northern Ireland, there are less than thirty industrial injury cases reported a year.

A discussion document issued by the Lord Chancellor's office in May 1986 considered various options in relation to the selection of decisions for report. It was particularly concerned to ensure that various welfare groups had as good an opportunity as the DHSS to make representations on whether a decision was worth reporting. To secure equality of treatment it provisionally favoured preventing any representation at all and leaving the Chief Commissioner to make his decision without any advice. However, the discussion document also recognised that the system of social security adjudication has exceptional features and these might make it desirable to pursue other options. One of these was to formally circulate all starred decisions to welfare organisations so that they might express their opinion upon them. Another option being considered was simply to do nothing and retain the present method of selecting decisions.

(b) Citation

The method of citation in the first three years of reporting differs from that presently employed, but a consistent feature has been the use of a system of numbers and letters to identify separate elements in the decision. *Reported decisions after 1950* – are distinguished by the prefix 'R' indicating that they are reported. There follows a letter in brackets indicating with which of the ten groups of benefits the decision deals. (For industrial injury this is '(I)' but, for example, for sickness and invalidity it is '(S)'.) Next appears the case number which represents its order amongst other reported decisions for that particular year, the number and year being separated by an oblique stroke. Finally if a decision is made by a tribunal of Commissioners this is indicated in this book by the addition of '(T)' rather than the full usage of '(tribunal decision)'. For example, *R(I) 12/75(T)* is the twelfth reported case on industrial injury in 1975 and is a decision of a tribunal of Commissioners.

Reported decisions from 1948-50 – use the reference allocated to the Commissioner's file of papers relating to an appeal. This begins with 'C' for Commissioner. Next if the case is Scottish or Welsh this is indicated by 'S' or 'W'. There follows the letter, but without brackets, indicating the type of benefit being considered, again for industrial injury this is 'I'. Finally appears the case number and year. The number represents the order in sequence in relation to other reported cases, but because only a minority of decisions were reported from the Commissioner's file, gaps appear in the numerical sequence of cases in the reports. Thus although *CWI 17/49* is the

---

[34] W. Robson, *Justice and Administrative Law* (1951) p. 210.

seventeenth case on file in 1949 of a Welsh claim for industrial injury benefit, it is immediately followed in the reports by CWI 20/49 and *CWI 26/49*. If these cases had remained on file and not been reported this will be indicated in this book by the addition of '(unreported)' after the citation.

Northern Ireland decisions – are cited in a similar way to the British except that until 1960 the prefix 'R' or 'C' was not used. The letters indicating which group of benefits the decision deals with also differ and are not given until the end of the citation. Industrial injury is represented by '(II)'. Thus *R 2/60(II)* and *3/49(II)* are both Northern Ireland decisions on industrial injury for the years 1960 and 1949 respectively.

Unreported decisions – are, in effect, numbered by the pre-1951 British method and appear, for example, as *CI 6/78* (unreported). (Former distinctions between numbered and unnumbered cases as discussed in *R(I) 12/75(T)* are no longer made following the Chief Commissioner's practice direction referred to above.)

(4) The relative importance of decisions as precedents

As with other areas of law, determination of a social security case is affected by a hierarchy of authority in which the decision makers in superior courts are able to impose their views upon those beneath them in the appellate structure. This is done in an attempt to secure uniformity of treatment and greater certainty in the application of the rules. It is important for claimants and their advisers to appreciate that under this system of precedent, decisions of the High Court must be followed by the determining authorities which includes all Commissioners. In turn Commissioners' decisions bind tribunals and adjudication officers. This gives Commissioners considerable law-making power because few decisions reach the superior courts. Whilst the social security system complies in most respects with the doctrine of precedent as applied elsewhere in the law, it has certain problems and peculiarities of its own.

(a) Workmen's compensation cases

Although decisions of the superior courts on the industrial injuries scheme are binding, rulings made by such courts before 1948 on the Workmen's Compensation Acts need not be followed. The attitude of the Commissioners to such decisions has not been consistent. In *CI 70/49* it was said that "it is as a rule unnecessary in deciding cases under the Industrial Injuries Act to refer to decisions under the Workmen's Compensation Acts for the purposes of comparison or contrast". But in practice Commissioners have often resorted to citing the earlier cases and, in the High Court, these have been much more frequently used than Commissioners' decisions themselves. Workmen's compensation cases were recognised as a guide to construction in *CWI 6/49*, and this was supported by *R(I) 34/57* where it was said that if the language in the statute being considered is the same as that under the earlier Acts then there is a strong implication that it carries the same meaning. Neligan, a retired Commissioner, has suggested that, although not bound to do so, Commissioners in practice always have regard to and follow Court of Appeal and House of Lords cases on the Workmen's Compensation Acts. However, Lord Denning in the court of Appeal in *R* v. *Industrial Injuries Commissioner, ex p. AEU (Re Culverwell)* (1966) whilst acknowledging that it was legitimate to look for guidance to these decisions, emphasised that the errors made by them should not be incorporated into the new scheme. In his view these errors included too narrow an interpretation of the legislation and a failure to appreciate its social significance such that workers were denied the compensation Parliament intended them to receive.

(b) Commissioners' decisions

Previous decisions of Commissioners do not bind other Commissioners, although there is pressure to achieve consistency where possible. According to *R(I) 12/75 (T)*:

> ". . . a single Commissioner follows a decision of a Tribunal of Commissioners unless there are compelling reasons why he should not, as, for instance, a decision of superior courts affecting the legal principles involved. A single Commissioner . . . normally follows the decisions of other single Commissioners (see . . . *R(I) 23/63)*. It is recognised however that a slavish adherence to this could lead to the perpetuation of error and he is not bound to do so."

For their part adjudication officers and tribunals must follow all Commissioners' and court decisions. The only exception is in the case of those Commissioners' decisions which are marked "medical" and consider the aetiology of certain conditions and diseases. They were recognised as offering only guidance and were not considered to be binding precedents in *R(I) 9/67*. All other decisions must be followed. If there is conflict, a decision of a tribunal of Commissioners – even if reached only by a majority – is to be preferred to that of a single Commissioner. Where the conflict is between single Commissioners, tribunals are not obliged to prefer the earlier decisions to the later one or *vice versa*. However, Lord Denning suggested in *R* v *National Insurance Commissioner, ex p. Stratton* (1979) that the High Court would not be as ready to interfere with a decision which has been followed for a long time and not changed by regulations or challenged in the High Court, compared to a more recent decision. Although decisions from Northern Ireland are not binding they may be used in support of argument. While Irish cases are not often cited in Britain, one such decision was persuasive enough to be preferred to an unreported British decision in *R(I) 14/63*.

(c) Unreported cases

R(I) 12/75(T) suggests that less weight be given to unreported decisions. This is because reported decisions have been specially selected and have been distributed more widely than unreported cases so that they are more important, at least in as much as they have been applied and followed without criticism. The practice direction of October 1982 indicates that adjudication officers will, so far as is possible, cite only from reported cases. If, as an exception to this rule, they rely on an unreported case they must supply a copy of that decision for the claimant to see before the hearing. Claimants also must give advance notice if they intend to rely upon such a decision.

A discussion document dealing with the availability of decisions was issued by the Lord Chancellor's department in May 1986. It suggested that the freedom to cite all Commissioners' decisions, including those which were not reported, might lead to excessive legalism in argument, and delay further the hearing of a case. To prevent this it put forward three options for consideration: firstly, the present requirement that advance notice be given of the intention to cite unreported decisions could be more strictly enforced; or secondly, leave could be made necessary in order to cite such a case; or finally, the citation of unreported cases could be banned altogether.

CHAPTER 2

WORKERS COVERED

1. THOSE INJURED IN BRITAIN

Each day of their working lives 21 million people are covered by the industrial injuries scheme in that, if they were to suffer a work injury, the scheme could provide them with compensation. All those working for an employer are covered from their first day at work. It does not matter how long they have been in their job, what hours they work, or what they get paid. Nor do workers have to qualify, as they do for other benefits, by paying a minimum number of national insurance contributions. However, not everyone in work can claim: the growing number of self-employed – now around 2.6 million – are usually excluded. This is because SSA s. 50(1) requires a beneficiary to be an "employed earner" injured whilst in "employed earner's employment". An employed earner is defined by SSA s. 2(1)(a) as

> ". . . a person who is gainfully employed in Great Britain either under a contract of service, or in an office (including elective office) with emoluments chargeable to income tax under Schedule E."

Who are included in these two groups of people comprising all "employed earners"?

(1) Office holders

This group is much less important than the other, very few employed earners being office holders. Most people dignified with the title "officer" are no more than employees, and are usually included in the industrial scheme by virtue of having a contract of service and thus being members of the other, larger group of employed earners. Statute has failed to define who might be an office holder, and caselaw has also left matters vague. However, the leading tax case, *Edwards (Inspector of Taxes)* v *Clinch* (1981), requires an office holder at least to occupy a continuing post, that is, one which is not personal to the identity of the incumbent, but which is filled by successive holders. This meant that an engineer appointed on a personal basis to hold an ad hoc public inquiry was not an office holder. However, other tax cases have held that, for example, company directors, accountants acting as company auditors, officers of trade unions and NHS consultants can all be office holders. Members of Parliament, judges and local councillors could also be included. In so far as an office holder occupies an unpaid, honorary post he may not be considered "gainfully employed'', and therefore not an employed earner as defined above.

Apart from cases on national insurance contributions,[1] the only social security decision to consider who might be an office holder is *CI 6/78* (unreported). In this case a storeman received benefit under the industrial scheme for an injury sustained at a college whilst he was attending a training course for shop stewards. At first it was thought that he was covered by the scheme because at the time of his injury he was employed in the separate office of shop steward. However, later he was considered to be attending the course as part of his contract of service with his union, and he was therefore entitled to benefit in any event. This case reveals that if someone is a part-time office holder, or can show that he has a second contract of service, in effect, he has two chances to establish that injury has occurred in the course of his employment.

(2) Those employed under a contract of service

There is a distinction, familiar to lawyers in a variety of contexts, between a contract for services under which an independent contractor is engaged, and a contract of service under which an employee works. SSA s. 2 defines an employed earner to include those working under the second type of contract, but not the first. This is the reason for the exclusion of the self-employed from the industrial scheme. Also omitted are, for example, volunteers working for charities, and students placed with employers during vacations.

In practice, it is usually easy to apply the distinction between the two types of contract in order to classify most workers. Generally, if wages are received and tax is paid under the Pay As You Earn system, work is done under a contract of service, and as an "employed earner". This is the work that most people do, for there are at least eight times as many employees as self-employed. However, in some cases the distinction between the contracts can be difficult to draw. Is a truck driver who provides his own transport really an independent contracter if he is buying his lorry on credit from the one "customer" for whom he works exclusively? Problems in drawing the distinction can arise in a variety of contexts and it has given rise to much litigation. Disputes may occur not only in social security, but also with regard to taxation, various aspects of labour law and in tort. In relation to the latter, for example, damages at common law are only paid by an employer for the negligent acts of those employed under a contract of service; they are not generally paid for acts done in pursuance of a contract for services. The textbooks in these areas[2] deal with the distinction in detail, and it is therefore considered here only in outline. Before examining the specific legislative provisions on the distinction, the more general rules developed by caselaw are considered.

(a) Caselaw

Although the distinction between the two types of contract has provided a fertile field for litigation in areas other than industrial injury, no decisions

---

[1]   For cases on contributions see D. W. Williams, *Social Security Taxation* (1982) p. 69.
[2]   B. A. Hepple and P. O'Higgins, *Encyclopedia of Labour Relations Law*, Vol. 1 chap. 3. R. W. Rideout, *Principles of Labour Law* (4th ed. 1983) chap. 2. P. S. Atiyah, *Vicarious Liability in the Law of Torts* (1967) pp. 35-69.

have reached the courts specifically with regard to its application in relation to the industrial scheme. One reason for this is that SSA s. 93(1)(d) requires disputes about the distinction in relation to social security to be resolved by the Secretary of State, and there is only a limited right of appeal to the High Court. However, outside of industrial injury, and even social security altogether, there is a large body of caselaw which may be employed to decide under which type of contract work is being done and, therefore, whether there is entitlement under the industrial scheme.

The courts have employed various verbal formulae to distinguish employees from the self-employed. Is the person subject to some control, at least over the way in which the work is done, or where and when it is carried out? Is the person an integral "part and parcel" of the organisation as a "matter of economic reality"? In its leaflet NI. 39 the DHSS rely (perhaps too much) upon the test of control. It describes a contract of service as one

> ". . . where there is a mutual agreement or understanding that, in return for some specified remuneration in money or in kind or some other benefit or privilege, the employee shall personally render services subject to the right on the part of the employer to control or direct him in the work he does and the method and performance of his duties."

Many factors are relevant in deciding whether someone is in business on his own account. They include, for example, who owns the equipment or tools of the trade; who takes the chance of profit and the risk of loss; whether piecework payments are made rather than wages paid by the hour or day; whether a substitute can be sent to carry out the work involved; and what view of the relationship is taken by the parties themselves. However, a final decision cannot be taken upon the basis of any one of these factors alone. A court must weigh them all together to find, on balance, which side of the line a case falls. Partly by the very nature of this exercise it has resulted in decisions which very much depend upon their own facts. In borderline cases they are only of limited assistance in deciding whether a claimant is in business on his own account or is covered by the industrial scheme.

(b) Statute

By contrast to the caselaw, there are two groups of regulations which give clear guidance as to whether certain workers are to be treated as employed earners.

(i) Categorisation of earners regulations

The Social Security (Categorisation of Earners) Regulations 1978 (SI No. 1689) were made in order to determine the contributions which different groups must pay into the social security system. Class 1 national insurance contributions are payable in respect of employed earners, but the self-employed pay the lower Class 2 contributions. As a result, the self-employed are entitled to fewer benefits, and cannot claim for their industrial injuries. Where the regulations define which class of contributions are to be paid, they also have the effect of deciding who are employed earners for the purpose of the industrial scheme. This is so even though the regulations were not specifically intended to deal with entitlement to industrial injury benefit, but instead had the purpose, for example, of making it more difficult to avoid paying contributions.

The regulations treat certain workers as employed earners even though they are not employed under a contract of service. These include ministers of religion, certain part-time lecturers and teachers, and cleaners of premises other than private houses. Most people employed through agencies, such as the office "temp." secretary, or the non-NHS nurse, are also included as employed earners. However, some of those supplied on an agency basis may be held to be self-employed. Examples given in the schedule to the regulations include certain outworkers and homeworkers, actors, musicians and models. DHSS leaflets NP. 21, NI. 192 and NI. 222 give guidance on most of the above employments.

There are a number of decisions in relation to these regulations which have been made by ministers or courts. Although depending on their particular facts, these cases can give some guidance and, for example, have determined that a sub-postmaster is self-employed. Other decisions[3] have concerned those such as agricultural workers, artists and performers, driving instructors, labour only sub-contractors, sales representatives and sports staff.

(ii) *Employed earners for industrial injuries purposes regulations*

The regulations which deal with the classification of workers specifically for the industrial scheme are the Social Security (Employed Earners' Employments for Industrial Injuries Purposes) Regulations 1975 (SI No. 467). Schedule 1 lists various employments as within the scheme including paid or volunteer members of fire and other rescue brigades, mine inspectors, special constables, taxi drivers who rent their cabs, workers on the continental shelf, and certain airmen and mariners. Apprentices are also included, even if not gainfully employed in the sense that they receive no remuneration for their work, as used to be the case with solicitors' articled clerks. Although trainees injured whilst working under the Youth Training Scheme may not be employed earners, in practice the Manpower Services Commission makes payments to those injured which are equivalent to those under the industrial scheme.[4]

The most important exclusions from the industrial scheme made by these regulations involve two types of domestic employment:

Being employed by a spouse – does not fall within the scheme if the wages paid are below the threshold at which Class 1 contributions first become payable. The contributions regulations which define this threshold are amended each year, and from 6 April 1987 the minimum wages required are £39.00. If the wages exceed the threshold, the employment is still not employed earner's employment if it is not done "for the purposes of the spouse's employment". This means that if a husband employs his wife, at wages above the contribution threshold, she is within the industrial

---

[3] For detailed discussion of the regulations see A. Booth, *Social Security Contributions* (1982) chap. 2, and D. W. Williams, *Social Security Taxation* (1982) chap. 3, and especially pp. 54-68 dealing with the relevant cases.

[4] Secretary of State for Employment, H. C. Deb., written answers, vol. 46 col. 215, 21 July 1983.

scheme if, for example, she drives him to his place of work, but not if she drives him to a football match or for some other purpose unconnected with his job.

Being employed by certain other relatives – again may fall outside the industrial scheme. This happens if the relative employing the worker is not the spouse, but lives in the same private dwelling house as the worker, and the work is not being done "for the purposes of any trade or business carried on" in the house by the relative. For example, if a son is rewarded with payment for completing his homework, he is not in employed earner's employment, but if he is paid by his mother to type a manuscript sent to the typing agency she runs from home he may be within the scheme irrespective of how little he is paid. Even if the employment is illegal and the contract of service void, the Secretary of State has power, under SSA s. 156, to direct that the work is still covered by the industrial scheme. This power may be especially important in relation to children because one survey suggests that up to 40 per cent of those aged from 11 to 16 are in some form of employment, and most of this work is done illegally. Almost a third of these children were found to have suffered some sort of accident whilst working.[5]

(3) Reform

The main question concerning reform has been whether the self-employed should continue to be excluded from cover. The Pearson Commission considered them just as deserving of compensation for work injuries as employed earners.[6] It therefore recommended that they be brought within the industrial scheme, anticipating that this would increase its costs by 4 per cent. However, the DHSS expressed reservations particularly about the difficulty of identifying the course of employment of the self-employed. Is it always easy to say when they are "off duty"? There has also been concern that if this more independent group of workers were entitled to benefit, there would be more dispute over uncorroborated evidence because there are less likely to be witnesses of their accidents. Although the Pearson Commission concluded that these problems were not overwhelming and had been solved in other countries, the White Paper accepted that there were sufficient difficulties to prevent extending the scheme to the self-employed. As it is, for example, the farmer driving his tractor is well advised to take out private insurance against injury because he is not entitled to industrial injury benefit.

2. THOSE INJURED ABROAD

There are territorial limits to the industrial injury scheme as with any regime of social security. Generally the scheme does not protect those injured abroad. Thus with regard to prescribed diseases, PD reg. 14 regards time spent working abroad as not being in employed earner's employment. The general rule against cover used to be subject to few exceptions. It meant, for example, that no industrial benefit could be paid

---

[5]   Low Pay Unit, *Working Children* (1985, pamphlet no. 34).
[6]   Vol. 1 p. 183.

to the carpenter injured whilst working in the British embassy in Moscow in *R(I) 44/61*. However, in recent years the scope of the industrial scheme has been extended and many accidents on foreign soil now fall within its scope. Although the general rule still excludes, for example, foreigners who have no connection with the country, the exceptions to the rule offer protection to those for whom UK national insurance contributions are collected, or who temporarily work in particular countries.

The territorial limit of the scheme is not confined to the British Isles. For industrial injuries purposes Britain includes Northern Ireland, the Isle of Man and the Channel Islands.[7] By SSHBA s. 44 injuries within the territorial waters are also included. Outside these areas a claimant must bring himself within one of the following exceptions in order to take advantage of the scheme. The first of these exceptions is the most recent and important; the others remain of value only in so far as they offer cover beyond the scope of this first exception.

(1) Workers for whom UK contributions are payable

Injuries to these workers when employed abroad were brought within the industrial scheme in 1986. The Social Security Benefit (Persons Abroad) Amendment (No. 2) Regulations 1986 (SI No. 1545) amend the principal regs., SI 1975 No. 563, as follows:

> "Where on or after 1st October 1986 a person to whom this paragraph applies sustains an accident arising out of, and in the course of, his employment, or contracts a prescribed disease due to the nature of his employment, such employment shall for the purposes of. . . (benefit for industrial injuries and diseases) be treated as employed earner's employment notwithstanding that he is employed outside Great Britain, and any benefit. . . shall be payable from the date of his return to Great Britain notwithstanding that the accident happened or the disease was contracted while he was outside it."

The regulations apply this paragraph in favour of two groups of workers: firstly, the few who pay Class 2 contributions as voluntary development workers overseas; and secondly, workers for whom Class 1 national insurance contributions are payable. This last group includes any worker in his first year abroad if he was ordinarily resident in Britain before taking up his appointment overseas, and if his employer has a place of business here. Class 1 contributions must be paid for that period because of reg. 120 of the Social Security (Contributions) Regulations 1979 (SI No. 591).

The reason for providing cover for these workers was that it was thought harsh to deny them benefits when contributions were still being levied. In addition, it was doubtful whether there was much force in the objection that evidence concerning the claim might be difficult to obtain because other countries have no formal obligation to co-operate in any inquiries. Even if there were no such liaison, corroboration still could be obtained in normal circumstances from the employer based in the UK.

---

[7] For co-ordination with Northern Ireland see SSA s. 142. The parallel legislation for Northern Ireland is the Social Security (Northern Ireland) Act 1975. For industrial injury arrangements in relation to the Channel Islands see art. 24 of SI 1978 No. 1527, and for the Isle of Man see SI 1977 No. 2150.

(2) Airmen, mariners and workers on the continental shelf

Even outside territorial waters crew members of a ship or aircraft may be covered by the industrial scheme. They must show that they are working on a British craft, or their contract of service was entered into in the UK, or their employer has his principal place of business in this country.[8] Although areas designated under the Continental Shelf Act 1964 may not be within Great Britain, workers there are also covered provided that their injuries are incurred in connection with obtaining the natural resources of those areas, including oil and gas from the seabed.[9]

(3) Workers in a country with which Britain has a reciprocal agreement

Many western countries have entered into arrangements with Britain to deal with their subjects' rights to a range of social security benefits.[10] These agreements vary in their scope, and not all of them include industrial injury benefit. For example, because workmen's compensation within the individual states of the USA, Canada and Australia is privately administered, it has not been possible to include such coverage within reciprocal arrangements with those countries. Apart from EEC countries there are 14 others which have agreements with Britain regarding the industrial scheme. They are Austria, Bermuda, Cyprus, Finland, Gibraltar, Israel, Jamaica, Malta, Mauritius, Norway, Sweden, Switzerland, Turkey and Yugoslavia. In addition the EEC has agreed to co-ordinate benefits with Algeria, Morocco and Tunisia. Leaflets for most of these countries can be obtained from the DHSS Overseas Branch, Newcastle.

(4) Workers in EEC countries

Reciprocal arrangements made with member states before Britain joined the Community have largely been replaced by EEC regulations.[11] These aim to co-ordinate the national systems of social security in order to promote unity and encourage the free exchange of labour. Migrant workers, for example, are not to be penalised by having benefits withheld because of their movement from one state to another. The regulations thus try to remove restrictions on the payment of benefit which depend upon the claimant's nationality, or upon territorial limits. However, it is still left to each country to determine its own range and level of benefits, and it is important for a worker to identify the "competent" member state

---

[8] For airmen's benefits see SI 1975 No. 469 and for mariners' benefits SI 1975 No. 470. See also sched. 2 of the Social Security (Employed Earner's Employments for Industrial Injury Purposes) Regulations 1975 (SI No. 467), and regs. 82 and 88 of Social Security (Contributions) Regulations 1979 (SI No. 591).

[9] Sched. 1 part 1 para. 7 of the Social Security (Employed Earner's Employments for Industrial Injury Purposes) Regulations 1975 (SI No. 467), reg. 85 of the Social Security (Contributions) Regulations 1979 (SI No. 591), and regs. 10C and 11 of the Social Security (Persons Abroad) Regulations 1975 (SI No. 563).

[10] The relevant legislation is listed in the *Index to Government Orders* in force on 31 December 1983, pp. 1457-59.

[11] Art. 6 of reg. 1408/71 of the EEC Council of Ministers. In so far as the agreements are of wider scope than the regulations, they are still in force. Some of them have been updated since Britain joined the EEC.

responsible for his benefit. Generally, this will be the state in which the worker is employed and which collects his national insurance contributions, even if the worker is normally resident and his employer is based in another state. For example, British construction workers who take up employment in Germany normally must pay their contributions to the German system, and it is from that system they must claim if they suffer an industrial accident.

There are exceptions to this general rule. It is still possible for a worker to regard Britain as his competent state if he is posted to the EEC by a UK-based employer and his foreign job is expected to last for no more than a year, during which time he remains liable to pay UK contributions. Special provision for others, effectively enabling them to claim under the British scheme, is made by articles 13-16 of reg. 1408/71 of the EEC Council of Ministers. Those who may benefit include workers involved in international transport, and members of the diplomatic service and the EEC auxiliary staff. Regulations require co-operation between states with regard to providing evidence of the circumstances of the accident for which a claim is made. Article 65 of reg. 574/72 also requires that medical reports be forwarded to the competent state. These reports may contain details of the claimant's present condition and an assessment of the permanent consequences of the accident. These provisions further reduce what was once considered the serious difficulty of obtaining corroboration for an accident which occurred abroad. According to the first report in 1985 of the Chief Adjudication Officer there were 19 cases in 1984 where the provisions of the EEC regulations enabled accidents which occurred in the territory of other member states to qualify for industrial injury benefit in this country.

CHAPTER 3

ENTITLEMENT FOR ACCIDENTS

To succeed under the industrial scheme a claimant must show either that he has suffered personal injury by accident, or that he has contracted a prescribed disease. In both cases there are provisions which require a connection with work to be shown, but these differ as between accidents and prescribed diseases. For the latter the work connection is established by confining the claimant to a list specifying a limited number of diseases which experience and medical expertise have shown to be typical risks for certain categories of employment. If the disease is on the list the claimant benefits from a presumption that it has been caused by his job. By contrast for accidents, although the system is open-ended in that no list exists to limit what may amount to an industrial accident, it is more difficult for the claimant to prove the work connection for there are no presumptions.

Entitlement under the accident provisions derives from SSA s. 50(1) which states that benefit shall be paid in respect of

"personal injury caused after 4th July 1948 by accident arising out of and in the course of his employment".

This formula establishing the work connection is the same as that which determined liability under the Workmen's Compensation Acts. Throughout this century it has given rise to an enormous volume of litigation. In an attempt to reduce its complexities various reforms have been suggested. For example, it has been thought too subtle to require that the accident arise both in the course of and out of employment. Instead it has been proposed that a claimant should only have to satisfy one of these two branches of the formula. A more radical change would be to substitute a new form of words altogether, by, for example, requiring the accident to be "attributable to employment". But overall the formula seems firmly entrenched. It has been recognised that the problems to which it has given rise are not the result of the particular form of words used, but are inevitable in the concept of the industrial scheme itself: it is not poor legislative drafting, but the very attempt to distinguish work accidents from others which has thrown up the mass of litigation. However, the formula has been modified in certain limited circumstances where legislation has extended the scheme by declaring specific accidents to be work-related when, formerly, there may have been dispute about them. This approach of specifically dealing with recognised areas of difficulty is one which could be further pursued given the particular problems identified in the course of this chapter. But this would not undermine the support which exists for the words used by the present general formula. When it was retained in the

1946 legislation the Minister of National Insurance said: "We have looked at many alternative phrases . . . but . . . I am convinced that it is better to stick to the devil we know than fly to the devils we know not of".[1]

To establish a claim five interrelated conditions must all be satisfied:

1. An "accident" must occur.
2. "Personal injury" must be suffered.
3. The accident must "cause" the injury.
4. The accident must arise "in the course of" employment.
5. The accident must arise "out of" employment.

1. AN ACCIDENT MUST OCCUR

In drafting the Workmen's Compensation Act 1897 it was hoped that the use of simple language would make detailed legal interpretation unnecessary.[2] But employing less technical language does not ensure that the words will be easy to apply. Forty years after the Act was passed Lord Macmillan observed that:

> "The amount of money which has been spent in trying to ascertain what is an 'accident' . . . must now have reached a surprising total . . . . The question lends itself to metaphysical subtleties."[3]

The difficulties have not lessened in the intervening years.

Although an accident in the popular imagination may conjure up some dramatic event causing the emergency services to turn out in an atmosphere of crisis or even disaster, it is apparent that under the industrial scheme many other types of incident not normally thought of as accidents are included within the term. These may be of the most trivial or unsensational nature and cause injury only in a stealthy manner. Thus, as discussed below, even the slow onset of disease in certain circumstances can be classified as an accident. Nor, as may popularly be supposed, need an accident be completely unexpected. It is true that in *Fenton* v. *Thorley & Co.* (1903) an accident was defined as "any unexpected personal injury . . . any untoward event which is not expected or designed". But an accident need only be unexpected from the worker's point of view. It does not matter that it could have been anticipated by an expert such as a doctor or engineer. Also it includes "an event which although intended by the person who caused it to occur, resulted in a misfortune to him which he did not intend". Thus in *CI 123/49* the farm labourer who deliberately handled frozen material throughout the day and then found that he had suffered frost-bite was able to claim. Even though other people deliberately cause the claimant's injury it can still be called an accident. Thus in *Trim School* v. *Kelly* (1914) a schoolteacher beaten up and killed by his pupils was held to have suffered an accident. There also have been a number of cases in Northern Ireland in recent years, such as *R 1/81 (II)*, where deliberate shootings have been held to be accidents for the purpose of the industrial scheme.

---

[1] H.C. Deb., Vol. 414, col. 270, 10 October 1945.
[2] Lord Halsbury in *Powell* v. *Main Colliery Co. Ltd.* [1900] A.C. 366.
[3] *Law and Other Things* (1937) p. 159.

(1) The relationship between accidents and diseases

The distinction between an accident and a disease appears fundamental to the industrial scheme. At first sight there seem to be separate provisions in the SSA 1975 to deal exclusively with each form of injury. Indeed SSA s. 76(5) prevents those suffering from a prescribed disease bringing their claim under the accident provisions. However, because there is no sharp dividing line between an accident and an illness, diseases which are not on the prescribed list can be considered accidents in certain circumstances. This overlap is important and has perhaps surprising effects, for there were four times as many claims for disease first recognised as falling within the industrial scheme in 1982-83 because they were considered accidents rather than because they were listed as prescribed diseases.[4] This is also a reflection of the history of the legislation which has placed great strain upon the meaning of the word accident. The term has been expanded to include certain diseases and other injuries which many claimants are surprised to find covered.

When the Workmen's Compensation Act was passed in 1897 it compensated only the accident victim. The failure specifically to refer to disease was soon discovered to be a major omission, and in 1906 the list system of compensation described in the next chapter was begun. However, it takes a long time for a disease to be added to the list, and when it is included it may be narrowly prescribed in relation to specific occupations only. The result has been that if victims of disease are to claim at all, often they must do so under the accident provisions. This has caused the meaning of accident to be stretched to its limit in some cases in order to accommodate an injury caused by disease for which no compensation could otherwise be obtained. Despite such interpretations many diseases which develop slowly and insidiously cannot be considered accidents and no compensation for them exists. Thus in the case of non-prescribed diseases there is a crucial distinction between those which are caused by accident, and those which are the result of some continuous "process" and fall outside of the industrial scheme.

(2) Factors involved in the distinction between injury by accident and by process

As a general guide to this distinction it can be said that whereas an accident requires an event, or a series of events, no matter how small to cause injury, process is less likely to be the result of particular incidents and is better associated with the general wear and tear involved in the continuous activity of a job. There have been a large number of decisions[5]

---

[4] DHSS *Social Security Statistics 1984*, table 20.50. The figures include awards of injury benefits which has since been withdrawn.

[5] Under the Workmen's Compensation Acts see Willis pp. 8-18. For decisions since 1948 holding the injury to have occurred by process so as to deny benefit (and which are not referred to in the text) see *CSI 21/49*, *CWI 43/50* and *CI 83/50*(T) (all dealing with tuberculosis); *CSI 24/49* (rupture of knee ligaments); *CI 257/49*(T) (Raynaud's disease, "white finger"); *CI 325/50* (pleural effusion); *11/50(II)* (Dupuytren's contracture); *4/51(II)* (progressive muscular dystrophy); *R(I) 35/56* (motor neurone disease); *R(I) 32/60* (carbon monoxide poisoning); *2/59(II)* (muscular strain); *R 10/84(II)*. The injury occurred by accident and benefit was paid in *CI 12/49*, *R(I) 24/54* and *R(I) 4/62* (abscesses of hands); *CI 211/49* (epidermophytosis); *CSI 20/49* (fracture of wrist); *CI 36/50* (boils); *CI 159/50* (poliomyelitis); *CI 196/50* and *R(I) 77/52* (tuberculosis); *7/59(II)* (angina); *10/59 (II)* (conjunctivitis); *R 5/62(II)* and *R 2/72(II)* (muscle strain); *R 6/63(II)* (bovine tuberculosis); *R 1/69(II)* (poisoning by di-isocyanate).

dealing with the distinction, including important cases decided under the Workmen's Compensation Acts. It is difficult to reconcile all of these cases, although *R* v. *Industrial Injuries Commissioner, ex p. Starr* (1974) emphasises that the distinction is one of fact and degree, and should not be elevated to law and principle so as to accumulate any great mass of authority. The decisions offer the following three guidelines as to what amounts to process rather than accident:

(a) Continuity

According to the House of Lords in *Roberts* v. *Dorothea Slate Quarries Ltd.* (1948) the important element of process, in gradually producing incapacity, is its continuity from day to day, though not necessarily from hour to hour. The case held that silicosis caused by continuous exposure to dust over a 20 year period was injury by process. Another example of injury by process emphasizing the continuous acts involved is *CI 125/50* where injury was caused by the repeated jerking of the handle of a chisel against the claimant's palm. It resulted in injury to the hand (Dupuytren's contracture). The claimant in *CWI 29/74* (unreported) was similarly denied benefit when, as a garment cutter constantly using scissors, she developed a traumatic oedema of her finger. But where such injury from using scissors came on suddenly it was held to be an accident in *R(I) 43/61*. This leads to consideration of the next factor.

(b) Length of time

According to *R(I) 4/62*: "The period of time over which the process has existed has generally been a lengthy one, reckoned in years rather than days". This can produce anomalous results for, in effect, it means that the longer the exposure and higher the risk, the more difficult it may be to claim under the industrial injury scheme. Thus a claimant was denied in *R(I) 7/66* where his injury was caused by exposure at work to various chemicals over a period of 18 years. Similarly an accident could not be found in *R(I) 32/60* where the exposure was to carbon monoxide over a period of a year. Working for two years in water wearing wet and cold gum boots which resulted in frost-bite and septic feet was also held injury by process in *R(I) 25/52*.

By contrast, given a short period, it is easier to hold that a condition should be regarded as having occurred by accident. In *R(I) 31/52* one morning's exposure to a continuous draught through a lorry's broken window enabled the driver to establish that his resulting attack of fibrositis was an accident. But injury by process has been held to occur after only three days during which the claimant stitched leather in *R(I) 19/56*. This case was distinguished in *R(I) 43/61* where it was said that process "seemed to contemplate a length of time much longer than 2 or 3 days". However, if the period during which the condition develops is some five months then it must have occurred by process according to *R* v. *Industrial Injuries Commissioner, ex. p. Starr* (1974).

In emphasizing these two factors of continuity and length of time the decisions have left matters vague in two particular respects. First, it has not been made clear whether the factors should be applied to the features in the employment which cause the injury, or whether it is the effects of the employment – such as the internal or physical process of the disease itself – which should be studied. Thus in *R. (Curry)* v. *National Insurance*

Commissioner (1974) it was questioned whether continuity had to apply to the process which produced noise, or the physical process of the effects of noise on the ears. Secondly, the relationship between these factors and their relative importance is unclear. Which of them is to take precedence? Continuity was emphasized in *CI 83/50*(T) but *CI 257/49*(T) concentrates upon the time period involved.

(c) Particular event causing injury

In order for injury by accident to occur there must be some particular event which causes injury. The event may be similar to several others, but it must be capable of being reasonably clearly identified as the cause of the trouble. In *R(I) 52/51* the claimant was unable to establish that the aggravation of his childhood injury (an unhealed tubercular hip) had been caused by any specific incident at work and he was refused benefit. Similarly in *CI 244/50* a bus driver suffered from conjunctivitis because of the continuous draught entering his cab, but unlike the claimant suffering from the same disease in *R 10/59(II)* he could not identify any particular occasion which could be regarded as an accident causing his injury. According to *CI 39/83* (unreported) a continuous draught cannot be regarded as an event, or series of events, causing personal injury. In *R 2/60 (II)* a riveter subject to vibration from his machine was unable to point to any particular incident causing his hand to become painful and swollen. Finally, in *Fraser v. Secretary of State for Social Services* (1986) although the claimant suffered from strain resulting from uncongenial working conditions, he could not show that any particular event constituting an accident was responsible for his nervous disorder.

However, it has been held that just because a claimant cannot identify with certainty the particular day on which an event occurred she will not be prevented from establishing that it did take place within a limited period of time and amounted to an accident. This was the basis of the decision in *CI 46/49* where a claimant developed cattle ringworm after being in contact with infected calves. She was able to show that her disease amounted to an accident without having to identify exactly when, within the seven weeks of her association with the animals, the disease began. But where no contact with a source of ringworm infection at work could be shown the claim failed in *R 1/63(II)*.

Because a particular event is required it does not mean that an accident must be confined to external incidents like mishaps with machinery. It can include an internal physiological change for the worse as long as it amounts to a personal injury as defined below. All that is required is that such a change was contributed to in a material degree by the claimant's work (as discussed under causation below). This means that a muscle strain, a ricked back, or a rupture caused by lifting a weight at work can all be accidents. No exceptional or violent exertion is required. Thus the claimant who "felt something go inside" whilst pushing a hand truck, and who was then found to be suffering from angina induced by strain, was able to claim injury by accident in *CI 27/49*.

(3) A series of accidents and an accident at the end of a process

The distinction between accidents and disease has been complicated by two arguments which have been used to bring claimants within the injury by accident provisions even if they are suffering from disease. The first argument is that injury need not flow from one specific and definite accident, but may be the result of a series of such accidents. Although injury may occur over a long period of time, benefit is payable if there are a series of incidents each amounting to a separate identifiable accident. On this basis the claimant succeeded in the following cases: in *Burrell* v. *Selvage* (1921) where blood poisoning and arthritis resulted from a series of cuts to the hands over a period of four months; in *R(I) 43/55* where a neurotic condition was the cumulative effect of the claimant being in the vicinity of a series of explosions each amounting to an accident; in *R(I) 77/51* where a hernia was caused by the continual operation of a stiff reversing lever on the engine of a train, each movement leading to a minute widening of a tear in the muscular wall and amounting to an accident; and in *CI 29/49* where a strain to the heart was brought about by lifting a weight many times a day to operate an air press. If injury by accident is to be found, according to *R(I) 32/60*, these incidents must not be too numerous or develop too insidiously, whilst *R. (Curry)* v. *National Insurance Commissioner* requires that the incidents amount to accidents and not merely be the ordinary wear and tear of work. In this case deafness caused by regular screeches of a high-pitched saw used for cutting pigs' carcases was held to be injury by process because "a series of incidents which are not accidents cannot become a series of accidents merely because the victim's injury is caused over a matter of hours, weeks or months rather than over a period of years". There is therefore a crucial distinction between accidents and incidents, but little guidance can be obtained from the cases as to its application in particular circumstances.

The second argument concentrates upon finding not a series of accidents but only one accident among a number of incidents. The argument accepts that it may be by process that the body's defences are worn down, but it suggests that the final event – such as the breakthrough by which infection penetrates the skin – can amount to injury by accident. The onset of disease can then be an accident. In *Brintons* v. *Turvey* (1905) one stray germ of anthrax entering the body via the eye amounted to injury by accident, whilst an abscess resulting from an infection in a cut hand used all day in dirty work was held an accident in *R(I) 75/51*. Similarly, if a harmful process culminates at a point at which a physiological change for the worse occurs, it can be argued that an accident has happened. On this basis in *R(I) 18/54* the claimant succeeded where pressure on a nerve from a buckle on a knee over a period of ten weeks culminated in numbness and paralysis in the leg. This argument is particularly useful if claimants are to be compensated for a work injury when at first glance they appear to be injured by process and fall outside the industrial scheme.

(4) Reform

The doctrine of process has long been criticised. It is harsh to deny compensation to those workers who suffer from the gradual effect of work upon their health especially when the work connection is all too clear. In *R(I) 7/66* the Chief Commissioner refused payment with some regret:

"If it be accepted that the first purpose of this legislation is to provide benefit when insured persons are injured or killed by their work, the result of the doctrine of process . . . is that that purpose is not fulfilled. The claimant must think the result of this case neither intelligible nor just . . . ."

In this case, although a widow could prove that her husband had died from many years exposure to toxic chemicals in his workplace, she could not establish injury by either accident or prescribed disease.

The doctrine of process often denies compensation to those for whom medical science has not progressed far enough to enable a decision to be made that a disease should be prescribed for a particular occupation. The IIAC only recommend that a disease be prescribed if it satisfies the criteria examined in the next chapter. The detailed investigations it makes can take years. The IIAC have joined with others in expressing concern about the delay involved. Meanwhile many workers fall through the gap in the system being neither able to establish injury by accident nor able to rely on the list of prescribed diseases. The IIAC have described this gap as "a serious flaw in the present scheme",[6] and has proposed certain reforms. In particular it suggests that a claimant should be allowed to go outside the list of prescribed diseases and prove that in his case alone the injury, even if resulting from process, was caused by his employment. The IIAC believe that this system of individual proof is the only way that injury by process can be brought within the industrial scheme because the accident provisions cannot be eased any further. The IIAC proposal is discussed at p.133. The proposal has been rejected by Government. No other reform is in the pipeline, nor is clarification of the doctrine of process proposed. It seems that the accident/process distinction will continue to be a major one, difficult to apply and limiting the coverage offered by the industrial scheme for some time to come.

2. Personal Injury Must Be Suffered

The industrial scheme offers no compensation for damage to workers' property. Only injury to person can found a claim. However, this has been given a wide meaning and covers not only physical injuries, such as wounds or external bodily injuries, but also internal injuries such as the rupture of a blood vessel. It also includes illnesses and contracting disease (although a claim will fail if this is not an accident as discussed above). If injury is not caused immediately, it may be important to seek a declaration that an industrial accident has taken place for its consequences may not be fully known, and symptoms of injury may not reveal themselves until some time later. This is discussed at p. 202. However, immediate injury to person has usually been an obvious feature of claims made under the scheme. There have only been a few decisions discussing the meaning of personal injury, but these show that it has been interpreted broadly to include not only the more dramatic forms of physical injury but also less obvious consequences.

(1) Strains

A worker who suffers some temporary pain, or feels the body strain

6   IIAC report, *Industrial Diseases* (1980, Cmnd. 8393) para. 160.

because of the stress imposed by the task in hand as in *R(I) 19/60*, is not able to claim personal injury unless there is some lasting physiological or psychological change for the worse. This means that someone who already suffers from disc trouble and experiences an increase in back pain whilst lifting at work is unable to claim unless there is a physical deterioration in the condition itself. Even if there is such a change *R(I) 1/76* requires it to be of some substance.

(2) Mental Injury

Injury to person includes mind as well as body. Although relatively few claims are made it is possible to obtain benefit for the onset of a psychological disorder resulting from an accident at work. In *R(I) 22/59* it was recognised that "damage to the nervous system may be just as much a personal injury as damage to the structure of the bones, muscles and tissues of the body". In *CI 4/49* a worker using a circular saw cut his fingers and, although the wound healed, he subsequently developed a neurosis which prevented his return to work. Despite his apparent susceptibility to such illness he was successful in making a claim. In *R(I) 43/55* the neurotic condition resulted from repeated explosions each of which could have indicated that a more serious and damaging explosion was about to take place. Although the claimant succeeded in this case, if the nervous disorder is the result of strains arising over a period of time from uncongenial working conditions, it is likely to be regarded as arising by process and not accident as in *Fraser* v. *Secretary of State for Social Services* (1986).

In *R(I) 49/52* the neurosis resulted from witnessing the accidental death of a fellow employee. Although the claimant was not immediately involved she was sufficiently close to the accident for her injury to be attributed to it. This successful claim was distinguished in *R(I) 22/59* on the basis that in that case the accident had not been seen by the claimant. Instead a father had been told at work that his son, a fellow slate quarryman, had been killed whilst working nearby. The shock inflicted was considered not to arise out of an accident within the father's employment,[7] but was the result of the natural distress which any parent would feel on receiving such news. Whether a claimant's refusal to return to work because of his psychological state – which may include a fear of further injury – is considered at p. 176.

(3) Damage to artificial parts of the body

The remaining decisions have considered whether damage to an artificial part of the body can constitute personal injury. *R(I) 7/56* required that a claim could only succeed if there were "injury to a living body of a human being". Damage to spectacles as in *R(I) 1/82*, false teeth, or an artificial limb were then excluded. But *R(I) 8/81* has reconsidered the position of damage to prostheses and holds that a claim can succeed if the artificial appendage is so intimately linked with the body as to form part of it. This is the case if a diseased part such as a kidney is replaced with living tissue, or where synthetic material such as an artificial hip joint is inserted into the living body. Just because a prosthesis is an external appendage will not

---

[7]   In establishing the causal connection see "arising out of employment" below at pp. 83 and Willis pp. 369-70.

prevent it being treated as part of the body, but this will be unlikely if it can be freely detached. Whether damage to an artificial limb amounts to personal injury now depends on whether it is intimately linked with the body on the facts of the particular case.

3. THE ACCIDENT MUST CAUSE THE INJURY

(1) General principles of causation

The industrial scheme has experienced problems relating to the philosophical doctrine of causation similar to those encountered elsewhere in the law. In *R(I) 43/52* the hope was expressed that in determining questions of causation in relation to industrial injury "too much subtlety" would not be introduced. But it is apparent that the scheme has arrived at complex solutions depending upon subjective and unpredictable formulae often similar to those found in the law of tort or crime. In order to establish entitlement to benefit the claimant must prove:

(a) That on the balance of probability the accident caused his injury. According to *R(I) 14/51* it must not remain a matter of mere speculation as to what happened.
(b) That "but for" the accident the injury would not have occurred (the *causa sine qua non*). Although this is a necessary condition it is not sufficient to establish a claim. The claimant must go on to prove –
(c) That the accident is a cause of some potency, amounting to an "effective" cause of the injury (the *causa causans*). It must not merely be the circumstance or condition of injury, but must contribute to a material degree. For the accident to be an effective cause there must be an unbroken chain of causation connecting it with the claimant's present incapacity.

The claimant does *not* have to prove:

(a) That the accident is the sole or even predominant cause of injury. It is sufficient that it is a contributory cause as emphasised in *R(I) 3/56*(T).
(b) That at the time of the accident the injury could be seen as a probable, direct or natural consequence – *R(I) 54/52*.

In practice the distinctions are by no means easy to draw. For example, the fact that an employee is drunk does not necessarily prevent an accident from arising "out of" employment. If the drunkenness is the sole and exclusive cause of the accident, then it does not arise out of employment. On the other hand, if the employment is sufficiently material to amount to an effective cause, then the accident arises out of employment notwithstanding that the employee, because of drunkenness, is less able to avoid the risk or its consequences. The distinction is one of degree and the dividing line cannot be defined clearly in general terms.

Although each case is decided upon its own facts the general principles can be illustrated by looking at decisions dealing with successive injuries or conditions which combine to establish injury. Most of these cases have either considered whether death benefit should be paid, or have been concerned with entitlement to the now abolished short-term injury benefit. The cases dealt with situations where it often must have been the case that no continuing loss of faculty was likely, and entitlement to disablement benefit would not arise. Nevertheless they applied general principles which are still relevant to a disablement benefit claim. There is an additional feature to such a claim in that, if the loss of faculty is the result of more than one effective cause, an offset is made to reduce benefit for any non-industrial cause, as discussed at p. 149.

(2) Later injury after the industrial accident

(*a*) *Falls*

The first line of cases considers what is to happen where, following an industrial accident, the claimant suffers another injury not immediately connected with his job. These later injuries have almost always been the result of falls away from the place of work. Are they to be considered as caused by the earlier industrial accident? In *CI 384/50* the claimant failed to show that her fall at home, which was the result of giddiness and a nervous state, was brought on by her earlier industrial accident when she had fallen at work. In *R(I) 16/55* the claimant was injured at work when nails pierced his foot. This caused him a few days later to walk along a beach in such a way that he twisted on his ankle and fractured a bone. This later non-industrial injury was a new intervening cause giving a new starting point to the incapacity and no benefit could be claimed. The case of *R(I) 59/51* was distinguished in that the later accident – a fall whilst doing remedial exercises in hospital – was considered to be the direct result of the earlier industrial injury. The claimant also recovered following a fall whilst walking through snow in the very act of returning to his job in *R(I) 3/56*(T), the leading case on causation in relation to injury benefit.

(*b*) *Attempted suicide*

A second example of a later injury which may be caused by the industrial accident is where, following his injury, the claimant attempts suicide and further injures himself. The cases[8] have dealt exclusively with claims for industrial death benefit, but it is likely that the principles of causation would be similarly applied if the claimant survived his attempt and claimed his greater injury resulted from his work accident. The crucial distinction is made by *R(I) 19/52*. If the depression and moodiness which results from the work accident

> ". . . is so acute as to deprive a man of the power of making conscious decision and place him entirely at the power of unreasoning impulse, then the suicidal act committed under the force of that unreasoning impulse can properly be said to result from the injury. On the other hand, if the depression is not such as to deprive him of will and reason and conscious decision, but merely throws him into a state of dejection in which he consciously decides that death would

---

[8] Claims succeeded in *CI 172/50, R(I) 2/57* and *R(I) 36/60* but failed in *CI 256/49, CWI 12/49, R(I) 38/51, R(I) 19/52, R(I) 23/57* and *R(I) 42/59*. There is a presumption against death being the result of suicide and this was not rebutted and the claim for death benefit succeeded in *CI 113/50, CSI 23/50* and *R(I) 47/59*(T). Whether this presumption against suicide as the cause of later injury would apply where the claimant was still alive to give evidence in applying for disablement benefit is open to question.

offer a means of escape, then his conscious decision creates a new precipitating cause. . . ."

(3) Earlier susceptibility to injury before the accident at work

A longer line of cases consider whether conditions which arose before the claim for the industrial accident and which made the claimant more susceptible to injury are to be taken into account. These cases often contain detailed guidance as to the aetiology of certain diseases and conditions. Many of them have concluded that the weakness of the claimant was the sole effective cause of injury (in which case no benefit is paid). However, in other cases the pre-existing condition has been considered either a contributory cause (in which case an offset may be made to reduce disablement pension), or not an effective cause at all (in which case there is entitlement to the full benefit).

If the injury would have occurred anyway and it merely happens that, for example, the heart attack began whilst at work, benefit will not be paid. The claimant cannot then show his work to be causally relevant; he cannot say that but for his work the accident would not have occurred. The accident does not arise "out of" employment. The crucial causation question asked in *R(I) 73/81* is "was it the disease that did it, or did the work that he was doing help in any material degree?" The work need only be a material not the predominant cause, so that compensation arises if a minor work incident has quite disproportionate physical results and the claimant suffers much more serious injury than would a normal worker. It does not matter then that the industrial cause is the "last straw which breaks the loaded camel's back", for the scheme takes its claimants as it finds them, including their pre-existing weaknesses. The rule in tort law that a plaintiff can succeed despite having an unusually "thin skull" which makes the effects of his accident much more severe is thus reflected under the scheme. It was applied in *R(I) 19/63* where a bakery assistant with a degenerative disc condition crouched down to put dishes under a table and this was the last straw which caused the complete prolapse of an already partially prolapsed disc. In *R(I) 16/62* a nick of the skin had such an effect upon the claimant's existing vascular condition that his foot had to be amputated. Benefit was nevertheless paid.

The decisions have emphasised the need to find some feature in the employment which brought about the injury so that it arises "out of" employment. (See also the cases cited under that heading at p. 83). The employment can be shown to be causally relevant in two particular ways:

(a) *The cause of strains and heart conditions*

If it can be shown that the work caused the strain which resulted in injury (and this is more likely if the work required special effort), then the claimant will succeed. According to *Clover, Clayton & Co.* v. *Hughes* (1910) an accident arises out of employment "when the required exertion producing the accident is too great for the man undertaking the work, whatever the degree of exertion or the condition of his health". On this basis the claimant who suffered a hernia whilst lifting a heavy steel plate succeeded in obtaining benefit in *8/59(II)*. In *R6/70(II)* the strain was a material cause of the claimant's injury despite his pre-existing osteo-arthritis which contributed to it. However, in *R(I) 11/61* the strain was not sufficient to amount to an effective cause to materially aggravate the pre-existing hernia. Nor in *CWI 50/82* (unreported) could it be shown that the strain caused to a nursing officer's back by rising from a chair arose out of employment. The chair was not defective and she had not been working for an abnormal length of time. It was merely fortuitous that the accident had happened at work and benefit was refused.

With regard to heart disease, claimants in the past encountered great difficulty in relating their injury to work. The problem gave rise to many decisions in the early years of the scheme,[9] but there have been hardly any since 1961. In most of the early cases benefit was refused even though heavy work was involved, as in the miner's job in *R(I) 16/56*. The difficult burden with which the claimant was faced is illustrated by a decision in which payment was made. In *CWI 30/59* (unreported) the Commissioner noted that the claimant's work must have tested his strength to the limit:

> "He succeeded in doing something which normally required the strength of two men. It was an effort of short duration, but severe while it lasted, and was utterly different in kind from his normal work. It seems to me to have been the sort of abnormal effort which, if followed within a few hours by a coronary occlusion may be regarded as having caused the occlusion."

But the last reported case to consider heart disease contains detailed medical evidence which is much more favourable to claimants. In *R(I) 12/68* a furniture remover was able to show that his myocardial infarction resulted from lifting a heavy wardrobe. The degree of exertion required in order to cause such injury and establish title to benefit was said to be only that which is excessive for the person concerned. The history of the change in attitude leading to the medical opinions expressed in this case is traced in an article by a former DHSS chief medical adviser.[10]

(b) The cause of falls and fractures

If the employee is injured by coming into contact with the employer's plant, premises or equipment the employment will be considered the cause. In *R(I) 11/80* the claimant with a blood pressure condition fell to the factory floor probably because of his hypertension. The injury caused by contact with the premises was held to arise out of employment. The decision is very favourable for claimants because the Commissioner stated that it did not matter whether the cause of the fall had been the state of the floor, the claimant's artificial leg, his carelessness or something else unexplained. Previous cases denying compensation because the fall had resulted from the claimant's epileptic condition were not followed. But just because a fall happens at work does not mean that the injury must arise out of employment if the injury did not result from coming into contact with an external object. Thus in *R(I) 6/82* it was emphasised that unexplained bone fractures suffered by an employee whilst walking, or a heart attack suffered

---

9   The claimant recovered in *CI 27/49*, *CI 39/49*, *R(I) 6/51*, *R(I) 14/51*, *R(I) 13/54*, and in the medical decisions *R(I) 42/53*, *R(I) 54/53*, *R(I) 42/54*, *R(I) 31/56*, *R(I) 12/68*. The claim failed in *R(I) 18/51*, *R(I) 20/51*, *R(I) 19/60*, and in the medical decisions *R(I) 43/53*, *R(I) 84/53*, *R(I) 99/53*, *R(I) 62/54*, *R(I) 1/55*, *R(I) 34/55*, *R(I) 16/56*, *R(I) 29/56*, *R(I) 32/56*, *R(I) 49/56*, *R(I) 21/57*, *R(I) 28/58*, *R(I) 25/59*, *R(I) 44/60* and *R(I) 5/61*.

10   Carmichael, "Medical Aspects of the Industrial Injuries Act: Some Illustrative Case Studies" (1974) 42 *Medico-Legal J.* 44.

whilst sitting down, are not compensated unless some specific aspect of the employment causes the injury. In *R(I) 12/52* this condition was satisfied. The workman had hopped over a shallow gully at work and this, together with his brittle bone condition, had resulted in a fractured leg. By showing that he had come into contact with the work premises in this way he had proven that his employment was a contributory cause of injury. However, no such work connection could be shown in the other brittle bone cases of *R(I) 73/51* and *5/57(II)*.

(c) The cause of other conditions

There are many other reported decisions dealing with whether the accident caused the injury in which the aetiology of certain diseases and conditions is considered. Many of these have been reported primarily so that the medical opinion can be published and their heading is marked as a "medical decision". Almost all of these decisions are more than 20 years old. Although care must be taken to ensure that their views are not out of date, they may still give guidance as to the medical factors taken into account in deciding whether an accident has caused injury and whether it arises out of employment. Although *R* v. *Deputy Industrial Injuries Commissioner, ex p. Moore* (1965) allows medical opinions given in other cases to be taken into account, *R(I) 9/67* emphasises that the medical decisions themselves offer only guidance and do not constitute binding precedents. As an example of this guidance in relation to the common injury involving intervertebral disc conditions[11] *R(I) 19/63* suggests three broad classes of case, the first being the most likely to fall within the industrial scheme:

"The first class is that of a person whose intervertebral discs are completely healthy but who suffers a sudden prolapse. Since the discs are controlled by extremely powerful ligaments, considerable violence is necessary in such a case . . . . The second class is at the opposite end of the scale. Here a claimant, one or more of whose discs would be described by doctors as degenerative, suddenly suffers a spasm of pain. This may indicate nothing more than that the discs are not in a healthy condition, and are becoming progressively worse, partly perhaps as a result of the ordinary stresses and strains of life . . . . [I]t would be difficult to say that there was anything that could be described as personal injury by accident, or that it arose out of employment . . . . A third and intermediate class of case [is] . . . where there is already a degenerative condition of one or more discs and, owing to some movement by the claimant at work, the claimant feels sudden pain which continues . . . . [Here] there must have been a physiological change for the worse as opposed to mere transient pain."

Apart from these disc conditions and other causes of injury discussed in the text, there are cases dealing with the following:[12] cancer, brain haemorrhage or thrombosis, eye or ear disease, bronchitis or influenza causing pneumonia, phlebitis, tuberculosis, arthritis, sclerosis, asthma, osteomyelitis, "trigger finger", hypertension and other conditions.

---

[11] A claimant recovered in *CI 94/50*, *R(I) 53/51* and *R(I) 19/63* but failed in *R(I) 20/56*, *R(I) 35/59*, *R(I) 12/60*, *R(I) 33/60* and *R(I) 4/65* affirmed in *R* v. *Deputy Industrial Injuries Commissioner, ex p. Moore* (1965).

[12] A claim for cancer failed in *R(I) 37/53*, *R(I) 74/53*, *R(I) 86/53*, *R(I) 19/54*, *R(I) 55/54*, *R(I) 67/54*, *R(I) 25/58*, *R(I) 14/59*, *R(I) 6/60* and *R(I) 25/60*.

4. THE ACCIDENT MUST ARISE IN THE COURSE OF EMPLOYMENT

Although in most accident cases the relationship with work is obvious, the formula used to inquire whether such connection can be made has given rise to more dispute than any other in social security law. If taken together with the other main problem area – that of reduced earnings allowance – cases dealing with "arising out of and in the course of employment" comprise the great majority of Commissioners' decisions on the scheme. The phrase has always been present to mark out the boundaries of workers' compensation. According to Lord Denning in *R* v. *National Insurance Commissioner ex p. Michael* (1977) the words "have been worth – to lawyers – a King's ransom. The reason is because, although so simple, they have been applied to facts which vary infinitely". As recognised in *R(I) 42/56* very subtle distinctions have been drawn by the cases and "attempted assimilation of the circumstances of the accident under review with those of other cases in the reports, if carried too far, becomes merely perplexing". Despite this in 1978 the Pearson Commission rejected the suggestion that the phrase should be substituted by "attributable to employment" because "a considerable body of case law has developed . . . and we should be reluctant to change the definition after such a long period of use".[13]

The caselaw may appear less confused following the guidance offered by the Court of Appeal in *Nancollas* v. *Insurance Officer* (1985). It emphasises that decisions on the course of employment are to be regarded only to a very limited extent as creating binding precedents. Because the incidence of employment is so varied, the cases cannot provide a simple formula to give a ready answer in particular cases.

> "[T]he reality is that none of the authorities purports to lay down any conclusive test and none propounds any proposition of law which, as such, binds other courts. They do indeed approve an approach which requires the Courts to have regard to and weigh in the balance every factor which can be said in any way to point towards or away from a finding that the claimant was in the course of his employment."

The approach to be adopted was compared to that of a jury: a yes or no answer was required to a broad question, and no one factor was to be conclusive. Athough this guidance may help explain away "difficult" decisions, it is of little assistance in predicting which way future cases will be decided. Much of this chapter therefore examines the relative importance attached to various factors taken into account in the past in

---

A claim for brain haemorrhage or thrombosis failed in *R(I) 53/53, R(I) 17/55, R(I) 21/55, R(I) 21/56, R(I) 9/58, R(I) 15/58* and *R(I) 15/59*.
All the following claims failed: for eye injury or ear disease in *R(I) 35/54, 10/59(II)* and *R(I) 39/59*; for phlebitis in *R(I) 70/53, R(I) 100/53* and *R(I) 101/53*; for tuberculosis in *R(I) 11/60* and *R(I) 23/60*; for arthritis in *R(I) 60/53*; for sclerosis in *R(I) 33/51*; for asthma in *CSI 1/48*; for osteomyelitis in *R(I) 2/61*; for "trigger finger" in *R(I) 10/60*; hypertension in *R(I) 2/61*; and for cervical spondylosis in *CI 39/83* (unreported).
Bronchitis or influenza causing pneumonia were considered unconnected with accident in *CI 147/50, CI 413/50* and *R(I) 9/52*.
Other claims failed in *CWI 3/50, CSI 82/49, R(I) 83/53, R(I) 19/54, R(I) 43/60* and *R7/61(II)*. They succeeded in *CI 5/49, CI 82/49* and *R 5/62(II)*.
[13] Pearson vol. I para. 896.

deciding whether injury occurs in the course of employment. These factors must be considered alongside the Court of Appeal's emphasis upon the circumstances of the individual case.

Relationship to "out of employment"

It is often difficult to distinguish the requirements that an accident must arise both "in the course of" and "out of" employment. What does the one part of the phrase add to the other? Both emphasise that the injury must be a risk of employment and there is authority noted in *R(I) 3/67* for viewing the phrase as a "composite expression". Despite this, it is more common for decisions to distinguish two separate elements in the formula. According to *R(I) 2/63:*

> "Whereas the question whether an accident arises in the course of the claimant's employment is, generally speaking but not always, a question of time and place, the question whether the accident arises out of employment is one of causation."

This distinction was applied in *R(I) 7/60* where an agricultural worker going about his job was struck by lightning. He was denied benefit (although the case would today be resolved differently by SSA s. 55, below p. 86). The reason the claim failed was that although he was in the course of employment (he was doing his job at the appropriate time and place), the injury did not arise out of it (the job did not cause the accident). Despite this example the distinction is by no means clear. There is confusion because both parts of the phrase often rely upon the same analysis of causation. The definition of the course of employment depends upon causation for it is not enough to rely upon the injury occurring at the factory during working hours. What the claimant was doing before he was injured can interrupt the employment unless it was reasonably incidental to the work he was employed to do and thus caused by it. "Did the work cause the injury?" is then as relevant to the course of employment as it is to arising out of employment. The overlap is illustrated by the claimant who is injured when his clothes catch fire because he smokes cigarettes at work, although he has been told not to do so. If he is to be denied benefit he could either be considered acting outside the course of his employment, or his injury might be thought not to arise out of employment.

Despite the potential confusion in distinguishing separate elements in the phrase, in practice the overlap causes few problems. Today if an accident is found to be in the course of employment it is almost certain to arise out of it. This is partly because of the statutory presumption, discussed later, that an act in the course of employment arises out of it. But more important is SSA s. 55 which was first introduced in 1961. This declared certain injuries in the course of employment, such as those resulting from another's misconduct, to arise out of employment. The section has prevented adjudication officers from bringing before tribunals certain problems of causation formerly debated as questions arising out of employment. The two branches of the phrase can be seen as more closely related than ever before. Despite this it will be convenient here to maintain the distinction between out of and in the course of employment in order to follow the traditional grouping of certain problems as discussed in the cases.

A question of time, place and activity

In considering whether the claimant was acting within the course of employment the first questions to be asked are whether the injury occurred at the place of work (examined under (1) below), and whether it happened during working hours (examined under (2) below). If the claimant's answers are satisfactory on these points a preliminary case for benefit is established. However, the time and place of the accident do not finally dispose of matters for it may be that the course of employment has been interrupted by the claimant performing some act for his own purposes and unconnected with his work. It is also possible for employment to be extended beyond the usual place and times of work if the claimant is doing something reasonably incidental to his work. The claimant's acts which may thus extend or interrupt his course of employment are examined under (3) below.

(1) The Place of work and access to it

The general rule formulated at the beginning of the century is that employment does not begin until the worker has reached the place of work or the ambit, scope or scene of his duty. It does not continue after he has left it and the periods of going and returning are generally excluded. This rule is subject to several exceptions such as where the employee travels in transport provided by the employer, as dealt with by SSA s. 53. The rule also cannot be applied where the employee's job is to travel, and where there is no fixed place of work. These particular issues are considered in relation to commuting accidents and travelling on duty at p.73 below. Here the discussion is confined to an examination of the course of employment for these who have a defined place and hours of work, that is, for most workers. To what extent can they succeed if injured in or near the employer's premises, although not actually at the immediate place where they perform their duties, and to what extent may they fail even if the accident occurs on their employer's property?

The general question to be asked is whether the injury is due to "a risk incidental to employment as distinguished from a risk to which all members of the public alike are exposed" as discussed by Lord Macmillan in *Northumbrian Shipping Co.* v. *McCullum* (1932). Injury is less likely to be the result of a risk to which the general public is exposed if it occurs at the claimant's place of work, or is upon other property such as the road to the factory which is controlled by the employer. Therefore, whether the employer owns the land upon which the accident happens is an important, although not conclusive, factor. Even if the accident occurs off the employer's property it may still be considered the result of employment if the claimant is injured in gaining access to his place of work and the public do not run such a risk. However, the further away in time and space from the hours and place of employment the more likely it is that the risk is shared by the general public and is outside the industrial scheme. The exact boundary line can be difficult to draw, however, and this is reflected in some of the contradictions to be found in the case law.

(a) *The place of work*

This is not confined to the employee's immediate site of production and can include a broad area. In *Holness* v. *Mackay* (1899) it was settled that a claim could succeed even though the employee was injured on the ground floor of a factory whilst going to his work on the upper floor. But a claim will fail if the employee is injured at a place where she has no business to be as in *CI 128/49*. The relevance of the claimant's activity at work in the context of where the accident takes place is considered in relation, for example, to baths, toilets and canteens at p. 63 below.

(b) Access and egress

The entry by employees to and from their place of work may also be protected by the industrial scheme. Access was defined in *R 2/75(II)* (T) as

> "a link between the place open to the public and the place where the employee has to work. It may be over the employee's premises, . . . or it may be over someone else's private property over which passage has been arranged solely by reason of the employment. A place which is open to the public is invariably excluded."

The distinction between an employment risk run in the course of leaving work and a risk run by the general public was further explored in *R(I) 3/72*:

> "The course of an employed person's employment normally ends when he leaves his place of work. This does not necessarily mean the particular building or part of the premises where he works. A workman is generally allowed time and space in which, so to speak, to 'disengage himself' from his employment. Thus a person who works at a particular place or building within an enclosed area of property will generally be regarded as still in the course of his employment until he reaches the exit gate . . . . In cases where that gate marks the boundary between private property and public thoroughfare, no difficulty arises . . . . The moment, or place of disengagement is less easy to determine in the case . . . where the employed has some distance to traverse between leaving his precise place of work and reaching the public road. In that situation, the answer generally depends on the extent to which the route or mode of egress is open to and used by the public."

These distinctions have been explored in a number of cases[14] where, in general, claimants have succeeded if the injury was on a private road, but have failed on public roads or private roads to which the public has access. This access need not be the result of a public right of way for it is enough that the public has only a licence to use the land. The test is whether the public in fact use the road or land in question. The mere existence of a power to exclude them will not suffice to establish a claimant's title to benefit if that power is not exercised and the public in fact use the road as in *R 3/61 (II)* and *R 10/83 (II)*. In *R(I) 20/57* although the use was much more frequent in summer it was sufficient to classify the pathway all year round. This meant that the claim failed even though the accident happened at a time when the public rarely used the path. Claims also failed where the public used the land in the leading cases of *Clark* v. *Stephen's Sutton* (1937) and *R(I) 21/59*. In *R 2/75 (II)* (T) the majority opinion fully reviews the workmen's compensation decisions on the subject and strictly enforces the

---

[14] The claim succeeded where the road was private, for example, in *R(I) 43/51, R(I) 41/57* and *R(I) 27/60*. The claimant failed where the road was public in *CI 331/50, R(I) 79/51, R(I) 1/53, R(I) 61/51* and *4/52(II)*. There was sufficient public use of a private road so that the claim also failed in *CI 39/50, R(I) 23/55, R(I) 6/64* and *R 3/61(II)*.

view that an accident on a public road before work has begun is outside the industrial scheme.

There are five related arguments which have enabled claimants to succeed in some cases despite their accident occurring on the public highway or on a private road to which the public also has access. These are that:

(i)   The use made of the road by the public is insignificant as in *R(I) 43/51* and *R(I) 1/68*.

(ii)   The only members of the public using the road do so in order to visit the employer on business as in *R(I) 41/57*. Thus in *5/51 (II)* an Irish civil servant obtained benefit following injury whilst riding his bicycle down an avenue a few hundred yards from his place of work at Stormont Castle. The avenue was only used by employees and members of the public having business at Stormont.

(iii) The road is private at the time the claimant is injured, although the public are not prohibited from using it at other times. This dual character of the road enabled the claim to succeed in *6/51 (II)*.

(iv)   The claimant has so nearly approached his means of access that it is reasonable to hold that he had returned to his sphere of employment. This argument was successful in *R(I) 3/53* and is referred to below in relation to mariners.

(v)   The claimant is entangled with employment and becomes involved in the duties of his job to such an extent that, although injured on the public highway, he has ceased to be an ordinary member of the public. On this basis the claim succeeded in *R 1/81 (II)* where the employee was shot outside a car park as he was making his way towards his place of employment. Benefit was paid despite the injury occurring on the public road because the claimant was making arrangements about the allocation of parking space at the time he was shot. Similarly, the minority opinion in *R 2/75 (II)* (T) emphasized that the frontier between the public and private place does not mark the separation between risks incidental to employment and those shared equally by the public. An attack on the road outside the place of work, such as an injury arising from crossing picket lines, might then fall within employment. However, the majority opinion strictly enforces the distinction to deny claims on property to which the public has access. The general rule that accidents on the road on the way to work are outside the industrial scheme was reaffirmed in *R(I) 4/79*. Other cases generally denying benefit to those injured whilst travelling to duty are considered at p. 73.

(c) Mariners

The above general principles can be illustrated by decisions relating to accidents occurring to dockers and seamen when a ship is in port. Injuries have occurred whilst going to or from the dock or the ship in harbour. It has been held that benefit may be paid if:

(i)   the claimant is injured whilst using a means of access which is not available to the general public. Thus a seaman injured whilst crossing a jetty not owned by his employers but which he, and not other people, was permitted to use in order to board his ship succeeded in his claim in *Northumbrian Shipping Co.* v. *McCullum* (1932), *CI 7/50* and *R(I) 21/54*. However, as in *R(I) 195/49*, *R(I) 61/54* (T) and *R(I) 6/64*, a claimant injured on property used by the public cannot claim unless –

(ii) the claimant has so nearly approached his means of access that it is reasonable to hold that he has returned to his sphere of employment. On this basis the claim succeeded in *R(I) 3/53* but failed in *8/50 (II)* and in *R2/73 (II)* when the accident occurred in the course of climbing the harbour gates only 25 yards from the ship.

No matter where the injury occurs – even if it is on board the ship itself – a claimant will fail if he was acting for his own purposes such as to take himself outside of employment. Thus a seaman was refused benefit when injured on leaving his ship in order to buy lemonade in *R(I) 10/81*. The claim similarly failed in *R(I) 75/53* where the seaman was injured whilst returning to the ship where he was lodging, having bought himself provisions on shore. By contrast it was suggested in *CSI 23/50* (T) that when at sea a mariner is continuously in the course of employment.

(d) Railwaymen and other employees of large landowners

Even though injury occurs on the employer's property to which the public do not have access, a claim will be refused if the claimant is not within the "ambit, scope or scene of his duty". This is a question of fact in each case and depends, for example, upon how far the claimant is from his job, and the times during which he is expected to perform it. If the employer is a large landowner, such as British Rail or British Coal, there is a greater likelihood that the claimant's injury is divorced from employment, even though it occurs on the employer's land. One such case is *R(I) 7/52* involving a farm worker, although nearly all the other decisions involve railwaymen or miners. The farmworker was denied benefit following injury whilst returning home after work. Although still on his employer's land he had sufficiently disengaged himself from his work such that he could not be said to be using a means of egress from it.

The decisions involving railwaymen using the railway line as a means of access to and from their work have been decided on their particular facts both for and against claimants.[15] A ground for denying benefit has been that the railwayman was injured whilst using a prohibited route as in *CSI 5/49* and *R(I) 28/55* (T). But the claim may succeed even in these circumstances if either the prohibition has not been effectively enforced as in *CI 220/49*, or if SSA s. 52 applies as in *R(I) 8/59*. These exceptions are considered further at p. 70 below. A railwayman may also take himself outside of the course of employment by using the railway line for his own purposes as where the claimant was injured whilst fetching tobacco from a nearby shop in *R(I) 27/53*.

(2) The hours of work

It has already been seen under the last heading that the course of employment can extend beyond the time during which work is actually being done. For example, in certain circumstances it can include injuries occurring whilst travelling to and from work. Just as an employee is allowed space to disengage himself from employment, he is also allowed time to do so. This means that the contract of service cannot be taken as

---

[15] Railwaymen were refused benefit in *5/49(II)*, *R(I) 67/52*, *R(I) 22/53* and *R(I) 30/53* but their claims succeeded in *R(I) 32/58* and *R(I) 5/67*.

defining precisely the hours within which the course of employment will be found to exist. Where the contract is vague as to the hours of work, or allows considerable discretion as to when tasks are carried out, correspondingly more emphasis must be given to whether the claimant's act is incidental to employment. However, for employees with a fixed place and hours of work the time of their injury is an important factor, although a certain latitude is allowed both before starting work and after finishing it. As recognised in *R(I) 5/77* "the course of a person's employment is not commensurate with the course of his work. It may start before the start of work, may bridge an interruption of work, and may continue after the end of work".

(a) Early arrivals

The leading authority is *R* v. *National Insurance Commissioner, ex p. East* (1976) which involved a worker arriving half an hour early at her factory in order to put on her work clothes and go to the canteen for refreshment before "clocking on". When she slipped and was injured in the canteen she was held to be within the course of employment. The following statement from Willis on *Workmen's Compensation* was approved as a good starting point in deciding cases:

> "The course of employment may be taken to have commenced although the hour for actual work has not struck, if the workman's arrival on the premises is either not unreasonably early, or is necessitated by the circumstances of the employment, or if, at the time of the accident, he is doing something on the employer's premises which is necessary to be done to equip himself for his work. . . ."

An earlier case also favouring the claimant is *R(I) 3/62* where a civil servant nearing retirement age arrived at work regularly one and a half hours early in order to avoid the London rush hour. She then read until the appointed time for her to begin her duties. She was injured whilst attempting to open a window before such time had arrived. She nevertheless succeeded in her claim. It was emphasized that she had arrived early not for her own convenience but out of practical necessity in that she sought to conserve her strength for the better performance of her duties at work. This helped to distinguish *R(I) 1/59* where the early arrival was in order to obtain refreshment, play billiards and chat to fellow employees. Benefit may therefore be refused if the claimant is acting entirely for her own convenience as in *R(I) 45/55* where a laundry worker was injured before "clocking on" when she deposited her own laundry at the place where she worked. On a similar basis miners failed in their claims when injured at the entrance to canteens before the start of work, although all these cases should now be read in light of *ex p. East*. In *R(I) 7/59* the miner was entering the canteen in order to buy soap to be used later in the pit-head baths, and in *R(I) 11/54* in order to collect sandwiches. This last case was distinguished in *R(I) 72/54* where the miner's visit was necessary to equip himself properly for work for he required a replacement boot lace from the canteen. The claimant also succeeded on this basis in *R(I) 53/54* where it was accepted that it was a necessity of employment that the mill worker leave her child at the factory nursery before the start of work.

(b) Late stays

These are dealt with on the same principles as early arrivals. As recognised in *R(I) 17/60* the course of employment does not necessarily come to an end when an employee signs off work. In *R(I) 22/56* a miner succeeded in his claim for injury which occurred after he had "clocked off" when he remained at the pit in order to avoid the rush hour. However, if there is a deviation such that the course of employment can be said to have come to an end benefit will be refused. This was the basis of *R 1/70* (II) where an employee of a department store, leaving work at the end of the day, stopped to make a purchase from the store herself. She was later injured at the public exit. Her claim for benefit was refused because her deviation in making the purchase had brought her course of employment to an end. Similarly claimants injured whilst visiting the canteen after the end of work were denied benefit in *CI 120/49, R(I) 52/52* and *R(I) 14/61*. However, there are three arguments which may now help such claimants:

(i)   The cases denying benefit must now be read in the light of the *ex p. East* (above) which adopts a more liberal attitude to injuries on work premises outside working hours.

(ii)   If it can be shown that the deviation is in order to obtain part of the employee's remuneration, such as a meal at the canteen, the claim may succeed as in *R(I) 15/55*.

(iii) If the claimant although intending to do so has not yet deviated from the route giving access from the place of work, benefit will be paid. Thus in *R(I) 60/54* the miner who after work slipped on icy ground succeeded in his claim because "he had not deviated towards the canteen".

Injuries suffered after work hours by a school teacher playing a game at a Christmas party, and a matron of a nursery hurt at the school's dance both led to successful claims in *R(I)62/52* and *CI 17/75* (unreported). The van driver in *R(I) 63/54* (T) who was injured while saving his employer's property from fire on his day off also obtained benefit. But a home help failed to show that her course of employment had been extended beyond her normal working hours when she was injured whilst shopping for a client in *R(I) 5/77*. The claim also failed in *R(I) 46/59* where the employee was injured after office hours when attending a meeting of his Staff Association.

(c) Official breaks

If the claimant is injured whilst acting reasonably during a break in work at his employer's premises the accident is likely to be within employment. Permitted activities within employment have included, for example, using the break in order to go to the toilet, have a meal, attend a union meeting and even to play sport. These are considered respectively by 3(*h*) (*j*) (*m*) and (*o*) below. For decisions considering the use of unofficial breaks and lulls in work see 3(*f*) below.

Whether a claimant has acted such as to interrupt his employment by, for example, overstaying his break period as in *R(I) 44/57* is considered below in connection with the leading case of *R* v. *Industrial Injuries Commissioner, ex p. AEU (No. 2) (Re Culverwell)* (1966). The general principles affecting a claim were noted in *R(I) 4/67*(T) where a bus driver was injured whilst having a cup of tea during a short break between journeys. In awarding benefit on the basis that the break had been used for the purpose intended by his employer and the claimant had not disentangled himself from employment, the tribunal stated:

> "Regard must be had to the nature of the employment, the duration of the break, the place at which the claimant was injured, the reason why he was there, whether or not he was there with the consent, express or implied, of his employers and any other relevant circumstances."

Injuries occurring whilst the claimant is travelling along a public road during a break in work or in between spells of duty are generally considered outside of employment.[16] For example, in *3/49 (II)* a postman was refused benefit following injury whilst carrying a personal message during his lunch break. The position can be complicated where claimants are employed to travel and these decisions are considered further at p. 73 below. In *R(I) 6/76* the break in work was caused by a bomb scare. Employees were told to leave the building and return an hour later. The claimant was injured whilst walking back to the building. Benefit was refused because the situation was said to be comparable to the position where a factory is closed at midday and employees go elsewhere for their meal. During this time they would be considered outside employment. The claimant was not to be treated as if he had been sent on an errand by the employer during the work break.

(3) What the claimant was doing

Although the time and place of the injury can establish whether at first sight an industrial accident has occurred, a final decision cannot be made until the claimant's activity leading to his injury is considered. If his acts were a part of, or reasonably incidental to, the work he was employed to do then his course of employment can extend beyond the normal hours or place of work. But if what he was doing was a material deviation from that which he was employed to do, it may place him outside the course of employment even though he was injured at his factory during working hours. The many decisions in this area are grouped under three headings: the first examines the general principles applied to decide whether an act is incidental to employment; the second, at p. 63, lists examples of particular activities which have been the subject of Commissioners' decisions; and the third heading, at p. 67, brings together those areas where statute has intervened to assist in the definition of the course of employment.

General principles as to what may be incidental to employment

The course of employment is not confined to the times during which the employee is doing that which is solely aimed at producing the goods his factory makes. Many acts may be done which are not directly relevant to production but which are an inevitable consequence of the employee spending up to half his waking hours at his place of work. From the earliest years of workmen's compensation it was recognised, for example, that taking a meal or going to the toilet were incidental to employment and should be included within the industrial scheme. The non-statutory test of

---

[16] *CI 331/50, CI 398/50, 4/52(II), R 1/64(II), R 3/64(II).*

whether the act is incidental to employment has been developed to extend the course of employment to take account of these additional activities. The test has also been applied to resolve cases where the employee is not only doing what his job requires but at the same time he is, for example, chatting or handing a sweet to another worker, or he is smoking. The scope of the industrial scheme has thus been extended in several directions by what has become a "doctrine of incidental activity".

The leading decision as to what is incidental to employment is *R* v. *Industrial Injuries Commissioner, ex p. AEU (No. 2) (Re Culverwell)* (1966). The factory worker in this case queued in the corridor outside a booth where smoking was permitted during a break period. He was struck by a truck whilst still waiting to enter the booth five minutes after his ten-minute break period had finished. The Court of Appeal held that by remaining in the corridor beyond the permitted time he had taken himself outside the course of employment. He had deliberately done something not permitted by his employer and this was too serious a breach to be considered merely as incidental to employment. Although he had overstayed his break by 50 per cent of the time allowed, the case does appear to be somewhat strict in demanding that employees be punctual, for the claimant was only five minutes late in returning to duty.

However, it would be a mistake to view the case generally as confining the course of employment. The judgments are favourable to claimants in several respects and they have encouraged a more liberal view to be taken of the course of employment. In particular, together with *Nancollas* v. *Insurance Officer* (1985), the decision emphasises that it is no longer necessary for the claimant to show that he acted in pursuance of a duty owed to the employer. He may be protected by the scheme even if he is acting for his own purposes, for this may be reasonably incidental to his employment. Thus Lord Denning said:

> ". . . if a man whilst at his place of work, during his hours of work, is injured by a risk incidental to his employment, then the right conclusion usually is that it is an injury which arises out of and in the course of the employment, even though he may not be doing his actual work but chatting to a friend or smoking or doing something of that kind."

Earlier he suggested that a negligent or even a deliberately disobedient act would not necessarily remove the claimant from the course of his employment unless the circumstances show that he is doing something different from anything he was employed to do. As recognised in *R(I) 4/73*, in fact the case signifies a less strict approach to the course of employment. Earlier Commissioners' decisions should be applied bearing in mind *Re Culverwell*'s inclusion of a more varied range of activities than perhaps would have been allowed in the past.

From the many decisions on the subject it may be helpful to list the main factors or principles which have influenced whether or not an act is within the course of employment, perhaps by being incidental to it. Not all the cases can be reconciled, and as recognised in *R(I) 13/68*, "opinion may differ widely as to what can fairly be regarded as incidental".

(a) Acting with the employer's consent

This is essential for the claim to succeed as recognised by Davies L J in *Re Culverwell*. But consent is not of itself sufficient so that, if permission had been given to the seaman to leave his ship to buy lemonade in *R(I) 10/81*, it would not necessarily have kept him within the course of employment. Consent may be expressly given or found to be implied. In *R(I) 1/77* tacit consent to the erection of Christmas decorations was implied from the employer's knowledge that it was common practice. This decision did not follow *R(I) 36/55* where benefit was refused despite the employer's "passive sympathy" to the same act. The employer's authority and consent to the employee's act is further considered in (*b*).

(b) Acting under orders from a superior

Although acting under orders is likely to be within employment, it need not necessarily be so. As recognized in *R(I) 24/52*: "While as a general rule the fact that a claimant is doing something which his foreman has ordered him to do is sufficient to prove that an accident arises out of his employment, there are clearly limits . . . ." These limits are that the orders must be given with the actual or ostensible authority of the employer, and the parties must intend that the work be done under a contract of service and not merely as an act of friendship. A restrictive approach to implying that the employer has authorised the orders was taken in *R(I) 36/55* where a claimant was refused benefit following an accident whilst erecting Christmas decorations at the request of his immediate superior. The claim similarly failed in *R(I) 8/61* where the claimant was injured whilst working at the request of his foreman on the latter's private property. The employer knew such jobs were being done but did not expressly authorize the practice, and the foreman's orders were viewed as beyond his ostensible authority. The Commissioner recognized that it is common for employees to be instructed to perform tasks which are outside the true scope of their employment, but which either because of a threat to their jobs, or because of a desire to be co-operative, they may find difficult to refuse. Nevertheless he warned that these employees would not be covered by the industrial scheme in carrying out such orders.

There is a restrictive approach in these cases to implying that the employer has authorized the orders. But as suggested in *R(I) 24/56* a claim will succeed if an employee can show that he reasonably believed such authority would be given, and there are a number of decisions under the Workmen's Compensation Acts in which the scope of employment was enlarged by the orders of a superior.[17]

(c) Acting in the employer's interest

This is likely to be regarded as incidental to employment. Thus in *R2/74(II)* the claimant succeeded despite being injured whilst making safe his own property which he had brought to work. This was because the property also presented a danger to passers-by and his actions in protecting the safety of the public were held to be in his employer's interest and within employment. If the claimant's act expedites the employer's business, for example, by increasing his production, it is even more likely to be in his

---

[17]   Willis pp. 56-7.

employer's interest and within employment. Claims therefore succeeded in *R(I) 11/56*, where a lorry driver delivering bricks was injured whilst helping to remove a concrete mixer from the site where the unloading was to take place, and in *R(I) 13/68* where an agricultural worker was injured while on his way to help an engineer repair the tractor he had delivered. A stricter view of the employer's interest was taken in *CI 326/50*. In that case a garage handyman was refused benefit when, in order to obtain a jack required by his employers, he assisted someone else using the garage and was injured. However, usually these injuries whilst in the process of obtaining equipment necessary for work – even if only a bootlace as in *R(I) 72/54* – are likely to be incidental to employment.

Whether the claimant acts in the employer's interest is also a relevant factor when considering what he has done in response to meeting something unexpected at work, or in otherwise taking the initiative and operating without specific instructions. These situations are considered under (*q*) and (*r*) below.

(*d*) *Acts relating to the necessities of employment*

These are more likely to be considered incidental to employment than acts relating to mere amenities provided only for the employees' benefit. Thus the claimant in *R(I) 53/54* succeeded in showing that the nursery provided at her cotton mill was a necessity of her employment, and her fall whilst taking her child there before the start of work was within the industrial scheme. However, claimants failed in *R(I) 18/52* and *3/53(II)* where injuries occurred at work whilst the claimant, in the first case, was fetching raffle tickets to promote a children's Christmas party and, in the second, was making a blood donation. In *R(I) 53/56* benefit was also refused to a claimant injured whilst making a telephone call about a sick colleague. This narrow definition of what is incidental to employment was not followed in *R 3/74(II)* where the telephone call was made by the claimant to her daughter in hospital. The Commissioner in awarding benefit suggested that *Re Culverwell* in effect had increased the work facilities which could be regarded as incidental to employment. Using the telephone was to be dealt with by the same principles as those dealing with eating at the canteen or going for a smoke.

(*e*) *Acts which are natural and reasonable*

These acts are more likely to be considered incidental – especially if they are almost instinctive – compared to acts which are the result of some deliberation or are unreasonable or unnatural. On this basis claims succeeded where employees were retrieving lost property in *R(I) 32/53*, *R(I) 57/54* and *R(I) 4/73*. But the claim failed in *R(I) 78/52* were in order to recover her lost coin the claimant moved some heavy billiard table slabs for "it is . . . a different matter when the action is not immediate and instinctive but is calculated, and is done after an interval, and plainly invokes some risk". The retrieval was similarly unreasonable in *R(I) 20/54* and in *R(I) 16/60*.

Where the claimant in *R(I) 36/59* sat at the edge of a tank of scalding liquid in a distillery, and then fell asleep and fell into the liquid he was nevertheless considered in the course of employment. His acts were natural ones and he had fallen asleep involuntarily. This was in contrast to the stoker in *R(I) 68/54* who was refused benefit because he had deliberately left his place of duty in order to sleep.

(f) Acts done for the claimant's own purposes

Even if such acts are negligent or deliberately disobedient, they do not automatically take the claimant outside the course of employment unless he was doing something different from anything he was employed to do, and his employment is interrupted as in *Re Culverwell* (above). According to *R(I) 4/73*

"it is proper . . . to consider whether the interruption was material in extent and also whether the risk was of a kind dissociated from the employment. In modern times the Courts and Commissioners have tended to take a less strict view of these matters than formerly".

If the pattern of work imposes a period of idleness upon the claimant who is injured whilst making reasonable use of this lull in work a claim will succeed. Thus, as recognized in *R(I) 24/63*, if a typist in an idle moment walked across the room to the window to take a breath of air she would not necessarily leave the course of her employment. Claims succeeded where the employee went to chat to another worker in *R(I) 46/53* and *R4/60(II)*, and where he went to help in other work of the employer in *R(I) 13/68*. Where a hospital worker was injured crossing the grounds in order to visit a friend who was a patient the claim was allowed in *R 1/68(II)*. The visit was during a lull in work and at a break which was in substitution for her normal tea-break. But the Commissioner would have decided the case differently if the claimant had asked for time off. Claimants have been denied benefit when acting for their own purposes as, for example, in accompanying another employee to the stores in *R(I) 1/58* or going to explore another part of the building in *R(I) 45/59*. The claimant must not avoid work when he should be doing it as in *Re Culverwell* and *R(I) 44/57*. On this basis the claimant was outside of the scheme when injured whilst showing a photograph to another employee in *R(I) 71/52* or when leaving the room where she worked in order to deliver a personal message in *4/50(II)*.

Smoking whilst working was recognized in *Re Culverwell* as capable of being incidental to employment, especially if permission has been expressly given as in *R(I) 3/67*. In *R(I) 2/63(T)* the claim succeeded, although it was agreed that not all injuries caused by smoking at work could be said to arise out of employment. The case refused to follow the reasoning which had led to the denial of benefit in *R(I) 68/52*, *R(I) 9/60* and *R(I) 30/60*. In *R(I) 4/64* the accident was held to arise out of employment where the claimant was burnt by a thread flicking hot ash from a cigarette into his eye.

(g) Acts away from the place of work

These should not be considered incidental to employment without careful consideration. Lord Denning's dictum to this effect in *R v. National Insurance Commissioner, ex p. Michael* (1977) was applied in *R(I) 5/77* and *R(I) 10/81*. In particular in *R(I) 4/79* the Commissioner said that

"I agree with the view that in some cases the doctrine of incidental activity will not enable an insured person to claim the protection of the industrial injuries insurance scheme if he is injured in a road accident while reasonably pursuing his own purposes, and that highway accidents occupy a special position in relation to the doctrine of incidental activity".

Further examples of whether particular activities are in the course of employment

Examples of what may be in the course of employment are found in the following decisions which are classified according to the specific activity involved:-

(h) Using toilet facilities

This has been held to be incidental to employment since *Rose* v. *Morrison* (1911). The cases have especially concerned injuries to bus drivers during break periods. The claims succeeded in *CI 21/50, R(I) 17/60* and *R(I) 4/67*(T) not following *R(I) 45/53*. But in *R(I) 45/59* the Commissioner observed that "it may be a different matter where in order to relieve himself an employee goes into some dangerous part of his employer's premises where his work does not take him".

(i) Taking a bath and using changing rooms

This was incidental to a miner's employment in *CI 22/49, CI 23/49, CI 26/49* and *CI 34/49*. Acts which are themselves incidental to taking a bath, such as the purchase of soap at the canteen, are excluded as in *R(I) 7/59*. Crossing a public road to leave or arrive at the baths was outside the course of employment in *CI 65/49* and *R(I) 16/63*. In *CI 190/52* (unreported) a fireman who injured himself whilst shaving during a break in duty was entitled to benefit because "to take refreshment, wash and tidy himself up for duty and to appear cleanly shaved were all things incidental to his employment".

(j) Taking a meal or other refreshments

This is the example often given of an act incidental to employment, it first being recognized as such in *Blovelt* v. *Sawyer* (1904). Claims have succeeded where injury has occurred on the employer's premises while the claimant is at, or going to or from, a canteen or other place where meals are taken. Benefit was paid in *Armstrong Whitworth & Co.* v. *Redford* (1920), *CSI 6/49, R(I) 25/55, R(I) 17/60* and *R4/70 (II)*. In these cases the accident happened during a break in work hours, but it may not be incidental to employment to go for a meal outside work hours as discussed in (2) above.

The place of injury is an important factor. It made no difference that the canteen or food trolley was owned not by the employer but by an independent contractor in *Knight* v. *Howard Wall* (1938), *CI 34/50* and *R(I) 3/63*(T). Nor did it matter that the canteen was physically separate from the employer's premises in *R(I) 11/53*. But there is a sharp contrast between these cases and those where injury occurs on a public road. Even if the claimant is only crossing the road to reach the canteen on the other side, as in *R(I) 34/52*, the accident will be held outside of employment. Cases on this point are considered under (*s*) below in relation to travelling in order to take a meal. Before and after crossing the road the employee may be within employment, but from the moment he sets foot on the public highway until he leaves it he is usually without the protection of the industrial scheme. Transport workers, in particular, must be concerned about the fine distinction involved. Its difficulties were referred to in *CI 248/50* where the Commissioner found that although an assault occurred whilst crossing the road to the canteen – rather than on the employer's premises itself – the injury was in the course of employment.

Making tea can be within employment as in *R(I) 21/53*, but in *R(I) 33/53* the claimant unreasonably exercised his discretion to make tea only ten minutes after the start of work, and benefit was refused.

(k) Using medical facilities

If these prove necessary within the ambit of employment they may be incidental to it. Successful claims were made in *R(I) 3/54* where the claimant felt ill and was made worse by the treatment he received in the factory's ambulance room, and in *R(I) 16/62* where the claimant was injured when he made use of a chiropody service provided by his employers. The claim may fail if treatment is given otherwise than through the service provided by the employer, such as where it was administered by another workman in *R(I) 43/57*. Although the service may not be provided by the employer, if he encourages and has an interest in employees making use of it they are protected by the industrial scheme when they do so. Thus in *R(I) 24/63* the claimant obtained benefit following injury on the way to a mobile X-ray unit temporarily stationed at his place of work. Employees who suffered a reaction to vaccine following immunisation carried out either at their employer's request, or because of their fear of being in contact with a disease at work, failed in their claims in *R(I) 15/61* and *R(I) 12/58*.

(l) Collecting pay or returning forms relating to employment

These acts have also been held incidental to employment. Claimants succeeded when injured at their employers premises in *R(I) 14/60* whilst completing a form required in connection with pay, and in *R(I) 48/56* whilst handing in a medical certificate and discussing return to work. This last case approved the statement from Willis on *Workmen's Compensation* that a "workman who has to return to his employer's premises for some legitimate purpose justified by the terms of his employment is, whilst so doing, acting in the course of his employment". Such a purpose would be in order to collect pay as in *Riley* v. *Holland* (1911). But injuries occurring outside of the employer's premises whilst the employee was seeking to cash his wages in the form of a money order, or whilst making inquiries about pay, were not within the industrial scheme in *R(I) 34/52* and *R(I) 8/60*.

(m) Participating in a trade union

This was held incidental to employment in *R(I) 9/57* where the claimant was injured at a factory whilst returning a union card to another employee. But there are limits. For example, injuries occurring on the picket line would be outside of employment. Most of the cases have had to consider whether a claimant injured whilst attending a union meeting is within the scheme. It has been held that benefit will be paid if the meeting takes place during a break period at the place of work, and it discusses matters with which the employer is concerned, as in *R(I) 63/51*. Benefit was refused in *R(I) 36/54* and *R(I) 46/59* where the meeting was held either at premises some distance away from the workplace or after office hours, and the topics of discussion were only remotely the concern of the employer. But in *CI 526/75* (unreported) the claimant succeeded when injured away from her place of work whilst attending a meeting at her union headquarters in London. The meeting was to discuss a wide range of topics affecting all the various premises of the employer, the Ministry of Defence. The Commissioner considered the meeting to be as important to the employer as to the union members the claimant represented. A more restrictive view of the employer's interest sufficient to bring a claim within the scheme was taken in *CI 1/81* (unreported), where benefit was denied to a nurse injured whilst attending her union's conference. The Commissioner acknowledged that it was important and in the employer's interest that union officials should be well versed in the proper conduct of industrial relations and the workings and problems of, in this case, the health service. But he continued, "although training may well be to the advantage of the employers, it does not follow from this that the training in question is in fact the work for which the trainees are employed. Indeed, nurses are employed to nurse, not to hold union office . . . ." Voluntary payment by the employer to the claimant for the leave of absence required to attend the conference made no difference to the definition of the course of employment in this case. It could not transform what was done into what the claimant was employed to do. Similarly in *R(I) 10/80* an accident at premises where a trade union course was being held on a day release basis was considered outside of employment. Although related to the claimant's contract of employment, the course was not incidental to the work of that employment. But if the claimant can establish a second contract of service by showing that he was also employed by his union during his attendance at the course the claim may succeed as in *CI 6/78* (unreported).

If a claimant is injured on the road whilst travelling off duty after the end of work to a meeting of conference the claim will be refused as in *R(I) 10/56* and *CI 1/81* (unreported). However, the former case was distinguished in *R9/63(II)* where benefit was paid to a civil servant who was injured during work hours in the course of attending a meeting of the Whitley Council.

(n) Using accommodation made necessary by employment

This can be within the course of employment even if work has ended for the day. The concern is whether the course of employment continues during off duty periods for those, such as resident medical staff, who remain under some form of control or supervision from their employers. Two factors assist in making this decision. The first is whether the claimant is required by the employer to use the accommodation concerned. This enabled the claim to succeed in *CI 83/49* and *CI 374/50* but benefit was refused where the employee was free to go elsewhere in *CSI 3/49, 7/50(II), 9/50(II)* and *5/54(II)*. However, this factor cannot be conclusive for *Re Culverwell* has made it clear that the claimant need not act in pursuance of a duty owed to the employer. Further in *R(I) 30/57* although free to go elsewhere the claimant succeeded when injured in a hostel provided by British Rail for their employees travelling on long journeys. The second factor is whether the claimant has duties to perform at the accommodation itself, even if the injury occurs during an off-duty period. On this basis the claim succeeded in *CI 374/50* but failed in *R(I) 22/54*.

In *R(I) 49/51* a resident cook slipped on a mat in her bedroom and succeeded in her claim. The case implies that a resident domestic servant's course of employment can be very broad, and may continue throughout the time spent in the employer's house. But in *R(I) 9/59* a level crossing keeper who lived in a gatehouse owned by British Rail failed in her claim following her fall on the garden path in the course of collecting milk for household purposes. Her act was considered not to be incidental to her employment but to taking a meal at her own home.

(*o*) *Participating in sport*

Sport has been held within the course of employment of a few employees, but a decision of the Court of Appeal now limits the possibility of extending these decisions to cover other jobs for which sport may be thought relevant. However, at least it is no longer essential for the claimant to show that his contract of service obliges him to play sport, and *R(I) 13/66* emphasises that, in so far as older cases require such a duty, they ought not to be followed. Nevertheless it is still important for the claimant, if possible, to establish an obligation to play. It was the determining factor in *R(I) 3/81*, as well as in several earlier cases[18] involving apprentices injured whilst attempting gym exercises at their day release in technical college. In the absence of an obligation to play it may help a claim if it can be shown that the employer encourages participation in sport, and that there are special circumstances in the work requiring a high degree of fitness. But jobs with such special circumstances which can bring sporting injuries within the industrial scheme will be harder to find as a result of the Court of Appeal decision in *R* v. *National Insurance Commissioner, ex p. Michael* (1977).

In that case a policeman injured on his rest day while playing rugby for his county force was denied benefit. The Court made it clear that those who play for their works or office teams are not in the course of employment unless a special case can be shown. With regard to policemen the fact that playing sport improved morale and fitness did not constitute such special circumstances. Nor did it make any difference that a player might be treated by his employer as on duty at the time of his injury. But the door was not closed on all sporting claims: it was suggested that an injury occurring whilst participating in activities which are part of police training (even though many may regard these as recreational, such as where mountaineering or car driving courses are involved) could be incidental to a policeman's employment. *Ex p. Michael* was distinguished in *R(I) 3/81* where police cadets were under an obligation to take part in swimming championships. However, in the absence of such an obligation it seems that, in future, it will be more difficult to claim for sporting injuries.

Ex p. Michael was applied in *R(I) 4/81* to deny benefit to an airline stewardess who was injured whilst playing tennis during a stop-over between flights. But this case did suggest that there was some scope for a claim, at least in the case of a fireman. It distinguished the successful claims in *R(I) 13/66* and *R(I) 68/51* on the ground that the nature of a fireman's employment – involving long periods of waiting and the need to be

---

[18] *CI 228/50*(T), *CI 314/50, R(I) 4/51, R(I) 31/53, R(I) 66/53* and *R 4/62(II)*.

exceptionally fit – was so special that the playing of volleyball at the station could be considered an integral part of the duties of the job. In older cases a fireman injured in his brigade's agility team (organised to give displays for recruitment purposes) successfully claimed in *R(I) 72/52*, but where the fireman attended only in order to watch the competition and not to take part he failed in *R(I) 41/54*. An employee who was injured when taking part in his work's fire brigade competition successfully claimed in *CWI 27/50*, but the railwayman injured while taking part in an ambulance competition failed in *R(I) 102/53*.

It was held in *R(I) 13/51* that playing football was within the course of employment of a nurse in charge of the recreation of mental hospital patients. However, the claim failed where the team consisted only of hospital staff in *CI 30/49* and where the main purpose of the game was to select a staff team in *R(I) 33/56*. But the nurse recovered in *R(I) 3/57* where it was accepted that the game's main purpose was to entertain patients and help in their recovery.

Other cases have awarded benefit to teachers hurt at the school's Christmas party game in *R(I) 62/52*, and when supervising a skiing party of pupils in Switzerland in *R(I) 39/56*. The lab technician injured whilst playing football at lunchtime in *R(I) 2/69* failed in his claim, but the professional footballer injured in a benefit match succeeded in *R(I) 80/52*.

(p) Attending a day release class or residential course

This may be within the course of employment of trade unionists as considered in *(m)* above. Sporting injuries occurring while at day release classes are considered in *(o)* above. Attendance at a day release class in motor mechanics was within the course of employment of an apprentice employed at a garage in *R(I) 2/68*, as was attending a self-defence course in the special circumstances of employment of a taxi-driver in *CI 36/67* (unreported). For a residential course the normal rule to determine the course of employment, as applied in *R(I) 2/80*, is to equate the syllabus timetable with normal working hours. Travelling to or from such a course is normally outside the course of employment as in *CI 310/50* and *R(I) 1/83*.

Examples also dealt with by specific statutory provisions

(q) Emergencies

Employees may have to respond to unexpected events at work. If they act reasonably in doing so they will not take themselves outside of the course of their employment even if they attempt something which they may not have been employed to do. They may be taken to have acted in an emergency when special rules apply. It would be a mistake to think that these rules operate only to benefit those working in the emergency services such as firemen and policemen. In fact, they apply in circumstances not commonly thought to give rise to any emergency at all. They can thus benefit many employees injured at work. Cases have usually been resolved by applying principles developed by the Commissioners themselves, or by the courts which dealt with workmen's compensation in the past.[19] However, SSA s. 54 supplements these general principles established by caselaw by extending the industrial scheme so that actions taken in certain emergencies are deemed to be within the course of employment. Before

[19] Willis pp. 74-5.

considering the scope of s. 54, the broader grounds established by the general principles must be examined.

(i) GENERAL PRINCIPLES APART FROM S. 54

What amounts to an emergency – The definition of emergency for the purposes of the industrial scheme is a broad one. The principles apply in unexpected circumstances. Although cases have included courageous attempts to save children from fires or road accidents, an emergency is not confined to where there is danger to life or limb, or even property. Nor does danger have to be imminent, or bravery called for. All that is required is that something occurs unexpectedly and that in response the claimant acts reasonably and in his employer's interest, for example, by ensuring that work is able to continue. This was stated in *Dermody* v. *Higgs and Hill* (1937) where a road labourer succeeded in his claim after he had been injured while helping a driver crank an engine. He was trying to start a vehicle which had unexpectedly broken down while transporting material to his site. Similarly the emergency principle has been applied in other cases which, to those linking the term with some dramatic circumstance, would not be thought to involve an emergency at all. These include *CI 280/49* where a pottery examiner was injured whilst helping builders hold up a window frame in the room where she was working; *R7/60(II)* where a butcher was injured in assisting a telephone engineer fit a wire at his employer's premises; and *CI 407/82* (unreported) where a general post office worker was injured in helping a cleaner fix the head of her mop.

Acting reasonably and in the employer's interest – Whether this requirement is satisfied depends in each case on an assessment of the extent of the risk as balanced against the object in view. In *R(I) 32/54* an emergency occurred in that unexpectedly employees were unable to gain access to their factory at the usual time. But this did not justify one of them climbing a pipe in order to get in through a window instead of waiting for a key. The interest of the employer has been broadly construed. It was satisfied in *Culpeck* v. *Orient S N Co.* (1922) where a baker employed on an ocean liner was held to act reasonably in protecting passengers from foul language by remonstrating with the swearer and later striking him in self-defence. In *R(I) 62/50* a night-watchman was injured in the course of helping a policeman investigate a building which was not the one where he was employed. His concern about general security was considered sufficient to satisfy the requirement that he acted in the employer's interest. But *R(I) 6/63* shows that there must be a limit to the employer's interest. The milkman in that case who tried to enter a burning bungalow to rescue some children could not show that his acts were for the benefit of his employer. He would have failed to obtain benefit had it not been for the application of s. 54 as considered below.

Acts incidental to employment – The employee's action in meeting the emergency must still be reasonably incidental to employment. This means that there must be some connection between his acts and the duties imposed on him by his job so that, for example, he is protecting his employer's interest, or doing something without which a normal day's work cannot be carried on. This was stated in *R(I) 52/54* where a civil servant visiting private houses failed in his claim when he was injured stopping a runaway child's tricycle. As in *R(I) 6/63* it was not enough in such a case to show that the employee acted with the best of intentions or with the approval of his employer had he known. If the employee is only doing what any member of the public might have done in like circumstances, as in *CI 35/50*, his acts may not be incidental to employment.

It is not necessary as it was under the Workmen's Compensation Acts that in order to be within the course of employment help must be given only to fellow employees. Thus benefit was paid to a lorry driver who was injured after he had stopped to assist another road-user in distress in *R(I) 11/51*. His action was held incidental to employment, but only because of a principle of reciprocity which was applied "having regard to the recognized behaviour of give and take between persons using the highway". The connection with employment was established by this principle on the basis that employers may reasonably expect their lorry drivers to help other motorists in order that they in turn will receive assistance when they require it. Other claimants who are unable to show that they too might receive aid from the sort of person they help may not obtain benefit. Thus the claim failed in the case of the above civil servant who was injured in stopping the child's tricycle, for there was no similarity of function between the helper and the person helped. With regard to road accidents *R(I) 11/51* has also been confined by *R 4/63(II)* to situations where assistance is given in removing an obstruction to the flow of traffic. Benefit will be refused a claimant who acts merely to alleviate the inconvenience caused to another by a vehicle failing to start.

At the time of the emergency the claimant need not act within the specific duties delegated to him by his employer. If, for example, he goes outside the property where his duties are normally performed he may still be able to claim. In *R(I) 46/60* an Admiralty policeman left his dockyard post to save a child in a runaway push-chair. Although he was injured outside of his employer's property benefit could be paid because the emergency justified the action of a policeman. In *R(I) 11/56* and *R5/64(II)* the claimants were lorry drivers. Both obtained benefit when injured whilst moving goods to enable them to make their delivery. Although a claimant may be outside of the course of his employment before the emergency, it may have the effect of bringing him back within it. Thus the claim succeeded in *R(I) 63/54* (T) where a driver was injured in rescuing his employer's van from a fire on a Sunday when he was not at work and had no duties to perform.

Travelling to work in response to an emergency – can be within the course of employment as in *Blee* v. *London & North Eastern Railway Co.* (1938) and *R(I) 21/51* where platelayers were called in from home to repair railway tracks at their steelworks. Whether or not payment is made for the time spent travelling is not conclusive, but the successful employee in *R(I) 27/56* was required to proceed to his place of work as quickly as possible by the shortest practicable route. Although responding to a request to be at work an hour early, the claimant in *R(I) 36/57* was not making a special journey in response to an urgent summons and the emergency principle was inapplicable. Travelling home after the emergency was outside the course of employment in *R(I) 48/52*. Other cases dealing with travelling on duty are considered under (*s*) below.

(ii) RESCUERS SPECIFICALLY DEALT WITH BY S. 54

This section may save a claimant where his case would otherwise fail under the above principles for SSA s. 54 states:

> "An accident happening to an employed earner in or about any premises at which he is for the time being employed for the purposes of his employer's trade or business shall be deemed to arise out of and in the course of his employment if it happens while he is taking steps, on an actual or supposed emergency at those premises, to rescue, succour or protect persons who are, or are thought to be or possibly to be, injured or imperilled, or to avert or minimise serious damage to property."

Although the section has been in operation since 1948 it has not proved of great importance, for almost all of the decisions have been made by applying the general principles. The only decision which discusses s. 54 in detail is *R(I) 6/63*. This case involved a milkman who, whilst delivering to a bungalow, discovered the building to be on fire and children to be inside. The injury he suffered in attempting to rescue those children was held to be within employment only because of s. 54. The section is broader than the general principles examined above in that it covered the milkman even though his act was not furthering his employer's interest, and was not incidental to his employment. But in other respects the section is of narrower application. For example, the emergency must relate to danger to life or limb, or to serious (not minor) damage to property. Therefore acting in order to maintain the employer's production on encountering some unexpected hindrance at work is not covered. The section also requires that the emergency occurs "in or about" premises where the employee is working. This means that in the above cases the van driver rescuing his employer's property on his day off is not within s. 54 for he was not working at the time. Nor can the employee injured whilst working on the road make a successful claim because he is not working at "premises", for this term does not include the highway.

(r) Acting contrary to order or without instructions under s. 52

Just as the claimant is not necessarily within the course of employment when carrying out the orders of a superior (see *(b)* above), he is not necessarily excluded because he has acted without, or even against, orders at the time he was injured. Even in the absence of special statutory protection, acting contrary to the rules of the job may not be outside of employment. A distinction is drawn between orders or rules which define what work is to be done, and those which merely describe how it is to be done and which, if broken, do not prevent compensation being paid. But if it appears that an employee will be considered outside of his employment by reason only of the fact that he has broken a rule, he may seek assistance from SSA s. 52. This states:

> "An accident shall be deemed to arise out of and in the course of an employed earner's employment, notwithstanding that he is at the time of the accident acting in contravention of any statutory or other regulations applicable to his employment, or of any orders given by or on behalf of his employer, or that he is acting without instructions from his employer, if –
> (a) the accident would have been deemed so to have arisen had the act not

been done in contravention of any such regulations or orders, or without
such instructions, as the case may be; and

(b) the act is done for the purposes of and in connection with the employer's
trade or business".

The section was applied in *CI 210/50* where a miner, finishing work
underground, hitched a lift on a tram heading towards the bottom of the
shaft. He was injured when the tram was derailed. His ride was illegal for it
was prohibited by a statute of 1911, but his claim succeeded because of the
equivalent of the present s. 52. The Commissioner followed Lord
Maugham in *Noble* v. *Southern Railway* (1940) in asking the following
three questions in order to discover whether the claimant could rely on the
section:

"(1) Looking at the facts as a whole, including any regulation or orders
affecting the workman, was the accident one which arose out of and in the
course of the employment?

(2) If the first question is answered in the negative, is the negative answer due
to the fact that when the accident happened, the workman was acting in
contravention of some regulation or order?

(3) If the second question is answered in the affirmative was the act which the
workman was engaged in performing done by the workman for the purposes
of, and in connection with, his employer's trade or business?"

Each question was answered in the claimant's favour for it was decided that
but for the prohibition he was acting for the purposes of his employer's
business and within the course of employment when making his way to the
shaft bottom.

Nature of prohibitions involved – For s. 52 to apply the rule that is
broken must relate to the claimant's employment. In *CI 182/49* the
employee was injured on the way home when alighting from a moving bus.
This was contrary not to the employer's regulations, but only to those of
the company operating the transport service by arrangement with the
employer. As a result s. 52 was held inapplicable. The case also noted that
s. 52 requires the rules or orders be made by or on behalf of the employer,
and this was not satisfied in *9/55(II)* where the warning came from a fellow
workmate.

The regulations must be made clear and brought to the attention of the
workforce; an employee who is given ambiguous instructions and chooses
the "wrong" course will not be outside of employment. The prohibition
must be enforced and not be merely a nominal rule which has been
habitually disregarded. The rule that railwaymen were not to cross the
tracks had been disregarded by the employees in *CI 220/49* and benefit was
therefore paid. A similar result occurred in *R(I) 96/53* where the rule was
that workers should not congregate at the factory gates shortly before they
were to be opened. There were many cases decided under the Workmen's
Compensation Acts[20] in which custom and practice, or the connivance of
employers at the breaking of the rule were sufficient to enable the court to
disregard it, as in *Mellor* v. *Ashton* (1921). But in *R(I) 7/57* a miner was not
allowed to rely upon a custom that permitted him to leave work early if he
were soaked to the skin. Such a custom was not well known, and was

[20] Willis pp.53-5.

unreasonable in that it left the employee to be the sole judge of a standard which was uncertain and variable. If the prohibition is imposed by statute, as in *CI 11/49* and *R(I) 17/61*, it is not relevant to consider whether it has been waived or relaxed.

The existing course of employment – The effect of Lord Maugham's question (2) set out above is to emphasize that s. 52 does not operate to extend the course of employment. A claimant can only receive help if, apart from the prohibition or lack of orders, he was doing his own job. If it were otherwise, disobedient employees could be in a better position than those who, although also outside the scope of their employment, conform to the rules involved in the prohibited work they are doing. The question to be asked is "ignoring the prohibition was he doing his job?" This can be difficult to answer. The precise circumstances of the decided cases need not be set out here but there are an equal number of them falling on each side of the line.[21]

Different conclusions have been reached even in cases with very similar facts. This is illustrated by two decisions dealing with dock labourers who were injured whilst driving trucks when they should not have been. In *R(I) 1/66* benefit was refused because it was decided that the employee's act was wholly different from that which he was employed to do, although it was his job to move the load involved. This decision was upheld on appeal in *R v. Deputy Industrial Injuries Commissioner, ex p. Bresnahan* (1966) although the Divisional Court indicated that it might have decided the case differently had it come before them on broader grounds of appeal. In *R(I) 1/70* the Commissioner managed to distinguish *R(I) 1/66* and find for the claimant on the ground that, in the case before him the prohibition had not been enforced as strictly as in the earlier case where, had the foreman known of the unauthorized driving he would have stopped it immediately. The Commissioner made this distinction because otherwise he felt himself bound by *Bresnahan's* case, despite the doubt cast upon it by the Court of Appeal in *Kay v. I T W Ltd.* (1968) where it was said to be inconsistent with the general line of authorities. Since 1970 two other decisions have cast further doubt upon *Bresnahan*: in *CI 407/82* (unreported) it was suggested that the case should only be cited with caution, whilst in *CI 9/74*

---

[21] The act was held to be within the course of employment and for the employer's purposes in the following cases involving:
(a) breach of statutory regulations — *CI 11/49* (miner taking a ride as in *CI 210/50*).
(b) breach of employer's regulations or orders – *CI 113/50* (miner opening gates of shaft cage); *R(I) 6/55* (kitchen porter hanging clothing near to ovens to dry); *R(I) 24/55* (taking short cut from canteen); *9/55(II)* (tea maker putting oil on fire to boil kettle faster); *4/57(II)* (using improper means of access from trench); *R(I) 8/59* (railwayman walking on track).
(c) acting without instructions – *R(I) 76/51* (ship's fireman helping seamen put hatches in place); *R(I) 41/55* (quarryman hole borer driving dumper truck).
The act was held to be outside of the course of employment in the following cases involving:
(a) breach of statutory regulations – *R(I) 12/61* (repairer coupling shot for shot-firer)
(b) breach of employer's regulations or orders – *CSI 5/49* and *R(I) 28/55*(T) (railwaymen walking on tracks); *R(I) 80/53* (using oil stove).
(c) acting without instructions – *CI 28/49* (visiting another part of the factory); *CI 47/49* (electrical engineer walking along wall near high tension cables); *CI 35/50* (railwayman freeing jammed door on train on way to work); *R(I) 8/52* (insurance agent driving prospective customer home); *R(I) 77/54, R(I) 8/55* and *R 6/62(II)* (using machines which were not part of the job); *R(I) 16/60* (retrieving drying clothing).

(unreported) *Bresnahan* was considered no longer to be good law. That case involved a driver of a coal lorry who, in order to make his delivery, did another employee's job. He injured himself in climbing a ladder to open a chute. Despite this prohibited act he obtained benefit. These decisions represent a more liberal approach in that they avoid limiting too narrowly the job the claimant has been employed to do. But in deciding whether, apart from the prohibition, the employee is within the course of employment much depends upon the particular facts of the case.

In applying s. 52 there appears to be a distinction between cases where an employee acts without instructions as opposed to doing something which is contrary to orders or statute. Where there are no instructions s. 52 in effect requires the act to be considered as if there were in fact instructions. Depending upon how such hypothetical instructions are formulated this seems to ensure that the act will be within employment. However, in cases where statute or orders have been broken there seems to be more scope for denying that the claimant was doing his job. Then the question to be asked is: "ignoring the prohibition is the act within the course of employment?" The act is not to be viewed as done under instructions and it is therefore easier to deny benefit. However, the decisions in this area have not fully examined this distinction which may favour unduly the employee who acts without instructions rather than contrary to orders. But at least it is appropriate here to emphasise that s. 52 has been cited in support of many claimants who have not broken any rules at all, but have acted on their own initiative and without instructions.

Acting for the employer's purposes – Lord Maugham's question (3) above seeks to apply SSA s. 52(b). It may appear to add little to s. 52(a) because in that context it is also relevant to consider whether the employee's act is done for the purpose of the employer's business in order to decide whether it is within the employee's course of employment. But in *R(I) 7/57* the Commissioner recognized that s. 52(b) was an additional requirement. Although the miner who left work early without permission may have been within the course of employment, his act was done for his own convenience and not for his employer's purposes. A similar decision to deny benefit is *R(I) 17/61*. This case distinguished *CI 210/50* because there the miner was leaving work at the proper time. This might also account for the claimant's success in *R(I) 8/59*. Decisions which have discussed s. 52(b) and found the employee's act unconnected with the employer's business include *R(I) 68/54* where the employee fell asleep, *R(I) 80/53* where an oil stove was moved to provide heat for the employee at lunchtime, and *R(I) 1/58* where during a lull in work the employee accompanied another to the stores.

(s) *Commuting to and from work and travelling on duty*

Commuting can seriously damage health. There are almost as many deaths caused by the daily journey to and from work as there are at work itself.[22] Commuters can be made ill by their daily travel as, for example, where the stress involved leads to heart disease. But whether it is illness or injury resulting from travelling, it generally falls outside the industrial scheme. The general position was restated in *R(I) 12/75*(T):

---

[22] L. Pickup and S. W. Town, *A European Study of Commuting and Its Consequences* (1983) p. 106.

"[N]ormally a person's employment begins when he arrives at his place of work and ends when the person leaves it, so that accidents on the journey from home to work before arrival at the place of work, or on the journey home from work after departure from it, do not arise in the course of employment."

In *Nancollas* v. *Insurance Officer* (1985) it was emphasized that although the course of employment requires relevant factors to be taken into account, none of them can be conclusive. Each case involves a balancing operation and depends upon its own particular facts. Subject to this qualification regarding the limited value of decisions as precedents, this section analyses the factors which have been taken into account in past cases. It finds that the above statement from *R(I) 12/75*(T) is subject to three important exceptions. The first has already been considered in relation to the place of work and access to it, and its details are not repeated here. It is that if an employee is injured whilst travelling on his employer's land or property from which other members of the public are excluded, his claim may succeed if he was injured in the course of entering or leaving his place of work. The second exception is that special provision exists for employees following a peripatetic occupation for which the hours and place of work may vary considerably. It would be unjust to exclude from benefit those, such as lorry drivers or salesmen, who are employed to travel and who are injured away from their base. The final exception, like the first, benefits all employees even if they have a fixed place and hours of work. It is that if they are injured whilst travelling in transport provided by the employer the connection with work is thought to be close enough for them to be included within the industrial scheme. Specific statutory provision to this effect is made by SSA s. 53.

(i) GENERAL PRINCIPLES APART FROM S. 53

Employees following peripatetic occupations – in so far as they are employed to travel are likely to be within the course of employment when doing so. Commercial travellers are typical examples of such employees who, if injured on the road in the course of their day's work, fall within the scheme. Such employees are likely to succeed if their accident occurs between one duty point and another, although the cases have rarely had to deal directly with such circumstances. Instead the problem posed has been whether the journey from home to the first call of the day, or the return home from the last call of the day, is within employment. The general problem for all employees injured whilst travelling was restated in *R(I) 18/55*: "The question at issue is whether on the particular journey [the claimant] was travelling in the performance of a duty, or whether the journey was . . . merely preparatory to the performance of it". In short, was the journey one on duty and within the scheme, or was it to or from duty? However, *Nancollas* v. *Insurance Officer* (1985) describes this duty question as "but one of the factors to be taken into account . . . albeit no doubt an important factor".

Successful claimants injured between home and their first or last call have had jobs which gave them discretion as to when and where their duties were to be performed. Another important factor in all but two of these cases was that the employee's home was considered the base from which the work was done. The exceptions are *R(I) 18/55* where an agricultural advisory officer injured whilst visiting a farm at the beginning of the day obtained benefit, and *Nancollas* v. *Insurance Officer*. Other successful claims have been made in respect of a newspaper representative in *R(I) 55/53*; a school inspector in *R(I) 59/53*; a chief fire officer in *R(I) 64/54*; a brewery cellar inspector in *R(I) 5/55*; an insurance agent in *R(I) 15/60*, but not in *R(I) 8/52*; a DHSS official making home visits in *R(I) 4/70*; a home care assistant employed by the council in *CI 28/85* (unreported); and commercial salesmen in *R(I) 22/51* and *R(I) 38/53*, although the salesman in *R(I) 51/51* was considered to be injured too far away from his area of operations to be within employment.

The claims failed in the case of a tubular scaffolder in *R(I) 9/51*(T); a meter reader in *R(I) 19/57*; a relief signalman in *R(I) 34/57*; and a court bailiff in *CI 18/73* (unreported). In all these cases the employee's home was held not to be the work base. These decisions have been reinforced by *R(I) 2/67* and *R(I) 12/75*(T) in which benefit was denied to home helps injured on their journey to their first house of the day. These decisions appear to have restricted the scope for basing a claim upon a peripatetic occupation. They emphasized that there was a clear distinction between a person employed to travel, and one who has definite work hours and a fixed place of work, even though it may vary and be more than one place in any day. The latter was thought to be travelling to duty rather than on duty, and therefore likely not to be within the course of employment despite the peripatetic nature of the work.

However, the exact scope of this limitation is unclear and the position of a number of employees is left in doubt. For example, even with regard to a home help it is still uncertain whether an injury which occurs whilst travelling to the second duty point of the day is within employment: *R(I) 12/75*(T) suggests that a claim will fail, but *R(I) 14/81*(T) indicates otherwise. In this last case the tribunal of Commissioners refused benefit to an itinerant disablement resettlement officer injured in the course of paying his first domiciliary visit of the day. However, this decision was overruled on appeal in *Nancollas* v. *Insurance Officer* (1985). The Court of Appeal considered that the tribunal were misdirected in believing that there were previous decisions binding them to decide the case as they did. Each case should depend on its own facts and the resettlement officer's claim succeeded on the evidence produced.

However, it is still necessary to identify factors relevant to these individual decisions. In doing so a number of difficulties are involved. For example, it is uncertain precisely which employees will receive more favourable treatment by virtue of their job being affected by the factor relating to peripatetic employees. If they are within the exception, it is again uncertain which of their discretionary decisions to travel will bring them within the scheme and, in particular, whether travelling between home and the first (or last) call of the day is a journey of duty or not.

The most recent case is *CI 28/85* (unreported). It awards benefit to a home case assistant returning home after her last call of the day. Emphasis was placed on the fact that her hours of paid duty began when she left home and lasted until she returned. The Commissioner accepted the following submission of a AO as to the effect of the *Nancollas* case:

> ". . . the Court of Appeal's judgment suggests strongly that where a person is called upon to travel between home and work at differing locations and makes the journeys each way during normal working hours, at the employer's

> expense and by a reasonable route in relation to where he has to perform his duty, the journeys can, in the absence of other factors to the contrary, reasonably be regarded not as journeys to and from work but as part of the work which he is employed to perform and thus he will throughout be in the course of his employment."

Although the Commissioner found for the claimant, he warned that he did not regard *Nancollas* as giving *carte blanche* to all travelling accidents even if the claimant has no fixed place of work.

Employees with a fixed place and hours of work – if injured whilst travelling generally fall outside the scheme. Among a number of cases supporting this finding[23] is *R(I) 3/71* where benefit was denied to a DHSS official who, having been temporarily seconded to another town, was injured after normal office hours when returning home for the weekend. The Commissioner referred to the Court of Appeal's decision in *Vandyke* v. *Fender* (1970) where the general rule was affirmed without any regret: "It would be a disservice to the common law as a whole unnecessarily to blur the line between the period of road and rail travel to the place of employment and the period of employment itself". The same basis led to the refusal of benefit in *R* v. *National Insurance Commissioner, ex p. Fieldhouse* (1974) where a relief manager of petrol stations was injured whilst travelling home on the route between the station where he had just completed his duties and the place where he had been assigned to work the next day. The Divisional Court refused to quosh the Commissioner's finding that the journey occurred after work was finished, and was preparatory to the next day's duty so that it fell outside of employment.

However, in *Ball* v. *Insurance Officer* (1985) the Court of Appeal emphasized that each case must depend on its own facts. Its approach could lead to greater flexibility and an increase in the number of claims for benefit. The Court allowed the appeal of a policeman who, although having a station as his usual place of work, was injured whilst travelling to give sailing instruction to police cadets at a reservoir. He was travelling directly from his home, having first telephoned his station to report for duty. He was riding his own motorcycle as approved by his senior officers and for which he was paid expenses. Looking at these facts as a whole the Court decided that the only consistent decision was that the policeman was in the course of employment.

The application of this factor relating to those with a fixed place of work is subject to a number of other exceptions where benefit has been paid because of special circumstances, especially if the journey was made to fulfil an express or implied term of the employee's contract of service. Some of the cases falling within these exceptions can only be reconciled with others by emphasizing that each depends on its own facts. Claims have succeeded where:

> (1) *The employer instructed the claimant to make the journey at the time in the manner that he did.* This was the basis for the successful claim of the dock worker in *R(I) 11/57*. He was implicitly required by the dock labour scheme to travel directly from an employer's office, where he had failed to obtain work, to the Dock Labour Board office.

---

[23] See for example, *5/48(II), CI 33/50, CI 310/50, R(I) 79/51, R(I) 48/52, 6/56(II), R(I) 10/56, R(I) 16/58, R 4/61(II), R 2/64(II)* and *R 3/83(II)*.

But where such direct travel was not required the dock worker failed in *R(I) 6/64*. In *R(I) 27/54* the employee was injured whilst waiting, as instructed, for the car to take him to the building site where he worked. Other successful claims were made in *3/58(II)* and *Paterson* v. *Costain and Press (Overseas)* (1979). This last case was decided by the Court of Appeal but *R(I) 1/83*(T) suggests that it depends upon its special facts. For employees who are asked to travel in response to an emergency see (*q*) above.

(2) *The employer arranged for the claimant to convey other employees to work.* In *R(I) 8/51*(T) the claim succeeded where another employee was carried as a public passenger on the claimant's motor cycle.

(3) *The claimant used or waited for transport provided by the employer* as in *R(I) 4/59, R(I) 34/59* and *R(I) 3/81*. In the last case a police cadet was injured whilst travelling in a police personnel carrier as she was obliged to do. Benefit was obtained, as in the other cases, without the necessity of applying the special provision made by SSA s. 53 which is considered below. In *R(I) 65/51* the claimant alighted from his employer's lorry taking him to work and was injured in crossing the road to reach the gates of his workplace. Benefit was paid on the basis that crossing the road was necessary to do what was required by his employers. This decision appears to be exceptionally favourable to claimants but it contrasts with the denial of benefit in, for example, *CI 65/49* and *R(I) 4/79*. It may be that the explanation for the cases is that where benefit was denied the claimants had not used transport provided by the employer before their injury on the road occurred.

(4) *The employee is considered to be on duty because his responsibilities continue whilst travelling.* Examples of the factors which give rise to such a conclusion are examined below. Again each of these factors cannot be decisive. In particular the course of employment cannot be determined by arrangements made between the employer and employee alone.

The first factor is that the claimant is paid whilst travelling. Several decisions have emphasized that these payments cannot be conclusive for, as noted in *R(I) 21/55* and *ex p. Fieldhouse* "it may be no more than a means of recompensing him for the inconvenience of travelling". The second factor is that the claimant carries goods relating to his work. This helped the claim succeed in *Shepherdson* v. *Hayward* (1940) and in *R(I) 17/51* where an electrician had been instructed to collect a sheet of metal and bring it with him to work the next day. But carrying a file or two home from the office is unlikely to suffice. Thus claims failed despite the carrying of work papers in *R(I) 39/53*, or tools in *R(I) 16/58* and *R 1/77(II)*, even where the tools impeded movement and caused the accident in *R(I) 78/53* and *R 1/65(II)*. The third factor is that the claimant is injured whilst on call. This has been the subject of recent cases which have considered in detail the scope of this exception to the general rule concerning travelling.

The first of these cases is a 1980 decision of the Divisional Court which at first seemed to extend the exception significantly. In *R* v. *National Insurance Commissioner, ex p. Reed* (1980) a policeman working in the station's control room took advantage of a privilege of his job by spending his meal-breaks at home. During this time he was on call for he remained responsible for station matters throughout his tour of duty. In cycling back to the station after lunch he was involved in an accident and claimed benefit. Earlier decisions had denied that policemen were in the course of employment in making their way to their stations to report for duty as in *R(I) 45/52*, *R(I) 12/74* and *3/50(II)*. But in *Reed's* case the claimant succeeded in establishing special circumstances to provide an exception to the trend of finding that travelling is not in the course of employment for those with a fixed place of work. The court realized that being on call, of itself, was not sufficient to amount to such special circumstances: claims on behalf of a chief fire officer in *R(I) 28/53* and a prison officer in *R 2/79(II)* had been refused despite the officers being liable to be called out in an emergency. However, by applying a fine distinction the court was able to place the policeman into a different category. "He was not standing by to be called back to duty . . . he was still performing his duty of standing by." On this basis the course of employment seemed to have been significantly extended because it appeared that it would have made no difference if the accident had happened at home. But two later decisions have exposed the limits of *ex p. Reed*.

In *R(I) 5/81* a fire officer was injured whilst on call in the course of making his way home from headquarters. Benefit was denied and *ex p. Reed* was distinguished on two grounds. First, it was said that the policeman's job limited his choice as to where his break might be taken, whereas the fireman was free to do as he pleased; and secondly, the policeman had, or might have had, duties to perform during his break. This approach was supported by a tribunal of Commissioners in *R(I) 1/83*(T) in which a policeman injured while returning home from a residential course was denied benefit because he was performing no duties at that time. *Ex p. Reed* was said to depend upon its special facts and in particular upon what was thought to be the debatable finding that the policeman's responsibility continued throughout the lunch break.

These decisions reduced the scope for claiming that a policeman was on duty when involved in a road accident. They were supported by decisions refusing benefit to officers in Northern Ireland. In *R 1/83(II)* a policeman was killed by a bomb which exploded under his car while he was travelling home. Although the bomb may have been planted when he was on duty it exploded when his duty had ended, and he was no longer in the course of employment. An off duty policeman can put himself on duty again, but only if he takes a conscious decision to do so or he does some act which is consistent with being on duty. The claimant in this case had no such opportunity. In *R 2/83(II)* an act consistent with being on duty could not be proven by a policeman who was shot in the back by a terrorist. The very circumstance of his shooting was said to reveal that he could only have put himself on duty, if at all, after he had received his injury. The questionable presumption applied here is that a policeman on duty does not turn his back on a gunman. Both these Irish decisions confirmed the trend of limiting the course of employment of policemen. However, this trend has been reversed by *Ball* v. *Insurance Officer* (1985) as discussed above. Despite having a fixed place of work and travelling from his home on his own motor cycle, the policeman succeeded in his claim. He had reported on the telephone for duty, and was paid travelling expenses. Each case must now depend very much on its own facts.

Travelling in order to take a meal or other refreshment – is dealt with in accordance with the rules outlined above in that an accident is generally considered to be outside of employment if it happens on a road.[24] This sharply contrasts with the position where injuries occur in the course of taking a meal on the employer's property as considered at p. 63 above. Even where an employee was only making a short journey across the public road to reach the employer's canteen benefit was refused in *R(I) 74/52*. An exception to this general rule is where the claimant's responsibilities continue throughout the mealbreak as in *R* v. *National Insurance Commissioner, ex p. Reed* (above). A more important exception exists in relation to those employed to travel, as in *R(I) 5/55*, where the itinerant brewery cellar inspector obtained benefit when injured on the road while going to get a meal.

A number of cases have involved claimants who are employed to drive or be driven in vehicles on the road. Bus drivers have succeeded in claims where they have shown that their job continues to affect them during the break in that, for example, it restricts where they may take their refreshment. A second factor is that, as in *ex p. Reed*, the drivers continue to have duties to perform during their break period. Thus in *R(I) 11/55* the claim succeeded where the driver was required to remain near his bus to be available if required, and in *R(I) 20/61* the driver had to take refreshment at a place where he could keep watch on the bus. By contrast the claims failed in *R(I) 10/52*, *R(I) 38/59* and *R(I) 4/79* where the drivers had no such duties and their movements were unrestricted until the time when their duties were to resume. The fact that the drivers in the last two cases were going to or returning from a canteen operated by their employer made no difference. The claim also failed in *R(I) 84/52* where a delivery van assistant was free to do as he liked on leaving the van to obtain his lunch. Where there was a deviation from employment the claim was refused in *CI 456/50* and *R(I) 6/53*. In these cases conductors left their buses *en route* in order to obtain refreshment in contrast to *R(I) 21/53*, where the claim succeeded because tea was taken only at the end of the journey and not during it.

Deviations from a journey on duty – can take the claimant outside the course of employment especially if he acts for his own purposes. Thus in *R(I) 40/55* benefit was denied where a furniture remover diverged from his direct route to visit a pub, although in *CI 148/49* and *R(I) 5/55* stopping to have a meal was within employment. Much depends on whether the employer would have permitted the deviation. In *R(I) 40/56* had the employer known he would have agreed to the employee accompanying another to obtain medical treatment and the claim therefore succeeded. In *R(I) 38/53* the deviation was against the claimant's will in that he had been detained in a police station and as a result he was found still on duty when he resumed his journey.

It is clear that more lattitude is given to employees who have no fixed hours or place of work. *R(I) 38/61* involved such a claimant. One evening he visited an acquaintance to obtain some spare parts for his lorries but he stayed for some hours, turning a business call into a social visit. He was injured whilst returning home, which was also the base from which he worked. His claim succeeded because his hours of work were not closely defined and he was considered to have resumed the course of his

---

[24] *Bell* v. *Armstrong, Whitworth & Co.* (1919), *CI 282/49*, *R(I) 1/53*, *R(I) 24/53*, *R(I) 89/53* and *R(I) 24/56*. See also the cases cited in relation to official breaks in work hours at p. 57 above.

employment when he set out for home. Just as in this case it was difficult to change what was primarily a journey on business into one which was not, so in *R(I) 70/51* the claimant was unable to show that a holiday in Paris had become a business visit only because he had extended his stay by one day in order to visit a factory there.

(ii) TRAVELLING IN THE EMPLOYER'S TRANSPORT UNDER S. 53

Under workmen's compensation if the employee was injured whilst travelling to or from work in a vehicle operated by, or on behalf of, the employer, a claim could be made only if there were a contractual obligation to use the transport involved. This obligation is no longer required for SSA s. 53 states:

> "(1) An accident happening while an employed earner is, with the express or implied permission of his employer, travelling as a passenger by any vehicle to or from his place of work shall, notwithstanding that he is under no obligation to his employer to travel by that vehicle, be deemed to arise out of and in the course of his employment if –
>   (a) the accident would have been deemed so to have arisen had he been under such an obligation; and
>   (b) at the time of the accident, the vehicle –
>   (i) is being operated by or on behalf of his employer or some other person by whom it is provided in pursuance of arrangements made with his employer; and
>   (ii) is not being operated in the ordinary course of a public transport service.
> (2) In this section references to a vehicle include a ship, vessel, hovercraft or aircraft."

In some ways this section has been restrictively interpreted. Although it no longer matters that the use of the vehicle is optional, the employer's permission to travel is still required. This must normally be given before the journey begins, although in some circumstances it may be that restrospective express permission will suffice. Permission is often implied if the employer knows of the circumstances and the means by which the employee travels and does nothing to stop it. But if the employer takes preventative action the requirement may not be satisfied and the claim will fail as in *R(I) 5/80*. In this case a bus service operated on behalf of the employer was used by the claimant in order to return home. The claimant was told by the driver that he would be taken the last few miles in the driver's own car. His subsequent injury was held to fall outside s. 53 because, unknown to the claimant, the driver had been warned not to carry passengers in that way. The employer had not given implied permission for the car to be used to transport bus passengers. An argument that the driver had ostensible authority to carry out the contract with the employer in the way that he did was also rejected. The Commissioner concluded that s. 53

> "embodies a very limited exception to the general rule that a person going home after the end of a day's work is not in the course of his employment. In my view, there can be no doubt that the exception was deliberately enacted in narrow terms . . . ."

The protection of s. 53 only extends to employees "travelling as a passenger by any vehicle". This means that the employee must be injured while actually being carried, for in *R(I) 67/52* the phrase was taken to exclude injuries which occur as the claimant approaches the transport involved. Thus benefit was refused where the claimant was injured crossing the road to board the employer's bus in *R(I) 79/51*, and where the claimant was walking towards one bus having alighted from another in *R(I) 48/54*. Waiting for a bus must also be excluded, but the claimant succeeded when injured in alighting from a moving bus in *CI 12/49*. In *R(I) 42/56* the claimant fell from a tractor taking him home. He was held to be travelling "as a passenger" under s. 53 even though he occupied a part of the vehicle not designed for the carriage of passengers. Had he been driving the tractor benefit would have been refused for he would not then have been a passenger. The claims of a motor-bike rider and a pedal cyclist were rejected because they were not passengers in *CI 49/49* and *R(I) 9/51*(T). Although drivers are thus excluded from s. 53 itself, they may succeed without its assistance if they carry other employees to work by arrangement with the employer. As in the case of the motor-cyclist in *R(I) 8/51*(T) the course of their employment will then normally include accidents which occur whilst conveying these passengers to work. A claimant may succeed despite being injured by a vehicle carrying him only part of the way to work as in *R(I) 8/62*.

A further requirement of s. 53 is that, if the vehicle is operated by someone other than the employer, it must be provided in pursuance of an "arrangement" with the employer. In *CI 101/49* the arrangement was made by the County Agricultural Committee and although the farmer employing the claimant agreed to it, he was considered to play no part in making the arrangement and benefit was refused. An arrangement is a vague term. Although it does not require a contract, the employer must make some specific provision for the transport and might be expected to have some measure of control over it by, for example, reserving the vehicle for the exclusive use of his employees. No such arrangement could be found in *R(I) 67/51* where all that existed was a suggestion or request by the employer that a train run to and from the colliery. But where another such loose agreement was involved in *R(I) 49/53* the claim succeeded. The difference between these two cases, as explained in *R(I) 15/57*, was that in the case of a vehicle provided by a public transport undertaking something more definite is required to constitute an arrangement. British Rail and public service bus companies are therefore treated differently from those who provide transport privately. This helps to explain why the claim succeeded in *R(I) 49/53*. There, the service was laid on not by a public transport undertaking, but privately by a building contractor who allowed employees of the sub-contractors on site to use his vehicles to get to work. Although the claimant's employer seemed only to agree and not actually devise the scheme, an arrangement falling within s. 53 was nevertheless found. Although it may be more difficult to establish an arrangement in the case of a public transport undertaking, successful claims were made in *R(I) 15/57* and *R(I) 3/59*. An arrangement was found in the first case because the employer had deliberately adapted the working hours to coincide with the bus schedules, and had permitted use of a private road. In return the bus company agreed to carry passengers directly into the factory. It was also important to note that the service did not run when the factory was closed.

If the agreement is merely a private affair and does not envisage that employees will be carried, benefit will be refused as in *R(I) 5/60* where the claimant's accident occurred whilst travelling in a car borrowed by his foreman from the employer. If an employee is ill and with permission of the employer is taken home by another employee, it is likely to be considered a private affair. But if a taxi is ordered and paid for by the employer rather than the employee then it may well be that an arrangement will be found.

Factors relevant to whether a vehicle was "being operated in the ordinary course of public transport" were examined in *R(I) 15/57*. In favour of such a finding was that members of the public were not carried; the service did not run when the factory was closed; it was not included in ordinary timetables; the bus had no destination indicator and it ended its journey along a private road. A claim therefore does not necessarily fail only because the public use the service. The claim succeeded in *R(I) 15/57* although the bus carried passengers who did not work for the claimant's employer. Even if a substantial number of members of the general public are carried, the vehicle may be found to operate privately on one section of its route and publicly on another. The claim thus succeeded in *R(I) 3/59* because the accident occurred whilst the bus was travelling on the private section of its journey.

The requirements of s. 53(1)(b) do not apply to an airman travelling to or from his place of work in any aircraft. This means that it does not matter that the airman takes a regular flight with other members of the public and no special transport arrangements are made by his employer. A similar provision exists in respect of mariners travelling by ship to or from the vessel where they work. If an airman or mariner is forced to return to the UK following loss or damage to his plane or ship, or because he is ill, he is deemed to be in the course of employment if he travels at the employer's expense.[25]

(iii) REFORMING THE COURSE OF EMPLOYMENT

Reform has focussed upon whether the industrial scheme should be extended to include all employees injured whilst commuting to and from work. This would be an important change which, according to the Pearson Commission,[26] would eventually increase the cost of the scheme by 7 per cent. The Commission thought the arguments were finely balanced, but by one vote they recommended that the scheme be extended. The majority were persuaded by the evidence of the Post Office Engineering Union that "the process of travelling to and from work is just as much a part of industrial and commercial activity as the work itself". However, this view has been rejected by the Government. The White Paper proposes to retain the existing boundary line. There are several reasons given for this. First the Government consider that the risks to which these travelling to work are exposed are no different from those faced by the public as a whole on the roads and railways. Secondly, if travel were included the concept of industrial preference would be placed under great strain for the position of certain non-industrial injuries would be seen as anomalous. Thirdly, it

---

[25] Reg. 3 of the Social Security (Industrial Injuries) (Airmen's Benefits) Regulations 1975 (SI No. 469), and reg. 3 of the Social Security (Industrial Injuries) (Mariner's Benefits) Regulations 1975 (SI No. 470).

[26] Pearson vol. I paras. 858-868.

would be difficult to define precisely what constitutes a commuting accident and much time might be taken up deciding whether, for example, a deviation to collect children from school or to consult the doctor are within the scheme. Finally, the investigation of claims would be made more difficult in that employers may not be in a position to give much information about the circumstances of the injury. Although schemes compensating commuters exist in other countries, the present limits to the UK legislation are therefore likely to continue for the foreseeable future.

5.   THE ACCIDENT MUST ARISE OUT OF EMPLOYMENT

(1) The "idea of causation"

The relationship between arising "out of" and "in the course of" employment has already been considered at p. 51. There it was suggested that the overlap in theory between the two parts of s. 50(1) in practice causes few problems: if an accident is found to be in the course of employment it is almost certain to arise out of it. Arising "out of" employment conveys "an idea of causation". According to *R(I) 10/52* it

> "signifies not only was [the claimant] working at his employment at the moment of the accident, but that his employment, or something incidental to it, actually caused the accident."

The nature of this relationship between the accident and the work is by no means clearly defined. On the one hand it has been said that the causal connection may be remote and only a "superficial nexus" with work need be shown. What has been called "active physical causation by the surroundings" is not required. According to *Cadzow Coal Co.* v. *Price (and Murphy)* (1943):

> "It is enough that the exigencies of the employment brought the workman within the range of the particular danger and exposed him to its impact, whereas but for his employment he would not have been exposed."

On the other hand the work has been required to be more than a *sine qua non* of injury and must amount to what has been variously described as a *causa causans*, or a "proximate", "efficient" or "effective" cause. Thus in *R(I) 12/58* a laundry worker handled blankets suspected of being contaminated by smallpox and was vaccinated against the disease. Her subsequent reaction to the vaccine was held not to arise out of employment. Although her work was a condition or *sine qua non* of injury, it was not the effective cause of it, for that was held to be the vaccination itself.

These general principles of causation have been examined at p. 45 in relation to the requirement that the accident cause the injury. That section considers in particular the important question whether a claimant suffering before the industrial accident from a condition which contributes to the later injury at work, can establish that the injury arises out of employment. If, for example, the claimant has a heart condition and suffers an attack at work, the accident does not arise out of employment if the job is merely the setting for the event. The work must amount to an effective cause of injury if the accident is to arise out of it, although it need not be the sole or dominant cause. Thus it has been held that a claim succeeds if work is the effective cause of injury by bringing about the strain which precipitates the attack.

(2) A risk of employment, or one created by the claimant?

The general principles of causation received a particular interpretation in the leading case of *R(I) 2/63*(T). Although the case only purported to deal with a claimant who could be accused of creating a non-employment risk by acting for his own purposes, certain views of the tribunal of Commissioners may be of wider application. For example, they emphasized that it may not be helpful to classify causes into various types. Instead causation cases could be treated primarily as involving questions of fact and resolved "in a broad commonsense manner". Nevertheless in relation to the claimant acting for his own purposes, the tribunal relied upon a specific formula as a substitute, in effect, for the requirement in other cases that the work amount to a proximate or effective cause. This was that if the *sine qua non* test is satisfied (so that it can be said that the accident would not have happened but for the employment), then the injury will be considered to arise out of employment "unless the claimant had added or created a different risk . . . and this different risk was the real cause of the accident". In *R(I) 2/63*(T) the claimant was injured by an explosion following his attempt to light a cigarette near a place where, unknown to him, gas was escaping. The danger of such an explosion was present before the claimant used his lighter, for there were other naked flames heating various machines near the escaping gas. The Commissioners held first, that the risk of explosion was clearly one of employment and was the *sine qua non* of the injury; and secondly; that although the claimant had acted for his own purposes in lighting his cigarette, he had not created a new or different risk from that which already existed. As a result the accident arose out of employment and benefit was paid.

In so far as decisions before *R(I) 2/63*(T) refuse benefit if a claimant acts for his own purposes, and fail to ask whether a new or different risk has been created which is the real cause of the accident, they ought not to be followed. According to this decision these earlier cases concentrate solely upon what the claimant was doing, whereas attention should also be paid to the circumstances in which the act was done. This is a more liberal approach and a claimant now finds it easier to establish that his injury is a result of an employment risk. This is illustrated by two cases, the one before and the other after the 1963 decision. They both deal with a claimant who acts for her own purposes in handing over a sweet to another employee and who is injured by a machine as a result. Under a stricter regime *R(I) 41/56* held the claimant's act was not incidental to her job and her injury did not arise out of employment. By contrast *R(I)17/63*, relying upon *R(I) 2/63*(T), could not find that a new or different risk from that of employment had been created and benefit was paid.

(3) A risk of employment, or one shared by the general public?

If a risk is not special to the job and is shared by the public as a whole the accident may not arise out of employment. For a claim to succeed it must be shown that the character of the employment and its surrounding circumstances create or magnify a risk which is special or incidental to that employment. Again the distinction can be difficult: employees are frequently exposed to risks in places where they would not be if it were not for their employment, but these risks may also be run by the general public. If an employee is struck by lightning it may be his job which brought him to the place where he was hurt but the risk of such injury was shared with the public at large. The most common problems to which the distinction gave rise have now been resolved by statute. Commissioners were troubled in a series of cases[27] where injury was either the result of an assault, or skylarking of another person, or was caused by an act of nature in that an animal, or insect, or even a bolt of lightning was involved. Did these accidents arise out of employment? Sometimes the fact that the claimant's job brought him to the particular locality was sufficient for him to succeed, but at other times a less generous attitude was taken and benefit was refused. The uncertainty that resulted has now been removed at least in relation to the specific examples given above. Since 1961 they have all been made risks of employment by what is now SSA s. 55. In so far as the old decisions deal with circumstances specifically covered by s. 55, they are now relevant only to illustrate how the general principles of causation apply. There have been almost no Commissioners' decisions upon the operation of the new section itself.

Although the area appears relatively free from dispute it is still possible for circumstances to occur which fall outside s. 55, and then the distinction between an employment risk and one common to the general public must be examined. Two areas highlighted by the old cases illustrate the difficulties to which the distinction could still give rise:

(a) Road accidents

Whether certain injuries occurring on public roads result from a risk of employment may still prove troublesome. For example, in *R(I) 62/53* injury was caused when something struck a lorry driver in the eye. He was denied benefit because there was nothing in his employment which exposed him to a greater risk than the general public. By contrast in *R(I) 67/53* a police motor cyclist struck in the eye by a piece of grit obtained benefit by s. 55(c). The Commissioner decided that the conduct was not of than other road users, and in travelling a greater distance because of his job the risks were proportionately increased.

(b) Exposure to the weather

Whether injuries resulting from weather conditions (other than lightning

---

[27] Injury caused by an assault was held to arise out of employment in *CI 3/48, CI 51/49, CSI 63/49, CI 88/50, CI 248/50, R(I) 47/51, R(I) 41/53, R(I) 71/53, R(I) 30/58*, but the claim failed in *CI 5/50, R(I) 41/51*(T), *R(I) 76/54, R(I) 23/56, R(I) 21/58* and its appendix being *R v. National Insurance Commissioner, ex p. Richardson* (1958), *R(I) 5/59* and *R(I) 26/59*.
Injury caused by other misconduct, skylarking or negligence of another was held to arise out of employment in *CI 334/50, R(I) 55/52, R(I) 63/52, R(I) 8/54, R(I) 9/54, R(I) 46/54* and *R(I) 16/61*, but the claim failed in *CI 170/49, R(I) 24/51, R(I) 25/51, R(I) 31/51, R(I) 76/53, R(I) 12/54* and *R(I) 75/54*.
Injury caused by an animal or insect was held to arise out of employment in *CI 3/49, CWI 6/49, R(I) 5/56, R(I) 10/57*, and *R(I) 13/60*, but the claim failed in *CI 101/50* and *R(I) 89/52*.
Injury caused by lightning was held to arise out of employment in *R(I) 23/58* but the claim failed in *R(I) 12/56, R(I) 11/58* and *R(I) 7/60*.

which is now covered by s. 55) are risks arising out of employment could still prove a difficult issue. (The problem also gives rise to difficulties in defining whether an accident has occurred and whether it in fact caused injury.) As to whether the injury arises out of employment there are cases where, on the one hand, being subject to the prevailing weather has been considered an ordinary risk of life and not protected by the industrial scheme. Thus in *CI 18/49* benefit was denied to a home help who was wringing out clothes in a garden on a cold day and caught a chill which developed into pneumonia. Similarly in *R(I) 32/57* exposure to cold over a period of several years was considered to be no more than incongenial working conditions and was insufficient to amount to a risk of employment. On the other hand, in *R(I) 3/51*(T) an employee who received "two bad wettings" as a result of heavy rain entering his workplace obtained benefit for his resulting attack of fibrositis. The incidents were held to be exceptional and not to be compared with ordinary drizzle and cold winds which others might encounter. The exceptional nature of the risk was also emphasized in *CI 123/49* where a farm labourer who suffered from frostbite following his pulling of sugar beet on a cold day received benefit because his job exposed him to a risk not shared by others.

These decisions reveal that it is not always easy to determine whether the risk is the same as that run by the general public. There is no scientific application of risk rates and in particular there may be no obvious comparitor by which the injury to the claimant can be measured. For example, in *CWI 6/49* and *R(I) 4/61* seamen died abroad, in the first case of malaria due to an infestation of mosquitoes in an African port, and in the second case of heatstroke suffered in the Arabian Gulf. In both cases these risks were shared by all others in the locality. Was the risk to the claimant to be compared with the general public in the area concerned, or with the risks to the public in the UK? It was decided in favour of the latter comparison so that benefit was paid for what were considered special risks of employment totally different from any which the employees would have run in this country. Based upon the overlapping criteria involved the conclusions were not easy to reach. Similar difficulties arise in settling upon suitable comparitors for the above road accident cases involving eye injuries. The problem is further illustrated by *R(I) 27/60* where an employee obtained benefit after she had been blown off her bicycle on her employer's premises by a freak gust of wind. She was said to run a greater risk of injury because she was compared not to other members of the public riding bicycles, but to other people walking in the locality, for they would not have been as vulnerable to the wind as she was. Although there is this scope for uncertainty in deciding whether an accident arose out of employment, the industrial scheme has not been troubled by it in recent years. It must be repeated that there have been no decisions in the area since 1960 and the most common problems that used to occur are now dealt with by SSA s. 55.

(4) Accidents caused by another's misconduct or by certain acts of nature and considered by s. 55

The impetus for the enactment of s. 55 was a 1958 decision which was thought to expose the uncertainty and possible unfairness of applying the distinction between a risk of employment (which was considered to be within the industrial scheme) and a risk shared by the general public (which was not). In *R(I) 21/58* a bus conductor was attacked by a gang of "teddy boys". The attack seemed to be indiscriminate because other members of the public had previously been assaulted by the gang. The claimant had not been singled out because of his job. For example, he had not been attacked because he carried money or wore a uniform. As a result the injury was held not to arise out of employment and benefit was refused. The decision was affirmed on appeal in *R* v. *National Insurance Commissioner, ex p. Richardson* (1958). After pressure for legislation to reverse the decision, the present s. 55 was introduced in 1961. This section dealt with not only cases of assault but also others in which the materiality of work had previously been questioned. Various risks, which had provided nearly all the problems requiring a decision of a Commissioner as to whether they arose out of employment, were grouped together and declared to be risks of employment. The reform is presently incorporated in SSA s. 55 which states:

> "(1) An accident shall be treated . . . as arising out of an employed earner's employment if –
> (a) the accident arises in the course of the employment; and
> (b) the accident either is caused by another person's misconduct, skylarking or negligence, or by steps taken in consequence of any such misconduct, skylarking or negligence, or by the behaviour or presence of an animal (including a bird, fish or insect), or is caused by or consists in the employed earner being struck by any object or by lightning; and
> (c) the employed earner did not directly or indirectly induce or contribute to the happening of the accident by his conduct outside the employment or by any act not incidental to the employment.
> (2) This section applies only to accidents happening after 19th December 1961."

There are only three decisions which have considered s. 55. In *R(I) 3/67* the claimant was taking a permitted smoking break in a factory corridor when he was hit by a snowball thrown by another employee. The claimant followed the assailant in order to remonstrate with him as to the danger of what he had done, but he was injured when the employee slammed a door in his face. Applying *Re Culverwell* (1966) the Commissioner held that the accident was in the course of employment but that *Culverwell* was not directly relevant to the question whether the accident arose out of employment. That question was to be decided by applying s. 55, but then the particular problem was whether the claimant, in following the assailant, had contributed to the accident happening so as to be denied benefit by s. 55(c). The Commissioner decided that the conduct was not of this nature and that benefit was payable, but the result would have been different had the claimant been found to have been indulging in horseplay. Benefit was denied on this basis in *R 1/71(II)* where the claimant was injured whilst watching, with a group of other employees, one of their number cause an explosion. The group had agreed to go to a place during their lunch hour in order to make these explosions. Although the claimant had not set them off himself he was denied benefit because he was considered to be contributing to the occurrence of the accident. In *R 1/81 (II)* it was held that being a reserve constable and member of the security forces in Northern Ireland did not contribute to being shot, and s. 55 could be applied so that the shooting arose out of employment.

The presumption applied by s. 55 is a conclusive one; it does not matter that in fact the work is immaterial to the accident, provided that the claimant was in the course of his employment and he does not contribute to his injury. The section is thus of broad scope and its potential may be further illustrated by applying s. 55 to the facts of a few of the cases which arose before it was enacted. The misconduct causing injury need not be that of another employee and can include a deliberate assault, so that injury resulting from a robbery committed by strangers, as in *R(I) 41/51*(T) and *CSI 63/49*, would now fall within the scheme. It no longer matters that there is nothing in the work which encourages an assault, so that a claim will succeed even if the assault is the result of another employee's disturbed mental state which is unrelated to his job as in *R(I) 76/54* and *R(I) 30/58*. Where the injury is caused by a fellow employee it is not relevant to ask whether that employee is acting in the course of his employment. *R(I) 16/61* emphasizes that the proper question is whether the claimant's injury arises out of the claimant's employment. Where an animal is involved the injury may result not only from its behaviour, but also from its presence. Thus an agent calling door to door may be protected by the scheme if he falls over a dog as in *R(I) 13/60*, as well as if he is bitten by a cat as in *CI 3/49*. Where the claimant is stung by insects there is no longer any need to prove that the work-place offers a special attraction to them as there was in *R(I) 89/52*. As for being struck by any object as well as lightning, s. 55 now assists the claimant injured by debris hurled by high winds, as well as the victim of an assassin's bullet as in *R 1/81(II)*. Finally it may be noted that the chain of causation connecting these various agents to the claimant's injury can be a lengthy one and the scope of s. 55 increased as a result. In *R(I) 9/54* a skylarking employee struck a match and to avoid it burning his fingers he threw it away, thus accidentally setting alight a bowl of benzine. To minimize the damage he tried to take the bowl to a safer place, but in doing so he spilt it over the claimant. It was held that benefit was payable because the injury was a direct result of the act of skylarking in striking the match.

(5) The presumption that an accident in the course of employment arises out of it.

Under the Workmen's Compensation Acts the burden of proving that an accident fell within the equivalent of SSA s. 50(1) lay upon the claimant. This could cause problems if the precise way in which the accident occurred was not known because, for example, the claimant suffered from amnesia following his injury. These difficulties were eased somewhat when the legislation brought into force in 1948 stated that:

> ". . . an accident arising in the course of . . . employment shall be deemed, in the absence of evidence to the contrary, also to have arisen out of employment."

Although this presumption is still to be found in SSA s. 50(3) it has had only a limited effect upon claims. This is because evidence can readily be put forward to prevent the presumption applying, and it in no way affects the burden upon the claimant of showing that his accident arose in the course of employment.

R v. *National Insurance Commissioner, ex p. Richardson* (1958) considered that s. 50(3) "either creates a conclusive presumption or gives rise to no presumption" because "if there is evidence . . . that the accident does not arise out of and in the course of employment, then there is no presumption at all . . . ." Evidence making the presumption inapplicable was required to be that which would be "fit to be left to the jury", and was further described in *R(I) 1/64* as being "something more than speculative inference although . . . something less than proof". That decision involved a post office engineer who could remember nothing between the time when someone opened the door of the telephone box in which he was working, and when he arrived home with a head wound. Although there were many possibilities as to how he had come by his injury these were dismissed as too speculative. As a result the evidence required to prevent the presumption applying could not be found and the injury was held to arise out of employment.

If there is evidence which goes beyond mere speculation the presumption does not apply. This was the case in *R(I) 39/59* where there was medical opinion that a detached retina could be caused by natural circumstances as well as by the strain of lifting heavy goods at work. Where the facts are fully known and the question is of applying the law to them then there is no room for the application of the presumption. Thus in *R(I) 6/82*, even though the precise reason for the claimant's twisting of his ankle and breaking it was not known, there was no uncertainty as to the other facts surrounding the accident. The presumption was then held inapplicable and the claim failed.

CHAPTER 4

ENTITLEMENT FOR PRESCRIBED DISEASES

1. INTRODUCTION

There are two ways in which those who suffer from disease may gain entitlement under the industrial scheme. Firstly, they may show that their disease amounts to injury by accident and thus qualifies for benefit under SSA s. 50(1), as discussed in the last chapter. In proving this they are faced with the rejection of injuries caused by "process". As explained at p. 39 this prevents payment for most diseases because they develop over a period of time and it is not possible to identify any specific event which could be called an accident. Instead resort must be had to the second method of compensation which is the subject of this chapter. This is that entitlement may be claimed under SSA s. 76 if the particular disease is "prescribed" for the claimant's occupation. This system allows claims only in respect of those diseases which appear on a statutory list. This is compiled on the basis that experience and medical expertise have shown the diseases to be particular risks for those following certain employments. For example, the rare disease called glanders is prescribed for occupations involving contact with horses of their carcases. The list was begun in 1906 and although it continues to be expanded it still covers only about fifty diseases.

If the disease is prescribed for the claimant's job there is a presumption that his incapacity results from his work. Proving that the injury has an industrial cause is therefore easier in the case of a prescribed disease than where an accident is involved. Partly because of this, there has been a reluctance to list a disease if there is doubt about its connection with work. The list has therefore been narrowly drawn and this has placed pressure upon the accident provisions to accommodate those diseases which are not listed. No overlap is permitted between accidents and listed diseases because SSA s. 76(2) refuses to allow a claim for a prescribed disease to be treated as if it were an accident. However, for the many diseases not listed, the accident provisions remain of vital importance. In fact in 1982-83 there were four times as many victims of disease compensated for being injured by accident compared to those diagnosed as suffering from a prescribed disease.[1] Two examples of compensation for disease via the accident provisions of SSA s. 50 can be given. Firstly, although non-infective dermatitis is one of the most common prescribed diseases and, as such,

---

[1]   DHSS *Social Security Statistics 1984*, table 20.50. The figures include awards of injury benefit which has since been abolished. See also the IIAC report, *Industrial Diseases* (Cmnd. 8393, 1981) para. 148.

cannot be considered under s. 50, the infective skin condition, dermatophytosis, is often regarded as having developed by accident. Secondly, according to the IIAC report in 1981 (Cmnd. 8383):

> ". . . where a man already had mild and non-incapacitating bronchitis and was then exposed to a pulmonary irritant which aggravated the bronchitis, that exposure would be accepted as an accident, as would an aggravation of an existing spondylosis of arthritis by a particular piece of work or movement occasioned by that work."

Other diseases held in particular cases to have been caused by accident have been considered in the previous chapter. They include ringworm, malaria, poliomyelitis, tuberculosis, typhoid fever, fibrositis, angina and conjunctivitis.

If the disease is neither an accident nor on the prescribed list then no benefit can be paid even if the claimant is able to show that his disability has an occupational cause. There have been proposals to change this system. These would have ended the exclusive nature of the list of diseases by allowing a claimant to show, in his particular case, that the non-prescribed disease from which he suffers is caused by his work. However, these proposals have been rejected by Government as discussed at p. 131.

Prescribed diseases accounted for about a quarter (36,000) of the 186,000 pensions current in 1983 (appendix A, table 1). Of these, pneumoconiosis accounted for two thirds (23,000) occupational deafness for one sixth (7,000) and the remainder of the prescribed diseases for only one sixth (6,000). Three out of four current pensions are for accidents and not prescribed diseases, but in any one year there are about 30 times as many initial assessments for accidents as opposed to prescribed diseases (appendix A, table 6). However, payment of benefit for an accident is not likely to continue for as long as that for a disease. This is the reason for the disproportionate accumulation of pensions for disease within the system compared to the relatively low number of initial assessments.

One of the conditions for making a claim is laid down by SSA s. 57(3): benefit is not available for a prescribed disease until 15 weeks after its date of onset. By PD reg. 6(2) this is "the day on which the claimant first suffered from the relevant loss of faculty on or after 5th July 1948". The date of onset can depend upon whether the disease is a recrudescence or fresh attack, as considered at p. 106. The other conditions for making a claim are considered at p. 97 below, and an outline of them is given in DHSS leaflet NI. 2. Special conditions apply to pneumoconiosis and occupational deafness and these account for the separate treatment given to them in this chapter. According to the first annual report of the Chief Adjudication Officer in 1985 determining entitlement in the case of a prescribed disease is one of the areas which cause AOs most problems.

2. How Diseases Are Prescribed

(1) The legislative basis

The legal basis upon which the list of disease is compiled has remained unchanged since it was laid down in 1946. According to SSA s. 76(2):

"A disease or injury may be prescribed in relation to any employed earners if the Secretary of State is satisfied that –

(*a*)   it ought to be treated, having regard to its causes and incidence and any other relevant considerations, as a risk of their occupations and not as a risk commmon to all persons; and

(*b*)   it is such that, in the absence of special circumstances, the attribution of particular cases to the nature of the employment can be established or presumed with reasonable certainty."

Although these criteria have never been examined by a court, they have been discussed by several committees over the years. Their history was traced in an IIAC report in 1981 (Cmnd. 8393), but the meaning of present formula was more fully examined by the Dale committee in its 1948 report (Cmd. 7557). That body considered that the criteria gave the Secretary of State a wide discretion whether to prescribe a disease. As a result the committee thought that it was not necessary to change the statute. In spite of this broad interpretation of the formula, it has since attracted the criticism that it has been applied narrowly and has hindered the prescription of diseases recognised as being caused by work.

(*a*) *SSA s. 76(2)(a): an occupational risk*

In considering this paragraph the Dale committee thought that the primary consideration should be

". . . whether the disease is specific to the occupations of the persons concerned or, if it is not so specific, whether the occupations of those persons cause special exposure to risk of the disease, such risk being inherent in the conditions under which the occupations are carried on."

The committee therefore considered that even if a disease were common among the general public, the Secretary of State still had power to treat the risk as work-related provided that it was a special risk of particular occupations. This was a change from the old workmen's compensation position where it had to be unlikely that the disease would be contracted outside work. The change meant that a common disease could be prescribed under the State scheme "having regard to its causes and incidence". The relative incidence of the disease in a group of workers compared to the general population is therefore of prime importance. However, it is sometimes forgotten that a disease may be prescribed even if there is little difference in incidence, provided that the disease is caused in such a way as to sufficiently identify those occupations where the risk is likely to be greatest. For example, tuberculosis was first prescribed in 1950 in relation to certain medical workers. It was prescribed not because of a clear increase in the incidence of the disease in that particular group, but because of the higher risk of infection run by medical workers in contact with tuberculosis patients. "Any other relevant circumstances" may also lead to a disease being listed although the legislation does not specify what these may be.

(*b*) *SSA s. 76(2)(b): attribution in individual cases*

Even if there is an increased incidence of a particular disease in a group of workers, it may only be prescribed in relation to them if para. (*b*) is also satisfied. The Dale committee justified this additional requirement by arguing that "no useful purpose would be served by prescribing a disease unless individual claims . . . stood a reasonable chance of succeeding". It was thought unsatisfactory to allow them to succeed only by applying the presumption that the disease was caused by the employment, as discussed at p. 105. Positive proof in each case was needed. Although this requirement of individual attribution may be dispensed with in "special circumstances" – the nature of which again is not specified – para. (*b*) has been seen as imposing a stringent limitation upon prescription. A minority report of the Beney committee in 1955 (Cmd. 9548) suggested that para. (*b*) should be replaced by a test asking whether "it can be presumed with reasonable certainty . . . that most of the cases in the field covered are occupational". In their evidence to the Pearson Commission the TUC pressed for the removal of para. (*b*), and have continued to argue that the standard applied for prescription is too high.

(c) Narrow interpretation of the criteria

It is open to question whether it has been the criteria laid down by s. 76(2) which has been responsible for limiting the number of prescribed diseases, or whether it has been the conservative attitudes adopted by successive Secretaries of State and the IIAC. The decision to prescribe depends upon the Secretary of State being satisfied that the conditions are met. He is thus given an exceptionally wide discretion which is subject to little control. However, only rarely has the discretion been exercised in a liberal fashion in favour of workers. Of but few examples, two can be given here to illustrate the potential for prescribing diseases quicker, more frequently and on a wider basis than has usually been the case in the past. The first example concerns dermatitis. When it was first listed the workmen's compensation criteria could have been interpreted to prevent the prescription of diseases commonly found amongst the general public. One of these is dermatitis because it can be contracted by coming into contact with a variety of non-industrial agents such as household detergents. It also may result from congenital skin abnormalities, or nervous conditions, both unrelated to work. In spite of the widespread nature of the disease it was prescribed. The second example of a more liberal interpretation of the criteria is occupational deafness. This disease was prescribed although loss of hearing can be caused by many factors, and in spite of it being difficult in some cases to satisfy para. (*b*)'s requirement of individual attribution.

Despite these examples, generally the criteria for prescription have been interpreted narrowly both by the IIAC and successive Secretaries of State. For example, para. (*b*) refers to the need for "reasonable certainty". In their reports and memoranda requesting evidence the IIAC have referred to this as a constraint upon their recommendations. However, in the past they failed to point out that, as interpreted by the Dale committee, "certainty" means only that it must be more likely than not that particular cases can be attributed to employment. Another example of narrow interpretation is where para. (*a*) is read as meaning that the non-industrial risk of disease must be small compared to the industrial risk. The IIAC admitted in their 1984 report on hepititis that prescription has often depended upon "a demonstrable and *substantial* increase in the incidence of disease in the workers concerned". For emphysema and bronchitis it called for an "exceptionally high" incidence in its 1973 report on pneumoconiosis. It is not surprising, therefore, that the TUC, in submitting its evidence on occupational lung cancer in 1983, described the requirements for prescription as "stringent".

It is not only the refusal to prescribe certain diseases but also the delay in listing several others which may be attributed to the narrow interpretation of the statutory criteria. An example of such delay is vibration white finger which attracted the attention of the IIAC four times between 1954 and 1981. Recently, rather than refuse or delay their prescription unduly, the IIAC have recommended that a few diseases be listed subject to certain limiting conditions. These conditions may be of five types: they may define a minimum level of severity of the disease below which there is no compensation; the type of work covered; the minimum period for exposure to the risk; the "period of onset" within which the disease must develop following exposure to the risk; and finally, they may exclude the statutory presumption that the disease has been caused by the employment. For example, in the case of vibration white finger only the most severe forms of the disease qualify for benefit, whilst for occupational deafness the claimant must have been employed for an aggregate of at least ten years in a qualifying occupation, and must claim within five years of leaving it.

Because it has been possible to impose these limiting conditions, certain diseases have been prescribed which otherwise might not have been listed at all. However, others continue to be excluded. Emphysema, for example, is a disease in which there is an abnormal amount of air retained in the tissues of the lung, the lining of which is gradually worn away. As the process continues, the trapped air enlarges the lungs and causes a struggle for breath. This places a severe strain on the heart. Although emphysema is found among the general population it particularly affects coalminers. Pressure from the National Union of Mineworkers for the disease to be prescribed has met with no success.[2] The conditions of s. 76(2) have been said not to be satisfied because diagnosis and attributability present grave problems given the current state of medical knowledge. Another recent example of a refusal to prescribe is in cases of tennis elbow, and rotator cuff syndrome of the shoulder.[3] The pain in both cases is caused by repetitive movements which may be associated with a job involving, for example, the constant use of a hammer. However, because the disease may also be caused by non-occupational activities such as tennis, prescription has been refused even for narrowly defined occupations. Overall the discretion to prescribe has not been exercised as generously as many would wish, particularly in the light of the increasing evidence offering many links between diseases and industrial processes both old and new.

(2) The role of the Industrial Injuries Advisory Council

SSA s. 141 gives the Secretary of State the power to refer to the IIAC any question he thinks fit concerning the industrial scheme. In addition he is obliged to seek advice from the Council if he proposes to make any regulations dealing exclusively with the scheme. However, this duty is subject to the exceptions made by SSA 1986 s. 61. These enable the

[2]   See J. Craw *et al*, *Coalworkers' Pneumoconiosis, Emphysema and Bronchitis* (1979), a report compiled for the National Union of Mineworkers.
[3]   See H.C. Written Answer, Vol. 52 col. 327, 20 January 1984.

process of consultation to be avoided if the Council agrees, or if the Secretary of State thinks that the matter is so urgent that "it is inexpedient" to refer the regulations. Despite this power, in practice the Secretary of State has exercised his discretion to prescribe a disease only after the IIAC's advice.

The membership of the Council is governed by SSA sched. 16. It must consist of a chairman and

> ". . . an equal number of persons appointed by the Secretary of State, after consultation with such organisations as he thinks fit, to represent employers and employed earners respectively."

At present the Council consists of a chairman and 15 members, although representatives of the Health and Safety Executive and the DHSS also attend as observers and to provide liaison. Although half of its membership is clearly drawn from both sides of industry, the emphasis in selecting the other half has been upon them having the necessary medical and technical expertise relating to disease. This emphasis is not surprising given the work traditionally done by the IIAC.

In practice the Council has almost always been concerned with the medical aspects of the scheme and, in particular, with the need to keep the list of prescribed diseases up to date. Only three of the 31 reports it has published since it was set up in 1946 (listed in Appendix B) have concerned subjects other than specific diseases being considered as potential candidates for prescription. This is in spite of the possibility of the Council offering advice on a wide range of other subjects. It is now in a better position to do this because in 1982 SSA s. 141(4) was added, making it unnecessary for the IIAC to request the Secretary of State formally to refer to it the subjects it wants to examine. Instead it can give advice on its own initiative "on any matter . . . relating to industrial injuries benefit or its administration". Suggestions as to what ought to be investigated can be made by the TUC, DHSS or any interested party. However, it is likely that, in spite of these powers, the Council will remain primarily concerned with medical matters. This was the view of the DHSS in its Discussion Document in 1980. It considered that, if the Council were to be given a more prominent advisory role in non-medical matters, it was unlikely to lead to any basic change in the character of the industrial scheme.

The full Council meets six times a year. Its method of work is to call for written evidence on the subjects it is investigating. The evidence usually comes from trade unions, industry and medical organizations and only rarely does a claimant directly submit any views on the system. The IIAC does not commission research itself. However, the Secretary of State has power to do this under SSA s. 115, and the Council can recommend that these powers be used to investigate particular problems. There is some evidence recently of the Council taking a more proactive role. For example, it has formed a working party on occupational deafness which itself gathers evidence by visiting factories.

Where the reports of the Council have recommended that changes be made, they have almost always been accepted by Government, and legislation has followed. This success is partly because the reports deal with relatively narrow matters in connection with the list of prescribed diseases; they do not review the working of the industrial scheme as a whole. In addition the changes usually can be made easily by statutory instrument. Occasionally more substantial reform has been suggested – as where the system of individual proof considered at p. 131 was proposed – but this has fared less well. However, any conclusion as to the power of the Council must note that its influence extends beyond the making of legislation to its interpretation: it has been accepted in *R(I) 2/85* that Commissioners are entitled to look at IIAC reports as a guide to the application of the legislation.

Two of the major criticisms of the Council have been that it is slow to make recommendations, and that it has reported in favour of listing too few diseases. The list was increased from its original six in 1906 to 41 in 1948. Since then only a further dozen or so new diseases have been added, although the terms of prescription have been extended for many others. The Pearson Commission noted that although the four most recent cases in which prescription had been recommended had taken less than two years from the beginning of the IIAC investigation, "others have taken much longer and there are examples of diseases being identified by medical experts as occupational in origin many years before they were scheduled". In its defence the IIAC can point not only to the restrictions within the legislation, but also to the difficulties in establishing the aetiology of the diseases it presently considers. The first diseases prescribed in 1906 were obviously the result of following particular employments, but since that time the problems of identifying the cause of disease have become progressively more difficult. For example, it is very difficult to identify occupational as opposed to other factors in cases of lung cancer, especially when the disease may be latent for many years. Its incidence can only be discovered by costly, exacting and prolonged investigations of groups of workers. The complex causes of disease account not only for the delays in prescription, but also for the refusal to prescribe at all. To speed up the process of prescription the Council has recently improved its organisation as explained at p. 132. However, the measures it has taken are insufficient for those such as the Society for the Prevention of Asbestosis and Industrial Diseases. A massive increase in resources has been called for to enable the Council to pursue a more investigative role and identify quickly the dangers arising from industrial processes and materials both old and new.

3. THE CONDITIONS OF ENTITLEMENT

In the case of a prescribed disease the following four conditions must be satisfied:

(1) The claimant must have been employed at some time since 5 July 1948 in an occupation listed in relation to the disease. (The "employment" question.)

(2) The disease suffered by the claimant must be one that is prescribed. (The "diagnosis" question.)

(3) The disease must be due to the nature of the claimant's occupation. (The "causation" question.)

(4) The disease must have resulted in a loss of faculty. (One of the "disablement" questions.)

The last condition is considered with the other "disablement" questions in the next chapter. It involves an inquiry into whether the claimant's loss of faculty results from the disease related to work, or whether it is caused by something else. The other three conditions are all considered in this chapter. The "employment" and "causation" questions are determined by the statutory and not the medical authorities. However, the latter have exclusive jurisdiction over the "disablement" question. Medical authorities also almost invariably determine the "diagnosis" question, although the AO also has power to do so in the circumstances considered at p. 102. If several questions fall within its jurisdiction a determining authority can decide them in any order, and if it finds against a claimant on any one of them it need not proceed to consider the others. If the "employment" and "diagnosis" questions are satisfied there is a presumption that the "causation" question is also satisfied. This can be rebutted by the AO.

(1) The "employment" question: is the disease prescribed for the claimant's occupation?

The answer to this question entirely depends upon the two columns of part I of schedule I of the PD regs. This is because by reg. 2(a)

> ". . . each disease or injury set out in the first column . . . is prescribed in relation to all persons who have been employed on or after 5 July 1948 in employed earner's employment in any occupation set against such disease or injury in the second column. . . ."

The two columns of the schedule are laid out in appendix E in a table containing two additional columns of annotation. In its first column the schedule lists over 50 diseases, but prescribes each only in relation to the specific occupations contained in its second column.

(a) Nature of the occupations contained in the schedule

These occupations in the second column of the schedule are defined either by reference to an activity or process involved in a job, or by reference to certain substances to which workers are exposed or come into contact. Occasionally the conditions laid down by these job descriptions are easily satisfied, as where tuberculosis is prescribed in relation to any occupation involving "contact with a source of tuberculosis infection". However the conditions are usually much more stringent and severely limit claims. For example, the dozen or so cancers[4] listed are related to very specific occupations. The fear is that if the jobs were defined in more general terms there might be a flood of claims upon which adjudication could be especially difficult.

In defining the qualifying occupations the schedule uses the chemical rather than the common names of substances to which claimants may be exposed at work. Although chemical names have the advantage of being precise, their use makes it difficult for the layman to know whether the work done involves risk, and in particular whether it is a prescribed occupation for benefit purposes. An IIAC report in 1983 (Cmnd. 8959) recognized that: "Many workers and doctors did not have the specialized knowledge of chemistry to know, in the first instance at least, whether a

---

4   Ten forms of cancer contained within the schedule were itemized by the Secretary of State for Employment in H.C. Written Answer, Vol. 970 col. 453, 17 July 1979. To these must now be added disease D8.

substance was one of those prescribed." The result is that many injured workers, together with their trade union advisers and even their own doctors, remain unaware that the illness is work-related and is covered by the industrial scheme. The IIAC has expressed its concern, but can only hope that effort is made to provide information on a wider basis about, for example, the link between particular diseases and certain chemicals.

The remainder of this section considers two matters relevant to the occupations listed in the schedule: firstly, the kind of evidence in practice which is needed to satisfy the conditions imposed; and secondly, the meaning to be attached to two important phrases used throughout the schedule.

(b) The evidence required in practice

In order for it to be held that a claimant has worked in a prescribed occupation his own work experience must fall within the description given in the schedule. As emphasized in *R(I) 2/77* each case must depend upon the worker's individual circumstances. Thus the case noted that certain evidence, although thought favourable to the claimant, may not be conclusive:

> "The fact that a number of people have contracted a disease at a particular factory may tend to suggest that some process there is conducive to it, but it is of no probative value on the question whether the disease is prescribed in relation to persons or any class of persons there. Even the fact that claims have been accepted when made by others proves little as their employment may have differed. . .".

Other factors which are relevant, although not conclusive of the "employment" question are the views of the employer and other employees as to what the claimant actually does; the description given in the contract of employment as to what the claimant ought to do; and the work normally being done by others possessing the claimant's skill, or in his part of the workplace. A claimant should ensure that an AO is fully aware of the work he has done. He may find, for example, that the official description of his job provided by the personnel office of his large employer does not adequately reflect the true nature of his duties. It may need to be supplemented by statements from his colleagues or shop steward in order to explain what the job actually entails.

In addition to the evidence outlined above, expert opinion may be required in some cases. For example, scientific analysis may be necessary in order to discover whether a substance handled by the claimant is one of those prescribed. Before this is obtained, claimants should bear in mind that under the Health and Safety at Work Act they have the right to discover the composition of materials handled at work. In addition on a claim for benefit, if there is doubt about the nature of a substance, the DHSS may arrange for a sample to be taken for analysis. The full report upon this can then be obtained by the claimant, although he may also wish to arrange for his own sample to be sent for independent analysis. In seeking the necessary scientific or technical assistance a claimant may contact organisations such as those listed in appendix C. If there is a disagreement between the analysis carried out by the DHSS on the one hand, and the claimant on the other, further samples can be taken in the presence of both sides as in *R(I) 36/53*.

(c) Meaning of phrases used throughout the schedule

Commissioners' interpretations of individual words used in the schedule as considered in appendix E. However, there are two phrases which recur in the list and which can be considered here.

(i) Interpreting *"any occupation involving. . ."*, for example, the use of particular substances, requires investigation of the work the claimant actually does, not that which he is supposed to do. Instead of referring only to the contract of service it must be shown, for example, that the particular substances are in fact being handled by the claimant. *CI 59/49* and *CI 60/49* both emphasize that the focus must be upon the work actually done. By contrast in *R 6/84(II)* the Commissioner refused to hold that work unofficially done could form part of the claimant's occupation.

In general the cases have adopted an intepretation of occupation which is favourable to claimants. For example, it is not necessary for the relevant occupation to involve the claimant exclusively in one of the listed process for, as recognized in *R(I) 3/78*, an occupation can involve carrying out more than one function and being part of several different processes. *R(I) 4/53* illustrates that exposure to a risk whilst carrying out a function which forms only a minor part of the occupation is nevertheless covered by the industrial scheme. The claimant suffered from pneumoconiosis but was only involved for three hours a month in the relevant qualifying work of trimming or tidying coal at a quayside. He did that work on his own initiative for his job was normally that of crane driver and labourer at a boiler house near the jetty. In awarding benefit the Commissioner held that an act done entirely at an employee's own volition may well not be "involved" in his work, but what the particular claimant had done was so closely akin to his normal duties that his occupation could be said to include coal trimming. The objection that the work occurred so infrequently and for so short a time that it ought to be disregarded was not sustained because

> "it does not seem . . . that work, even though only for half-an-hour, if it recurs regularly each month on several occasions can properly be regarded as so negligible that it cannot be taken into account."

By contrast in *R(I) 8/57* benefit was refused where only two days out of seven years service had been spent in doing the qualifying work. Similarly the work was insufficient in *R 6/75(II)* but not in *CI 265/49*, *CWI 26/49*, *CI 114/50* and *R(I) 1/78*.

(ii) The *"use or handling of"* various substances means, according to *R(I) 15/75*(T), that the claimant himself must use or handle them, so that unless provision otherwise exists, no claim can be made if another employees uses such substances and exposes the claimant to a risk in doing so. However, the claimant's "handling" has been broadly construed and is not confined to working with the mere hand. It can include using tools on the raw material, as where a shovel or brush was used to move coal in *CSI 69/49* and *CWI 26/49*. A claimant may also handle a substance by touching articles covered with it so that, for example, coal was handled by the colliery lamp attendant who checked and collected miners' lamps covered in coal dust in *CI 114/50*. The substance was also handled by the claimant who collected the tools used upon it in *CI 12/66* (unreported). However, a distinction can be drawn between where the claimant handles the substance itself and where he only handles a formula containing the substance, when according to *R(I) 2/72*, he may not qualify for benefit.

(2) The "diagnosis" question: is the claimant suffering from a prescribed disease?

As with the "employment" question the answer here depends upon whether the disease is listed in part I of schedule I of the PD regs. The first column of the table in appendix E must be closely examined. The diseases are classified into four sections depending upon whether they are caused by a physical, biological, chemical or other agent. There are now over 50 entries. However, about two fifths of these relate to various forms of poisoning, whilst very few infectious diseases are included. The list thus may appear somewhat idiosyncratic.

The list covers injuries which many workers may not consider diseases at all. Thus a typist who, because of work, develops a chronic cramp in the hand and arm may be surprised to find that there may be compensation for industrial disease. Other workers may discover that, although their condition is not specifically listed, it is nevertheless covered because the condition is caused by a disease which is prescribed. This is considered in (*a*) below, whilst in (*b*) some guidance is given to the medical literature which can help interpret the technical descriptions given in the schedule. Finally, in (*c*) below the jurisdiction to decide the diagnosis question is considered.

(*a*) Resulting conditions

PD reg. 3 requires that if the claimant is suffering from a condition which has resulted from a prescribed disease, this condition, even if it is not listed, must be treated as if it were a prescribed disease. This means that compensation is available for a much wider range of conditions than is indicated in the schedule itself; the list is extended to include the sequelae or after-effects of disease. The sequel of disease can be long delayed and can affect quite a different part of the body. Again this may account for workers being unaware of their right to benefit.

Examples of sequelae are noted in relation to the listed diseases in the publications on diagnosis referred to under the next heading. The most common example is infective dermatitis which may be a sequela of D5, non-infective dermatitis. Another example is carpal tunnel syndrome which occurs in the wrist, affects the hand and may be a sequela of disease A8 tenosynovitis. Although it is agreed that lung cancer can develop from C4 arsenic poisoning or D1 asbestosis, a connection with pneumoconiosis was rejected in *R(I) 10/75* and *CI 169/81* (unreported). Perhaps most dramatic are the sequelae of C12 poisoning by methyl bromide, for these include hallucinations, amnesia and even insanity. The saying "as mad as a hatter" originates from C5 poisoning by mercury nitrate which was used in making hair into felt hats. Specific provision is made for conditions which are associated with pneumoconiosis, as considered at p. 130.

(*b*) Useful publications on diagnosis

Advisers dealing with industrial claims occasionally need to refer to medical publications. Knowledge of the sources of medical opinion can enable a case to be presented more effectively. In particular a medical board can be influenced by the citation of such opinion. General practitioners on these boards are unlikely to have any specialist knowledge, or even rudimentary training in occupational medicine. They may be unaware of recent developments especially in a field where research proceeds at a pace which makes it desirable that up to date material on diagnosis be consulted. Even before the relatively expert body, the MAT, some investigation of the medical background can help a claimant establish that he is suffering from a disease related to his work.

In addition to strengthening claims brought, some access to medical knowledge is important in instigating a claim in the first place. Many claims are not brought because of ignorance of the true extent of the existing schedule of diseases; its full potential is not being exploited. If the anatomical and pathological descriptions of the diseases are carefully investigated and are combined with analysis of the listed substances and processes, more conditions would be found to fall within the present scheme than may at first be anticipated.

DHSS publications – These consist of a booklet and several leaflets which, although listed as being for medical practitioners, are available to the general public. *Notes on the diagnosis of occupational diseases* (revised edition 1983) can be bought from HM Stationery Office. The fifty-page booklet briefly lists not only the aetiology and diagnosis of most prescribed diseases, but it also identifies their prognoses and resulting conditions or sequelae. It does not deal with a few diseases which are considered in the following publications available free from the DHSS at the address given in appendix C. These are booklet ND. I for occupational deafness, leaflet NI. 238 for asthma, and the important 40 page leaflet NI. 226 for pneumoconiosis. The latter also deals with those disease, usually affecting the lung, which require special adjudication and which are listed at p. 103.

Other publications – These are usually stocked only by specialist libraries, but they may also be obtained on loan by a local library at a reader's request. As a general textbook D. Hunter's *The Diseases of Occupations* (6th ed. 1978) is a classic text which, although lengthy and discursive, is written in less technical language than others. The book is used to compile two lists by P. S. Barth and H. A. Hunt in *Workers' Compensation and Work-Related Diseases* (1980) (MIT Press): the first list is of occupations, each with its associated diseases; the second list is of diseases each with its associated occupations. As alternatives to Hunter there are W. N. Rom (ed.), *Environmental and Occupational Medicine* (1983) and H. A. Waldron, *Lecture Notes on Occupational Medicine* (2nd ed. 1979). For a general reference encyclopaedia consult the International Labour Office, *Encyclopedia of Occupational Health and Safety* (3rd ed. 1983). Finally, to illustrate those books which deal with particular diseases, mention may be made of W. R. Parkes, *Occupational Lung Disorders* (2nd ed. 1982) and the more concise W. K. C. Morgan and A. Seaton's *Occupational Lung Diseases*. For skin disease reference should be made to A. W. G. Griffiths, *Occupational Dermatitis* (1985).

(c) Adjudication of medical questions

The flow chart on p. 104 indicates those who may adjudicate upon diagnosis. In practice the question is usually determined by a medical board. However, in some circumstances the AO is given power to make the decision by Adj. reg. 45(2). The AO does so only after receiving a doctor's report. Adj. regs. 43 and 44 require him to seek such a report in each case unless one already exists. There may already be a report if, for example, the claimant has previously applied for benefit in respect of the same disease, or if a work's or hospital doctor has sent a report to accompany the claim. If the AO requires a medical report in the case of a common disease such as dermatitis, in practice he normally contacts a general practitioner. However, in an unusual case such as one involving lead poisoning, a consultant's opinion is obtained. If the AO makes the diagnosis himself, a claimant has only 10 days within which to appeal against it to a medical board. This comparatively short time limit is imposed by Adj. reg. 2a and can easily result in late or missed appeals.

The AO's jurisdictions to make the diagnosis decision is limited in two important ways: firstly, by Adj. reg. 45(4), if the AO thinks a disablement question arises in addition to one of diagnosis he must refer both questions to a medical board; and secondly, in the case of certain diseases regs. 32 and 43 require the AO to refer the diagnosis question to a special medical board, having first obtained a report from a specially qualified doctor. This procedure is required in the case of eleven diseases, mostly affecting the lungs. These are D1 pneumoconiosis, D2 byssinosis, D3 diffuse mesothelioma, D7 asthma, D8 lung cancer, D9 pleural thickening, and those involving poisoning by C15 nitrous oxide, C17 beryllium, C18 cadmium, C22(b) nickel cancer and B7 alveolitis, a disease including farmer's lung.

Even if the AO has jurisdiction to decide the diagnosis question he may still refer it to a medical board. This should happen frequently because there are often questions arising on diagnosis which can only be resolved by those with medical knowledge. For example, if a claimant states that he is suffering from a specific disease and the AO recognizes that it is not one of those prescribed it may appear that no entitlement to benefit arises. However, it is possible that neither the claimant not the AO is aware of the true nature of the illness. The case should be referred to a medical board for diagnosis. Thus in *R(I) 3/74* and *R 1/74(II)* although the claims were in respect of the unlisted disease osteoarthritis, it was recognized that the claimants could have been suffering from disease A4, cramp of the forearm due to repetitive movements at work. Similarly it is desirable that AOs refer to a medical board the many cases where an unlisted condition could be the result or sequela of a prescribed disease, as discussed in (*a*) above.

The constitution and procedure of the medical authorities is considered in chapter 9. They must not exceed their jurisdiction in relation to diagnosis. While a knowledge of the claimant's history of employment and conditions of work may assist a MAT to determine diagnosis, it must confine its decision to the factual issue of diagnosis and not, as in *R(I) 18/63*, set out to decide whether or not the claimant worked in a prescribed occupation. That is not a decision for the medical authorities.

(3) The "causation" question: is the disease due to the nature of the occupation?

The general principles of causation which determine whether a connection with work can be shown are the same for both disease and accident, and are discussed at p. 45. On the basis of these principles the claimant in *R(I) 10/53*(T) did not have to show that his employment was

AUTHORITIES WHO MAY DETERMINE A DIAGNOSIS QUESTION (ADJ. REGS. 43–50)

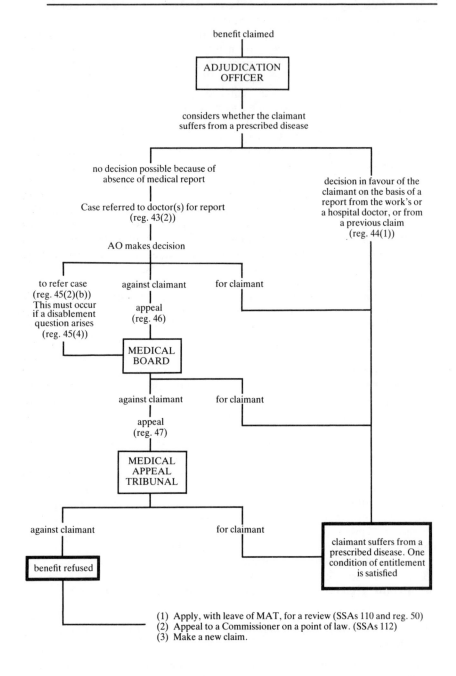

the sole cause of his disease, but only that it was a substantial or "effective" cause. However, causation in relation to a prescribed disease differs from that of an accident in one fundamental respect: there is a presumption which greatly assists a claimant to establish that his disease is caused by work. PD reg. 4(1) states:

> "Where a person has developed a disease which is prescribed in relation to him . . ., that disease shall unless the contrary is proved, be presumed to be due to the nature of his employed earner's employment if that employment [is listed in the schedule] . . . and he was so employed on, or at any time within one month immediately preceding, the date on which . . . he is treated as having developed the disease."

To take advantage of the presumption a claim should be made promptly, even though PD reg. 6(2) allows the date on which a claimant is treated as having developed a disease to be as early as when the loss of faculty is first suffered. A prompt claim helps a worker not only to be diagnosed accurately but also to establish that the loss of faculty was suffered within the time limit of one month after leaving the prescribed employment. The decision whether the disease is a new attack or a recrudescence, as discussed under the next heading, can also affect whether the presumption applies by changing the date of onset relative to the date of leaving employment.

To rebut the presumption the AO must show, on the balance of probability, that the claimant has no title to benefit because the disease is due to something other than the employment. The AO failed to do this in *R(I) 20/52* where the claimant obtained benefit for disease B3, leptospira contracted from rats, despite evidence of rats being near his home as well as his work. In getting evidence to rebut the presumption the AO may ask the medical board, when considering the diagnosis question, also to provide medical evidence as to whether the disease is due to the nature of the occupation. This non-statutory function of boards is acknowledged in the DHSS medical handbook. Such advice assisted in the refusal of benefit in *R(I) 16/52*, *R(I) 37/52*(T), *R(I) 65/53* and *8/55(II)*, all these cases dealing with tuberculosis. However, the claim succeeded where the presumption was not rebutted in *R(I) 38/52*(T) despite evidence that the claimant was suffering from tuberculosis before she began working in the prescribed occupation.

In the following exceptional cases the presumption applies even if the claimant is not employed in a relevant occupation in the month preceding the outbreak of the disease. However, there are other conditions which may limit such claims:

A10 occupational deafness – employment for an aggregate of ten years in a relevant occupation is required for the presumption to apply, and benefit is refused if the claimant has not worked in such an occupation in the five years immediately preceding the claim. This is discussed at p. 115.

B5 tuberculosis – employment for at least six weeks in the relevant occupation is required for the presumption to apply, but then it continues to operate for up to two years after the claimant leaves the occupation. This threshold exists because, as recognized by the IIAC in their 1950 report (Cmd. 8053), the disease cannot be contracted as a result of the occupation and reveal itself within a six-week period. The requirement was not satisfied in *R(I) 30/55*.

D1 pneumoconiosis – employment for an aggregate of two years in a scheduled occupation is required, but the presumption then continues to apply without time limit. For unscheduled occupations the presumption is excluded.

D2 byssinosis – the conditions here are the least stringent. Employment for any period is sufficient, and again there is no time limit within which the disease must develop in order for the presumption to apply.

The presumption does not apply at all and the burden of proving the causal link is always upon the claimant in claims relating to the following two diseases:

D4 inflammation of the nose, throat or mouth, and
D5 non-infective dermatitis.

4. RECURRENCE OF THE DISEASE: FRESH ATTACK OR RECRUDESCENCE?

A claimant may suffer from more than one attack of the same disease. Such attacks may be found either to be caused afresh, or to be a continuation or outbreak of the old disease, when the term "recrudescence" is used. This important distinction is the subject of PD reg. 7. However, it is not relevant in certain cases of chronic disease from which full recovery cannot be expected: it is not applicable where there is pneumoconiosis, byssinosis, mesothelioma, occupational deafness, asthma, lung cancer or thickening of the pleura.

The importance of distinction is that if the disease is considered to be a fresh onset it must satisfy the conditions of benefit for a new claim. It is as if it were a new accident. This means that a claimant must wait 15 weeks from the new date of onset before gaining entitlement to benefit. However, if the alternative view is taken and the attack is considered a recrudescence, then provided that the qualifying conditions have previously been met, there is immediate entitlement to benefit.

A second important use of the distinction is in connection with the "causation question", for it can help determine whether the presumption that the disease has been caused by the employment applies. If this presumption arising under PD reg. 4 is to operate the claimant usually must have been working in the relevant occupation in the month before the date of onset of the disease. That date is determined by whether the disease is considered a recrudescence or fresh attack. A finding of recrudescence gives rise to an earlier date of onset and this is more favourable for claimants.

These subtleties in classifying further attacks of the disease can be especially troublesome to the medical authorities. The difficulties involved in practice were illustrated in the dermatitis cases of *R(I) 10/53*(T) and *R(I) 30/51*. The problems in making the distinction are reduced by PD reg. 7 which provides for one of two presumptions to operate. The first is that if the further attack occurs during the period covered by an existing assessment of disablement, it is presumed to be recrudescence of the old disease unless it is proved in fact to be a fresh contraction. Where this presumption is not rebutted, any question of increasing the existing assessment is dealt with by way of review. The second presumption is that if the further attack occurs after the end of the period of assessment it must be treated as a fresh contraction. Here the presumption is conclusive and the claim must be started from the new date of onset.

The decision about the nature of the further attack is made by the same authorities who decide the "diagnosis" question. If either the recrudescence or diagnosis questions are coupled with that of disablement Adj. reg. 45(4) requires the AO to refer the matter to a medical board for determination. Adj. reg. 46(3) gives the medical board the power to re-open the diagnosis issue when considering a recrudescence question.

5. THE SCHEDULE OF PRESCRIBED DISEASES AND RELEVANT OCCUPATIONS

Part I of schedule I of the PD regs. appears in roman type in appendix E. The information in italics is not part of the legislation, but is the author's annotation. This falls into four sections: in the first column the annotations indicate the more common or shorthand descriptions of the disease; in the second column, the sort of occupations from which the diseases may result; in the third column, the relevant symptoms to which the diseases may give rise; and in the fourth column, any interpretations of the schedule by Commissioners and others.

Reform of the schedule

A few of the reforms presently being considered by the IIAC have been referred to in appendix E in the individual annotations of diseases in the schedule. Thus it has been noted that investigations are continuing into disease A1, involving the dangers from radiation; disease C24 involving the effects of exposure to VCM; and diseases D2 byssinosis and D7 asthma. However, other extensions of the schedule being considered relate either to diseases which are not listed in any form, or range over several of those presently prescribed. These proposals are better dealt with separately here, whilst more general changes brought about following the IIAC's 1981 report are considered in the final section of this chapter.

(a) Halogenic aliphatic hydrocarbons

Some effects of tetrachlorethene and methyl bromide are considered in disease C10 and C12. The present IIAC investigation is into the long term effects of, amongst others, methyl chloride, carbon tetrachloride and trichloromethane (chloroform).

(b) N-Hexane neuropathy

This chemical is used as a solvent or thinner in a wide range of industries including those producing footwear, furniture, chemicals, pharmaceuticals and tyres. It is feared that it may affect the nervous system and cause weakness and paralysis. As with (a) above, the Council received evidence from February to August 1985.

(c) Emphysema and chronic bronchitis

At present these diseases can only be compensated if they increase the extent of disablement in a pneumoconiosis case as discussed at p. 130. In 1973 the Council concluded that there was insufficient evidence to support prescription of these conditions in their own right (Cmnd. 5443). This decision is now being reviewed by the Council and suggestions that the diseases are especially associated with mining, quarrying, welding and foundry work are being examined. In November 1985 the Council also announced that as part of its investigation into respiratory diseases in textile workers it is examining evidence on chronic bronchitis.

(d) Occupational lung cancer

Prescription presently exists in relation to asbestos (diseases D1, D8 and D9) and nickel production (disease C22). Lung cancer is also an accepted sequela of arsenic poisoning (disease C24). In 1986 the IIAC reported on the links between lung cancer and other occupations (Cm. 37). It recommended that the prescription of lung cancer be extended to tin miners; those exposed to the chromates of certain chemicals; and to those exposed to BCME. The Government accepted these recommendations and intends to make the relevant reforms in 1987.

(e) Cancer of the larynx

This is being investigated in relation to those whose job involves contact with asbestos. Evidence was requested to be submitted before October 1986.

(f) Psittacosis and Q fever

These diseases are being investigated and evidence was required to be submitted before October 1986. Psittacosis is a disease usually affecting the lungs and is often associated with birds. Q fever is an infectious disease, similar to viral pneumonia, and in the most serious cases can damage the valves of the heart. Workers potentially at risk from these diseases include those such as vets or farm workers who come into contact with animals in the course of their job.

6. OCCUPATIONAL DEAFNESS

(1) Introduction

Occupational deafness merits a section of its own in this chapter for several reasons. First its prescription has been accompanied by special rules which have given rise to particular problems. Secondly the large number of claims for deafness emphasise its importance. It accounts for over 7,000 of the pensions currently in payment, constituting one sixth of all those for prescribed diseases. Only pneumoconiosis is responsible for more (appendix A, table 1). Thirdly all the pensions for occupational deafness have been obtained since 1975 when its prescription first took effect. The disease is of such contemporary importance that in recent years unions have had to work hard to keep up with deafness claims. For example, these now comprise the majority of ASTMS's current industrial injury files. A final reason for highlighting the disease is that it illustrates a common feature of the industrial scheme in relation to diseases in general: the extent of the compensation provided often depends upon what is administratively feasible within the constraints of a limited expenditure, rather than upon a full recognition of the extent to which health may be impaired by work.

(a) Sources of information

DHSS leaflet NI. 207 outlines the conditions of entitlement to benefit and the claims procedure involved, whilst booklet ND. 1 offers clinical notes on the disease. Deafness also merits a separate section in the DHSS medical handbook. The IIAC have issued four reports on the subject: in 1969 there was an appraisal of the research done (Cmnd. 4145); prescription was recommended in its report in 1973 (Cmnd. 5461); and the terms of prescription were relaxed following reports in 1978 (Cmnd. 7266) and 1982 (Cmnd. 8749). Acoustical aspects which are important in the diagnosis and assessment of deafness are considered in R. Taylor, *Noise* (3rd ed. 1979), and a general guide to the disease is provided by ASTMS's *Prevention of Occupational Deafness* (1981).

(b) Effects of noise

Although noise appears less dangerous to many people than, for example, working with chemicals, its effects upon health are both serious and widespread. In 1978 the Department of Employment figures indicated that one in ten of the six million workers subject to the Factories Act were exposed to noise levels of 90 dB or more for at least six hours a day. This noise level is equivalent to working only 20 yards from a pneumatic drill. If noise is not too loud and exposure is not prolonged there may be only a temporary reduction in hearing. However, workers can become accustomed to a noise level which, after continued exposure, can cause permanent damage to the cells of the inner ear. This impairs the hearing of sound at certain frequencies. Hearing aids can only magnify the sound and cannot restore the ability to hear at the normal frequencies. Another serious condition resulting from noise is a continuous ringing in the ears known as tinnitus. For many workers the result of prolonged exposure is that long before they reach retirement age they have the hearing of an elderly person. According to the 1973 IIAC report:

> "Deafness is a condition which only rarely leads to incapacity or affects earning power, but we are satisfied that it can become severely disabling socially and in our view is a proper subject for compensation."

(c) History and basis of entitlement

Although until recently there was almost no investigation of the number of workers who suffered as a result of noise, the dangers of exposure have been recognized for many years. In the last century "boilermakers' disease" was a common description given to loss of hearing because of its association with the manufacture of steam boilers. Although such links were made with industry, little was done to prevent injury and nothing was done to compensate for it. One reason for this was that deafness affected earning capacity less than other injuries. The first major report on noise was not completed until 1963 (Cmnd. 2056). A programme of medical research followed, and this was evaluated by the IIAC in 1969. The Council was then asked to investigate whether occupational deafness should be prescribed and, four years later, they reported in favour of doing so. Following this 1973 report legislation was prepared which made compensation available from 1975 for occupational deafness as a prescribed disease.

However, this is not the only means by which loss of hearing can be compensated under the industrial scheme. If deafness is caused by a sudden event – such as an explosion – it has always been possible to claim that an injury by accident has occurred. Entitlement then arises under SSA s. 50. However, it is difficult to satisfy this section if, as is often the case, loss of hearing has been caused by exposure to noise over a long period of time. The injury is then likely to be considered the result of a "process" and not an accident. This distinction is fully explored in chapter 3. It led to an unsuccessful claim for benefit based upon the accident provisions in *R. (Curry)* v *National Insurance Commissioner* (1974). Instead of such an approach, workers must usually resort to claiming for occupational deafness as a prescribed disease. The extent to which there is compensation for deafness outside of the industrial scheme, where private agreements between certain unions and insurance companies may be involved is considered at p. 268.

(d) Changing limits upon claims

The IIAC recommended prescription of occupational deafness only if it were governed by a series of special rules aimed at restricting claims. The Council's concern was to avoid placing an undue burden upon the limited specialist and audiological facilities of the NHS. It noted that in 1973 consultants, technicians and machines were already under pressure in meeting commitments for hearing aids; they could be overwhelmed by the examinations required if unlimited claims for deafness under the industrial scheme were allowed. Therefore restrictions upon claims were imposed in order to prevent examinations for benefit purposes exceeding 10,000 a year. In fact these restrictions have proved far too severe. The examinations required have been at most only a third of those anticipated by the IIAC. Of those who have applied for benefit only a quarter have been successful. The rules have therefore been relaxed in recent years.

However, the basic framework for these restrictions remains intact. Each of the following conditions must be satisfied: firstly, a claimant must work in one of the occupations narrowly defined by the legislation; secondly, the occupation must be followed for a minimum period of time; thirdly, benefit must be sought within a limited time of the claimant last working in a prescribed occupation; and finally the claimant must suffer a loss of hearing of at least a certain amount. Further restrictions aimed at saving medical time include preventing an applicant from making another claim within a certain time of an earlier one being refused by a medical board, and preventing a successful applicant from applying for reassessment of hearing loss on the basis that it has become worse since the last examination.

This framework of restrictions is examined in detail in the remainder of this chapter. The rules have been devised on a trial and error basis and the IIAC is committed to keeping the scheme under constant review. It has set up a standing working party on noise. This pursues an investigative role with more vigour than in the case of other diseases. It visits factories, gathers evidence on its own account and maintains a close link with the Health and Safety Executive. The Pearson Commission viewed the restrictions on claims and the link of diagnostic experts as unfortunate. In agreeing with this the IIAC have indicated areas where some future relaxation of the rules may be expected, and these are referred to in the course of the following pages.

(2) Basis of entitlement

(a) Diagnosis

The schedule requires that a minimum amount of hearing loss be shown in order to qualify for benefit. It does so by defining occupational deafness as follows:

> "Substantial sensorineural hearing loss amounting to at least 50 dB in each ear, being due in the case of at least one ear to occupational noise, and being the average of pure tone losses measured by audiometry over the 1, 2 and 3 kHz frequencies."

"Sensorineural" loss of hearing results from the failure of the auditory receptor organ to transmit the sound message to the brain. This is distinct from "conductive" hearing loss which results from the malfunctioning of the organs between the outer and inner ear, or the obstruction of the passage of sound. The air conduction levels recorded by audiometry show the hearing loss attributable to both conductive and sensorineural elements, while the bone conduction levels show the hearing loss attributable only to the sensorineural elements. Tinnitus or "ringing in the ears" is not itself prescribed, but may be an associated condition for which an increased assessment can be made. Further guidance as to the clinical conditions is contained in the DHSS booklet ND. 1.

In practice the 50 dB threshold prevents many claims being made. According to ASTMS it is such that: "If you have been disabled to the point of hearing only half of what is said, then under the current rules you are declared fit and undeserving of compensation." The IIAC have agreed to reconsider the threshold at their next review but, in order to extend the scheme, the Council thinks that it is more important, for example, to ease the time limit on claims, or reduce the number of years which must be worked in a qualifying occupation. However, 6,600 of the 15,500 claims received up to the end of 1981 which were referred for a specialist otologist's report were rejected because the hearing loss was insufficient.[5]

(b) Occupational cover

In its 1973 report the IIAC refused to define the relevant occupations for this disease as simply those which were "very noisy". That would have meant applying a subjective and imprecise standard. The fairest and most precise test of which occupations should be covered would rely upon the level of noise to which a particular job exposed a worker. However, the Council considered that such a test was impractical given that information on noise levels – particularly relating to a worker's past history of employment – could not be obtained. Although such information could become available in the future, the Council considered that the only way to proceed in the meantime was to provide a list of what it considered the main relevant occupations. Additions to this list could be made from time

[5] Annual Report of the Chief Medical Officer of the DHSS *On the State of Public Health For The Year 1981* (1982) p. 27.

to time so as to expand coverage. However, as yet this complex and time consuming process of change has produced a list of occupations which is still a narrow one. It seems especially limited when compared with the health and safety regulations which assume that noise is a widespread hazard in many kinds of industry. Because the occupations are defined in detail the list also produces certain anomalies. For example, in *R(I) 13/81* the Commissioner refused a claim on the basis of para. (*c*)

> ". . . with some regret as I do not think that the distinction I have felt obliged to draw is an attractive one; and I find it incongruous that a person whose hearing has been affected by a weaving machine should, but a person whose hearing has been affected by a similar knitting machine should not, be entitled to benefit. . . ."

Similarly in *R 3/84(II)* the Commissioner was dissatisfied with having to draw illogical distinctions between the various occupations which co-operate in the building of a ship.

However, on occasions Commissioners themselves have been responsible for keeping claims for occupational deafness within narrow bounds. In several cases they have referred to the intention of Parliament to confine claims for benefit. Trade unions have been dissatisfied with their interpretation, for example, of what amounts to the "immediate vicinity" of relevant tools. Commissioners have also been criticized for their hesitancy as to whether machinery is included in the meaning of "tool". (Both of these examples are examined further in the definition section in (*ii*) below.) Against this background it should be noted that recent amendments of the schedule have extended its scope, and this may encourage broader interpretation.

(*i*) *The scheduled occupations*

Occupational deafness is prescribed by part I of schedule I of the PD regs. for "any occupation involving" the following:

> "(a) the use of, or work wholly or mainly in the immediate vicinity of, pneumatic percussive tools or high-speed grinding tools, in the cleaning, dressing or finishing of cast metal or of ingots, billets or blooms; or
>
> (b) the use of, or work wholly or mainly in the immediate vicinity of, pneumatic percussive tools on metal in the shipbuilding or ship repairing industries; or
>
> (c) the use of, or work in the immediate vicinity of, pneumatic percussive tools on metal, or for drilling rock in quarries or underground, or in mining coal, for at least an average of one hour per working day; or
>
> (d) work wholly or mainly in the immediate vicinity of drop-forging plant (including plant for drop-stamping or drop-hammering) or forging press plant engaged in the shaping of metal; or
>
> (e) work wholly or mainly in rooms or sheds where there are machines engaged in weaving man-made or natural (including mineral) fibres or in the bulking up of fibres in textile manufacturing; or
>
> (f) the use of, or work wholly or mainly in the immediate vicinity of, machines engaged in cutting, shaping or cleaning metal nails; or
>
> (g) the use of, or work wholly or mainly in the immediate vicinity of, plasma spray guns engaged in the deposition of metal; or
>
> (h) the use of, or work wholly or mainly in the immediate vicinity of, any of the following machines engaged in the working of wood or material

composed partly of wood, that is to say: multi-cutter moulding machines, planing machines, automatic or semi automatic lathes, multiple cross-cut machines, automatic shaping machines, double-end tenoning machines, vertical spindle moulding machines (including high-speed routing machines), edge banding machines, bandsawing machines with a blade width of not less than 75 millimetres and circular sawing machines in the operation of which the blade is moved towards the material being cut; or

(i)   the use of chain saws in forestry."

(*ii*) *Commissioners' decisions on the list of occupations*

"Any occupation involving" is a general phrase used throughout the schedule and is considered at p. 100.

"Wholly or mainly" can only be satisfied if a claimant spends more than half his working time within the vicinity of the prescribed tools. However, the amount of time these tools must actually be in operation while the claimant is working has proved a problem, and differs according to which paragraph is being considered. For (*a*) and (*b*) *R(I) 2/85* holds it sufficient that the tools are used for a non-negligible part of the claimant's working time. However, to fall within the terms of (*d*) *CI 67/85* (unreported) requires that a claimant must spend more than half of his time in the immediate vicinity of a drop-forging plant which is actually in operation. Any period when the hammer is not working is to be disregarded.

PD reg. 2(c) provides that where a person

". . . has been concurrently employed in two or more of the occupations described in . . . paragraph A10 those occupations shall be treated as a single occupation for the purposes of determining whether that person has been employed wholly or mainly in work described. . . ."

"Immediate vicinity." An important change to the regulations was made in 1979 to overturn the effect of *R(I) 15/75* and *R. (Horner)* v *Chief National Insurance Commissioner* (1979). These cases held that only those actually using the tools in question and not workers otherwise exposed to their noise were within the prescription. The revised terms of paragraphs (*a*) and (*b*) now make it sufficient for benefit that a claimant is in the immediate vicinity of the relevant tools; they do not have to be used by the claimant.

However, the meaning of immediate vicinity has been limited with the result that a worker can be excluded from benefit even though exposed to considerable noise arising from one of the prescribed processes. This happened in *R(I) 7/76* where it was decided that "immediate vicinity" was not to be identified by any acoustical means because this would require the authorities to receive technical evidence at an early stage in the claim. Instead the relevant area depended upon, for example, the distance between the area of the plant where the noise was generated and where the claimant worked. Whether there were walls, screens, or intermediate buildings was a relevant consideration although their effect upon the reduction of noise did not matter. It is therefore possible for a claimant to be exposed to a noise level much higher than the threshold limit and for it to arise from one of the few processes listed, but for benefit to be denied because of a measurement of distance rather than exposure. This distinction is fundamental to the scheme's provision for deafness and the IIAC consider that no alternative approach is practical at present.

However, two recent decisions have interpreted the "immediate vicinity" more in favour of workers. In *R 1/84(II)* although the Commissioner agreed that the regulations do not contemplate any scientific measurement of noise, he found it hard to accept that the amount of noise was irrelevant. He relied upon *CSI 5/76* (unreported) to justify taking into account the noise generated by a drop-forging hammer, and decided that a claimant who worked up to 50 feet away was in its immediate vicinity. In *R(I) 8/85*(T) the tribunal also found for the claimant, but it did not discuss whether the noise generated was relevant. The difficulty in the claim was that there was a physical structure between the drop forge and the claimant. However, the tribunal held that this should not be used as the sole criterion to establish immediate vicinity and that, on the facts of the case, it could not outweigh the distance factor. Because this particular claimant worked very near to the noisy machinery he was therefore able to obtain benefit.

"Pneumatic." According to *R(I) 6/83* whether a tool is pneumatic is a question of fact depending upon the essential nature of the tool, for it must be decided whether its driving force is predominantly compressed air or something else. However, in *CI 162/84* (unreported) a restrictive interpretation was adopted with regard to hybrid tools powered by more than one source. It was said that benefit would be refused if pneumatic power was not dominant and some other source of power was more than merely ancilliary to the working of the tool. In *CI 16/80* (unreported) the absence of air or wind used in the operation of a punching machine meant that it was not pneumatic.

"Percussive" has received a broad interpretation and applies to tools even if they produce no noise as in *R(I) 8/76*. According to *R(I) 5/76* the test depends not upon the use to which the tool is put, but upon how, in mechanical terms, it performs what it does when in use. This meant on the facts of the case that a rotary action tool used to tighten nuts was percussive but in *R 7/83(II)* a side light cutting machine was not.

"Tool." Although this appears to be a straightforward term it has proved a source of difficulty. All Commissioners have agreed that an implement held in the hand can be a tool, but the extent to which a machine is also inlcuded in the term has been a matter for dispute. At first it was emphasized in *R(I) 30/59* that although the meaning of tool may have been extended, it still has limits. Thus in *R(I) 3/80* although it was accepted that simple machines such as lathes and upright grinders may be called tools, in general a tool was hand-held. However, *R(I) 13/80* and *R(I) 3/83* disagreed with this and preferred a broader interpretation which recognized that the test had to be modified to take account of advancing technology. The machines in these cases were not simple lathes but complex contrivances and yet they were still found to be "tools". There was further support for this in *CI 162/84* (unreported) where it was also agreed that a machine can embody a tool as a component part. Whether a grinder is a "high speed" tool cannot be established by an absolute objective standard, but sufficient evidence enabled the claims to succeed in *R(I) 3/80* and *R(I) 13/80*.

"Cast metal" according to *R(I) 3/82*(T) does not include forged metal. Weld metal, however, is covered according to *CI 79/84* (unreported), not following *CI 420/75* (unreported). *R 4/83(II)* suggests that the regulation intended to specify processes involving cast metal plus certain of its

derivatives, or types, which it expressly mentions; it was not intended to include mild steel in any form.

"Ingot" was held in *R(I) 1/80* to be metal still in the form of raw material and could not be a finished product ready for use such as a rivet.

"Cleaning dressing or finishing." The use of the specified tools in any one of these operations is sufficient, and *R(I) 2/78* notes that para. 2(*a*) is not to be confined to the metal manufacturing industry.

"Shipbuilding or ship repairing of industries" does not include firms who do no more than manufacture products to be put into ships as in *R(I) 3/79*.

"Underground" means at a place where the surface of the earth is immediately above, as in the case of a tunnel. It does not mean below ground level though there may be excessive noise reverberation there as in *R(I) 4/84*.

"Mining coal" is not confined to the actual drilling of coal but can include work done in testing and repairing tools used by others in the mining of coal as in *CI 362/82* (unreported).

"Drop." Each of the drop processes in para. (*d*) involves a machine. This meant that the use of hand-held hammer on an anvil did not qualify in *R(I) 5/85*.

"Weaving" according to *R(I) 13/81* is different from knitting, which is not a prescribed occupation.

"Bulking up" in paragraph (*e*) was discussed in *CI 17/80* (unreported). It included not only high speed false twisting but also a process whereby the tow was crimped and heat set for it to resemble natural fibre. However, a drawer and spinner in the jute industry failed in his claim in *CSI 37/84* (unreported). The Commissioner stated that bulking up

> "should be regarded as applying to the texturing processes which impart a permanently bulked up finish to the yarn in question with a view to enhancing its properties for manufacture and use; and that it would not be right to apply a generalised dictionary meaning of the expression, which is not recognised in the jute industry, merely because its processes cause some increase in bulk in the fibre."

"Metal nails" is used in a generic sense of a piece of wire or metal used for holding things together and is not confined in a narrow sense to metal nails driven in with a hammer. Therefore in *R(I) 5/83* rivets were included.

(iii) Employment for ten years in a qualifying occupation

PD reg. 2(c) requires the claimant to have been employed for a minimum aggregate of 10 years in one or more of the qualifying occupations. Work done before 1948 can be taken into account. The 10-year period was reduced from 20 years in 1983 with the result that claims were expected to increase by 20 per cent a year. However, the conditions can still operate as a trap, forcing a deafened worker to remain in a noisy environment in order to qualify for compensation.

R(I) 2/79(T) offers guidance as to how the 10-year period is to be calculated. A claimant cannot rely upon the obligations in his contract of employment alone because the only time which counts is when the qualifying work is actually being done. However, normal short-term breaks in work need not be deducted from the total period because otherwise the calculation would be very burdensome. As a result weekends, holidays, and absences caused by sickness, or industrial troubles, all count. However, an interruption of work for an abnormal period must be deducted. What constitutes such an interruption depends upon the facts of each case, but it is very likely to include a break for three months, no matter what the reason for it.

(*iv*) *Employment in a qualifying occupation within five years preceding claim*

PD reg. 25 requires a claim to be made within five years of the claimant last working in one of the qualifying occupations. As recognized in *R(I) 2/79*(T) and *R 4/84(II)* this time limit is absolute. No late claims are allowed even if there is some good cause for the delay in applying for benefit. Again time runs from when the claimant actually last worked in the qualifying occupation, and not from when his contract of employment came to an end. Any period of absence before leaving the job can be included to make up the five-year period and defeat the claimant. It does not matter what caused this absence or how long it was.

The time limit was extended from one to five years in 1983. The IIAC expected that this would increase claims only by 10 per cent. There has been a reluctance to remove the requirement altogether because of the fear of causing administrative problems if a large number of people – many of whom may have retired some time ago – were brought within the scheme.

(*c*) *Causation*

To satisfy the final condition of entitlement the claimant must show that the hearing loss in at least one ear is due to noise at work. In doing so the claimant can rely upon PD reg. 4(5).

> "Where a person in relation to whom occupational deafness is prescribed. . . develops occupational deafness the disease shall, unless the contrary is proved, be presumed to be due to the nature of his employed earner's employment."

If the AO wishes to rebut this presumption he may seek guidance from a medical board. The board is asked to inquire particularly into the claimant's history. According to the DHSS medical handbook "noisy hobbies such as musketry and listening to amplified pop music should not be overlooked". Other causes of deafness noted in DHSS leaflet ND. 1 include congenital disease, an illness such as meningitis, and the taking of certain drugs.

(3) Adjudication, further claims, appeals and reviews

The adjudication of claims for deafness is similar to other diseases except that there are certain special provisions which aim to save medical time and counter the fear that the system might be flooded with claims. When a claim is received the DHSS make inquiries of the employer to establish whether or not the employment conditions are satisfied. The AO makes the actual decision on this, and it is subject to the usual rights of appeal. If the employment conditions are satisfied the claimant is referred to an otologist. If that report indicates that the conditions relating to minimum hearing loss are not satisfied and the AO disallows the claim, the claimant may appeal to a medical board. If the otologist's report indicates that the hearing loss satisfied the definition of the disease, the claimant is referrred to a medical board which makes the diagnosis decision. If the board refuses the claim, PD reg. 27 prevents another claim being made for three years. However, this does not apply to a claimant who has given up work in one of the qualifying jobs if, by waiting for three years, his claim would be barred because it would be outside of the five year time limit for making a claim.

For appeals the major difference from other diseases is that there is no right of appeal to a MAT following the medical board's initial assessment of disablement. However, by reg. 32 the Secretary of State can refer such a decision to a MAT. A further restriction is imposed on applications for review. PD reg. 30 prevents a review on the ground of unforeseen aggravation until five years have elapsed since the beginning of the assessment period. Even then reg. 31 requires that leave be sought from a MAT for the review if it involves an assessment made for life. There can never be a review for unforeseen aggravation if the assessment is for less than 20 per cent.

(4) Assessment

(a) *In general*

By PD reg. 29(a)

> ". . . every initial assessment of the extent of the claimant's disablement in respect of occupational deafness shall be a provisional assessment and the period taken into account by such an assessment shall be a period of 5 years."

Although the IIAC would prefer the period to be shorter than five years it considers that, if reassessment were allowed sooner, it would probably impose an unacceptable burden upon the medical facilities available.

According to the IIAC report in 1973 loss of hearing should be assessed without regard to the ability to lipread, or the availability of hearing aids. This contrasts with the general principles of assessment with regard to artificial aids as discussed at p. 142. Although a precise mathematical method for assessing loss of hearing is laid down by PD reg. 34(2) some allowance is made for a more flexible approach by reg. 34(4). This provides that the assessed percentage can be varied "as may be reasonable in the circumstances of the case" if it "does not provide a reasonable assessment", bearing in mind that there are other indications and factors relevant to assessment in general. These are discussed at p. 141. However, a starting point for any assessment is the two stage mathematical formula contained in PD reg. 34(2) and sched. 3.

This formula begins by calculating the loss in each ear upon the basis of the following table:

Average hearing loss (dB) over 1, 2 and 3 kHz	Degree of disablement per cent
50–53 dB	20
54–60 dB	30
61–66 dB	40
67–72 dB	50
73–79 dB	60
80–86 dB	70
87–95 dB	80
96–105 dB	90
106 dB or more	100

The second stage of the formula then uses these percentages to assess the combined loss of both ears by working out the following equation:

$$\frac{\left(\begin{array}{c}\text{percentage of disablement}\\ \text{of better ear}\end{array} \times 4\right) + \begin{array}{c}\text{percentage of disablement}\\ \text{of worse ear}\end{array}}{5} = \text{assessment}$$

To illustrate how this two-stage formula works suppose a claimant barely satisfies the conditions for making a claim in that the threshold for hearing in his better ear is 50 dB, and in his worse ear is 53 dB. The calculation is then as follows:

Stage 1: (a) 50 dB = 20 per cent
(b) 53 dB = 20 per cent

Stage 2: $\dfrac{(20 \times 4) + 20}{5}$ = 20 per cent assessment

In practice the formula means that, provided the minimum threshold of hearing loss is reached, the initial assessment must be for at least 20 per cent.

The DHSS medical handbook deals with a particular situation where there may be more than one cause of deafness. It provides that if the claimant satisfies the minimum hearing loss requirement and there is another ear condition (even if not caused by work) which produces other than sensorineural deafness and the condition makes the industrial deafness worse, it can be taken into account to increase the assessment. Resulting or connected conditions such as vertigo, tinnitus or chronic suppuration may also justify increased assessments in accordance with the general principles of assessment discussed in chapter 5. No offset is now made for presbyacusis, which is the natural effects of age upon hearing.

(b) Reassessment

By PD reg. 29(*b*)

"... the period to be taken into account by and subsequent reassessment of the claimant's disablement in respect of occupational deafness, if not limited by reference to the claimant's life, shall not be less than 5 years."

Again the purpose of this regulation is to reduce the pressure upon medical facilities.

Damage to the inner ear is a permanent condition and on reassessment an improvement may not be expected. Despite this there are several provisions designed to exclude from benefit those who, although obtaining payment after their first assessment, fail to meet the necessary conditions on reassessment. The usual reason for this failure is not that hearing has improved, but that the first test was inaccurate. Inadequate equipment may have been used. This accounts for the fact that in 1981 a third of those reassessed failed to satisfy the minimum loss requirements. This may happen because of PD reg. 34(5):

"Where on reassessment . . . the sensorineural hearing loss is less than 50 dB in each ear, being due in the case of at least one ear to occupational noise, the extent of disablement shall be assessed at less than 20 per cent."

For assessments below 20 per cent reg. 34(6) provides that neither disablement benefit nor REA is payable. In arriving at the assessment reg. 3(3) of the Social Security (Industrial Injuries and Diseases) Miscellaneous Provisions Regulations 1986 (SI No. 1561) provides that the rounding up provisions, described at p. 140, are not to apply if the reassessment is below 20 per cent. Also excluded in such circumstances is the provision enabling percentages of disablement to be aggregated, as discussed at p. 148. Finally, PD reg. 33 provides that if on reassessment disablement is assessed below 20 per cent it is to be the final assessment.

(c) In accident cases

A different method of assessment is used where a claim under SSA s. 50 is made for hearing loss caused by an accident. This may happen where, for example, deafness results from an explosion at work. Schedule 1 of the Benefit regs. indicates that for absolute deafness an assessment of 100 per cent is appropriate. In practice in an accident case, but never for the prescribed disease, the following table is used. It appears in the DHSS medical handbook which, although not forming part of the legislation, is often more readily accepted by boards than references to the regulations themselves.

Degree of hearing attained	For both ears used together Per cent
Shout not beyond 1 metre	80
Conversational voice not over 30 centimetres	60
Conversational voice not over 1 metre	40
Conversational voice not over 2 metres	20
Conversational voice not over 3 metres	
(a) one ear totally deaf	20
(b) otherwise	Less than 20

In addition the handbook notes that, where the hearing in one ear is normal, complete deafness in the other ear affects the detection of sound and an assessment of 20 per cent is reasonable. These suggested assessments apply to deafness only, and do not include any allowance, for example, for tinnitus. Such additional factors, as considered above in relation to the assessment of the prescribed disease, may justify higher assessments.

7. PNEUMOCONIOSIS INCLUDING SILICOSIS AND ASBESTOSIS

(1) Introduction

There are two main reasons for devoting a separate section of this chapter to pneumoconiosis: firstly, ever since the original scheme for compensation was established in 1918 there have been special rules which apply to this disease alone; and secondly, pneumoconiosis is by far the most important of the prescribed diseases, accounting for more pensions than all the others combined, and representing over one in eight of all disablement pensions whether for accident or disease (appendix A, table 1).

DHSS leaflet NI. 3 gives an outline of the conditions of entitlement to benefit and the claims procedure involved. The 40-page leaflet NI. 226 offers notes on diagnosis and describes the work of special medical boards. (It is best obtained from the DHSS, Norcross, Blackpool.) The IIAC have issued two reports on pneumoconiosis, the first in 1953 (Cmd. 8866) and the second in 1973 (Cmnd. 5443). Although the SSA 1986 removed the right to disablement benefit for assessments below 14 per cent, an exception was made for byssinosis, and diffuse mesothelisma pneumoconiosis. By PD reg. 20(1), as substituted by SI 1986 No. 1561, these diseases continue to attract compensation provided that disablement is assessed as at least 1 per cent. Special provision is also made for claims of REA in cases of pneumoconiosis, but this is discussed only at p. 172 and not in this chapter.

Although over 600 workers are annually diagnosed as new sufferers from pneumoconiosis (appendix A, tables 4 and 5), most pensions currently in payment first began many years ago, and they are now paid to elderly recipients. Of the pensions current in 1983, half began at least 20 years earlier, and half were being paid to people over the age of 70 (table 3). There has been criticism of the rules governing compensation ever since the disease was first prescribed. The National Union of Mineworkers remains unhappy with the details of the present scheme.[6] Although many of its suggestions for reform have been rejected,[7] reference is made to some of them in the course of this section.

(2) Basis of entitlement

(a) Diagnosis

Pneumoconiosis is a comprehensive term covering a group of dust-associated diseases of the lung, including silicosis and asbestosis. As

[6]   J. Craw *et al., op.cit.*
[7]   H.C. Written Answer, Vol. 973, col. 434, 12 November 1979.

recognized in *R(I) 10/67* it is the consequences of dust in the lungs, not its mere accumulation, which constitutes pneumoconiosis. These consequences include the laying down of fibrous tissue which brings about a pathological change in the lung, usually producing shortness of breath and coughing. As noted in *R(I) 44/54* and *R(I) 9/56* the condition does not improve and may grow progressively worse.

Although the disease is no longer defined by the PD regs., the original 1946 Act definition is retained by SSA 1975 sched. 20:

> "Fibrosis of the lungs due to silica dust, asbestos dust or other dust. The expression includes the condition of the lungs known as dust-reticulation."

In its leaflet NI. 226 the DHSS agrees that this definition has led to confusion and is best avoided. The IIAC report in 1973 recommended that the definition be changed to

> ". . . permanent alteration of the lung structure due to inhalation of mineral dust and to the tissue reactions of the lung to its presence but does not include bronchitis and emphysema."

This change would reflect the fact that fibrosis is not necessarily always present, that conditions can affect the lung lining, or pleura, as well as the lung itself, and that the relevant dusts are mineral rather than, for example, cotton dust or pollen.

Even if this change of definition received statutory recognition, it would still exclude two particular types of injury. The first of these related to what is known as category 1 pneumoconiosis. There are three categories used in measuring the extent of dust in the lung and for the lowest of these pneumoconiosis is not usually diagnosed unless the worker is young. This is category 1 and according to the IIAC represents only dust retention and a nearly normal position. However, the National Union of Mineworkers view the dividing line as arbitrary and a cause of many miners not being certified as having pneumoconiosis in spite of good radiological evidence of the presence of the disease.

The second type of injury excluded by the definition relates to claims in respect of the pleura. This is the thin membrane covering the surface of the lung and chest wall and is considered anatomically different from the lung itself. This distinction meant that many workers suffering from the effects of asbestosis were excluded from the pneumoconiosis provisions, for up to half of the refusals to award benefit by medical boards in asbestos cases were because only the pleura was affected. Following an IIAC report in 1982 (Cmnd. 8750; supplemented in 1984 by Cmnd. 9184) changes in the pleura were prescribed in their own right as diseases D8 and D9. However, pleural changes are not covered by the prescription of pneumoconiosis as disease D1.

(b) Occupational cover

Pneumoconiosis is prescribed by PD reg. 2(b) in relation to employed earners who have worked since 1948 in one of two groups of occupations. A claimant must have worked in either of the following:

Either *a scheduled occupation*, being any occupation listed in part II of schedule I of the PD regs. as reproduced in (ii) below. A claimant employed in one of these jobs for not less than an aggregate period of two years can take advantage of the presumption under reg. 4(3) that his pneumoconiosis is due to the nature of his employment. Coalmining and working with asbestos account for over 90 per cent of the cases in which a medical board first diagnose pneumoconiosis. (See appendix A, table 4 which also indicates the wide range of other occupations in which the disease may be contracted.)

Or *an unscheduled occupation*, being "any occupation involving exposure to dust" except for those scheduled occupations in (ii) below. This second group was added following an IIAC recommendation in 1953. However, in practice it is of little importance: it comprises only 1 per cent of all new cases examined by medical boards each year. Workers in unscheduled occupations are particularly unlikely to prove their claim, only two out of 64 such claimants being diagnosed as sufferers in 1984 (appendix A, table 4). This lack of success is because claimants suffer from two particular disadvantages compared to those who claim for a scheduled occupation. Firstly, they cannot take advantage of the presumption under PD reg. 4 which means that the burden of proving that the pneumoconiosis is due to the occupation rests with the claimant. The second disadvantage is that, before the AO refers the diagnosis question, PD reg. 24 requires the claimant to satisfy the officer that "there is reasonable cause for suspecting the claimant is suffering or has suffered from the disease. . . ." Despite these difficulties there have been a few claims which have succeeded as in the case of a forge hammerer in *R(I) 30/59*, and a clerk in a railway station who was affected by dust from the wagons used to transport china clay in *CI 300/83* (unreported).

(*i*) *"Exposure to dust" in unscheduled occupations*

Whether an occupation involves "exposure to dust" has proved difficult to resolve. In relation to the scheduled occupation "substantial" exposure is required, but that word is not used for unscheduled occupations and it is implied that a lesser degree of exposure will suffice. However, what this level is to be is uncertain. As recognized in *R(I) 1/85*:

> "It is in the circumstances somewhat surprising that the material legislation does not prescribe more closely the level of exposure to dust which is to count and the basis on which a qualifying level is to be assessed."

In the absence of a scientifically determined norm as to the level of exposure required Commissioners have developed the following general principles. According to *R(I) 1/60(II)* the dust need not be in excess of that met with in many other industrial occupations, but it must not be so trivial that it can be ignored as in *R(I) 40/57*. In that case a watchman at an ammunition dump claimed to have developed silicosis from using a hut containing a coke stove placed on an earth floor from which dust rose. However, the amount of dust was considered too trivial for the occupation to qualify. In refusing benefit the Commissioner also states that the dust must be "in excess of that met with in the ordinary course of life", and this has proved a difficult test to apply.

The test was examined in detail in *R(I) 1/85*, a case actually dealing with disease D4. The Commissioner was especially concerned whether the "ordinary course of life" involved a subjective or objective assessment. If it is subjective then two workers living in different neighbourhoods, or parts of the country, but meeting exactly the same levels of dust in their jobs could find that only one of them is entitled to benefit. The reason for this is that the unsuccessful claimant lives in an industrial area where the "ordinary course of life" dictates that he encounters a level of dust similar to that at work, whilst the other employee lives in the countryside. On the other hand if the test is objective, what is to be the base level with which dust at work is to be compared? The Commissioner avoided this difficulty by stating that decisions whether the dust was out of the ordinary were ones of fact to be determined by the reasonable man. He did, however, incline towards an objective test by suggesting that any special susceptibilities of the claimant and the relative toxicity of different dusts were to be ignored. Similarly he rejected any suggestions that a worker in a "dark satanic mill" should satisfy a higher burden of proof than one in a "rural paradise". However, confusingly the Commissioner also seemed to abandon the "ordinary course of life" test altogether by concluding that adjudicators should

". . . exclude from their evaluations conditions elsewhere than in the immediate work-place, . . . notwithstanding that the claimant may incur significant exposure to dust elsewhere than in his work-place in the course of his ordinary daily life."

The precise basis upon which an unscheduled occupation will be found to involved exposure to dust therefore remains uncertain. Each case is to be decided on its own facts.

(ii) The scheduled occupations

These are defined by part II of schedule I of the PD regs. as follows:

"1. Any occupation involving—
   (a) the mining, quarrying or working of silica rock or the working of dried quartzose sand or any dry deposit or dry residue of silica or dry admixture containing such materials (including any occupation in which any of the aforesaid operation are carried out incidentally to the mining or quarrying of other minerals or to the manufacture of articles containing crushed or ground silica rock);
   (b) the handling of any of the materials specified in the foregoing subparagraph in or incidental to any of the operations mentioned therein, or substantial exposure to the dust arising from such operations.
2. Any occupation involving the breaking, crushing or grinding of flint or the working or handling of broken, crushed or ground flint or materials containing such flint, or substantial exposure to the dust arising from any of such operations.
3. Any occupation involving sand blasting by means of compressed air with the use of quartzose sand or crushed silica rock or flint, or substantial exposure to the dust arising from such sand blasting.
4. Any occupation involving work in a foundry or the performance of, or substantial exposure to the dust arising from, any of the following operations:-
   (a) the freeing of steel castings from adherent siliceous substance;
   (b) the freeing of metal castings from adherent siliceous substance;
      (i) by blasting with an abrasive propelled by compressed air, by steam or by a wheel; or

(*ii*) by the use of power-driven tools.

5. Any occupation in or incidental to the manufacture of china or earthenware (including sanitary earthenware, electrical earthenware and earthenware tiles), and any occupation involving substantial exposure to the dust arising therefrom.

6. Any occupation involving the grinding of mineral graphite, or substantial exposure to the dust arising from such grinding.

7. Any occupation involving the dressing of granite or any igneous rock by masons or the crushing of such materials, or substantial exposure to the dust arising from such operations.

8. Any occupation involving the use, or preparation for use, of a grindstone, or substantial exposure to the dust arising therefrom.

9. Any occupation involving-
   (*a*) the working or handling of asbestos or any admixture of asbestos;
   (*b*) the manufacture or repair of asbestos textiles or other articles containing or composed of asbestos;
   (*c*) the cleaning of any machinery or plant used in any of the foregoing operations and of any chambers, fixtures and appliances for the collection of asbestos dust;
   (*d*) substantial exposure to the dust arising from any of the foregoing operations.

10. Any occupation involving—
    (*a*) work underground in any mine in which one of the objects of the mining operations is the getting of any mineral;
    (*b*) the working or handling above ground at any coal or tin mine of any minerals extracted therefrom, or any operation incidental thereto;
    (*c*) the trimming of coal in any ship, barge, or lighter, or in any dock or harbour or at any wharf or quay;
    (*d*) the sawing, splitting or dressing of slate, or any operation incidental thereto.

11. Any occupation in or incidental to the manufacture of carbon electrodes by an industrial undertaking for use in the electrolytic extraction of aluminium from aluminium oxide, and any occupation involving substantial exposure to the dust arising therefrom.

12. Any occupation involving boiler scaling or substantial exposure to the dust arising therefrom."

(iii) Commissioners' decisions and other notes on the list of occupations

Para. 1

"Working" means performing some operation on the silica or admixture with a view to bringing it to a certain condition in order that it may be used. Benefit was therefore refused where the claimant only encountered silica in cleaning out ink drums in *CI 110/49*; in "glazing" iron castings with a wheel covered in emery dust in *R(I) 21/52*; in dismantling brickwork in *CWI 53/50*; and in decarbonizing the tops of retorts as part of gas maintenance in *R(I) 14/55*. However heating an electric rod coated with silica in order to weld articles together was working with it in *R(I) 27/51* and *R(I) 2/58*, whilst using sand as a bed in which steel plates were heated was also sufficient in *R(I) 22/52*.

"Silica rock" according to PD reg. 1(2) means

". . . quartz, quartzite, ganister, sandstone, grit-stone and chert, but not natural sand or rotten rocks."

Ironstone is not silica rock *R(I) 32/52*, nor is dolomite in its natural state.

Burnt dolomite is not a "dry admixture" containing silica rock *R(I) 36/52*, nor is cement *R(I) 46/51*, but the reverse is the case with basic slag *R(I) 26/55* and ultramarine in its dry state *R(I) 13/59*.

"*Dried quartzose sand*" means sand which has been subjected to a drying process for the specific purpose of extracting the moisture. Natural sand used in cement making had not been subjected to such a process and benefit was refused in *R(I) 46/51*, but in *R(I) 28/57* it was sufficient that the sand had been cooked, even though it had been done for reasons other than extracting the moisture. There is no specific yardstick to judge whether the sand has been sufficiently dried. At least some sand had dried and the claims succeeded in *R(I) 83/52* and *R(I) 47/53*.

"*Admixture*" means according to Slesser LJ in *Gledhill* v *Dalton Mains Collieries* (1934)

> ". . . not a chemical combination transferring the constituent parts of the new combination into something quite other than those of which the constituent parts are composed, but a physical or mechanical mixture in which each mixing part retains its own identity."

Thus bricks and cement were not an admixture in *CWI 53/50* nor were welding rods after the free silica had become combined with the metal in *R(I) 35/52*. The mixture must be artificial and not compacted by nature as in *R(I) 32/52*, but the fact that its constituent parts are so compacted does not prevent it from being an admixture according to *R(I) 15/51* and *R(I) 27/51*. It can be a bi-product of an industrial process for it need not be made on purpose. This meant that basic slag incidental to the manufacture of steel could be considered an admixture in *R(I) 26/55*. This decision together with *R(I) 2/58* illustrate that only a very small amount of silica etc. need be found in the admixture.

Para. 2

"*Breaking, crushing or grinding*" does not include blasting so that the labourer handling flints which had been broken by blasting when they were quarried was not covered in *R(I) 82/52*.

Para. 3

"*Silica rock*" is considered in relation to para. 1 above.

Para. 4

"*Foundry*" according to PD reg. 1(2) means

> ". . . those parts of industrial premises where the production of metal articles (other than pig iron or steel ingots) is carried on by casting (not being diecasting or other casting in metal moulds), together with any part of the same premises where any of the following processes are carried on incidentally to such production, namely the drying and subsequent preparation of sand for moulding (including the reclamation of used moulding sand), the preparation of moulds and cores, knockout operations and dressing or fettling operations."

"*Substantial exposure to the dust*." Work for one to two hours a day in a foundry was sufficient in *R(I) 5/51*. The meaning of "dust" was not limited to dust sufficiently fine to be dangerous according to current medical opinion. The degree of exposure required is discussed at p. 122 in relation to unscheduled occupations.

"*The freeing of . . . siliceous substance*" must be the object of using the tools and not merely be the incidental result as in *R(I) 30/59*.

"*Siliceous*" in relation to parting powders used by iron moulders is to be interpreted in the sense in which it is used in the trade so that less than 3 per cent of free silica was insufficient in *CI 354/50* and *R(I) 36/53*.

"*Blasting with an abrasive*" was not being done by an iron dresser who used a chipping tool driven by compressed air to remove the siliceous substance in *CI 100/50*.

"*Tool*" is considered in relation to occupational deafness at p. 114.

Para. 5

"*Incidental to*" is considered in relation to para. 10 below. A lodgeman who checked goods into a pottery works and controlled the time-keeping of the operatives was held not to be involved in work "incidental to" the manufacture of china or earthenware in *R(I) 11/52*.

Para. 6

"*Mineral graphite*" was not contained in the printing ink used in *CI 110/49*.

Para. 8

"*Grindstone*" did not include a hand grinder in *R(I) 21/52*. According to reg. 1(2) it means

> ". . . a grindstone composed of natural or manufactured sandstone and includes a metal wheel or cylinder into which blocks of natural or manufactured sandstone are fitted."

Although a gas maintenance fitter used a grindstone wet in order to clean his tools, his claim still succeeded in *R(I) 14/55*.

Para. 9

"*Asbestos.*" The claim may succeed despite the amount of asbestos being small as in *CSI 68/49*, where a man sorting non-ferrous metals, including some cables with asbestos covering, was "handling" asbestos. The claim of an asbestos lagger succeeded in *CWI 53/50*, but failed in *R(I) 4/53* because the work done for a very short while about twice a year could be ignored as too trivial.

Para. 10

As recognized in *CWI 4/50*: "Continual and substantial exposure to coal dust is not, in itself, a qualification for benefit" under the scheduled occupations. In particular in relation to mining there are a number of restrictive decisions as to what constitutes work "at a mine" and operations "incidental thereto". They mean that benefit may be denied even if there is evidence of exposure, for example, at an opencast coal working.

"*Underground in a mine*" normally means what is colloquially referred to as "down the pit", so that a worker at a breaker-house a mile from the mine where shale was produced was not covered even though he worked below ground level in *R(I) 38/59*

"*Mine*" is defined by PD reg. 1(2) to include

> ". . . every shaft in the course of being sunk and every level and inclined plane in the course of being driven, and all the shafts, levels, planes, works, tramways and sidings, both below ground and above ground, in and adjacent to and belonging to the mine, but does not include any part of such premises on which any manufacturing process is carried on other than a process ancilliary to the getting or dressing of minerals or the reparation of minerals for sale."

According to *CWI 4/50* an opencast site is not a mine. In construing the definition *R(I) 38/59* found that a breaker-house is a "works" which "belonged to" a mine not because of common ownership but because of the functional association involved. "Adjacent to" in the definition does not mean contiguous but does imply reasonable proximity. On this basis it included work at a coal screening plant a quarter of a mile from the mine in *R(I) 52/56*.

"*Coal mine*" is defined by reg. 1(2) as

". . . any mine where one of the objects of the mining operation is the getting of coal (including bituminous coal, cannel coal, anthracite, lignite and brown coal)."

"*At*" *any mine* means adjacent to it so that places not within the curtilage of any mine are excluded. This meant that claims failed in the case of workers at a boiler-house three quarters of a mile from the mine in *CWI 14/50*, at coke ovens only 100 yards from the pit shaft in *CI 274/49*, and at a screening plant at a closed colliery in *R(I) 70/54*, but not as an open one in *R(I) 52/56*.

"*Incidental to*" means "some subordinate activity closely connected with the processes concerned". The older decisions upon the present schedule may require to be further examined in the light of the more liberal construction under SSA s. 50(1) as to what is incidental to employment, as discussed at p. 59. The following have been found not to be operating incidental to the working of coal: a telephone operator and clerk at colliery offices in *R(I) 39/51*; a driver of a stationary engine hauling trams in *R(I) 2/54*; a worker engaged in the maintenance of the railway track between two collieries in *CWI 17/50*; and a worker at a coke oven near the pit shaft in *CI 274/49*. In relation to slate a wages clerk was also refused benefit in *R(I) 14/52*, but a porter employed by a billiard table maker was operating incidental to the dressing of slate in *CI 265/49*, as was a labourer manhandling wagons of slate in *R(I) 15/52*.

"*Trimming*" according to *R(I) 4/53* means the tidying of coal.

"*Splitting . . . of slate*" does not require that it be done preparatory to commercial use. This meant that a worker removing unsafe rock at a disused slate mine was covered in *R(I) 13/52*.

(c) Causation

The legislation gives no help to a claimant in an unscheduled occupation to prove that his disease is due to his employment. However, for a worker in a scheduled occupation who contracts pneumoconiosis PD reg. 4(3) states that

". . . the disease shall, unless the contrary is proved, be presumed to be due to the nature of his employed earner's employment if he has been employed in one or other of the occupations set out in [the schedule] for a period or periods amounting in the aggregate to not less than 2 years in employment which either –
(a) was employed earner's employment; or
(b) would have been employed earner's employment if it had taken place on or after 5th July 1948."

An AO can rebut this presumption by proving on the balance of probability that the disease is not caused by the job. In practice this is an almost impossible task.

(3) Adjudication

(a) *Special medical boards and procedure*

Although adjudication in pneumoconiosis cases is similar to that for other diseases, there are a few special features. In particular decisions upon diagnosis and disablement are matters for special medical boards (formerly pneumoconiosis boards) involving specially qualified adjudicating medical practitioners. The boards also operate in the ten other cases, mostly involving lung disease, noted at p. 103. The number of new cases they diagnose each year is considered in appendix A, table 5. The procedure in all these cases of disease, including pneumoconiosis, is as follows.

If the employment conditions are satisfied the claimant must be sent for a chest X-ray. However, in the case of an unscheduled occupation PD reg. 24 also requires that before sending for an X-ray an AO be given reasonable cause to believe that the claimant is suffering from the disease. Together with the claimant's medical and occupational history the X-ray is examined by a doctor drawn from a special medical panel. If this doctor's report reveals no trace of the disease the AO disallows the claim, although an appeal can be made to a special medical board. This X-ray scrutiny procedure is said to enable straightforward claims to be cleared quickly and saves medical time. It is omitted in claims involving slate dust, byssinosis and asbestosis because, at least in the case of the latter, radiographic abnormalities are a comparatively late manifestation of the disease. If there is sufficient evidence of the presence of the disease the claimant is referred by an AO to one of eight special medical boards. These are situated in Cardiff, Glasgow, London, Manchester, Newcastle, Sheffield, Stoke and Swansea. The boards are staffed by 24 full-time and 28 part-time specially qualified adjudicating medical practitioners. A board consists of at least two of these doctors. Its duties are to make the diagnosis decision and assess the extent of disablement. Appeal lies to a MAT under Adj. reg. 51(3). It used to be that no such appeal could be made. Although this was changed, there remained a restriction that an appeal could not be made within two years of a MAT last hearing the claimant's appeal. However, this restriction has now been removed by SI 1986 No. 1374.

(b) *Criticism of special medical boards*

It has been said that special medical boards rarely give the claimant the benefit of any doubt and that they are "mean" in their attitudes. It is true that they refuse benefit in a high percentage of cases: of the 2,300 new claims for pneumoconiosis they receive each year three quarters are rejected. There are regional variations and Newcastle, for example, seems more generous to claimants in rejecting only 60 per cent of claims compared with Glasgow's 88 per cent.[8] There are accounts of disabled workers who have successfully sued their employer and obtained damages at common law, but for the very same disease they have still failed to persuade successive medical boards that they are entitled to benefit under the industrial scheme. In addition it is said that all too frequently the disease is not diagnosed during the claimant's lifetime but is revealed only

---

[8]   Secretary of State for Social Services, H.C. Written Answer, Vol. 980, col. 231, 5 March 1980.

on a post-mortem. Finally, it is argued that the doctors who staff the boards may lack expertise because they are more likely to be junior doctors rather than consultants. The DHSS admits that it has had difficulty in recruiting doctors, but it defends the expertise of the panels.

(c) Powers to issue advice and suspend from employed

Special medical boards used to have the power to issue certificates suspending claimants from their employment. This could encourage sufferers to hide the onset of their disease. Eventually boards used their power very sparingly, issuing only 24 certificates in 1974. After that year the power was revoked but PD reg. 39 allows any certificates which have been issued to remain in force, although by reg. 40 these may be varied or revoked. Although there are other procedures intended to safeguard workers and these are still in force, they are less likely to deter genuine claims. For example, claimants are required by reg. 38 to submit to regular medical examinations.

If pneumoconiosis is diagnosed the special medical board writes to the claimant to advise him whether or not he can safely continue with his work, and if so, under what conditions. In coal mining cases the claimant may be advised that he can continue in his current job underground provided that he works in dust approved conditions. Alternatively he may be advised to work where exposure to harmful dust is minimal, such as above ground, or it may even be recommended that he leave the industry. According to the National Union of Mineworkers those advised to change their place of work are usually told too late for it to have much effect upon subsequent events. Provided that the claimant consents, his employer is told of the diagnosis and is asked to safeguard the claimant's conditions of work. The claimant's own doctor is always notified even if a claim is disallowed on the basis of the X-ray. However, again the union considers that this notification is inadequate because the standard form letters sent to general practitioners give no useful clinical information and are couched in legal rather than medical terms. Even in colliery districts most doctors are said to have only a poor understanding of the pneumoconiosis problem.

(4) Assessment

The special medical board usually makes a provisional award for a year or two: only one in eight current pensions is for life (appendix A, table 3). This ensures that claimants are re-examined at regular intervals, but it also means that more than three quarters of the work of special medical boards involves reassessment rather than diagnosis of new claims (appendix A, table 4). On first certification two thirds of all coalworkers are assessed at the minimum level of 10 per cent, and in nine out of ten cases the assessment is not more than 20 per cent. By contrast in other industries only one third of initial assessments are as low as 10 per cent.[9] This is explained partly by the fact that pneumoconiosis produced by other than coal dust is often more disabling. However, generally assessments are low and, of those current for all industries, only about two fifths are for more than 25 per cent (appendix A, table 2).

Pneumoconiosis claimants are better placed than most other victims of industrial disease in the following four respects:

[9]   Health and Safety Executive, *Statistics 1981-82* table 10.6.

(*a*) *Entitlement despite an assessment below fourteen per cent*

The SSA 1986 removed the right to disablement benefit for any worker assessed as less than 14 per cent disabled. PD reg. 20(1), as substituted by SI 1986 No.1561, allows compensation to continue to be paid for all levels of pneumoconiosis provided that the minimum assessment is at least 1 per cent. This exception is of considerable importance to the industrial scheme because 40 per cent of those receiving a pension for pneumoconiosis are presently assessed at only 10 per cent disabled (appendix A, table 2). For the calculation of the payment due at these low levels of assessment see p. 253.

(*b*) *Diagnosis and the one per cent rule*

Before 1954 benefit for pneumoconiosis was only payable if the assessment of disablement amounted to 5 per cent or more whereas for other diseases 1 per cent was sufficient. Following the 1953 IIAC report this was changed by what is now SSA s. 78(3):

> "A person found to be suffering from pneumoconiosis shall be treated . . . as suffering from a loss of faculty such that the assessed extent of the resulting disablement amounts to not less than one per cent."

The effect of this section is to place a few victims of pneumoconiosis in an especially favourable position. This happens where category 2 pneumoconiosis is diagnosed, but as yet no discernable respiratory disablement arises from it. Instead of receiving a nil assessment a claimant can rely upon s. 78 to obtain an award of at least 1 per cent. The position is then exaggerated in practice because a minimum award of 10 per cent is made, as explained in (*c*) below. In 1983 the IIAC disapproved of the 1 per cent rule because its effect was to fail to distinguish between whether there was a loss of faculty on the one hand, and whether this loss resulted in disablement, on the other.

(*c*) *Assessment in steps of ten per cent*

There is a non-statutory administrative practice which makes all assessments of disablement in cases of pneumoconiosis in steps of 10 per cent. The reason for this is that it is difficult to calculate with any greater precision the degree of disablement suffered. However, this rule is applied even at the lower level of assessment. It therefore ensures that a 10 per cent pension is paid even to the victim, referred to in (*b*) above, who suffers no disablement although is diagnosed as having contracted the disease. This is also the effect of the provision with regard to the rate of benefit for low assessments of pneumoconiosis, byssinosis and diffuse mesothelioma as discussed at p. 253.

(*d*) *Including associated conditions such as emphysema and bronchitis*

A claimant may suffer from some other condition, such as chronic bronchitis or emphysema, which although not arising from the pneumoconiosis may make it more disabling than it otherwise would be. The special medical board may then make an increased assessment to take account of the extent to which the pneumoconiosis is made more disabling by the connected condition. This is in accordance with the general principles of assessment discussed at p. 149. However, there are also two regulations specially dealing with the extent to which conditions associated with pneumoconiosis are to be taken into account. These regulations are made under SSA s. 78.

The first of them is PD reg. 21:

> "Where any person is found to be suffering from pneumoconiosis accompanied by tuberculosis, the effects of the tuberculosis shall be treated . . . as if they were the effects of the pneumoconiosis."

This regulation is along the lines of others made as long ago as 1919. Although the incidence of tuberculosis has declined, as late as 1972 three per cent of newly diagnosed cases of pneumoconiosis were also accompanied by tuberculosis.

The second regulation is PD reg. 22. This provides that if the claimant's disablement resulting from pneumoconiosis alone (or with tuberculosis) would be assessed at 50 per cent or more, and he is also suffering from chronic bronchitis or emphysema, the effects of these last two diseases are treated as though they were the effects of pneumoconiosis. In contrast to reg. 21 this rule was first introduced only in 1967.

In its 1977 report the IIAC viewed this regulation as making generous provision. However in practice it can only benefit those one in seven recipients of a pension who are assessed as at least 50 per cent disabled (appendix A, table 2). The reason for the regulation is that at the 50 per cent level the disablement is so severe that it is difficult to apportion responsibility for it between different causes. In addition, the IIAC regarded the 50 per cent level as "the transition from simple pneumoconiosis to the more severe form of complicated pneumoconiosis." However, the difficulty of distinguishing between the diseases is said also to arise at much lower levels. The National Union of Mineworkers wants both the level to be lowered to 30 per cent, and emphysema to be more readily acknowledged as caused by pneumoconiosis. This possibility is currently being investigated by the IIAC.

(5) Other sources of compensation

These are all considered in chapter 11. For pneumoconiosis it should be noted that outside the industrial scheme there is a private no-fault compensation agreement between the unions and British Coal. In addition if an employer is no longer in business compensation may be available under the Pneumoconiosis (Worker's Compensation) Act 1979. Within the industrial scheme old cases may be compensated under the Pneumoconiosis, Byssinosis and Miscellaneous Diseases Benefit Scheme 1983. About a quarter of the supplementary payments under the Workmen's Compensation (Supplementation) Scheme 1982 are paid to victims of pneumoconiosis who were in receipt of benefit before 1948. For those coal miners contracting the disease before 1970 a supplement may be payable under the Colliery Workers' Supplementary Scheme.

8. Reform and a System of Individual Proof

In 1979 the Secretary of State asked the IIAC to carry out the first major review of the schedule of prescribed diseases since 1958. In effect it was required to look into three matters: the removal of restrictive conditions applying to those diseases already listed; the possibility of speeding up the process of prescription; and whether a system of individual proof should be introduced alongside the list system.

The result of the Council's deliberations was the blueprint for reform contained in its report published in 1981 (Cmnd. 8393). The report's proposals on the first two of the three matters investigated were accepted by Government and the relevant legislation was passed in 1983. However, on the third matter the Council made its major recommendation that a system of individual proof be introduced. This was rejected by Government. If the proposal had been implemented it would have marked a significant departure in principle from the present basis for compensating victims of disease.

(1) The removal of restrictive conditions

This involved making changes to the prescribed list by extending and clarifying the description of diseases and the range of qualifying occupations. The reforms have been taken into account in the descriptions given in appendix E and the course of this chapter. Together with these piecemeal changes the Council made a more general re-organization of the schedule in order to distinguish respectively between the physical, biological, chemical and other causes of disease. However, this was not done to bring the list into line with that recommended by the Commission of the European Community.[10] To achieve that objective was thought to require changes too complex to be included in the 1981 report. Instead the IIAC recommended that the European list be examined in detail sometime in the future. However, at present there is no prospect of another substantial reorganization of the list taking place soon.

(2) Speeding up the prescription process

Most of the IIAC suggestions which were made in order to speed up the prescription process have also been implemented. Some of these involved making changes to the Council's internal organization to ensure that it has adequate information and operates efficiently. For example, a research librarian has been appointed, and a working group has been formed to establish priorities for Council investigations and to keep it up to date with research information. In addition the Council can now more easily investigate matters on its own initiative for it no longer needs to wait for a formal reference from the Secretary of State.

However, one proposal which would have helped reduce the problems caused by delays in the prescription process has been rejected by Government. The Council recommended that a claimant's entitlement to benefit should date from when the Council submits its report rather than from when the relevant regulations are presented to parliament. The refusal to accept this suggestion means that nothing has been done to deal with the delay involved in a case such as vibration white finger. That

---

[10] Annex 1 to the EC Recommendation of 23 July, 1962. See Appendix II of the IIAC report 1981 (Cmnd. 8393).

disease was not prescribed until four years after the IIAC recommended that it be listed. Workers suffering during the intervening period are not entitled to benefit for that time.

(3) A system of individual proof

The list system has the merit of certainty in that it gives a clear indication as to whether or not a disease is included in the industrial scheme. Because of this the system is relatively cheap and easy to run. However, it is also open to criticism. A definitive schedule has also proved to be an inflexible one. It is changed only slowly and can be accused of failing to keep up to date with the introduction of new materials and processes into the workplace. To counter this tendency the IIAC put forward its most important recommendation in its 1981 report: it suggested that the exclusive nature of the list system be abandoned and a mixed system be instituted. This would involve adding a system of "individual proof" enabling an employee to establish in his particular case that his disease, even if not prescribed, was work related. Unlike in the case of a prescribed disease there would be no presumption to help a claimant prove the work connection. The onus would be upon the claimant to gather the relevant medical and work evidence, and present a case for the payment of benefit. Although this proposal was rejected by Government, it requires further examination here because its importance is such that it dominates any discussion about the future of compensation for industrial disease.

Trade unions have pressed for a system of individual proof almost since the beginning of workmen's compensation. As the IIAC noted:

> "The idea that industrial injuries compensation should be freely available to those who contract industrial diseases as it is to victims of industrial accidents is not a new one. . . . On each occasion [that it has been raised] both the equity of the principle and the practical problems of putting it into effect have been acknowledged."

Such a system had been rejected by previous committees in 1920 and 1955.[11] Despite this, the IIAC saw individual proof as the only way of providing a remedy for "a serious flaw in the present system" whereby benefit was not available for certain industrially caused diseases and injuries. In particular individual proof was thought the only practicable means of incorporating injuries by process into the industrial scheme.

The objections to individual proof are, firstly, that it would involve frequent conflicts in medical evidence and lead to inconsistent decisions and a litigious atmosphere; and secondly that it would open up a flood of claims which could overwhelm the medical and administrative resources. To meet these objections the IIAC recommended that limits be placed on the system to restrict the number of claims to a manageable level, by excluding those which would present the greatest difficulties. To do this three possibilities were investigated:

   (*a*) It was suggested that the claimant should have to prove that the disease was a particular risk of his occupation in that his job led him to

---

[11]   The Holman Gregory Committee 1920 (Cmd. 816) and the Beney Committee 1955 (Cmd. 9548).

run a greater risk than that to which the public was exposed. However, this was rejected as too complicated and unworkable. It is not practical to expect local DHSS offices to spend time and money to discover the extent to which the incidence of a particular disease can be traced within the population as a whole, and then compare it with the rate of that disease for other people doing the claimant's job. The IIAC itself has difficulty in performing this task.

(*b*) The Council considered whether it should confine the new diseases for compensation to a second list. This would recognize that they could be caused by work, but claimants would not be given the benefit of the presumption that they had been so caused, as they are with regard to those on the existing schedule. However, this idea was rejected because it could present the same kind of problems concerning the development of a rigid list system as found in the existing formula.

(*c*) The solution adopted by the IIAC was to propose a fully open system of proof, subject to the specific exclusion of certain common diseases. This exclusion was to be achieved by another list. This would contain those diseases which were thought not primarily occupational in origin, and which were likely to produce claims too numerous or complex for the scheme to deal with. The claimant would then be faced with three alternative situations: his disease might appear on the present list and a claim could then be made with the aid of a presumption; his disease might appear on the new second list for which no claim could be made; or finally, if his disease were on neither list it would be open to him to establish entitlement by individual proof.

In making this recommendation the IIAC was very concerned to avoid putting too much strain upon administrative and medical resources. Its approach is thus comparable with that for occupational deafness. In both cases the Council also suggested that the restrictions on claims could be relaxed in the future and regular reviews of developments should take place. The Council's initial restrictions on individual proof were severe in that it was proposed to place on the list of excluded diseases heart disease, strokes, lung cancer, high blood pressure, bronchitis, ulcers, arthritis and rheumatism, and certain mental disorders. It was recognized that many people believed these illnesses could be caused by work, but the IIAC report was quite blunt in its assertion that often there is little or no evidence for such a connection to be made. Occupational deafness, except to the extent that it was already prescribed, was also to be excluded from individual proof for fear of imposing too great a burden on the NHS. The list of exclusions was such as to cause doubts as to whether individual proof would have had much effect in practice upon the present scheme. These doubts may be echoed in other European countries where an individual proof system operates. The number of claims brought have been few, and when they have been made they have had little chance of success.[12]

---

[12]   The IIAC suggest the figures be treated with caution but only one in ten claims are successful in Germany and one in five in Luxembourg. The IIAC does not cite figures from Sweden, although the Pearson Commission report, vol. 3 para. 600, indicates that before 1977 up to 2000 claims a year were made for non-scheduled diseases and 75 per cent were successful.

Nevertheless the Council's recommendation could be seen as an attempt to decentralize decision-making with regard to the compensation of industrial disease by transferring some of the power from the Council to the determining authorities and, indirectly, to claimants themselves.

The Conservative Government rejected the Council's proposal on individual proof in 1984. It stated that:

> "While the concept had obvious attractions there could be considerable practical difficulties of assessment and administration giving rise to disproportionately high costs in relation to the benefit gained; and the resources to launch such a scheme are not available."[13]

---

[13]   H.C. Written Answer, Vol. 52, col. 774, 20 January 1984.

CHAPTER 5

ASSESSMENT OF DISABLEMENT

The disablement questions

According to *R* v. *MAT, ex p. Cable* (1968) the statutory chain of causation giving rise to entitlement under the industrial scheme is based upon the following elements:

1. an accident arising out of and in the course of employment, resulting in
2. an injury, resulting in
3. a loss of mental or physical faculty, resulting in
4. one or more disabilities, resulting in
5. disablement.

The statutory authorities may determine only the first two of these, the others being the preserve of the medical authorities and the subject of this chapter. It is to the medical authorities that the AO must refer all "disablement questions". This is required by SSA s. 108 which defines the disablement questions as

"(a) ... whether the relevant accident has resulted in a loss of faculty;
(b) ... at what degree the extent of disablement resulting from a loss of faculty is to be assessed, and what period is to be taken into account by the assessment ... ."

These three disablement questions form the basis for the organization of this chapter.

The assessment of disablement affects not only whether there is entitlement to benefit, but also its amount. For example, not only is an assessment of at least 14 per cent usually required for entitlement to a disablement pension, but the weekly rate of that benefit is also dependent upon the percentage assessed. How assessments are translated into payment is discussed in chapter 10.

1. HAS THE ACCIDENT OR DISEASE RESULTED IN A LOSS OF FACULTY?

(1) Loss of faculty distinguished from disability and disablement

The claimant must show on balance that the industrial injury has caused some loss of faculty and that, in turn, this has produced one or more disabilities which, taken together, amount to disablement. Loss of faculty is therefore "a cause of disabilities to do things which in sum constitute disablement". It was described as the total or partial loss of "a power or function of an organ of the body" in *Hudson and Jones* v. *Secretary of State for Social Services* (1972). Loss of faculty is to be judged by comparing the claimant's condition resulting from the accident with his condition apart from it. According to *R(I) 7/67* this should be done without considering whether the effect of the loss can be reduced by the claimant using some artificial aid, such as spectacles. However, as discussed below, such aids are taken into account in assessing disablement.

As defined in *R(I) 3/76*:

> "... 'disability' means inability to do something which persons of the same age and sex and normal physical and mental powers can do; 'disablement' means a collection of disabilities, that is to say the sum total of all the relevant disabilities found present in a given case."

Technically loss of faculty must be distinguished from both disability and disablement. Thus in considering the disablement questions *R(I) 5/84* (T) requires the medical authorities to give a full account of what constititues the loss of faculty. Only then must they give details of whether any disability results, and what percentage of disablement is appropriate, if any. The AMA's findings with regard to loss of faculty can be important if, for example, the claimant appeals that his assessment is too low because it only takes into account the physical effects of the industrial injury and has omitted the psychological consequences.

However, in practice the distinction between loss of faculty and disablement is usually of little importance because the concepts overlap. It is true that loss of faculty could differ from disablement if there were a loss which did not prevent the claimant from following normal everyday activities. However, this is most unlikely to happen. It may be thought that a potential example is where an accident causes the loss of a kidney. The claimant may still be able to live normally day to day and without any apparent handicap. Nevertheless an organ has been lost and because of this *R(I) 14/66* requires that a loss of faculty be found. Is this a case therefore where the distinction can be made? That is, can the medical authority find that, despite the loss of faculty, no disablement results? The answer according to the DHSS medical handbook is no. Disablement exists because the loss of reserve function must be taklen into account. This means that even where the other kidney is functioning normally, MATs have assessed disablement at between 5 and 10 per cent.

Even in the rare case where it may be possible to find a loss of faculty and yet no disablement, statute has intervened to blur the distinction. In *R(I) 6/61* the possibility was canvassed that the MAT had found that the claimant suffered from dermatitis (the loss of faculty), but was handicapped only in that he had to wear gloves in order to handle milk bottles, and this did not amount to disablement. In fact the MAT found that disablement did result, but they assessed it at less than one per cent. This meant that no loss of faculty was deemed to result. This confusing result was the product of SSA s. 57(3) which provides:

> "... there shall be deemed not to be any relevant loss of faculty when the extent of the resulting disablement, if so assessed, would not amount to 1 per cent."

However, when making their findings the medical authorities were urged to keep clear the distinction between loss of faculty and disablement because of the possibility, explained above, that their process of reasoning may be subject to appeal.

There is one other reference in the 1975 Act which is relevant in deciding whether a loss of faculty has occurred. SSA sched. 20 defines the loss as including disfigurement "whether or not accompanied by any actual loss of faculty". However, disfigurement is not of itself a disability, but only a potential cause of disability. This means that it is possible here to find that a loss of faculty has occurred (because of the statutory definition) but that no disablement results (because, for example, the scar is small and on a hidden part of the body).

Finally in the DHSS medical handbook AMAs are reminded that, although signs of a prescribed disease may no longer be present, there may still be a continuing loss of faculty due to the disease. For example, an attack of non-infective dermatitis, disease D5, may have lessened the claimant's skin resistance to such an extent that it is undesirable that he should be exposed to particular substances again, whether at work or elsewhere. This susceptibility can constitute a loss of faculty which can be taken into account in reaching a decision on any resulting disablement.

(2) The cause of the loss of faculty

It is for the medical authority to decide whether the claimant has shown, upon the balance of probability, that the loss of faculty results from the relevant accident or disease. The principles of causation apply as discussed at p. 45. The accident or disease must be shown to be an effective cause of the loss, although it need not necessarily be the only one.

The non-medical authorities have jurisdiction to determine that an accident has occurred and that it caused injury. However, as discussed at p. 229, their findings do not bind the medical authorities. This means that it remains open for an AMA to conclude that the loss of faculty does not result from the accident but instead is the product, for example, of a congenital condition or non-industrial injury. This freedom for the AMA to decide as it thinks fit applies even where the accident and the injury appear to be one and the same, for example, where a claim is made for a hernia. In effect the AMA is able to contradict the findings of the non-medical authorities. This is allowed by SSA s. 117 which also provides that an AMA is not bound by earlier medical determination of the claimant's condition even if they were given by a MAT. Disablement questions are to be considered afresh each time. However, if there is a difference from earlier views the reasons should be clearly stated.

2. At What Degree is the Extent of Disablement to be Assessed?

Disablement is the overall effect of the relevant disabilities. It involves considering whether the claimant is able to perform the everyday activities of life and whether he has lost the health, strength and power to enjoy a normal existence. It can only be assessed by an AMA if it is satisfied that, on the balance of the evidence, there is a loss of faculty resulting from the relevant accident. However, as stated above, it is not bound by any earlier findings of an adjudicating authority.

Although a medical authority is therefore allowed a wide measure of discretion in making an assessment of disablement, it must take certain principles into account as discussed in (2) below. In particular, the medical authority is guided by a percentage tariff which is prescribed as that normally applicable for certain injuries. The tariff, discussed in (3) below, is laid down by statute and is supplemented by the guidelines in (4). These guidelines lack the force of law, but are issued to the medical authorities by the DHSS. There is a presumption which helps decide the causation aspects involved in an assessment: according to *Hudson and Jones* v. *Secretary of State for Social Services* (1972) and *R(I) 2/74* if the claimant can prove that his loss of faculty was the result of the accident, "he is presumed to suffer all the disabilities which a normal person would suffer from such a loss of faculty unless the contrary is shown". As examined in (7) below this presumption can be displaced if the claimant's condition appears to be partly the result of non-industrial factors. A reduction of benefit may then be made. The problems which arise if an accident results in multiple injuries, or if there are successive industrial accidents, are considered in (5) and (6) below.

It should be noted that most assessments are for low percentages. Almost half of the pensions current in 1983 were for less than 25 per cent, and less than one in ten pensioners were assessed as over 55 per cent disabled (appendix A, table 2).

(1) A percentage calculation treated as a round figure

All assessments of disablement must be expressed as percentages as required by SSA sched. 8 para. 5. If they are for more than 13 per cent their exact figures may be treated as higher or lower depending upon the following provision for rounding them. It treats all assessments over 13 per cent as being made in multiples of 10 by rounding upwards the single figures between five and nine, and rounding down those from two to four, except in the case of 14 per cent which is treated as 20. It means that 35 is treated as 40, 34 as 30, 15 as 20 but 13 remains unchanged. This is all the result of SSA s. 57(1B), as inserted by the SSA 1986:

> ". . . where the assessment of disablement is a percentage between 20 and 100 which is not a multiple of 10, it shall be treated —
> (a) if it is a multiple of 5, as being the next higher percentage which is a multiple of 10; and
> (b) if it is not a multiple of 5, as being the nearest percentage which is a multiple of 10,
> and where it is a percentage of 14 or more but less than 20 it shall be treated as a percentage of 20."

The rounded figure determines, in particular, the amount of pension to be paid as discussed in chapter 10. However, rounding is only applied to the total assessment of all disablement arising from the industrial injury; it does not affect each constituent assessment where more than one condition is taken into account. In addition, for practical purposes medical authorities record the exact percentages not only for the individual disabilities, but also for the total assessment of disablement. This enables later authorities to appreciate how the total assessment was determined, for this would not be apparent from the rounded figure alone. This can be important, for example, in an application for review on the basis of unforeseen aggravation.

(2) General principles of assessment

The principles employed by the industrial scheme in assessing disablement are modelled upon those established for war pensions. An objective approach is adopted which contrasts with the partly subjective approach of the common law in awarding damages for injuries in tort. In *R* v. *MAT, ex p. Cable* (1968) Diplock L J emphasized that in construing the industrial scheme

> "the Court must be continually on guard against the fallacy of applying to the assessment of 'benefit' the principles applicable to the assessment of damages of compensation – a task with which it is so much more familiar."

The McCorquodale committee in 1965 (Cmnd. 2847) rejected the general use of subjective factors in industrial injuries assessment. Such factors "apart from being impossible to quantify, would clearly have no place in the determination of equitable and consistent assessments . . . ."

The objective nature of the industrial injury assessment is established by SSA sched. 8 para. 1 which applies the following principles:

> "(a) save as hereafter provided in this paragraph, the disabilities to be taken into account shall be all disabilities so incurred (whether or not involving loss of earning power or additional expense) to which the claimant may be expected, having regard to his physical and mental condition at the date of the assessment, to be subject during the period taken into account by the assessment as compared with a person of the same age and sex whose physical and mental condition is normal;
>
> (b) . . .;
>
> (c) the assessment shall be made without reference to the particular circumstances of the claimant other than age, sex and physical and mental condition;
>
> (d) the disabilities resulting from such loss of faculty as may be prescribed shall be taken as amounting to 100 per cent disablement and other disabilities shall be assessed accordingly."

The assessment is made in relation to the claimant's loss of health, strength and power to enjoy life. Perhaps its most important feature is that loss of earnings is not directly relevant, although such a loss may give rise to entitlement to reduced earnings allowance. Loss of the ability to work is taken into account in only a very general way, and no allowance is made for the specific occupation which the claimant follows. This means, for example, that assessment of dermatitis is the same whether it is for a wages clerk or a bricklayer, even though it might force the latter to give up his skilled trade. Thus in *R(I) 3/61* the claimant injured his Achilles tendon and was prevented from working on ladders, an indispensable feature of his regular occupation. However, his assessment was not increased to take account of his reduced prospects of employment and earnings. Again in *Murrell* v. *Secretary of State for Social Services* (1984) the Court of Appeal held that in making the assessment it was not relevant that the claimant had become unemployable as a result of a combination of his industrial injury with earlier non-industrial disabilities. Account could not be taken of unemployability because it would involve examining the claimant's particular circumstances.

The objective nature of the assessment is further illustrated by the refusal to award higher compensation to those who suffer a disproportionate loss because, before their accident, they were exceptionally fit and lived an especially full and active life. Unlike a damages claim at common law no account is taken of the claimant's inability to pursue any particular hobby which he enjoyed before his injury.

One subjective factor which is relevant is the claimant's age. An older person of normal physical ability is less able than his younger counterpart and this may mean that, for certain conditions, a lower assessment may be made for older claimants. However, in practice at least with regard to anatomical losses, medical authorities generally award the same amount whatever the age of the claimant. The claimant's sex is another relevant subjective factor. It is particularly important in cases of facial disfigurement where, as admitted in a committee report in 1947 (Cmd. 7076), the practice of the medical authorities is to make higher assessment for a woman than for a man.

Sched. 8 states that there is nothing in the principles of para. *(c)* above to prevent further regulations being made specifying different assessments for arm and hand injuries, depending upon whether the claimant is left or right handed. However, such regulations have not been made and the prescribed assessments treat each arm equally. Despite this it may be possible to argue that if the dominant hand is lost an AMA should exercise its discretion to increase an award, as discussed under the next heading. However, changing the legislation specifically to allow for an increase in such circumstances was not approved by the committee which reported in 1965 (Cmnd. 2847). It considered that this subjective factor should be ignored because, in its view, the non-dominant hand can easily replace the one which is lost.

Apart from cases where there are multiple causes of a claimant's condition, as considered in (6) below, the general principles of assessment have rarely been considered by Commissioners. In one of the few cases, *R(I) 30/61*, it was pointed out that assessments of 100 per cent do not require claimants to be totally disabled. Most awards of benefit relate to only temporary periods of disablement and there may be a tendency to make too low an assessment of a severe but not permanent injury. *R(I) 30/61* reminds AMAs that they "must not be misled by the fact that a very serious disability is expected not to last long. The answer to that situation is high assessment for a short period". It could be argued for example, that a claimant who is only temporarily confined to bed because of his injury is more disabled during that time than an amputee who has adapted to the loss of both legs.

Two cases have affirmed that assessments of disablement can be reduced because artificial aids are available to the claimant. The medical authority was allowed to take into account that, following the accident, the claimant could wear spectacles to correct his defective vision in *R(I) 7/63*(T) and *R(I) 7/67*. However, the first case added the qualification that an award would still be appropriate even if the defect could be cured. This was partly because

"... however much a person may be accustomed to wearing glasses, there may be accidents, emergencies, and other circumstances when the glasses are not available for short or long periods, or where they constitute a serious inconvenience, as they do to some people in rain and other conditions."

With regard to artificial limbs the DHSS medical handbook suggests that it may be necessary to modify an assessment where a limb is to be worn, but has not yet been fitted. The assessment then should be provisional and at a higher rate than the set tariff (prescribed in the next section). This should last until the claimant has been fitted with an artificial limb and has been allowed a reasonable time to get used to wearing it.

(3) Conditions for which there are prescribed degrees of disablement

Para. (*d*) above requires assessment to be made by relating the claimant's disability to conditions which are specifically prescribed as amounting to 100 per cent. In fact only seven such conditions are listed by Benefit reg. 11(6) and sched. 2, but a range of 48 other less serious injuries are also listed with their tariffs ranging as low as 1 per cent. The schedule mostly deals with amputations of limbs, or parts of limbs, and is related to stump lengths. It has been used for war pensions since 1914. The detailed basis of this tariff system has been considered by two committees: in 1947 the Inter-departmental Committee on the Assessment of Disablement due to Specified Injuries reported (Cmd. 7076), and in 1965 the McCorquodale Committee on the Assessment of Disablement reported (Cmnd. 2847).

It must be emphasized that the prescribed degrees of disablement are not to be mechanically applied. The medical authorities are given considerable discretion to change the assessment to take account of individual circumstances. For example, if a hernia is caused by the strain of using an artificial limb, or if ulceration or paralysis is due to the use of crutches, an unscheduled assessment can be given. By Benefit reg. 2(6) the medical authorities may make

"... such increase or reduction ... as may be reasonable in the circumstances of the case where [the prescribed degree] ... does not provide a reasonable assessment of the extent of disablement resulting from the relevant loss of faculty."

Subject to this over-riding power the following table contained in sched. 2 of the Benefit regs. applies:

Description of Injury	*Degree of Disablement* *Per cent*
1. Loss of both hands or amputation at higher sites	100
2. Loss of hand and a foot	100
3. Double amputation through leg or thigh, or amputation through leg or thigh on one side and loss of other foot	100
4. Loss of sight to such an extent as to render the claimant unable to perform any work for which eyesight is essential	100
5. Very severe facial disfigurement	100

6. Absolute deafness	100
7. Forequarter or hindquarter amputation	100

Amputation Cases — Upper Limbs (either arm)

8. Amputation through shoulder joint	90
9. Amputation below shoulder with stump less than 20.5 centimetres from tip of acromion	80
10. Amputation from 20.5 centimetres from tip of acromion to less than 11.5 centimetres below tip of olecranon	70
11. Loss of a hand or of the thumb and four fingers of one hand or amputation from 11.5 centimetres below the tip of olecranon	60
12. Loss of thumb	30
13. Loss of thumb and its metacarpal bone	40
14. Loss of four fingers of one hand	50
15. Loss of three fingers of one hand	30
16. Loss of two fingers of one hand	20
17. Loss of terminal phalanx of thumb	20

Amputation Cases — Lower Limbs

18. Amputation of both feet resulting in end-bearing stumps	90
19. Amputation through both feet proximal to the metatarso-phalangeal joint	80
20. Loss of all toes of both feet through the metatarso-phalangeal joint	40
21. Loss of all toes of both feet proximal to the proximal inter-phalangeal joint	30
22. Loss of all toes of both feet distal to the proximal inter-phalangeal joint	20
23. Amputation at hip	90
24. Amputation below hip with stump not exceeding 13 centimetres in length measured from tip of great trochanter	80
25. Amputation below hip and above knee with stump exceeding 13 centimetres in length measured from tip of great trochanter, or at knee not resulting in end-bearing stump	70
26. Amputation at knee resulting in end-bearing stump or below knee with stump not exceeding 9 centimetres	60
27. Amputation below knee with stump exceeding 9 centimetres but not exceeding 13 centimetres	50
28. Amputation below knee with stump exceeding 13 centimetres	40
29. Amputation of one foot resulting in end-bearing stump	30
30. Amputation through one foot proximal to the metatarso-phalangeal joint	30
31. Loss of all toes of one foot through the metatarso-phalangeal joint	20

Other injuries

32. Loss of one eye, without complications the other being normal	40
33. Loss of vision of one eye, without complications or disfigurement of eyeball, the other being normal	30

Loss of:
A. *Finger of right or left hand*

   Index finger:
34. Whole   14
35. Two phalanges   11
36. One phalanx   9
37. Guillotine amputation of tip without loss of bone   5

   Middle finger:
38. Whole   12
39. Two phalanges   9
40. One phalanx   7
41. Guillotine amputation of tip without loss of bone   4

   Ring or little finger:
42. Whole   7
43. Two phalanges   6
44. One phalanx   5
45. Guillotine amputation of tip without loss of bone   2

B. *Toes of right or left foot*

   Great toe:
46. Through metatarso-phalangeal joint   14
47. Part, with some loss of bone   3

   Any other toe:
48. Through metatarso-phalangeal joint   3
49. Part, with some loss of bone   1

   Two toes of one foot, excluding great toe:
50. Through metatarso-phalangeal joint   5
51. Part, with some loss of bone   2

   Three toes of one foot excluding great toe:
52. Through metatarso-phalangeal joint   6
53. Part, with some loss of bone   3

   Four toes of one foot, excluding great toe:
54. Through metatarso-phalangeal joint   9
55. Part, with some loss of bone   3

(4) Non-prescribed conditions

If the claimant's condition falls outside of the schedule the medical authorities have even more freedom in their assessment. Their decision is one of fact, and depends upon what is appropriate in the circumstances. *Murrell* v. *Secretary of State for Social Services* (1984) emphasizes that it is not sufficient to base an appeal against a MAT assessment only on the ground that it seems low. Courts and Commissioners will not interfere unless the assessment was so wrong as to indicate that there must have been an error of law. This is very difficult to establish given that the medical authorities have such a wide discretion. Whilst Benefit reg. 2(8) requires them to "have such regard as may be appropriate to the prescribed degrees of disablement", *R(I) 30/61* suggests that an assessment for a non-prescribed condition should not be tied too closely to the schedule. The difficulties of comparing conditions with scheduled assessments were recognized in the 1965 report (Cmnd. 2847).

> "There are no medical means of proving exactly that the effects of say, a diseased kidney, are more restrictive in their effects on ability to lead a normally occupied life than loss of a foot, any more than there is of so proving the effect of loss of a kidney in relation to the effects of a prolapsed disc or pneumoconiosis. But so long as the law provides for all assessments to have regard to the common denominator of the condition of a normal healthy man of the same age, all concerned . . . are under a duty to see that as far as possible assessments are mutually fair between pensioners suffering from all kinds of disabling conditions. The schedule thus occupies a central position in the framework within which unscheduled assessments are made."

In addition to the schedule there are non-statutory guidelines for assessment. These are set out in appendices 7 and 8 of the DHSS medical handbook. They include the following:

(*a*) *Ankyloses* (immobility of joints)

If a joint becomes fixed in a position which causes the least disability (these optimum positions are defined in the handbook) the following assessments are appropriate, although AMAs are reminded that all depends upon the individual claimant.

	Per cent
Shoulder	40
Elbow	40
Wrist	30
Hip	60
Knee	30
Ankle	20

(*b*) *Aphakic eyes*

MATs have taken into account the degree of tolerance and sensitivity to the wearing of a contact lens.

	Per cent
Unilateral aphakia with reasonable correction by a contact lens	15-24
Bilateral aphakia with reasonable correction by a contact lens	25-30

(*c*) *Other eye conditions*

The following table is of assistance:

Valuation Table reproduced from Report of the 18th International Congress of Ophthalmology, 1958. Reduction of Vision: Compensation Rates (Figures in percentages)

		6/6	5/6	6/9	5/9	6/12	6/18	6/24	6/36		6/60	4/60	3/60	
		1-0.9	0.8	0.7	0.6	0.5	0.4	0.3	0.2	0.15	0.1	1/15	1/20	-1/20
6/6	1-0.9	0	0	2	3	4	6	9	12	16	20	23	25	27
5/6	0.8	0	0	3	4	5	7	10	14	18	22	24	26	28
6/9	0.7	2	3	4	5	6	8	12	16	20	24	26	28	30
5/9	0.6	3	4	5	6	7	10	14	19	22	26	29	32	35
6/12	0.5	4	5	6	7	8	12	17	22	25	28	32	36	40
6/18	0.4	6	7	8	10	12	16	20	25	28	31	35	40	45
6/24	0.3	9	10	12	14	17	20	25	33	38	42	47	52	60
6/36	0.2	12	14	16	19	22	25	33	47	55	60	67	75	80
	0.15	16	18	20	22	25	28	38	55	63	70	78	83	88
6/60	0.1	20	22	24	26	28	31	42	60	70	80	85	90	95
4/60	1/15	23	24	26	29	32	35	47	67	78	85	92	95	98
3/60	1/20	25	26	28	32	36	40	52	75	83	90	95	98	100
	-1/20	27	28	30	35	40	45	60	80	88	95	98	100	100

These assessments are for defective vision without special features and are based on the visual defect as measured, *after correction with glasses,* by the ordinary test only. The degree of tolerance to the wearing of contact lens should be taken into account.

(*d*) Removal of spleen

This may lower natural resistance to certain organisms. MATs have assessed the loss at between 2 and 5 per cent.

(*e*) Removal of testicle

Again the resulting loss of reserve function has been assessed at between 2 and 5 per cent.

(*f*) Removal of kidney

The loss of reserve function has been assessed at between 5 and 10 per cent.

(*g*) Deafness

This is considered at p. 117.

(5) Multiple injuries

Where the accident gives rise to more than one injury, although the medical authorities are entitled to specify the degrees of disablement resulting from each injury, *R(I) 42/55*(T) requires that the assessment should be one embracing the whole extent of the loss of faculty resulting from all injuries for any one period. If the one injury has become incorporated into the other, Benefit reg. 2(6) requires that the scheduled tariff for the more serious disability be used. If the injuries are separate, and their tariffs individually are listed in the schedule but nothing is given for their combination, the degree of disablement need not be the aggregate of their individual tariffs. Instead, according to *R(I) 40/60*(T) and *R(I) 39/61*, the assessment should be made as for non-prescribed conditions, and be based on the particular circumstances of the case. This means, for example, that if an index finger has been lost (scheduled at 14 per cent) and two phalanges of the middle finger (scheduled at 9 per cent), the assessment for the injuries combined is not necessarily their aggregate when taken separately. If it were so it would amount to 23 per cent and be more than the 20 per cent scheduled for the loss of two fingers. Instead, it is for the AMA to determine the appropriate amount on the facts of each case.

(6) Successive industrial injuries

In determining whether the threshold of 14 per cent which triggers payment of a disablement pension has been reached, disablement caused by earlier industrial accidents or diseases may be taken into account. For accidents SSA s. 57(1A), as inserted by SSA 1986 sched. 3, states:

> ". . . there may be added to the percentage of the disablement resulting from the relevant accident the assessed percentage of any present disablement of his resulting from any other accident after 4th July 1948 which arose out of and in the course of his employment, being employed earner's employment, and in respect of which a disablement gratuity was not paid to him under this Act after a final assessment of his disablement."

A similar provision is made by SSA s. 77(4) and PD reg. 15A in relation to assessing the disablement from a prescribed disease after there has been an earlier prescribed disease or industrial accident. By s. 57(1C), s. 77(5) and PD reg. 15B the rounding up provisions, discussed in (1) above, are to apply only to the aggregate percentage of disablement, not to the assessments for the individual injuries.

In the case of successive industrial accidents SSA s. 91 limits the amount of benefit that may be paid. It prevents a claimant receiving, by way of two or more disablement pensions, an aggregate weekly amount in excess of that paid for a 100 per cent disablement pension. In calculating this maximum *R(I) 3/73* required that any payments for REA be included. However, it may now be argued that they should be left out of account, because the SSA 1986 made REA independent of a disablement pension and no longer merely a supplement to it. The other supplements, for constant attendance and exceptionally severe disablement, are also excluded because of the specific wording of s. 91.

Entitlement to constant attendance allowance will not be refused only because the individual assessments for the successive injuries are each below 100 per cent. Provided that the combined assessment is for at least that amount, Benefit reg. 39(3) provides for payment to be made. Of course, only one such allowance can be claimed even if the claimant suffers from several industrial injuries.

By Benefit reg. 11(5) where there is a connection factor between successive accidents it is to be taken into account only in the assessment of the latest of them. This means, for example, that higher pension for the earlier period cannot be claimed. The connection factor is discussed next in more detail.

(7) Multiple causes of a condition and offsetting benefit

Assessment has proved especially difficult where there are disabilities resulting not only from the industrial accident, but also from other causes. The general principle is that the industrial scheme should not have to bear the costs of the disablement not attributable to work. To achieve this a system of apportionment allows an offset to be made; the overall assessment can be reduced to take account of the non-industrial causes. However, where the disability resulting from the industrial accident is made greater because of its connection with other conditions, there is also provision for attributing the extra disablement resulting from the connection alone to the industrial scheme.

The problems in applying the relevant legislation were recognized by Lord Denning in *R* v. *MAT, ex p. Cable* (1968):

> "Judges have been at their wits' end to know what some of these provisions mean. There have been acute differences of opinion amongst them. If judges find this difficult I can imagine how impossible it must be for those who have to apply them. They are for the most part, not lawyers, but medical men and civil servants. No wonder they have developed their own peculiar terms such as 'connection factor' and the like, which they may understand but no one else does."

Wilmer L J was similarly upset.

> "I regard it as deplorable that in a matter which so vitally affects the lives and welfare of working men and women there should be so much obscurity and so much room for doubt."

(a) General principles and the connection factor

In the assessment of disablement the claimant may benefit from the presumption that in the absence of evidence to the contrary, the whole of his disability is to be taken as arising from the accident. However, if this presumption is displaced then Benefit reg. 11 seeks to apportion the total loss by separating the percentage of disability resulting from the industrial accident from that which is attributable to the other effective but non-industrial causes. Causes may be distinguished as occurring at different times, or as resulting in different forms of injury. Thus if an earlier non-industrial accident causing a claimant to lose his finger is followed by a later industrial accident causing him to lose the rest of his hand, an assessment of the total disability is made, followed by an offset to reduce the pension in order to take account of the earlier injury which contributes to the present disability.

What is the connection factor and how does it affect this calculation? It is not referred to expressly by the legislation but, instead, is derived from a form used by the AMA to record its findings. The form was described in *R(I) 23/61* as explaining the terms used to describe the "relevant conditions", that is, those to be taken into account in an assessment of disablement:

> " 'Fully relevant' means that all the disablement from the condition described results from the accident; for example injury to a limb which was previously normal. 'Partly relevant' means that only part of the disablement results from the accident; for example a previously damaged joint rendered worse by the injury or the loss of a previously deformed limb. 'Connected' denotes a condition which does not itself result from the accident but which makes a fully

or partly relevant condition more disabling than it would be in a normal person. 'Unconnected conditions' means abnormal conditions which are not regarded as relevant conditions, and which are therefore not to be taken into account in making the assessment."

The "connected condition" occurs when the relevant cause and the other effective cause affect different parts of the body and, taken together, these produce a disability greater than that which results from the total of their individual assessments combined. The combined individual total is increased by the extra disability caused by the injured parts being complementary in function. It is this that is the "connection factor". For example, the loss of an eye is substantially greater for a man who has already been deprived of sight in his other eye, compared with one whose sight in the other eye is normal. Similarly the combined loss of thumb and forefinger is greater than the total disability if each digit is taken separately. Again, as in *Murrell v. Secretary of State for Social Services* (1984), it may be more severe for a blind man to suffer an industrial injury to his hand than if he were a sighted person, for example it may prevent him using braille. On the facts of the case this led to an increase in his assessment from 15 to 30 per cent although the Court of Appeal considered that the increase for this connection factor in the case of blindness to be on the low side.

Whether disablement benefit will be increased because of a connected condition (now recorded by AMAs simply as a "C condition"), depends upon the detailed construction of the regulations set out below. They are based upon a distinction between, on the one hand, cases in which the non-industrial (i.e. "other effective") causes occur before the relevant industrial accident (resulting in what AMAs record as "O (Pre) conditions"), and on the other hand, cases in which the non-industrial causes occur after the accident (resulting in "O (Post) conditions").

(b) Where the other effective cause occurs BEFORE the industrial accident
Benefit reg. 11(3) states:

"Any assessment of the extent of disablement ... in a case where the other effective cause is a congenital defect or is an injury or disease received or contracted before the relevant accident, shall take account of all such disablement except to the extent to which the claimant would have been subject thereto during the period taken into account by the assessment if the relevant accident had not occurred."

To illustrate this let us suppose a claimant has suffered losses in the following chronological order and as assessed in accordance with the schedule:

(a) non-industrial loss of a foot assessed at 30 per cent.
(b) industrial loss of a hand assessed at 60 per cent.
(c) combination of (a) and (b) assessed at 100 per cent.

The connection factor here is 10 per cent being the figure by which (c) exceeds the total of the individual assessments (a) and (b). The assessment requires all disablement to be accounted (i.e. 100 per cent) except that to which the claimant would have been subject had the industrial injury not occurred (i.e. 30 per cent). The result is that the claimant is assessed at 70 per cent and therefore, in the case of a later industrial accident, he will always benefit from any connection factor which may be present.

(c) Where the other effective cause occurs AFTER the industrial accident

Benefit reg. 11(4) is somewhat more complicated. It states:

> "Any assessment of the extent of disablement . . . in a case where the other effective cause is an injury or disease received or contracted after and not directly attributable to the relevant accident, shall take account of all such disablement to the extent to which the claimant would have been subject thereto during the period taken into account by the assessment if that other effective cause had not arisen and where, in any such case, the extent of disablement would be assessed at not less than 11 per cent if that other effective cause had not arisen, the assessment shall also take account of any disablement to which the claimant may be subject as a result of that other effective cause except to the extent to which he would have been subject thereto if the relevant accident had not occurred."

To continue the above example, if the injury in (*a*) is preceded by that in (*b*) the calculation is as follows. According to the first half of reg. 11(4) all disablement is to be taken into account (i.e. 100 per cent) except that which the claimant would have been subject to had the other effective cause not arisen (i.e. 40 per cent). So far this gives an assessment of 60 per cent. All incapacity arising from the second injury has been discounted. In contrast to the inclusion of the connection factor by reg. 11(3), so far here it is excluded because it is taken to arise as a result of the latest and non-industrial cause. Until 1970 this exclusion was total because this was as far as reg. 11(4) went. This was in spite of the IIAC recommendation in a 1956 report (Cmnd. 9827) that the assessment should take account of half of the greater incapacity caused by the later accident.

However, in 1970 the position was changed to bring into account the connection factor. Although this was to be done only in part, the compromise solution enacted was not that recommended by the IIAC in 1956. Instead it took the form of what is now the second half of reg. 11(4). This allows the claimant to benefit from the connection factor provided that the industrial disablement is over 10 per cent. It states that if the figure arrived at under the first half of the regulation is 11 per cent or more (as it is in the example) the assessment must "also take account of any other disablement . . . as a result of that other effective cause" (i.e. the remaining 40 per cent including the connection factor), except for that which would have been present if the earlier accident had not happened (i.e. to give this meaning this must be 30 per cent, excluding the connection factor). By adding the resulting 10 per cent to the 60 per cent reached under the first half of the regulation we arrive at a final total assessment of 70 per cent. The difficult wording of the second half of the regulation seems specifically intended to deal with the connection factor problem although it does not expressly use that term. The claimant is always to benefit except where a low initial assessment is involved and then the rather arbitrary 11 per cent *de minimis* requirement comes into play. Indeed regs. 11(3) and 11(4) will differ only if this arbitrary figure of 11 per cent is not reached for then, unlike reg. 11(3) no connection factor will be included in the calculation under reg. 11(4).

(d) Where the disablement amounts to 100 per cent

Benefit reg. 11(7) confers a discretion on the medical authorities not to reduce an assessment because the claimant would have been subject to some disablement even if the industrial accident had not occurred if they are

> ". . . satisfied that, in the circumstances of the case 100 per cent is a reasonable assessment of the extent of disablement from the relevant loss of faculty."

Because it is relatively easy to attain a 100 per cent assessment this discretion is needed to ensure that in cases of very serious disablement the offsetting provisions will not reduce benefit. The DHSS medical handbook gives the following example. Suppose a person already lacking vision in one eye suffers an industrial injury to the other eye and is made sufficiently blind to be unable to perform any work for which eyesight is essential. The AMA has power to decide that the 100 per cent assessment suggested by the schedule is a reasonable assessment despite the fact that, even if the accident had not occurred, the disablement would have been assessed at 30 per cent. The AMA may take this view especially if the loss of sight is greater than that for which 100 per cent is prescribed, as it would be, for example, if the claimant were made totally blind. On the other hand it may take the opposite view and make a considerable offset. This may happen where, for example, a minor industrial injury raises disablement to 100 per cent when it would have been assessable at a high level in any event.

(e) *What constitutes a disability justifying an offset of benefit*

On a first reading the whole purpose of reg. 11 seems obscure. In fact the mathematical formula eventually reached is quite simple and despite the complex wording of the regulation once its overall aim is understood it would appear to do its job effectively. However, when considered in detail the regulation has given rise to further problems of interpretation because the definition of a disability justifying an offset has proved difficult. Not only are there inevitable factual problems of medical diagnosis, but there have been legal disputes with regard to whether a disability is present. We may now know the formula to employ when there is a multiple cause of loss of faculty, but are we sure that the claimant was suffering from, a "disability" before the accident occurred? Perhaps it was merely some dormant physical condition and not a true disability and therefore not relevant to the question of offset. The often asked question "would the claimant have suffered from a disability had the accident not occurred?" is more complicated than it first appears.

The problem is illustrated by *R(I) 3/76* where a 50-year-old woman struck her face against the side of an office filing cabinet and detached the retina of her eye. A MAT awarded her a gross assessment of 12 per cent for life, but then made an offset of 5 per cent because in any event it was thought the claimant had "a high degree of probability of spontaneous retinal detachment". An appeal to the Commissioner was allowed. He stated that the tribunal should have distinguished between a disability and pre-disposition to disability for the latter did not trigger the offset. Other cases have similarly emphasized that a disability does not include a pre-existing constitutional or congenital defect which would not have caused any disablement if there had been no accident. Thus in *R(I) 8/74*, although the claimant suffered from a hysterical disposition such as to make her industrial back injury worse, it did not justify an offset being made unless her mental state would have become apparent as a disability even if she had not suffered an industrial accident. (Mental states causing the exaggeration of symptoms were further explored in *R(I) 13/75* where distinctions were made between malingering, hysteria and "functional overlay".) Again in *R(I) 1/81* the Commissioner decided that the MAT should not have made an offset because of the claimant's liability to develop multiple sclerosis. That constitutional defect was wholly symptomless and corresponded to the concept of loss of faculty in that it was a potential cause of disability but not itself a disability.

In this last case the Commissioner was disturbed because, as far as he could judge, MATs were commonly making mistakes with regard to offsetting. He considered that the errors were caused by a failure to appreciate the underlying purpose of the regulations which was to apply the common law principle that the accident victim must be taken as found, with his own physical or mental condition, even if he has an "eggshell" skull or personality. Another cause of mistakes is the failure of medical authorities to take into account the age of the claimant. This is important because if a condition is normal in someone of the claimant's age no offset should be made. For example, although hardening of the arteries or arthritis would be unusual in a young person, these conditions might be regarded as normal for an older worker, in which case there should be no reduction in the assessment. Claimants have been particularly upset by the offsetting provisions where they have resulted in the reduction of benefit because of some condition of which no one was previously aware but which, in the opinion of the medical authority, would have flared up in the future. Because of both this concern of claimants, and the medical and legal difficulties of operating the offsetting regulations, it is likely that they will continue to be a source of much dispute.

(8) Reform of assessment

Official reports have offered few criticisms of the assessment of disablement. The McCorquodale committee which reported in 1965 (Cmnd. 2847) concluded that the relationship between scheduled and unscheduled assessments was satisfactory, and concentrated attention largely upon the technical aspects of amputation assessments. The DHSS Discussion Document was similarly content with present methods: "The loss of faculty basis . . . was given an almost universal welcome in 1948 and has remained popular ever since". Again, no change was proposed by the White Paper which followed, although it did suggest that the scale of assessment be revised in favour of the seriously disabled as discussed at p. 254. However, these official views have not fully reflected the nature or extent of the criticisms which have been made of the methods of assessment.

Assessment was criticized in general by claimants in the only empirical investigation of their attitudes towards the industrial scheme which has been carried out. The few surveyed were unanimous in their opinion that the system was "ludicrous".[1] It is often uncertain as to what is an appropriate assessment and, apart from amputation cases, there is a great deal of room for conflict. Certain injuries, such as those involving back pain, are extremely difficult to assess, and yet an appeal is unlikely to succeed because

---

[1] M. Blaxter, *The Meaning of Disability* (1976) p. 187.

of the considerable discretion vested in AMAs. The TUC in its evidence on the Discussion Document noted that this discretion is exercised such as to result in low assessments; insufficient weight is given to medical evidence presented on behalf of claimants; and excessive reductions are made in some cases to take account of pre-existing conditions. A partial solution to these problems would be to extend the existing schedule and make it less arbitrary by specifying a wider range of injuries for which there is a prescribed assessment. The TUC suggested that the IIAC investigate this possibility as well as considering other criticisms of the method of assessment. As yet there is no prospect of such an investigation taking place.

Other criticisms of assessment have been more fundamental in that they have attacked the loss of faculty approach as out of date and inappropriate because it represents a limited and clinically orientated view of what it is to be disabled. Instead it has been suggested that, for example, the approach of the American Medical Association should be adopted.[2] The scheme devised by that Association does not depend exclusively upon a simple list of "loss of faculty" equivalents. Instead it also asks what loss of function results – what does the injury prevent the claimant from doing? It thus takes account of the inability to perform the activities of daily living. It also makes allowance for the psychological and social consequences of impairment, as well as for such factors as whether persistent pain is suffered. In short, it involves a more sophisticated and complex set of criteria. Although it involves a wider range of objective tests, it results in an assessment geared more to the specific circumstances of the individual, and therefore requires a more subjective analysis of impairment than under the present industrial scheme. Such a detailed assessment would not only be more expensive to operate, but its subjective nature could make it less reliable, and more open to discretionary value judgments. In taking into account the social effects of injury it would reduce the extent to which reliance is placed upon medical expertize. A study carried out for the DHSS is particularly concerned about these features and doubts whether such an approach "would be sufficiently reliable and acceptable for people to regard the resulting assessments as dealing equitably between eligible applicants".[3] For similar reasons the Discussion Document rejects any move towards greater subjectivity in assessment.

3. WHAT PERIOD IS TO BE TAKEN INTO ACCOUNT BY THE ASSESSMENT?

SSA sched. 8 para. 4(1) requires the medical authorities to assess the disablement for "the period during which the claimant has suffered and may be expected to continue to suffer from the relevant loss of faculty". Definite dates must be given. The beginning of the period cannot be earlier than when entitlement arises, and by SSA s. 57(4) this must be at least 90 days, ignoring Sundays, after the accident. This means that at least 15 weeks must elapse. The end of the period is when the medical authority expects the disability to end, and this may be either at some definite date, or at the end of the claimant's life. However, sched. 8 para. 4(2) makes special provision

[2]   American Medical Association, Committee on Rating Mental and Physical Impairment, *Guidelines to the Evaluation of Permanent Impairment* (1971).
[3]   D. Duckworth, *The Classification and Measurement of Disablement,* DHSS Research Report No. 10 (1982) p. 91.

for the end of a period of assessment when the claimant's disablement is below 14 per cent. Then the period

"shall not end earlier than any date by which it seems likely that the extent of the disablement or the aggregate will be at least 1 per cent."

Assessing the period of disablement inevitably involves making an estimate, but the medical authority must decide whether its decision is to be a "final" one, or is only "provisional". If the prognosis is certain, it may be possible to make a final assessment. The period then may be stated to end, for example, in as little as six months, or it may be for as long as several years. However it is unusual for a limited period to be definitely stated as lasting for a specific number of years. Instead it is much more common for final assessments, to be limited by the maximum possible period so that they end only on the claimant's death. These final assessments "for life" can be made because there is no upper age limit for the receipt of disablement benefit. As discussed at p. 229, a forecast by a medical authority that the disablement will last for life can be challenged by evidence that the loss of faculty no longer exists. A revised determination may then be made by the statutory authority.

If the medical authority believes the claimant's condition is liable to change it can make a "provisional" assessment for a limited period only. SSA sched. 8 para. 4(1) gives this power:

"Provided that if on any assessment the condition of the claimant is not such, having regard to the possibility of changes therein (whether predictable or not), as to allow of a final assessment being made up to the end of the said period –
(a) a provisional assessment shall be made, taking into account such shorter period only as seems reasonable having regard to his condition and that possibility: and
(b) on the next assessment the period to be taken into account shall begin with the end of the period taken into account by the provisional assessment."

By SSA s. 108(4) the claimant must be re-examined before the period taken into account by the provisional assessment comes to an end. There should be no need for the claimant to apply for this examination. This contrasts with the end of a period of final assessment when the claimant must apply if he wants the period to be extended and a further assessment to be made. Claimants who were awarded gratuities for a short period were often unaware of the possibility that, if the disability continued, there was further entitlement to benefit at the end of the final assessment period.

In the early years of the scheme the medical authorities were reluctant to state on first examination that the assessment was final because they wanted to give the claimant every encouragement to undergo treatment to improve the condition. However the proportion of provisional awards has become less: whereas in 1951 80 per cent of awards were provisional, this had fallen 10 years later to 50 per cent, and in 1983 to 20 per cent. These figures also reflect the build up of life awards which by their nature are likely to continue longer than provisional assessments. More than half of all current pensions have been paid for at least the last 15 years (appendix A, table 3).

In 1983 there were 38,000 provisional awards out of a total of 186,000 pensions in payment (appendix A, table 1). Most of these related to prescribed diseases, with only 7 per cent of pensions for accidents being provisional. Occupational deafness accounted for 3,000 of the provisional awards, largely because PD reg. 29 requires that intital assessments for loss of hearing be provisional. Half of all provisional assessments were for pneumoconiosis, a disease where prognosis is especially difficult and where there is a need for claimants to be regularly re-examined. Apart from those for pneumoconiosis almost all current pensions first assessed before 1973 are now final awards for life (appendix A, table 2). Indeed of those pensions which are final almost all of them are made for life.

Most disablement pensions are awarded for injuries which are not permanent. Between 1970-1975 as many as 60 per cent were no longer in payment only 18 months after first being monitored.

Pearson Commission Vol. 2, table 7

Years since award	½	1½	2½	3½	4½	5
Percentage of pensions continuing	71	39	32	29	28	28

CHAPTER 6

DISABLEMENT BENEFIT AND ITS SUPPLEMENTS

1. INTRODUCTION

Following the SSA 1986 there are to be only two benefits provided by the industrial scheme. Disablement pension accounts for 60 per cent of the total expenditure and reduced earnings allowance for the remainder. The former is considered here, whilst the latter is dealt with by the next chapter.

A disablement pension is awarded for the physical or mental disability suffered as a result of a work injury. It is based upon a medical assessment of the degree of disablement from the "loss of faculty" as discussed in the last chapter. The claimant is compared "with a person of the same age and sex whose ... condition is normal". The pension can be increased by supplements to take account of factors not considered in the medical assessment. These supplements are listed and their relative importance is indicated in the table at p. 5. Until recently there were five of them, but the SSA 1986 reduced this number to two. Only the allowances for constant attendance and exceptionally severe disablement survive the changes made. The supplements for hospital treatment and unemployability were withdrawn by the Act from a date yet to be stated. However, all four of these allowances, even when taken together, were of limited importance because only about one per cent of disablement pensioners obtained any of them. Nevertheless, for those who did receive them, they could be of considerable value. For example, the two supplements still available can more than double the value of a 100 per cent disablement pension. These remaining supplements, and the reasons for the withdrawal of the others, are considered later in this chapter.

The fifth supplement, the special hardship allowance, was by far the most important. The SSA 1986 renamed it reduced earnings allowance to better reflect its objective. It was also made independent of disablement benefit. Because it is no longer a supplement, and due to its complexity and importance, this benefit is considered separately in the next chapter.

The final section of this chapter deals with industrial death benefit, being the provision made by the scheme for widows whose husbands had died as a result of a work injury. The benefit was quite separate from disablement pension and its supplements. It was also withdrawn by SSA 1986 from a date not yet stated. It is noted here not only because it completes the picture of the industrial benefits which were available until the 1986 Act, but also because entitlement to it may continue to affect benefit in certain cases.

2. DISABLEMENT PENSION

This is the main benefit provided by the industrial scheme as indicated by the table at p. 5. There are about 10,000 new pensions awarded each year. Pensions accumulate within the scheme so that in September 1983 there were 186,000 in payment (appendix A, tables 2 and 8). The benefit is awarded to compensate for the effects of work injury upon mind or body, irrespective of whether the claimant is capable of working or whether earnings are reduced. Entitlement is founded upon SSA s. 57(1):

> ". . . an employed earner shall be entitled to disablement benefit if he suffers as a result of the relevant accident from loss of physical or mental faculty such that the assessed extent of resulting disablement amounts to not less than 14 per cent."

The 14 per cent threshold was substituted for 1 per cent as from 1 October 1986 by the SSA 1986, although there is entitlement to a pension no matter what the degree of disablement from pneumoconiosis, byssinosis or diffuse mesothelioma. The previous chapter has considered what amounts to a "loss of faculty" and how disablement is assessed. Earlier chapters dealt with the meaning of "employed earner" and which accidents or diseases are relevant to the scheme.

The loss of faculty does not have to be permanent but it must last for some time because entitlement does not arise until 15 weeks have passed since the accident or onset of the disease. This threshold is imposed by SSA s. 57(4):

> "Disablement benefit shall not be available to a person until after the expiry of the period of ninety days (disregarding Sundays) beginning with the day of the relevant accident."

Claims should be made no later than six months after the accident or onset of the disease otherwise benefit may be lost as explained at p. 205. The pension can continue to be paid for as long as the loss of faculty lasts, and this may be for the claimant's lifetime; it can continue through incapacity, unemployment and retirement. Although in practice most pensions last for only a year (see table at p. 156), half of those currently being paid began at least 15 years ago.

Because of the changes made by the SSA 1986, payment of all benefits under the industrial injuries scheme must take the form of a pension. The provision whereby a lump sum could be awarded for assessments below 20 per cent was abolished. The rates of payment for the pension are examined in chapter 10, and can range from under £10 to over £60 a week depending upon the percentage of the claimant's disablement. All payments are free of tax. There may also be benefits, such as those for sickness, invalidity, unemployment or retirement. As chapter 11 explains, these are usually paid in full on top of the pension. For those very seriously injured the pension itself may be increased by the supplements considered next.

3. Supplements for Constant Attendance and Severe Disablement

(1) Constant Attendance Allowance

(a) Objective

An assessment of 100 per cent disablement is not intended to represent total disablement. It can be attained, for example, if both hands are lost or if the claimant is made completely deaf. The maximum assessment thus covers a wide range of severe disablement from total helplessness to disablement which, though severe, does not prevent the claimant from carrying out a full-time job. This lack of differentiation between severe disablements is deliberate because in the more serious of the 100 per cent cases constant attendance allowance and exceptionally severe disablement allowance are also available. They can more than double the maximum value of the disablement pension. The number of recipients for the different rates of constant attendance allowance is given at p. 5. In 1983 of the 3,660 people assessed at 100 per cent disabled, 2,170 received this allowance.

(b) Entitlement

Entitlement arises under SSA s. 61(1):

> "Where a disablement pension is payable in respect of an assessment of 100 per cent, then, if as a result of the relevant loss of faculty the beneficiary requires constant attendance, the weekly rate of pension shall be increased by an amount determined in accordance with regulations by reference to the extent and nature of the attendance required by the beneficiary."

In establishing whether the claimant is 100 per cent disabled Benefit reg. 20 allows account to be taken of any disablement which has given rise to a war pension or an earlier industrial injury payment. The regulations prescribe four different rates for the allowance and two of these may be further increased by the addition of exceptionally severe disablement allowance. The rates are given in at p. 250. They depend upon the extent of both the disablement and the need for attendance, and vary according to whether full or part-time attendance is required. A minimum condition is laid down by Benefit reg. 19 which requires that for entitlement to the lowest rate the claimant must be

> "to a substantial extent dependent on [constant] attendance for the necessities of life and is likely to remain so dependent for a prolonged period."

Neither these words nor the other conditions of payment of the various rates have received interpretation from any Commissioners or courts. This is because questions on the allowance were not decided by the usual statutory authorities but by the DHSS on behalf of the Secretary of State. (This has now been changed, as discussed at p. 237.) The cases were not reported and there was no effective right of appeal. Although in deciding them the DHSS used internal guidelines, these were not released to the public. Despite this, some of the factors previously considered relevant are revealed in appendix 3 of the DHSS medical handbook:

"The phrase 'the ordinary necessities of life' is interpreted liberally. It clearly includes eating, drinking and natural functions, but in addition an applicant can expect to have a reasonable degree of physical and mental comfort. The nature of the disability itself may create special needs for help, e.g. frequent feeding, attention for bed-sores, incontinence, vomiting, insomnia. The allowance is not granted however in respect of help in housework or other purely domestic purposes, or for only slight intermittent attendance such as help in dressing or undressing."

The medical handbook also suggests that "a prolonged period" is one that lasts for at least six months. The words of the regulation do not seem to require that the claimant should actually receive attendance, but only that the claimant be dependent upon it. Although the provision of attendance is some evidence of the need for it, severely disabled claimants should not be refused only because they live on their own. Nor will the fact that the attendance is provided by a spouse or other relative prejudice a claim, for the attendance need not come from outside. Those entitled to the attendance also qualify for a pensioner's Christmas bonus under SSA 1986 s. 63 and sched. 6.

(c) Reform

When the allowance was introduced in 1948 there was no equivalent in the main social security scheme. However, since 1971 a similar allowance has been available to the public at large irrespective of the cause of disability. This main scheme provision has different conditions of entitlement and usually provides benefit at a much lower rate. However, there are almost 200 times as many recipients, with over 415,000 allowances being in payment in 1983.

The Pearson Commission was not in favour of these separate arrangements in industrial and non-industrial cases:

"We felt that, at these extremes of disablement, cause is less important than effect, and that on grounds of both principle and administrative expediency the two types of attendance allowance should be rationalised."

The White Paper accepted this view and proposed to abolish entitlement under the industrial scheme, leaving injured workers to rely upon the attendance allowance paid irrespective of cause under the main scheme. Those receiving the part-time and normal maximum rates would receive the lower rate of attendance allowance under the main scheme, whilst those obtaining the intermediate and exceptional rates would receive the higher rate.

In its Consultation Paper of 1985 the Government continued to think that the White Paper provided a sensible rationalization of the two different schemes. Others, including the IIAC and TUC, were opposed to the levelling down of benefit for the seriously disabled. Because of this opposition the Government changed its view and decided not to proceed with the proposal in the White Paper. However, the Minister for Social Security stated that the need for the two separate benefits and ways of bringing them together would continue to be examined closely. The SSA 1986 makes it easier for changes to be made. It gives the Secretary of State the power to make regulations to modify, or even abolish, constant attendance allowance by making SSA s. 35 — relating to the main scheme's attendance allowance — effective in its place. However, in the debate on the Bill the Minister stated that the Government, at that time, had no prepared plan, nor had made any decision as to how the new power might be used.[1]

(2) Exceptionally Severe Disablement Allowance

(a) Objective

This allowance is the only one to be added to the industrial scheme since 1948. It was introduced in 1966 following the recommendation of the McCorquodale committee on the Assessment of Disablement (1965; Cmnd 2847). The committee considered that constant attendance allowance did not provide "a wholly adequate recognition of disablement which is extremely severe even within the class of 100 per cent pensioners". Rather than modify the scale of assessment the committee favoured the introduction of a new flat-rate supplement to disablement pension. In 1983 there were 710 beneficiaries, being a third of all those receiving constant attendance allowance. As indicated in the table at p. 5, of those receiving the higher rate of constant attendance allowance, over 90 per cent obtained the supplement for exceptionally severe disablement. It is paid at the same weekly rate as a the normal (not the exceptional) maximum for constant attendance allowance. For the year beginning 6 April 1987 this is £25.80.

(b) Entitlement

Entitlement arises under SSA s. 63(1) which requires that a disablement pension be payable and that two other conditions be satisfied. These are that the claimant

> "(a) ... is or, but for having received medical or other treatment as an in-patient at a hospital or similar institution, would be entitled to an increase of the weekly rate of pension ..." [for constant attendance allowance exceeding the amount of the lower rate].

Thus the claimant must be exceptionally severely disabled and entitled to the higher or intermediate rates of benefit. These are paid to around 40 per cent of those receiving constant attendance allowance. Although a stay in hospital may bring constant attendance allowance to an end, s. 63(1) allows the supplement for exceptionally severe disablement to continue. The supplement is especially valuable in that it is not considered to overlap with other benefits and is not offset against them.

The second condition of entitlement laid down by s. 63 is that with regard to the claimant,

> "(b) his need for constant attendance of an extent and nature qualifying him for such an increase ... is likely to be permanent."

There are no cases which have been reported so as to help interpret these conditions for, as discussed in relation to constant attendance allowance, decisions on entitlement were made by the DHSS on behalf of the Secretary of State and there was no effective right of appeal.

[1]   H. C. Deb., Standing Committee B, col. 1828, 29 April 1986.

(c) Reform

The Pearson Commission recommended that the allowance should eventually be abolished together with that for constant attendance, and that industrial injury victims should be left to rely upon the residual provision for attendance in the main national insurance scheme. This recommendation was based upon the argument, only occasionally adopted by the Commission, that at the extremes of disablement there should be no distinction in benefits based upon the cause of disability.

Although the 1981 White Paper followed this aim by proposing to abolish constant attendance allowance, it sought to retain exceptionally severe disablement allowance. This was because

> "the government consider that there is a continuing case for such a special allowance as an extra provision for a small number of beneficiaries who are the worst affected by their industrial injury."

Because of the proposal to abolish constant attendance allowance, the qualification for receiving the supplement was to be that the claimant was entitled to receive the higher rate of attendance allowance under the main scheme, and that such need was likely to be permanent. However, the Government are no longer committed to withdrawing constant attendance allowance, although it may soon be modified by regulations. The future of the allowance for severe disablement will obviously be closely related to any such change, but is has not been directly discussed since the White Paper.

4. BENEFITS WITHDRAWN BY THE SOCIAL SECURITY ACT 1986

(1) Unemployability supplement

The purpose of this supplement to a disablement pension was to provide benefit for the few industrial injury victims who lacked sufficient national insurance contributions to qualify for sickness or invalidity benefit. Entitlement lay under SSA s. 58 and only arose if the claimant was incapable of work and likely to remain so permanently. The supplement could not be paid together with any allowance for reduced earnings, but it could be increased in the same way as an invalidity pension to take account of dependants. The reason for the supplement was removed in 1982 by SSHBA s. 39 which amended SSA s. 50A by waiving the contribution requirements so as to give industrial injury victims automatic entitlement to national insurance benefits for incapacity for work.

This supplement was withdrawn subject to two exceptions. It can still be obtained firstly, by about 300 people receiving it before para. 4 of sched. 3 of SSA 1986 (which withdrew it) came into force; and secondly, by para. 16 of that schedule, by those whose disablement arises because of an injury before 1948 and who may not be entitled to national insurance benefits.

(2) Hospital treatment allowance

This supplement is also withdrawn from a date yet to be stated. It had the objective of encouraging workers to obtain in-patient treatment for their industrial injury by providing increased benefit at a time when wages might be lost. During their stay in hospital SSA s. 62 raised the value of their pension, or gratuity, to that for a 100 per cent pension. In practice this cost only £200,000 a year, for the stay in hospital was usually brief. However, this did not allow the supplement to escape criticism. It was said to be no longer necessary because, since its introduction in 1948, there had been an improvement in other benefits which could be paid during in-patient treatment. Thus, there had been an increase in the value of benefits for sickness, and of the coverage of occupational schemes. Further, the social security system normally requires benefit to be reduced if the claimant goes into hospital. Because the allowance was the only benefit to be increased in such circumstances it could be regarded as an anachronism. The Minister of Social Security introducing its withdrawal therefore described it as having an "antique flavour".

An incidental benefit of the allowance was to save administrative cost by making some applications for review unnecessary. Because of the automatic increase in benefit an AMA was not required to consider a review on the ground of unforeseen aggravation if the claimant's condition deteriorated such as to require in-patient treatment. However, the saving on costs was limited because if the claimant's condition remained poor after leaving hospital a review was still required. The DHSS Discussion Document suggested that, on the withdrawal of the allowance, it might be necessary to curb the right to review by not taking into account any short period spent in hospital during which the condition deteriorated. Regulations to this effect have not been made.

(3) Industrial death benefit

Until the SSA 1986 if a man died as a result of a work accident or disease his widow could claim industrial death benefit. However, subject to safeguarding existing rights, the Act withdraws this benefit from a date yet to be stated. Industrial widows are to be treated no differently from others. All must rely upon the provision made for them by the main national insurance scheme. This includes a £1,000 tax-free lump sum on bereavement, and a weekly pension if there are dependant children or if widowhood takes place over the age of 45. Death benefit has been withdrawn largely in order to save the costs of administration for these have been out of all proportion to the small extra payment the scheme usually offered. However, the Act also removed anomalies even though it meant the end of certain substantial payments. For example, it abolished both the award of a lump sum to an industrial widow on her remarriage (about 100 widows a year received a sum of up to £2,000), and the award of a pension to a childless widow under the age of 40 (there were between 200 and 300 new widows a year who received a weekly pension of £11.49.). Such provision was considered contrary to the spirit of Beveridge and finds no parallel in the main scheme.

Overall this withdrawal of special payment in the case of an industrial death amounts to only a minor cut in benefit. It was of little practical importance in spite of the fact that there were about 30,000 widow's benefit pensions in payment each year, and expenditure in cases of death comprised one seventh of that for the whole industrial scheme. The value of death benefit to beneficiaries was much less than these figures make it appear for two reasons: firstly, unlike other industrial injuries benefit, death benefit was subject to tax; and secondly, it had a counterpart — widow's pension — under the main national insurance scheme. This greatly reduced its real value because even if there were no special provision for an industrial death, widows would still be entitled under the main scheme for up to 90 per cent of the monies distributed as industrial death benefit. The main scheme paid benefit at almost the same rate, its widow's pension was only 55 pence, or 2 per cent, less than that of the industrial scheme. The White Paper therefore estimated the amount of preference given by the industrial scheme in the event of death as only £3 million a year. This contrasted sharply with the £410 million spent in 1985-86 on disablement benefit and REA. These benefits have no main scheme equivalent and are entirely preference.

In safeguarding existing rights SSA 1986 sched. 3 continues to make it important to benefit that death has been caused by work in the following two cases:

(a) By para. 9 widows entitled to industrial death benefit before its withdrawal are able to claim entitlement, in appropriate cases, to widow's allowance, widowed mother's allowance, widow's pension or retirement pension. This means, for example that widows younger than 45 may gain entitlement under the main scheme whereas they will not do so if they are not entitled to industrial death benefit before the Act comes into force. Paras. 11 and 12 similarly make provision for those who are not widows but who were entitled to industrial death benefit before its withdrawal. Thus the Secretary of State is given power to make regulations to provide for the payment of prescribed amounts in prescribed circumstances to those dependent relatives formerly entitled to a pension (in practice amounting to less than £1 a week) or a gratuity (which could not have exceeded £78).

(b) By para. 10 the contribution conditions for a widow's entitlement to benefit under the main scheme are to be taken as satisfied if it can be shown that her husband died as a result of an industrial accident or disease. This provision is required because industrial death benefit was non-contributory whereas this is not the case with benefits under the main scheme. This protection given to the few widows who, because of insufficient contributions, would not otherwise be able to claim provides the only case where it continues to be relevant to benefit that a death, occurring after the relevant part of SSA 1986 comes into force, has been caused by work.

CHAPTER 7

REDUCED EARNINGS ALLOWANCE

1. INTRODUCTION

(1) Outline of entitlement and organization of chapter

Reduced earnings allowance, formerly known as special hardship allowance, compensates for loss of earning capacity. Entitlement arises where the claimant's injury makes him incapable of following not only his regular occupation, but also any other suitable employment which offers equivalent pay. For example, if a coal face worker suffers an accident which forces him to accept lighter work above ground he may suffer a reduction in gross earnings. It is upon this difference in remuneration that entitlement is founded, although the allowance is subject to a maximum which, in practice, prevents 90 per cent of recipients from recovering all of their lost wages. The basic conditions for an award are laid down by SSA s. 59A(1):

> ". . . an employed earner shall be entitled to reduced earnings allowance if –
> (a) he is entitled to a disablement pension or would be so entitled if that pension were payable where disablement is assessed at not less than 1 per cent;
> (b) as a result of the relevant loss of faculty, he is either –
>   (i) incapable, and likely to remain permanently incapable, of following his regular occupation; and
>   (ii) incapable of following employment of an equivalent standard which is suitable in his case,
>   or is, and has at all times since the end of the period of 90 days [after the accident or onset of the disease], been incapable of following that occupation or any such employment."

The award was made independent of entitlement to a disablement pension by SSA 1986. This means that it can still be paid even where a pension is refused because disablement is assessed below 14 per cent. (However, para. (a) requires that even in such a case REA can only be paid if there is an assessment of at least 1 per cent.) Although in all other respects entitlement to a disablement pension is a condition for obtaining REA, this one difference from disablement benefit is of crucial importance. This is because many awards of REA follow low assessments, half of the pensions awarded in 1983 being in respect of disablement assessed below 20 per cent (appendix A, table 7).

Most of this chapter is devoted to an examination of the further conditions of entitlement established by para. (b) of the above s. 59A(1). Firstly, when will a claimant be held "incapable" of the relevant jobs? This involves investigation of the requirement that the claimant must either show that for the future he is permanently incapable, or show that, for the past, he has been continuously incapable since the end of the 15 week waiting period for benefit after his injury. Secondly, causation is examined. The loss of earning capacity must be the result of "the relevant loss of faculty", that is, the product of an industrial accident or disease. Thirdly, the "regular occupation" is considered. This can be difficult to establish if the claimant did more than one job, or changed jobs, or argues that overtime ought to be included as part of the work he once did. The final two headings dealing with entitlement consider what is meant by "equivalent" and "suitable" employment. They answer important questions, such as how to calculate the "standard" of remuneration for each job, and whether a claimant can be expected to move to another part of the country to find comparable work.

Following this long section on entitlement the chapter concludes by examining two other matters. The first of these is how the amount of the allowance is calculated and for how long it may be paid. In particular, this involves considering what is the effect of the ceiling upon the award, for at its maximum, it may not exceed 40 per cent of a disablement pension. The rate of the allowance may also be frozen on retirement. The final section considers the reforms made by the SSA 1986 and the plans for the future of the allowance.

The difficulties of interpreting and applying the legislation dealing with REA have made it one of the most criticized features of the industrial scheme. The DHSS stated in its memorandum to the Pearson Commission:

> "The administrative problems involved, the burden on the employers and the Department's staff, the complex case law which has developed all make this a comparatively costly benefit to administer, bearing in mind that in many cases the finely sifted results achieved could, even if compensation were in full, only bear a tenuous and sometimes hypothetical relationship to what would have happened but for the industrial disablement."

Although several important reforms have been made since this statement was made, REA continues to constitute one of the most complex areas of social security law.

(2) Aim of the allowance

A disablement pension is awarded for loss of faculty without regard to the effect of the injury upon earning capacity. As such it makes insufficient provision for workers whose pocket is more affected than their person. To take an extreme example, a worker may suffer a minor injury, but it may force him to give up his job. He may have to accept lower paid work or, perhaps, none at all. There is then a disproportionate loss of earnings compared to the extent of the loss of faculty. The example that used to be given of this was where a compositor lost an index finger, making him unable to continue in his occupation. The intention behind the 1946 legislation which set up the industrial injuries scheme was to make available a special allowance for such a loss. In a side-heading to the Act the allowance was described as payable "in case of special hardship", revealing that the original aim was to compensate only where there was a disproportionate loss of income. "Special hardship" continued to be used to identify the allowance until it was renamed by the SSA 1986. However, the old name was quite inappropriate because the original intention was soon forgotten, and the wording of the Act always made the allowance available for any loss of pre-accident earning capacity, no matter how small. It is not and never has been necessary for any disproportionate or special loss to be suffered. In fact there need be no financial loss at all, because the compensation is paid for loss of earning capacity, not actual monetary loss. This means that a claimant may be entitled to the allowance even if his actual losses are made good, for example, by other social security benefits.

(3) Importance to the industrial scheme

The allowance is anything but the minor feature of the scheme that some people originally envisaged that it would be. It accounts for 40 per cent of the total expenditure. In 1983 there were 145,000 recipients of the allowance. Over half of them had suffered lesser disablement and were receiving REA following assessments of less than 20 per cent disablement. For most beneficiaries the allowance represents the major part of their income from the industrial scheme. Although it fully replaces the gross loss of earnings in only about 20 per cent of cases, this figure rises if the actual loss suffered by the claimant is considered. This is because firstly, the allowance itself is not taxable, and secondly, it is based upon the difference in gross earnings without deduction for tax and national insurance contributions. Its value is also increased by the fact that it may be paid for many years; it can last through incapacity for work, through unemployment and into retirement.

2. INCAPACITY

(1) What constitutes incapacity

As defined in *CI 99/49:*

> "A person is incapable of work if, having regard to his age, education, state of health and other personal factors, there is no work or type of work which he can reasonably be expected to do."

The burden is upon the claimant to show that he is unable to do what his regular occupation normally requires. It is not enough for the claimant to rely only upon, for example, his registration as a disabled person as in *R 2/62(II)*. Instead, evidence of the kind produced in *R(I) 39/55* is required. The claim succeeded in that case because a joiner, who had suffered an injury to his back, could show that he was only able to work indoors and could not undertake the heavier outdoor tasks which his job normally required.

In determining incapacity several reports could be relevant. The first of these involves the medical evidence upon which much usually depends. The claimant may rely upon his own doctor's report, but the AO may employ the services of the medical authorities. They may offer advice as to the extent of the claimant's abilities. However, their report is more open to challenge here than it is, for example, in relation to whether a prescribed disease can be diagnosed. It can be attacked if it conflicts with the report given when the claimant was assessed for a disablement pension. However, it is more likely to be unreliable for the following reason acknowledged by the DHSS in its evidence to the Pearson Commission:

> "It cannot be expected that doctors will be in a position to exercise the same level of expertise when they come to consider the secondary question regarding the effect the disablement may have had on the individual claimant having regard to the particular nature of his work. Much will depend on the extent to which doctors are seized of the precise nature of all the tasks involved in the occupation concerned."

The AO may therefore seek another report, this time from the employer. This will deal with the nature of the claimant's job and the physical effort needed to perform it. However, at times these reports also may prove inaccurate. If, for example, the report is prepared by the employer's administrative staff, they may not appreciate the true nature of the job involved. The claimant himself may wish to guard against any under-estimation of the task by introducing evidence from colleagues who have had direct experience of the work. Finally, the AO may seek other reports, such as those from a disablement resettlement officer, as to the work which the claimant could do.

It may be easier to establish incapacity if the claimant does not go back to his previous job. If he does return it is strong evidence that he is capable of the work involved. However, this evidence can be rebutted, especially if the return is only for a short period. His claim can still succeed if he can show his ability to perform his regular occupation, or its equivalent, has been substantially impaired even though he briefly returned to it. This test is most obviously satisfied if the claimant, by continuing his work, endangers himself or others as in *R(I) 15/74*. But it is uncertain which other less extensive forms of impairment justify a finding of incapacity. Commissioners have used differing criteria in assessing where the line is to be drawn. Some have asked how many duties of the regular occupation can the claimant now perform, while others have inquired what hours can be worked, or how much money can now be earned. Thus in *R(I) 13/56* the claimant could still perform 86 per cent of her normal duties and was held not incapable, but in *CI 444/50*(T) and *R(I) 6/66* the claimants were only capable of working less than 70 per cent of their previous hours and this entitled them to REA. Although inability to work normal overtime did not constitute incapacity in *CI 443/50*(T), the claims succeeded in *R(I) 10/65* and *R 8/84(II)*. This was because the overtime involved heavier work, different from that done during normal hours and, as held in *R(I) 43/52*, if an occupation can be divided into two parts the claimant must be able to perform both in order to be found capable of it. This contrasts with *R(I) 10/59* where the fact that the claimant could not perform a particular skill of his occupation did not make him incapable. This was because there remained a wide range of work he could still do. The DHSS expressed its views on incapacity and overtime in a note on REA which it submitted to the Pearson Commission. The allowance may be paid if the claimant's inability relates to overtime which is part of the job in that the employer would not normally employ anyone who could not do it; but if the overtime is entirely voluntary the claimant's inability will be disregarded in assessing his capacity.

For piece-workers the test of incapacity is whether the claimant is capable of attaining his former standard of remuneration. In *R(I) 4/77* a one-sixth reduction in earnings following the accident was sufficient to gain entitlement, and this was similarly achieved in *R 6/82(II)*. The earlier cases of *CI 445/50*(T), *CI 447/50* and *CI 448/50* were not considered. These held that the allowance was not payable if the claimant was still able to fulfil the employer's requirements for the job, although he worked more slowly and lost earnings as a result.

Even if a claimant not only returns to his old job for a time, but also works the same hours and receives the same wages as before, he may still not lose entitlement if he later finds that he is unable to continue with the work. He may be found incapable of his regular occupation throughout the period he has in fact worked at it. It depends upon what he can do, not upon the name of the job he purports to perform. All the circumstances must be examined for, as recognised in *R(I) 29/52*(T), the claimant may be "a mere passenger who is only nominally at work and who is carried along by the charity of his workmates or is paid the wages he receives by the charity of his employer". Because of this REA was payable in *R(I) 39/52* and *R(I) 26/53* where workmates helped, and in *CI 445/50*(T) where the sympathetic employer had allowed the claimant to return to his old job. In *R(I) 5/58* the claimant succeeded after showing that he could only keep up by paying other to do his share of the work. SSA s. 59A(5) and Benefit reg. 17 make specific provision for treating a claimant as incapable of following an occupation despite his working at it. This is considered in relation to the continuing condition under the next heading.

(2) The incapacity must be either permanent or continuous

The claimant must show that for the period of the claim he is incapable of following both his regular occupation and any suitable employment of an equivalent standard. In addition he must satisfy one of the two conditions laid down by s. 59A(1): either first, with regard to his regular occupation only, that in the future he is likely to remain permanently incapable of following it (the permanent condition); or second, with regard to both his regular occupation and employment of an equivalent standard, that in the past he has been incapable ever since the end of the 15 week waiting period for benefit after the accident or onset of the prescribed disease (the continuous condition). An illustration of how these conditions operate is where the claimant suffers only odd weeks of incapacity for his regular occupation. He will then be refused REA because he has neither been continuously incapable, nor is he likely to remain permanently incapable of doing his work.

(a) The permanent condition

It is easier to satisfy this condition, which is described above, if the claimant's disablement is assessed as lasting for life. However, if there is only a provisional assessment and not one for life, this can still be consistent with a finding that the claimant is likely to be permanently unfit for his regular occupation. This happened in *R(I) 33/59* and the point is further emphasized in the DHSS medical handbook. The permanent condition is therefore less onerous than it first may appear.

The claimant cannot show that he is permanently incapable only because he has suffered a permanent loss of faculty; it is the ability to do the job which counts. In assessing this, account can be taken of the prospect of any improvement in the claimant's condition. If there are such hopes, it may be that the claimant will again become capable of performing his job despite the permanent loss of faculty. On this basis REA was refused in *R(I) 86/52*. The hope of improvement is the reason why doctors are often reluctant to certify that the permanent condition is satisfied. The argument was taken further in *R(I) 7/53*, where it was accepted that account should be taken of the possibility of a medical operation improving the claimant's condition. However, this was ignored in *4/59(II)* because the claimant was considered reasonable in his refusal to undergo such treatment. In *R 2/61(II)* the claim also succeeded because the operation failed to bring any hope of improvement in the condition.

To satisfy the permanent condition the ability to perform only the regular occupation need be considered. As far as equivalent employment is concerned, the claimant does not have to show that he has been, or will be, incapable for any period before or after that of the claim. This means that it does not matter that he could have worked at equivalent employment shortly after his accident and before the present claim. Such an ability would usually prevent him from satisfying the continuous condition, but the permanent condition enables a claim to succeed. This means that the permanent condition is of particular importance in the two circumstances noted in *R(I) 5/69*: firstly, where the condition of the claimant who was capable after the accident becomes worse, so that he cannot now do the job; and secondly, where the equivalent employment which he could do after the accident now no longer exists, or its wage rates have changed so that it is not now of the same standard as the regular occupation.

(b) The continuous condition

Claimants have found difficulty in satisfying the permanent condition because doctors have been reluctant to certify permanent incapacity unless they have been quite sure that there is not going to be a sufficient improvement in the condition for the claimant to resume work. In 1948 this difficulty prompted the introduction of the continuous condition as an alternative method of establishing entitlement. It is easier to assess whether this condition will be satisfied for, unlike the permanent condition, it does not involve any estimate of the claimant's future. Instead it relies upon an assessment of the past and present ability to work. It must be shown with regard to both the regular occupation and employment of an equivalent standard that the claimant has been incapable ever since the end of the 15 week waiting period following the accident or onset of the disease. The condition is likely to be more easily satisfied if the claimant has been unable to return to any work or has accepted a lower paid job, and he has continued to receive a disablement pension for his injury.

However, if there is a gap in a period of assessment during which the claimant does not receive a disablement pension, the claimant may fail to satisfy the continuous condition, with the result that any later claim for REA fails. This happened in *R(I) 29/58* and *R(I) 33/59* where there was a gap between the end of a fixed period of assessment and the time when the claimant was able to re-establish title to benefit by showing there had been an aggravation of his condition. However, claimants may take advantage of an important qualification to this rule which was applied in *R(I) 9/66*: if the gap is the result only of the rule that the medical authorities cannot backdate an assessment for more than three months, the continuous condition can still be satisfied and entitlement to REA established.

Periods of work disregarded

Even if a claimant returns to his regular occupation it may still be possible for him to satisfy the continuous condition if he later withdraws from the work finding that he cannot cope. This is because the claimant may be found to have become incapable of the requirements of the job and to have been kept on only because of the charity of his workmates, or employer, as discussed at p. 169. There is a similar rule applied in the case of a claimant who has followed an equivalent employment only for an exceptional period as discussed at p. 185. In addition, statute protects the right to REA in three circumstances. These are, firstly, where the claimant works for a trial period to see if he has recovered; secondly, when he works for rehabilitation purposes; and, finally, where he works before obtaining surgical treatment. Benefit reg. 17 made under SSA s. 59A(5) provides this encouragement to return to work. It states that, in determining the continuous condition, it will be disregarded in certain circumstances that the claimant has worked in his regular occupation, or in a suitable employment of an equivalent standard, since the end of the 15 week period after the accident. (That period is from when entitlement to industrial injuries benefit could first be claimed.) There are two such sets of circumstances, each having differing periods for which work may be disregarded:

> "(a) for the purpose of rehabilitation or training or of ascertaining whether he had recovered from the effects of the relevant injury."

The period to be disregarded is that

> "(i) . . . during which he worked thereat for any of the said purposes with the approval of the Secretary of State or on the advice of a medical practitioner, and
> (ii) . . . during which he worked thereat for any of the said purposes and which did not exceed six months in the aggregate. . . ."

The "advice of a medical practitioner" has been broadly interpreted in favour of claimants here, in contrast to (b) below. It is not necessary for a doctor specifically to direct the claimant to return to work and refer to the purposes mentioned in the statute. Instead it is sufficient if the doctor only has such purposes in mind. It has been implied that a doctor must have been thinking of these purposes when allowing the claimant to return to work in *R(I) 69/53* and *R(I) 97/53*. However, in *R(I) 35/58* it was suggested that being under the general care of a doctor may not be enough to establish the necessary advice to return.

A narrow view of the regulation was taken in *CI 254/50* where "rehabilitation" was confined to restoring the claimant to his previous condition; it did not include an attempt to prevent the injury from becoming worse pending an operation. After the case para. (b) below was introduced to cover the claimant in such circumstances. An interpretation of para. (*a*) which was favourable to claimants was taken in *R(I) 13/61* and *R(I) 1/69*. It was decided that a trial period for ascertaining whether recovery had taken place covered the circumstance where the claimant did not return specifically to discover whether he had recovered from his injury as such (for his doctor may know that he had not), but only to find out how he got on from the point of view of his ability to work. It was held in *R(I) 5/66* that if a period of work is to be disregarded, the qualifying purpose for which that work is done must continue throughout the period in question. This means that if the claimant is no longer on trial the continuous condition is not satisfied.

> "(*b*) before obtaining surgical treatment for the effects of the said injury."

The period to be disregarded is that

> "(i) . . . during which he worked thereat and throughout which it is shown that having obtained the advice of a medical practitioner to submit himself to such surgical treatment he was waiting to undergo the said treatment in accordance therewith, and
> (ii) any other period during which he worked thereat and throughout which it is shown that he was in the process of obtaining such advice."

R(I) 81/53 requires the advice in (*b*)(i), in contrast to (*a*), to be that a doctor should give "a definite opinion that surgical treatment should be carried out as soon as this could conveniently be arranged, and a claimant should have accepted that advice and should intend to give up work and undergo the treatment as soon as the arrangements have been made". In *R(I) 35/57* this was also taken to imply that the claimant "should use reasonable zeal and expedition in trying to secure surgical treatment", so that where over four years had elapsed since the advice, extremely strong and clear evidence was required to show that the claimant satisfied the condition. On the facts of the case the allowance was refused because the claimant had put aside the question of treatment and was content to go on working for as long as he could.

By contrast the period in (ii) was interpreted more in favour of claimants in *R(I) 13/56*. A period of three months during which the claimant received out-patient hospital treatment was discounted, even though the advice to have manipulative treatment was not given until the end of that period. ("Surgical treatment" was given a broad meaning here. It included manipulation and thus was not confined merely to the use of the knife.) However, in *R 9/83(II)*, although the claimant consulted his doctor at the time of the accident, surgical treatment was not considered until a year later. This prevented the claimant from relying upon both (*b*) (i) and (ii) because he failed to show that "throughout" the relevant period he was waiting for the treatment or was in the process of obtaining the relevant advice.

(3) Special provision for pneumoconiosis

The legislation makes special provision in the case of pneumoconiosis to decide whether a claimant is incapable and whether the permanent and continuous conditions have been satisfied. Cases interpreting this legislation have also helped to define the regular occupation and suitable alternative employment for these purposes. The relevant regulation, PD reg. 23, was recognized in *R(I) 35/60* as fulfilling two purposes, each being discussed here in turn. These purposes are

> "First . . . instead of the claimant having to prove that he is incapable, the insurance officer is required to prove that the claimant is capable. Secondly, if he decides to continue in his regular occupation but eventually gives it up he is to be in no worse a position than if he had given up immediately on receiving notice."

The first purpose is achieved by reg. 23(*a*) which sets up the following rebuttable presumption:

> "Where a beneficiary in receipt of a disablement pension in respect of pneumoconiosis receives advice from a special medical board that in consequence of the disease he should not follow his regular occupation unless he complies with certain special restrictions as to the place, duration or circumstances of his work, or otherwise, then. . .
> (*a*) the beneficiary shall be deemed, unless the contrary is proved by evidence other than the aforesaid advice –
>   (i) to be incapable of following his regular occupation and likely to remain permanently so incapable, and
>   (ii) to be incapable of following employment of an equivalent standard which is suitable in his case;"

A "letter of advice" from a special medical board is issued to everyone diagnosed as suffering from pneumoconiosis except for those claimants who, because of their age or illness, are unlikely ever to work again. The letter may advise the claimant to work in a dust free atmosphere, or that he may continue work in his normal job provided that certain conditions are fulfilled. If, following receipt of this advice, he changes his job reg. 23(a) provides that for the purposes of claiming REA he is deemed to be incapable. However, as is discussed below, this presumption can be rebutted.

The presumption is particularly important to coalminers. About one in five of all miners who are newly diagnosed as suffering from pneumoconiosis and assessed at the minimum level of 10 per cent, are advised that they may continue their normal job provided that it does not involve work in the most dusty conditions. Any time after receiving such a letter a miner may decide, for whatever reason, to move to less onerous and less well paid work. When he claims REA it is then presumed that he moved because he was incapable of his normal occupation. This applies even if he was working in a dust approved area when he received the advice as in *R(I)69/54*.

The presumption can be rebutted by attacking either branch of reg. 23(a), that is, with regard either to (i) the regular occupation or (ii) the employment of an equivalent standard. The attack on the first branch was discussed in *R(I) 35/60* where it was recognized that the presumption "leaves it open to the insurance officer to prove by any evidence (except the 'letter of advice') that the claimant is not incapable of following his regular occupation". This happened in *R(I) 69/54* where it was shown that the claimant was still capable of his regular occupation and the real reason for his change of job was that his former post had been abolished. However, twenty years after that case the DHSS, in its memo to the

Pearson Commission, stated that the presumption will only be challenged if, for example, the claimant faces redundancy, or if he is within two years of retirement, or suffers from some other incapacitating condition.

If the presumption is challenged it becomes necessary to determine the claimant's regular occupation in order to decide whether he is capable of it. This caused a problem in one case where it was argued that the regular occupation could include work in dust approved areas. Although the claimant had received advice to change to such work, the argument would have led to the refusal of REA because there would have been no change in the regular occupation. However, this argument was rejected and the issue decided in the claimant's favour in *R* v *National Insurance Commissioner, ex p. Langley* (1976). It was held that the regular occupation was to be narrowly defined as that of face worker. This excluded work only in dust approved conditions and therefore there had been a change in the regular occupation. However, *Langley's* case is now of little assistance to claimants who move to controlled areas. Their claims can still be defeated by the next argument.

This argument attacks the second branch of reg. 23(a), by showing that the claimant is capable of following suitable employment of an equivalent standard. It was successfully used in *R* v *National Insurance Commissioner, ex p. Steel* (1978) to circumvent *ex p. Langley*. Although the case agreed that the regular occupation did not include work in dust approved conditions, it found that work in such conditions could constitute suitable alternative employment. This meant that the presumption could be defeated and REA refused. In considering whether, on the facts, the alternative employment is in dust approved conditions, it does not have to be shown that dust levels can be guaranteed at all times as below the approved amount. Instead, as held in *R(I) 12/67* and *R(I) 2/76*, it is sufficient that the dust count is within the approved limits on routine dust sampling.

The second part of reg. 23 deals with what period of work maybe disregarded when considering whether the claimant has satisfied the continuous condition. Reg. 23(b) states that

> ". . . where the beneficiary has ceased to follow any occupation to which the aforesaid special restrictions were applicable, the fact that he had followed such an occupation in the period between the date of onset of the disease and the date of the current assessment of his disablement, or for a reasonable period of trial threafter, shall be disregarded."

This regulation prevents it being argued that the claimant is capable of following his regular occupation because of the sole fact that he has done so since the date of onset of his pneumoconiosis. Instead, to defeat a claim, other arguments must be produced to show that the claimant is capable despite his present physical condition. To do this, in theory, reliance can be placed on the claimant following his regular occupation for longer than "a reasonable period of trial". However, it was held in *R(I) 74/54* and affirmed in *R(I) 35/60* that any period of trial, of whatever length, is reasonable in pneumoconiosis cases.

3. THE CAUSE OF INCAPACITY

SSA s. 59A(1) requires the incapacity to arise "as a result of the relevant loss of faculty". This means that it must be caused by the disablement arising from the industrial injury and no benefit will be paid, for example, if the incapacity arises from an illness unconnected with work. Whilst the medical authorities determine what amounts to loss of faculty, it is for the statutory authorities to decide whether this loss is the cause of the incapacity. This distinction in jurisdiction is discussed at p. 229. In making their decision the statutory authorities must apply the general principles of causation as discussed at p. 45. In brief, these require the loss of faculty resulting from the industrial accident or disease to be an effective cause of the claimant's incapacity, although it need not be the only or even the major cause. It is sufficient if it is the "last straw which breaks the loaded camel's back". In addition to these problems of law there are also difficult factual issues to resolve. As the years pass since benefit was first awarded it becomes progressively more difficult to disentangle the claimant's loss of faculty from the other illnesses or conditions from which he may suffer. In examining the caselaw the following discussion illustrates not only the legal principles of causation, but also the difficult factual issues which the statutory authorities are required to resolve.

(1) Cases where claims have failed

If the industrial cause has worn off so that it is no longer an effective cause of incapacity the allowance cannot be paid. This may happen if the claimant has recovered from his industrial injury and his present condition is entirely caused by some other factor. This could be the onset of old age as in *R(I) 55/51*, *R(I) 49/54*. *R(I) 22/61* and *R(I) 4/76*; the reappearance of a condition to which the claimant was already subject before the accident as in *R(I) 26/52* and *R(I) 64/52*; or a condition which has arisen since the accident but which is unconnected with it as in *R v National Insurance Commissioner, ex p. Steel* (1978) and *R(I) 5/84*.

Claimants can still be held capable of their regular occupation or equivalent employment even if there is no such work locally, or if they have only a remote prospect of obtaining it. In these circumstances REA was refused in *CI 99/49* and *R(I) 29/53* because the incapacity must arise at least in part from the loss of faculty. A claimant is not therefore incapable if he has sufficiently recovered from his injury for it to be reasonable to expect him to move to an areas where suitable employment exists. Such employment is defined in *R(I) 24/57*(T) and considered at p. 190 below. For similar reasons REA was denied to a seasonal worker in *R(I) 56/53*. In that case the argument that there was incapacity was based only upon the claimant being unable to work during the part of the year when work was not normally done.

(2) Cases where claims have succeeded

If the claimant is to succeed the industrial injury must remain an effective cause of incapacity. Then it will not matter that there is another cause which also prevents the claimant from doing his job. *R(I) 2/56* expressed this simply by stating that once there is total incapacity for work there is no element of incapacity that can be taken away. Entitlement to REA has therefore been unaffected by the appearance after the accident of the following additional causes of incapacity: the onset of old age in *R(I) 29/51* and *R(I) 56/51*, or some other constitutional condition in *7/51(II)*, *R(I) 17/59*, and *R(I) 1/62*; a later non-industrial accident in *R 7/62(II)*; the disappearance of the claimant's former job in *R(I) 1/62*; and the claimant reaching an age at which he would have retired from the job in *R(I) 14/62*(T).

The last case extensively reviews the authorities for it was of considerable importance whether the loss of faculty could continue to be considered a cause of incapacity for work after the age of retirement had been reached. The decision of a tribunal of Commissioners ensured that elderly people would continue to receive REA. At the time of the case the allowance was being paid to over 25,000 people over the minimum retirement age. By 1979, according to the White Paper, this number had increased to 50,000, a third of all beneficiaries. However, as noted at p. 198 below, the SSA 1986 freezes the rate of the allowance on retirement and offsets it against earnings-related pension. Eventually this can mean that entitlement to the allowance is lost.

The rule which refuses to regard retirement, of itself, as ending incapacity can also be applied in favour of claimants who might be well below the deemed retirement age for a State pension. The rule can benefit those who are injured whilst doing heavier and better paid work in their younger years, which they could not be expected to do when older. The fact that they pass the normal retirement age for the job will not affect their title to benefit. If, for example, a professional footballer is forced to give up the game because of an injury received in a match, he can continue to have football classified as his regular occupation long after the time when age would have forced him to retire. Because of *R(I) 14/62*(T) his entitlement can continue even whilst he is an old-aged pensioner, provided that his injury is still an effective cause of his incapacity.

(3) The claimant's fear as a cause

An important group of cases consider whether REA is payable if the claimant is unable to work not because of the physical effects of the accident upon him, but because of the fears which it produces. These fears cause the claimant either to refuse to accept medical treatment which, if successful, could again make him capable of work or, more commonly, to refuse to return to the work itself because of the danger of further injury. There are three ways in which incapacity may be established because of these fears:

(*a*) If the claimant's refusal is the result of a nervous state caused by his accident he may succeed if the psychological condition is considered part of his loss of faculty as in *R(I) 45/54*. Thus in *R(I) 32/59* a collier received cuts to the face following a shot-firing accident and would not return to the coal face. It was held that the terrifying experience had caused a neurotic condition which, although of little effect in assessing the percentage of disablement, was sufficient to make the claimant incapable of his regular occupation and entitle him to REA. However, in *R(I) 12/80* and *R(I) 5/84* benefit was refused because the medical authority had not included any mental condition in its assessment of the loss of faculty and this prevented the statutory authorities from finding that the claimant was incapable. Unlike in (*b*) and (*c*) below it is not necessary for the claimant's fear to be reasonable. The test is a subjective one and it does not matter, for example, that in fact there may be no realistic danger to the claimant if he were to resume work.

(*b*) If the claimant's refusal is objectively a reasonable one a claim may succeed. This means that the claimant can refuse medical treatment which could restore his capacity for work if he reasonably believes that it could result in danger to his health or exceptional suffering. This is illustrated by *R(I) 23/59* and *4/59(II)*. Where the fear is of further injury if work is resumed claimants have found it difficult to establish that their refusal to return is reasonable, although the more specific argument produced in (*c*) below has improved the prospects of their success. An early case in which REA was paid is *R(I) 66/52*(T) where a majority of a tribunal held that a miner who had lost an eye underground and who refused to return to the coal face to run the risk of total blindness was acting reasonably. However, in *R(I) 15/74* this decision was said to give a somewhat extended meaning to the word incapable. It was characterized in *R(I) 12/80* as "not a success", and it has been suggested that the decision should be limited to its special facts. Refusals based upon fear of risks other than total blindness were rejected in *R(I) 85/52, 1/56(II), R(I) 8/56* and *R(I) 6/59*. In these cases the claimants had suffered only a partial loss of vision in one eye as a result of their accidents. This proved sufficient to distinguish *R(I) 66/52*(T) and REA was refused.

(*c*) If the claimant cannot continue the work without danger to himself or others incapacity may be established. The Commissioner in *R(I) 15/74* considered this argument to have quite a different basis from that in (*b*) above, although both involved objective tests. Again the problem involved the impaired vision of a miner, but with this argument the claim succeeded. The Commissioner was much influenced by the medical board's attribution of incapacity to the danger factor, although the AO had pointed out that assessment of danger was not a matter within the specialized knowledge of doctors, and such advice should be treated with caution. The test has since been applied in two other cases. The allowance was refused in *R(I) 12/80* because it could not be shown that the danger to the claimant had increased since the accident. However, in *R(I) 2/81* the claim succeeded even though there was danger of another accident, instead, there was a risk of further injury occurring by process, in that the claimant feared further gradual deterioration of his hearing if he returned to his job.

4. REGULAR OCCUPATION

(1) General principles

There are two particular reasons for determining the regular occupation: first, in order to establish the work in respect of which the test of incapacity is to apply; and secondly, in order that a pattern of earnings can be formulated to provide a comparison with the post-accident employment. Shortly after the accident on the first claim for REA it is usually relatively easy to establish the regular occupation. Generally, it is the job which the claimant was doing at the time of the accident or the onset of the prescribed disease, as acknowledged in *CI 440/50*(T). If there is a variation in earnings around that time which makes the period untypical it can usually be resolved as only a minor difficulty. However, more serious problems are caused in some cases, considered in (2) below, where the claimant has changed jobs shortly before the accident, or left his occupation before the disease caused a loss of faculty. Further difficulties may occur if the claimant derives earnings from several activities or from overtime, as considered in (3) below. However, as when determining incapacity, the problems are more likely to arise as the years pass and the need to re-establish the regular occupation continues. Since the accident there may have been a change in the relative value of the occupation, or it may have evolved into quite different work. In extreme cases, it may have disappeared altogether. The result may be that, as illustrated in (4) below, some cases are determined more by guesswork than any easy to apply formula. However, as considered at p. 186, the SSA 1986 has introduced the use of indices to reduce the problem of calculating the standard of remuneration for the relevant occupation. Despite this, predicting the future remains a feature of the allowance. This is especially reflected in the rule, considered in (5) below, that the claimant's prospect of promotion must be taken into account. The final heading in (6) below deals with another recent reform that enables REA to be obtained even if there is no regular occupation.

Before these particular problem areas are considered it is worth emphasizing that Commissioners have generally adopted a flexible approach to defining the regular occupation, and they have tried to reflect the realities of the claimant's work. For example, after stating that the question was mainly one of fact and depended upon the actual work being done, the Commissioner in *R(I) 6/75* continued:

> "The particular label which the employer or employee attach to the occupation is not conclusive, and too much weight should not be given to it. . . . Nor is the regular occupation for this purpose necessarily governed by trade union rules or understandings or agreements between them and the employers. . . . [A] fair and realistic view must be taken in the light of the work which the claimant was doing and was required to do and all other circumstances including the claimant's reasons for doing the work he was doing and his intentions for the future."

To illustrate the flexible approach in these matters it has been held that even self-employment can constitute the regular occupation. In *R(I) 15/56*(T) a jobbing mason was injured whilst temporarily employed as a farm labourer. It was held that his regular occupation was that of a self-employed mason. Despite the industrial scheme normally excluding the self-employed, the allowance was payable because the claimant was injured whilst temporarily an employed earner. A flexible approach has also been necessary to take account of the number of different sources or ways by which some people obtain their earnings. The regular occupation has been taken to include part-time employment and work in more than one job, as considered under the next heading.

(2) Changing jobs before the accident

If the claimant was transferred to a new job or undertook different duties just before the accident the regular occupation may be more difficult to identify. It is not enough to focus upon the job the claimant was doing at the time of the accident. Instead his general work history must be examined and the amount of time he spent at each occupation must be taken into account. Particularly relevant factors are the work the claimant intended to do and his prospect of obtaining such employment. Did the claimant abandon his previous job for a new regular occupation, or was the work he was doing before his accident merely a temporary expedient from which he would have eventually returned?

If the claimant has followed an occupation for a long time immediately before his accident there is a presumption that it is his regular one. Thus the jobs in which the claimant worked before the accident for three years in *R(I) 22/52*, and five years in *R(I) 65/54*, were both held to be the regular occupations. But the jobs done for only a year in *R(I) 34/51* and *R(I) 5/52*, and for two years in *CI 80/49*, were held to be merely temporary changes of work and not the regular occupation.

The intentions of the claimant are relevant, as revealed by *R(I) 44/52*. In that case the claimant viewed work as a storekeeper as an experimental trial which, if it failed, would cause him to return to his earlier job as a bus driver. It was held that because of this motive he had not abandoned his job as a driver. The claimant's intention can weigh more heavily than the length of time during which the job has been done. This was made clear in *CWI 55/50*:

"The length of time a person has been following an occupation is irrelevant if it is his regular occupation in the sense that it is what he intends regularly to do. Evidence might prove that a man sustained an injury within an hour of being promoted to a new job, which both he and his employer intended should thenceforth be his regular permanent job; in that case, employment for an hour, or perhaps even the offer and acceptance of a new job, might make the new job the man's permanent occupation."

However, no matter what the claimant's intention if he attempts a new job and finds it beyond his power, it cannot be held to be his regular occupation, especially where he could only work at it for one day as in *R(I) 18/60*.

Specific statutory provision has been made where an occupation has been abandoned following contraction of a prescribed disease. Normally, as in *CI 440/50*(T), the regular occupation is that followed at the date of the onset of the disease. However, if the claimant has been forced to give up his occupation as a result of the relevant disease, but before its formal date of onset, PD reg. 17 states that the abandoned occupation may be treated as the regular occupation. This regulation is needed because symptoms of the disease may appear before the formal date from which the medical authority states that its assessment begins. The claimant may have been encouraged to give up his job to prevent more serious effects developing. If the claimant changes jobs and suffers a further attack of the disease, even if it is considered a fresh attack and not a recrudescence (as discussed at p. 106), *R(I) 4/69* allows the claimant to rely upon reg. 17 provided that the earlier outbreak was the cause of his change of job. This decision emphasizes that the change of job does not have to occur as a result of the current outbreak of the disease, and that the earlier abandonment of occupation will be taken into account. However, where the claimant could not show any causal connection between the abandonment of a job in coal-mining and the development of pneumoconiosis the claim failed in *R(I) 8/58* and *R(I) 13/58*.

(3) Overtime or work in other jobs

If a claimant takes on additional work it must be determined whether his increased earnings are to be attributed to the regular occupation or whether they are to be discounted because they derive from what is, in effect, a separate job. The additional work may arise in a variety of circumstances: it may take the form of overtime in the usual job; it may involve quite a different activity done either for the same employer or someone else; or it may even be self-employed work done in addition to that of an employed earner. If the extra work is considered part of the regular occupation here again there may be an exception to the general rule of *CI 440/50*(T) that the claimant's job at the time of the accident is to be deemed the regular one.

In exceptional circumstances several jobs can combine to form the regular occupation. However, jobs which constitute subsidiary occupations must be excluded. This is because SSA s. 59A(3) states that:

> ". . . the reference to a person's regular occupation is to be taken as not including any subsidiary occupation. . . ."

Although this distinction is one of fact, the cases in the area appear to be in conflict, for the line is difficult to draw. Generally it can be said that the closer the second job is to the first in terms of the time spent and money earned, the more likely it is to be considered part of the regular occupation and not a subsidiary employment. Because of the time and the pay in *R(I) 33/58* the claimant succeeded in showing that two jobs – one as a shop assistant, the other as a tote operator for greyhound racing – formed a regular occupation, even though they were done for different employers. The argument in this case that the claimant's regular occupation was that of a housewife, and that her part-time employments were subsidiary, failed. This was because *CI 441/50*(T) decided that only gainful occupations were relevant, thus excluding any consideration of the claimant's housework.

There are several cases involving miners in which it has been found that their second activity formed part of their regular occupation. It was relevant that the work was done for only one employer, British Coal, but the cases also emphasize that if the work is all done in normal work hours, as in *R(I) 43/52*, it is more likely to be held all part of the regular occupation. However, even where the work was done at weekends, or as an overtime shift, it was included in the regular occupation in *R(I) 24/55*, *R(I) 10/65* and *R 8/84(II)*. This was because the overtime involved a different kind of work to that normally done. (If the overtime merely involves the same work but for a longer period the claimant may not be able to show that he is incapable. Benefit will then be refused as in *CI 443/50*(T). This is discussed at p. 168.)

Other cases have held the separate activity to be a subsidiary occupation, even if it is labelled overtime and done for the same employer. This was the result in *CWI 30/50* and *R(I) 48/51* because the work was done after normal work hours and was voluntary (although *R(I) 10/65* viewed the distinction between voluntary and compulsory work as misleading). Similarly voluntary overtime where the claimant participated in the work's fire brigade or civil defence teams did not form part of the regular occupation in *R(I) 58/54* and *R(I) 13/62*, and work for another employer was discounted in *R(I) 2/70*. Little time was spent on the activity in such cases compared to the regular occupation, but in *R(I) 45/51* the "overtime" was held a subsidiary occupation even though it amounted to over 20 hours a week.

R(I) 54/54 illustrates that a claimant may be prevented from showing that the extra work is part of his regular occupation by it being held either a subsidiary occupation, or too spasmodic or casual to be called regular. The claimant, an electrician, tried to include within his pre-accident earnings a large amount in repsect of overtime and for the work he carried out in private houses on a self-employed basis in his spare time. It was held that the prospect of earning overtime was too spasmodic to be taken into account and his contract work was a subsidiary occupation.

(4) Changes in the regular occupation since the accident

If a claimant is injured when young his entitlement to REA may continue for several decades. During this time considerable changes may take place not only in the nature of the work involved in the claimant's regular occupation but also in its relative value. In the past the DHSS have had to continue to identify the claimant's former job and monitor its fluctuating wage rate, or obtain some criteria by which an estimate of its value can be made. Often such efforts were artificial and, at their worst, they amounted to little more than inspired guesswork. The problems have now been eased by index-linking the earnings as discussed at p. 186. However, it is still necessary to identify the claimant's former job to see if he remains incapable of it, although he is not to lose entitlement only because that job changes character or even disappears. Thus in *R(I) 10/59* the Commissioner stated:

> "Changes in technique come in from time to time in various occupations and it would not be right to hold that a man, who had no experience of a technique which was only in its infancy at the time of the accident, had a regular occupation which excluded the use of that technique."

In *R(I) 88/52* and *R(I) 16/54* the job had disappeared, but was still held to be the regular occupation. In the former case, the claimant's post as a fitter was abolished after his contraction of pneumoconiosis. Although it remained his regular occupation it caused no great difficulty in making the required earnings comparison because a fitter was a well recognized grade within the coal industry, and information on earnings could be easily supplied from other pits. The method of calculating the remuneration in similar circumstances was also considered in *R(I) 11/65* and *R 3/69(II)*. As the years pass a percentage increase could be allowed for the higher salary that might be expected, or recourse could be had to comparison with the increases for other workers following similar jobs. This is now specifically permitted by SSA s. 59A(10) as discussed at p. 186. But the potential difficulties involved in this exercise are revealed by *R(I) 10/54* where not only was the claimant's job eventually abolished, but so were the remaining other posts. Inquiries elsewhere failed to produce a job comparable with that of the claimant, and the calculation had to be based upon the earnings of the claimant's former colleagues, although they had now been dispersed to a variety of jobs. The Commissioner understated the problems that could be involved: "Absolute accuracy is unobtainable: Probability must be the guide." No doubt this will influence the new approach involving the index-linking of the earnings levels.

(5) Promotion and the prospects of advancement

Further predictions are required to take account of the likelihood that a claimant would be advanced or promoted in his job. Subject to certain safeguards to limit the potential uncertainties involved in making such estimates, the claimant's regular occupation can be taken to be that which he might have attained. The earnings comparison eventually can take account of the higher pay which would have been received if the accident had not happened, and the promotion had taken place. This can occur because SSA s. 59A(4) provides:

> ". . . a person's regular occupation is to be treated as extending to and including employment in the capacities to which the persons in the occupation (or a class or description of them to which he belonged at the time of the relevant acident) are in the normal course advanced, and to which, if he had continued to follow that occupation without having suffered the relevant loss of faculty, he would have had at least the normal prospects of advancement; and so long as he is, as a result of the relevant loss of faculty, deprived in whole or in part of those prospects, he is to be treated as incapable of following that occupation."

This provision was introduced in its present form in 1961. Before that time the prospect of advancement was confined to promotion within a particular occupation, so that cases such as *R(I) 44/51* and *R(I) 29/55*, had refused to allow a regular occupation to include promotion to another job or grade. Because of this, those obtaining the benefit of the earlier rule were usually apprentices or trainees.[1] They were able to have the earnings of a fully qualified worker taken as their own. However, in *R(I) 3/60* the allowance was refused because the office boy could not show that he was an apprentice who would eventually have qualified as a skilled worker, and in *R(I) 6/57* the trainee was refused because there was clear evidence that he would not have qualified anyway.

Under the section as presently enacted a claimant must satisfy three conditions in order for the promoted grade to be classifed as the regular occupation. *R(I) 8/67*, followed in *R 4/72(II)*, requires affirmative answers to each of the following:

> (1) In general are persons in the claimant's position normally promoted or advanced to a higher grade? (An objective test.)

---

[1] Apprentices succeeded in *CI 93/49, CI 442/50*(T), *R(I) 2/52, R(I) 52/53, T(I) 31/58* and *R(I) 4/60*. After the rule was extended it continued, of course, to benefit trainees such as the carpenter in *R(I) 6/75*.

(2) If so, did the claimant have at least the normal prospects of such promotion or advancement? (A subjective test.)
(3) If so, is the claimant at least in part deprived of those normal prospects as a result of the relevant loss of faculty?

Of these questions it has been (1) which has been the subject of two notable decisions which have refused REA. This has happened because it involves an objective test. In *R(I) 8/73* the claimant was a town planning assistant who suffered an accident shortly before he was to move to a more senior appointment with another employer. The injury prevented the change from taking place, and the claimant resumed work with his old employer. His claim for the allowance was refused because the Commissioner found that the new job was not one to which others in the claimant's position were normally promoted. The claimant's (presumably) exceptional abilities could not be taken into account even though on the actual facts he had been offered the higher post.

In *R(I) 8/80* the claimant contracted pneumoconiosis whilst a pit deputy, but he still managed in later years to be promoted to overman, and then undermanager. However, despite s. 59A(4) the regular occupation at the date of the development of the disease was held to be that of deputy. Again this was because the Commissioner was not satisfied that deputies were in the normal course of events promoted to the jobs in fact eventually done by the claimant. It was emphasized that the legislation rarely assists a claimant where the predominant factor in advancement is selectivity. Instead the advancement must be automatic. Although the rule limits the amount of speculation as to what heights the claimant might have attained but for his accident, it can operate harshly where, as in the above cases, claimants actually are offered, or even follow for some years, the jobs which they seek to be defined as their regular occupations.

The application of the relevant section has been further limited by *R(I) 12/81* which considered the meaning of "advancement". This normally occurs when there is promotion to a higher position. More rarely there may be an advancement where there is no improvement in status but pay is increased because of seniority as where yearly increments are paid to those in Government employment.

> "However, the mere transfer from a lower paid job to a higher paid job does not necessarily constitute advancement. The higher paid post may carry with it certain unattractive features, for which the increased remuneration is intended to compensate. The movement then is not upwards but, if anything, sideways. There is a change of job but not an advancement."

(6) Absence of regular occupation

SSA s. 59A(2) states:

> "The Secretary of State may by regulations provide that in prescribed circumstances employed earner's employment in which a claimant was engaged when the relevant accident took place but which was not his regular occupation is to be treated as if it had been his regular occupation."

This clause was first introduced by SSA 1985 s. 14. It arose following the efforts of Mrs Beckett MP on behalf of a schoolboy injured whilst lawfully working on a farm. Although he had intended to become a full-time farmworker on completing his education, this could not yet be called his regular occupation. He was therefore refused REA in *CI 188/83* (unreported), despite having suffered a loss of earning capacity and being entitled to a disablement pension.

The only regulation to be made as a result of the new power is reg. 2 of the Social Security (Industrial Injuries and Diseases) Miscellaneous Provisions Regulations 1986 (SI No. 1561). As might be expected, it deals with the problem which gave rise to the power by providing cover for students or school children doing part-time jobs. It allows the work which the claimant was doing at the time of the accident to be treated as the regular occupation

> ". . . where the claimant, at the time the relevant accident took place, had no regular occupation but was pursuing a course of full-time education, either by attendance at a recognised educational establishment or, if the education is recognised by the Secretary of State in accordance with section 2(1A) of the Child Benefit Act 1975, elsewhere."

In determining whether a course of full-time education is being pursued

> ". . . any temporary interruption of that education not exceeding a period of 6 months, or such longer period as the Secretary of State may in any particular case determine, shall be disregarded."

To prevent REA being paid when, for example, the child or student could still be expected to be in full-time education there was another clause in the 1985 Act. This prevented REA being paid under s. 59A(2) for any period during which the claimant "would not normally be engaged in full-time employed earner's employment". However, this clause has been omitted from the relevant part of the SSA 1986, and has not been included in the above regulations.

5. EMPLOYMENT AT AN EQUIVALENT STANDARD OF REMUNERATION

REA compensates not for the loss of a particular job, but for the loss of the ability to earn. The conditions of entitlement laid down by s. 59A(1) therefore prescribe that a claimant must not only show that he is incapable of his regular occupation, but also that he is "incapable of following employment of an equivalent standard. . . ." Employment is equivalent if it provides the same "standard of remuneration". As held in *R(I) 48/53* the job need not, for example, be of equal permanence. It is the remuneration which counts and how this is calculated is considered in (2) below.

Although *R(I) 2/70* recognizes that the claimant's actual earnings are the best evidence of his earning capacity, the claimant's job after the accident does not always provide a reliable guide as to the standard of which he is capable. To obtain an assessment of his true potential for work an AO may make enquiries of the Department of Employment. An AO may also consult, for example, a disablement resettlement officer, especially if the claimant has never worked since the accident. Following this advice the AO may then suggest a job or series of jobs as equivalent to the work that used to be done. For any job suggested the claimant must be prepared to make one of three arguments: he must show that he is incapable of performing the tasks involved; or that the job is not suitable; or that it is not equivalent. In considering equivalence, although the key factor is the job's remuneration as considered in (2) below, the suggested employment must not be of an exceptional character. This is considered next.

(1) Employment not of an exceptional character

On the one hand the AO is allowed to suggest certain jobs which may be subject to some restrictions or limitations such as those imposed because of the claimant's loss of faculty. This meant that work underground in a mine, even if only in dust approved conditions, could amount to equivalent employment after the claimant had contracted pneumoconiosis in *R* v *National Insurance Commissioner, ex p. Steel* (1978). On the other hand the AO may not rely upon special jobs – perhaps created for the claimant out of reasons of charity – which do not reflect the claimant's ability to obtain employment on the open market. Thus in *R(I) 7/58*, after he had contracted dermatitis, a small arms expert did special work where no oil was involved. When that work finished he was transferred to other duties at a lower wage. It was held that his ability to perform the special work was not proof that he was capable of work equivalent to his regular occupation. The Commissioner stated:

> "Employment of an equivalent standard must. . . refer to some recognised occupation. It does not mean a limited class of jobs within an occupation for the exclusive performance of which persons are not normally employed, unless the limitation on the claimant's capacity is so slight that it would not preclude the claimant from obtaining employment at the occupation in question in the labour market."

In *R(I) 6/77* this meant that the sheltered employment of a machinist at Remploy factory was exceptional and not equivalent to the claimant's regular occupation. The earnings were not to be taken as a basis for a comparison of what the claimant could now earn on the open market.

If a claimant follows an occupation for any length of time it is progressively strong evidence of his capacity to perform it. However, as when capacity is considered in relation to the regular occupation, there still may be some opportunity for the claimant to suggest that he is incapable, even though he has done the work and received equivalent earnings. This will be the case if the work is done for an exceptional period and the claimant in fact has little chance of obtaining such earnings on a regular basis. Because of this there was no equivalent employment in *R(I) 42/52*, *R(I) 45/61* and *R(I) 73/52*. In the last case a mining engineer was forced to give up his job following his accident at work. He was not considered capable of equivalent employment just because, for three weeks in the summer, he was able to earn as much as a singer as when he was an engineer. However, where the employment involved work of a recognized kind which was not exceptional REA was refused in *R(I) 42/61* and *R(I) 48/53*.

(2) Calculating the standard of remuneration

For the claimant to establish that there has been a loss of earning capacity for the purposes of s. 59A(1) he must show that he is incapable of employment offering an equivalent standard of remuneration. The gross amount received from the regular occupation must be compared with that which the claimant could probably now earn.

(a) Index-linking the earnings

In calculating the probable standard of remuneration a considerable administrative burden is placed upon the DHSS. Until the SSA 1986 information about earnings had to be gathered from employers not only at the initial claim, but also at the periodic reviews of the allowance. Both the pre-accident and post-accident probable levels of earnings had to be checked to discover whether the claimant remained entitled and, if so, exactly what amount should be paid. Over 200,000 inquiries of employers were made each year to establish wage levels. These inquiries could be dispensed with if it were clear that the difference would at least amount to the maximum rate of REA. This rate is paid in 90 per cent of awards. According to the DHSS evidence to the Pearson Commission the maximum "reduced the guesswork to more manageable proportions". However, the minority of cases not involving the maximum award could involve tortuous investigations. These were especially difficult where the accident occurred some years ago. Where jobs had no modern counterpart highly artificial decisions were reached as to their standard of remuneration. However, the reforms enacted in 1986, foreshadowed in the White Paper of 1981 and the Consultation Paper of 1985, may considerably ease the burden upon the DHSS.

The White Paper suggested that the pre-accident earnings upon which the original award was made be uprated in line with the general increase in earnings. An adjustment could still be made for promotion prospects (as considered in the above section) but thereafter it would be index-linked. The Consultation Paper suggested taking this further so as to index all REA earnings calculations, including post-accident earnings, except for that made at the first calculation of the allowance. To take some account of earnings movement in different industries it was suggested that a separate index of the main industrial groups could be used rather than one general index. The TUC and IIAC broadly supported this proposal, subject to there being periodic reassessments of actual earnings levels. The reform also makes it easier to raise the maximum amount of REA without imposing an excessive administrative burden upon the DHSS. The possibility of making this change is considered at p. 199.

The legislation to implement the index-linking proposal was contained in the SSA 1986. This amends the SSA 1975 by including s. 59A(10):

> "On any award except the first the probable standard of his remuneration shall be determined in such manner as may be prescribed; and, without prejudice to the generality of this subsection, regulations may provide in prescribed circumstances for the probable standard of remuneration to be determined by reference –
> (a) to the standard determined at the time of the last previous award of reduced earnings allowance; and
> (b) to scales or indices of earnings in a particular industry or description of industries or any other data relating to such earnings."

One of the problems that may arise after a period of time is that the amount determined by indexation may not reflect the claimant's actual earning capacity if, for example, his physical condition has since changed. In reply to a parliamentary question in April 1986 the Minister for Social Security stated that beneficiaries are to be given the right to have the award reviewed if they feel that, as a result of indexation, the allowance no longer accurately reflects their earnings loss. However, no such regulations have yet been made. Indexation will reduce the difficulties in establishing remuneration as examined in the remainder of this section.

(b) Effect of short-term changes

Defining the standard of remuneration is necessary, not only for establishing title to the allowance under s. 59A(1), but also for quantifying the amount to be paid as prescribed by s. 59A(8) and discussed at p. 191. However, the phrase has been interpreted somewhat differently for each section. For s. 59A(1) a longer view must be taken – even up to a year as in *R(I) 76/52*. Short term changes may have no effect. Thus in *R(I) 31/59* and *R(I) 5/62* the trade recession in the claimant's regular occupation which temporarily reduced his earnings below that of his existing employment did not destroy entitlement to the allowance; it only affected quantification under s. 59A(8) by reducing the amount payable to nil for the period of the reduction of earnings. However, it is true of both s. 59A(1) and s. 59A(8) that when the standards of remuneration are compared the rate per hour, or per shift is not to be used. Instead, as stated by Lord Denning in *R* v *National Insurance Commissioner, ex p. Mellors* (1971):

> ". . . when you speak of 'standard of remuneration' you use the word 'standard' in the same sense as the phrase 'standard of living'. It means the level of remuneration which a man earns week by week or month by month as the case may be."

(c) Relevance of factors personal to the claimant

A second difference between the two sections is that in quantifying the allowance under s. 59A(8) factors which are personal to the claimant are more likely to be taken into account. These are considered in detail at p. 192 where, in particular, the position of part-time workers is discussed. By contrast for s. 59A(1) the comparison is only to be drawn between the jobs in question and not the particular claimant's personal experience of them. An objective impersonal standard is applied. As described by Buckley LJ in *ex p. Mellors* the standard of remuneration is that

> "which an employee of normal efficiency and industriousness. . . would be likely to earn working in that employment for such a number of hours in a week or other period which can be regarded as normal for persons employed in that employment. . . ."

This means that neither the wages paid by one or two exceptional employers to one or two employees, as in *R 7/63(II)*, nor payments made during an exceptional period, as in *R(I) 42/52*, are to be taken into account.

Although the standard of remuneration is based upon an impersonal assessment, some allowance is made for the sort of claimant involved in the following two respects. First, s. 59A(3) states that

> ". . . in assessing the standard of remuneration in any employment, including a person's regular occupation, regard is to be had to his reasonable prospects of advancement."

This is discussed at p. 182 above in relation to s. 59A(4) and defining the regular occupation. Secondly, the comparison in earnings must be taken at the place where the claimant is living, not at some other part of the country where there are higher wage rates for the job in question. In deciding this the Court of Appeal in *R* v *Deputy Industrial Injuries Commissioner, ex p. Humphreys* (1966) required that "like should be compared with like". This meant on the facts of the case that the actual earnings received by the claimant from temporarily working elsewhere could be discounted in favour of those available at the place where he had returned to live. This case is considered further at p. 191 below.

(d) Defining remuneration

Payments normally made for the job and forming part of its remuneration have included a bonus for working in difficult conditions in *CWI 30/50*; an incentive bonus in *R(I) 66/51*; and a subsistence allowance in *R(I) 24/59*, except where it was met by extra expenses in *R(I) 1/54*. Prizes, tips or other customary payments are included even if they are not paid by the principal employer. For example, in *R(I) 47/54* these included the prizes won by a riding instructress at horse shows. However, in *R(I) 60/52* it was said that payments from other than the employer should be closely scrutinized and may be ignored if they are illicit, or encourage neglect of duty, or if casual, spasmodic or negligible in amount. If overtime is a normal feature of the job it is included in the remuneration. This made the employment equivalent and title to benefit was lost in *R(I) 1/72*. A similar result followed when overtime was no longer a feature of the regular occupation in *CI 81/49*. However, in *R(I) 7/51* overtime increased the loss of earning capacity by affecting the value of the regular occupation. If the employment does not usually involve overtime it will be left out of account as in *R(I) 45/61*. Overtime is further considered in relation to defining the regular occupation at p. 180 above.

Remuneration was defined in *CWI 17/49* as "the amount of money (or its equivalent) which a person receives in return for his services". This highlights two particular features of the calculation. First, payments received other than in return for services are to be excluded. Thus in *CI 308/84* (unreported) concessionary rail travel for a railway employee was left out of account. More importantly social security payments for sickness and invalidity are also excluded. (However, there are proposals to change this as discussed at p. 199, and the earnings related element of invalidity benefit is now set off against REA as discussed at p. 197.) Disablement pension was also left out of account in *CI 330/50* and *CI 441/50*(T). This means that it is possible for a claimant to obtain more money after the accident by a combination of wages, disablement pension and REA, than was received by wages alone before the injury.

The second feature highlighted by the quotation from *CWI 17/49* is that, if received in return for services, benefits in kind are to be included as remuneration provided that a monetary value can be placed upon them. Benefits taken into account have included food and lodging in *R(I) 47/52* and *R(I) 47/54*; the use of a van in *R 1/79(II)*; concessionary coal in *R(I) 3/58*; and uniform in *R(I) 7/51*, except where it was worn not in return for services, but only to comply with the employer's wishes in *R(I) 33/51*. In *CI 11/80* (unreported) the provision of subsidized meals and a discount on goods purchased from the employing company formed part of the remuneration. However, the prospect of receiving an issue of shares in the company was excluded as being too remote. The value of social and club facilities was also excluded on the particular facts, but it was suggested that if the employer, for example, had paid for membership subscriptions these might have been included.

Having arrived at a total figure representing the full gross income, a deduction can be made for the expenses incurred in obtaining it. These have included the cost of the materials used in carrying out the work in *R(I) 79/52*, and payments passing directly through the claimant's hands to those who actually do the work in *R(I) 5/58*. However, the expense of travelling to and from work was held not to be deductible in *R 8/63(II)*.

6. Suitable Employment

Any comparison with the claimant's regular occupation can be rejected unless the alternative employment is suitable for the claimant. Suitability is assessed subjectively. It takes into account not only the claimant's capacity in terms of physical and intellectual powers, but also education, training, experience, age and employment history. Generally if a job is done for an appreciable time it will be held suitable for the claimant, as in *R(I) 29/52*(T). However, as discussed at p. 171, there are certain periods of work done by the claimant since the accident which may be disregarded. A job may be found suitable even though the claimant has never done it or was even aware of its existence. Nor did it matter in *CI 99/49* and *R(I) 29/53* that there was no such work locally or that the claimant had only a remote prospect of obtaining it.

The procedure by which an AO may make inquiries and obtain a report from the Department of Employment as to what other work is suitable for the claimant can be seen as bizarre. It has not gone without criticism:

> "It is difficult to see why a report by someone who has never seen a claimant, that he is suitable for a job which he has never been offered, and a job of whose availability he is totally unaware, and where there is no evidence that there are any vacancies in the job, still less that the claimant could successfully apply for one, can be regarded as cogent evidence."[2]

The cases discussing the suitability of employment fall into the following two groups:

(1) Mental or physical capacity for equivalent employment

Whether the claimant is capable of the equivalent employment has already been discussed under incapacity. The test involved in assessing incapacity is different from that involved in suitability because it requires the claimant's inability to result from the loss of faculty caused by the industrial accident. By contrast, employment can be held unsuitable if the claimant is incapable of it because of a disability from which he was already suffering before the accident. Thus in *R(I) 1/74* it was held that the suggested employment could be unsuitable because the claimant was blind

[2]   H. Street, *Justice in the Welfare State* (1975) p. 30.

in one eye, although this resulted from a condition contracted in childhood and not from the industrial accident.

However, *R(I) 33/55* and *R(I) 22/61* contrast the position where the incapacity arises after the industrial accident and is not connected with it. In the last case the claimant was prevented from following an equivalent employment because of osteoarthritis of the hips which had developed since the industrial accident to his wrist. REA was refused because he could not "show that such incapacity is a result of the relevant accident. He cannot rely on that supervening incapacity as a basis for saying that the employment in question is not suitable in his case".

In logic the distinction between the relevance of the claimant's condition before and after the accident seems to have little to commend it. However, in practice it has an important result: it prevents many claims from succeeding when injured workers grow older, and it is their age which prevents them from following the equivalent employments which are suggested as suitable. The logic of the distinction between conditions arising before and after the accident was recognized as presenting difficulties in *R(I) 4/76*(T), but the earlier decisions were followed. This was because many other cases had been decided in the same way, and it was thought that if the rule were to be changed, this should be done by a higher authority. This decision, refusing REA, was affirmed on appeal as *R v National Insurance Commissioner, ex p. Steel* (1978). The claimant in this case was incapable of equivalent employment not because of the industrial accident, but solely by reason of hypertension which had arisen after the accident, and was unconnected with it. As a result for REA purposes the claimant failed to show that he was incapable of work, or that the work was unsuitable even though he could not do it.

(2) Equivalent employment in another part of the country

Whether a job some distance away from where the claimant lives constitutes suitable employment, thus causing REA to be refused, depends on the facts of the case. Because of a Court of Appeal decision in 1966 a decision against a claimant is less likely, but it may still happen. The earlier authority in favour of finding such work suitable is *R(I) 27/57*(T). This case decided that employment elsewhere will be suitable only if a reasonable interval has elapsed since the claimant became capable of the work involved. However, this interval is only to be as long as the time it takes for the claimant to find out that there was no suitable employment in his home district, and to make arrangements to move to where such work was to be found. The relevant factors include:

> ". . . the locality of her home, and the distance and means of travel between her home and the place where employment exists. . . . [This factor is] of greater or less weight according to the circumstances. For instance, a man accustomed to moving from place to place could reasonably expect to accept without delay employment in a distant place . . . but a claimant with a long record of employment in his regular occupation in one locality could not be expected to move so readily. . . ."

The decision is to be based upon the claimant's character as a worker, and is not dependent upon personal family ties. This can mean that it does not matter that the claimant has a family, with perhaps a spouse who is ill, or does not wish to move. Further, as Salmon LJ stated in *R* v *Deputy National Insurance Commissioner, ex p. Humphreys* (1966), once employment is considered suitable

> "it is immaterial . . . that there is no suitable accommodation for the workman and his family in the place where such employment is available . . . just as it is immaterial that perhaps because of a depression he is unable to find any such available employment at all."

Where after the accident the claimant had returned to his home in another part of the country, employment where the injury had occurred was considered suitable in *R(I) 46/56*.

However, in *ex p. Humphreys*, without discussing *R(I) 24/57*(T), the Court of Appeal placed restraints upon the ability of the AO to suggest that a claimant move elsewhere. Lord Denning MR even suggested that suitable employment does not mean at any place in England, but only at the place where the claimant lives. All the judges agreed that the remuneration for a job must not be calculated on any basis other than that which exists where the claimant lives. This means that a difference in wage rates for the same job in different parts of the country cannot affect a claimant because "like must be compared with like". Although Davies LJ agreed with this, he still considered that the existence of the job elsewhere, if not its remuneration at that place, could constitute suitable employment.

7. THE AMOUNT AND PAYMENT OF THE ALLOWANCE

(1) Comparing the standards of remuneration

If there is entitlement to an award of REA under s. 59A(1)(b) the amount of the allowance is to be calculated by applying the similarly worded s. 59A(8). It states that the rate of REA is to be determined

> ". . . by reference to the beneficiary's probable standard of remuneration during the period for which it is granted in the employed earner's employments which are suitable in his case and which he is likely to be capable of following as compared with that in the relevant occupation. . . ."

The difference between the future probable standards of remuneration of the relevant employments should be expressed in round figures. This is because, as *R(I) 7/69*(T) appreciates, s. 59A(8) "necessarily provides for a rough and ready form of compensation and finicky calculations are not appropriate". As acknowledged in *R 4/75(II)*: "Actual earnings at any particular time will usually be a relevant consideration but a strictly mathematical calculation taking account of every fluctuation in rates or differentials, however temporary or fortuitous, and correct to the nearest penny is not required. . . ." This statement has now been reinforced by the SSA 1986 which allows the use of index-linking to calculate the respective level of earnings. This is discussed at p. 186 where the general method for calculating the standard of remuneration in relation to s. 59A(1) is examined. This discussion is fully relevant to the calculation to be made under s. 59A(8). However, there are two particular changes to be made when making the required comparison between pre and post-accident earnings. The first of these is that short term changes are more likely to be taken into account to quantify the standard of remuneration under s. 59A(8), whereas they may not affect the basic entitlement under s. 59A(1). Even if, for example, there is a temporary reduction in wage rates, which reduces the value of an award under s. 59A(8) to nil, entitlement may continue because s. 59A(1) is based upon a longer term assessment of the remuneration.

A second and more problematic distinction between the sections is that a more subjective assessment of the standard of remuneration maybe allowed for s. 59A(8). The personal work experience of the claimant is more likely to be taken into account, even if it differs from that which the job normally holds. By contrast, it is settled that for s. 59A(1) the remuneration is based upon an objective impersonal assessment of what might normally be expected from the respective jobs. This suggested distinction between the two sections has been undermined by the Court of Appeal in *R* v *National Insurance Commissioner, ex p. Mellors* (1971) as discussed below. However, the distinction continues to pose difficult problems, and has again troubled the Commissioners in recent years.

An objective assessment has the advantage of not requiring any extensive investigation of either the claimant's particular work experience, or the conditions of the work itself. Only the remuneration normally to be expected counts. In *ex p. Mellors* Lord Denning applied this objective approach to s. 59A(8):

> "In making the comparison, you look at the financial remuneration for a normal working week. You do not look at the conditions of the work. You do not look to see whether it is a high rate per hour because it is hazardous . . . or a low rate because it is safe . . ., nor whether the work is burdensome or easy; light or heavy; long hours or short hours; paid by the hour or by the piece; paid extra for overtime, or not. None of these things come into the calculation. The only thing that matters is the level of remuneration which week by week he would probably have been receiving if he had not been injured, compared with what he is probably capable of receiving after the accident."

On the facts of the case, the claimant as a miner had previously earned £28 for a 36-hour week. After the accident he worked as a lorry driver, earning only a couple of pounds less but this was for a 65-hour week. The hours of work were normal for both jobs. There was clearly entitlement to REA under s. 59A(1), but the question arose as to how the amount was to be calculated. The claimant asked for the allowance to be based upon the difference in the average earning per hour instead of the much smaller difference in the total weekly wage for each job. Applying the impersonal standard the Court of Appeal rejected the claimant's contention. The result has been criticized by the former Chief Commissioner:

> "The propositions that, if a man by working double the hours in a new occupation can earn the same money, that employment is of an equivalent standard and the difference between the two standards of remuneration is nil, are to me totally unjust and unacceptable."[3]

---

[3]   R. Micklethwait, *op.cit.* p. 108.

Although *ex p. Mellors* has been seen as favouring the imposition of an impersonal standard for s. 59A(8) as well as for s. 59A(1), it should be noted that, on its facts, it was not necessary to take account of any personal factors associated with the claimant's own work experience. An impersonal standard was applied in that the hours worked were normal for both jobs in question. It was not necessary to decide whether the claimant's own particular pattern of work could affect the calculation once it was accepted that the different jobs were not to be judged on a common time basis. In addition the Court of Appeal accepted that the personal factor could be taken into account if a claimant worked only part-time. Lord Denning agreed that such cases fall into a special category:

> "If it is 'probable' that the man or woman will work part-time after the accident, as he did or she did before, then you make the comparison by taking the part-time level of remuneration before and after."

In making this allowance for the part-time worker, the Court of Appeal supported the two earlier cases of *R(I) 6/68*(T) and *R(I) 7/68*(T). Both of these decisions have been considered further in cases which have been reported since *ex p. Mellors* and they are discussed next.

In *R(I) 7/68*(T) before her accident the claimant worked for only 28 hours a week as a home help. It was agreed that it was unfair to compare this part-time employment with an alternative full-time occupation which the claimant had never done. Instead the standards of remuneration were compared on a common time basis, with the result that the allowance was the difference between that received for the work as a home help and the rate of pay for 28 hours of factory work. *R(I) 3/83* reinforces this approach and further strengthens the claims of part-time workers for REA. The claimant worked 24 hours a week in her job before the accident, but in the suggested alternative employment no part-time workers could work more than 20 hours a week. It was held that the probable earnings from the alternative employment should not be scaled upwards from 20 to 24. A common time basis could not be used because it was not possible for the claimant to work 24 hours. The comparison was to be made with only 20 hours of factory work and this meant an increase in REA.

These cases dealing with part-time work can still be seen as applying an objective standard: there is an impersonal assessment of remuneration based upon a comparison of the jobs in question, and not the particular claimants' following of them. However, *R(I) 6/68*(T) – the other case approved in *ex p. Mellors* – does take into account the claimant's own work experience. There the claimant worked shorter hours than was normal so that he could carry out various public duties. He did this in both his regular occupation before the accident, and in the alternative employment afterwards. He chose to work part-time in a job which others did full-time. Nevertheless his allowance was based upon the difference in remuneration between the two jobs as done part-time by the claimant. The actual subjective work experience of the claimant was taken into account in assessing the rate of REA under s. 59A(8).

This case received further support in *R(I) 9/80*. There it was held that a subjective standard should be applied in that the actual experience of the claimant in any post-accident employment should be taken into account when estimating the probable standard of remuneration. The claimant worked for only 36 hours a week before the accident, but afterwards for 40 hours in the alternative employment. It was held that his post-accident remuneration should not be scaled down to equate with the 36-hour rate. A contrast was drawn with *R(I) 7/68*(T) where the claimant had never worked in the alternative employment, and in considering the probable future remuneration it could not be expected that the claimant would work more hours than he had done before the accident. Although actual post-accident experience was thus held relevant by *R(I) 9/80*, the Commissioner considered that this should not enable a claimant to increase the amount of REA by choosing to work only part-time after the accident, and asking for the remuneration to be compared with that from the former regular occupation which was worked full-time.

To conclude, *ex parte Mellors* assesses the difference in remuneration for the purposes of quantifying the allowance under s. 59A(8) by means of an objective impersonal standard, related only to the respective jobs, but not the detailed work conditions, nor the particular claimants involved. However, it allows part-time workers to be treated as a special case. What other exceptions will be allowed is unclear. For example, if a claimant earns overtime or bonus payments which are normal (in that they can also be received by others doing the work and they are not a sporadic feature of the job), *R(I) 1/72* confirms that they may be included in the remuneration. But what is to happen if these payments are not usually received by others, but are particular to the claimant's own experience? Whether a subjective standard will be applied to include such payments in the remuneration remains uncertain.

(2) The maximum allowance

The Pearson Commission considered that the costs of administration and the legal difficulties involved in establishing title to the allowance were very considerable and were only being kept within reasonable bounds by the low financial limit on awards. The DHSS evidence to the Commission suggested that the limit "reduces the guesswork to more manageable proportions". This is because the maximum rate is obtained by 90 per cent of beneficiaries, thus removing the need for the earnings loss to be precisely calculated in the many cases where it is apparent that the loss is well in excess. The index-linking of the earnings, as introduced by the SSA 1986, further eases the administrative burden. It also makes it possible for the ceiling on the allowance to be raised. This has been done in one minor respect by the 1986 Act as discussed in (*b*) below. However, the major change to the maximum, envisaged in the White Paper and discussed below at p. 199, has yet to be enacted.

The rate of REA is the difference between the gross earnings before and after the accident, but it must not exceed either of the two limits contained in SSA s. 59A(8), as introduced by the SSA 1986. These are:

(a) The maximum for REA alone

REA alone must not exceed a rate which is specified in the annual up-rating order, and which, traditionally, has been equivalent to a 40 per cent disablement pension. This restriction does not prevent the acquisition of more than one award of REA where there are several industrial accidents or diseases. This is because a claimant may suffer from several earnings losses as in *R(I) 2/56*. The 40 per cent limit applies only to each individual loss, but the aggregate of allowances and disablement benefit is subject to the further limit imposed next.

(b) The maximum for REA and disablement pension combined

When added to a disablement pension (but ignoring entitlement to the allowance for constant attendance and severe disablement), REA must not exceed 140 per cent of the maximum for a disablement pension alone. This was raised from 100 per cent by the SSA 1986 and will take effect from 6 April 1987.

In practice, the new limit will only restrict the claims of those receiving more than one award of REA. This is because, given the limit in (*a*) above, a recipient of a single award cannot obtain more than 140 per cent in any event. A greater restriction was imposed by the previous limit of 100 per cent. The reason for this limit was that, before the SSA 1986, the allowance was technically an increase in disablement benefit and could not be paid independent of it. The limit meant that those receiving the maiximum disablement pension were not able to obtain REA, whilst those assessed at between 70 and 90 per cent disabled had their entitlement curtailed. The 1986 Act removes this limit upon the ability of the more seriously injured claimants to obtain REA. Although this change may be welcomed as an improvement in benefit to those most in need, very few will actually gain from it. This is because only about one in twenty pensioners are assessed at over 65 per cent disabled (appendix A, table 2). In parliament the Minister of Social Security admitted that only 3,700 disablement pensioners (2 per cent of the present total) would be able to obtain more money.

(3) The duration of the allowance

By SSA s. 59A(6):

"Reduced earnings allowance shall be awarded –
(a) for such period as may be determined at the time of the award; and
(b) if at the end of that period the beneficiary submits a fresh claim for the allowance, for such further period as may be determined."

By the subsection (7) an award cannot be made for any period beyond that specified by SSA sched. 8 para. 4. This refers to the limit on the period to be taken into account by the assessment of disablement. It is discussed at p. 154. The period is thus not to exceed that during which the claimant may be expected to continue to suffer from the relevant loss of faculty. Definite dates for the beginning and ending of that period must be given except where the maximum period for an award is made, when it may be limited only by the claimant's lifetime. The potential for confusion and injustice caused by an open-ended award as in *R(I) 6/68* no longer exists. Of course, at the end of the period a fresh claim can be made. However, there is no automatic renewal. Instead, as the above subsection 6(b) and *R(I) 6/62*(T) emphasize, if a claimant wishes to continue to receive REA he must apply for it.

Although the legislation thus gives the authorities considerable discretion as to the duration of the allowance, caselaw offers some guidance as to the usual period for an award. *R(I) 73/53* suggests that where there is permanent disablement the award should be made for a considerable period. This not only enables a claimant to know where he stands, but also avoids the necessity for constant renewals. For these reasons *CI 81/49* suggested that normally REA should be awarded for a year at a time, except where a change of circumstances can be anticipated and then a shorter period may be more appropriate. As explained at p. 242, there is a reluctance to review a decision during the period for which it is still current.

(4) Reductions on receiving retirement pension or invalidity benefit

The SSA 1986 substantially changes the amount of REA to which people receiving a retirement or invalidity pension are entitled. It reduces REA by the amount of earnings-related additions to these pensions and, on retirement, it freezes the rate of REA. Each increase of the additional pension will be offset against REA until eventually all entitlement to the allowance may be lost. This affects not only future claimants, but also present beneficiaries because they are offered only limited transitional protection by the Act. Although the offset is only to be made after 6 April 1987 with regard to either new awards or increases of the additional pension, it can be made against all beneficiaries, including those presently receiving the allowance. These number about a third of the present total, for according to the 1981 White Paper, there were 50,000 beneficiaries of REA over the minimum age of retirement.

Although the TUC and IIAC objected to this attack upon established rights, they joined with others to give wide support to the reform with respect to future beneficiaries. It had long been recognized as anomalous that the allowance should continue at a time when employment would have finished and loss of earning capacity ceased. The DHSS had challenged the position in *R(I) 14/62*(T), but as discussed at p. 176, the payment of REA beyond pension age was upheld in that case because of the absence of any clear legislative intent to do otherwise. The Commissioners noted that it was open to parliament to change the rule, but it was not until the 1981 White Paper that any reform was proposed. It put forward the suggestion that payment of REA should be stopped when a person retires for national insurance purposes, or in any event, on the deemed retirement age of 70 for men and 65 for women. However, there was a particular difficulty with this: some recognition would have to be given after retirement to the earnings lost during the working life for otherwise there would be a reduction in earnings-related pension. The SSA 1986 therefore does not follow the White Paper by ending all entitlement on retirement. Instead from that time it freezes the rate of REA and offsets it against earnings-related addition to the pension. In focussing upon earnings relation the Act also takes the opportunity to offset REA against payments for invalidity, as described below.

(a) *Freezing the allowance on retirement*

The SSA 1986 sched. 3 reforms REA by inserting a new s. 59A into SSA 1975. The rate on retirement is frozen by s. 59A(11) and (13). The first of these subsections states that a person who reaches pensionable age and retires after the Act comes into force

". . . shall be treated as entitled as from the day on which he retires from regular employment to reduced earnings allowance at a rate not higher at any time than that at which the allowance was payable to him immediately before he retired from regular employment."

Existing beneficiaries in retirement are also affected. If before the Act was passed they were receiving REA under its former name of special hardship allowance, the rate is to be frozen as from the date when s. 59A(13) comes into force. This will probably be 6 April 1987. For future beneficiaries the relevant date is laid down by subsection (11) above as the date of retirement.

(b) *Offsetting the earnings-related additions to the pensions*

The main provision for offsetting is made by s. 59A(14):

"Where . . . a person is entitled both to reduced earnings allowance and to an additional pension of a long-term benefit or, if the long-term benefit is invalidity pension, to either an invalidity allowance or an additional pension, or both, his reduced earnings allowance shall be reduced in respect of the period falling on or after 6 April 1987 by the amount of any increase in the additional pension or invalidity allowance . . . taking effect on or after that date."

REA is thus offset against any award or increases in the "additional pension" – this is the earnings-related element – "of a long-term benefit". This is defined by SSA 1975 sched. 20 to include both the contributory retirement pension and invalidity pension. In the case of invalidity the section goes on to offset REA against not only the earning-related increase of invalidity pension, but also the invalidity allowance. This is the flat-rate addition to the pension payable to claimants whose incapacity began five years or more before pensionable age.

The offsetting provisions also ensure that a claimant will not avoid this reduction in REA if he receives the earnings-related addition from a private occupational pension scheme instead of from the State. Contracting out of the State scheme does not affect the claimant's right to the basic State pension. However, the earnings-related element of that pension will be reduced by what is known as the guranteed minimum pension, that is, the separate right to a minimum amount of occupational pension. If such a reduction is made there could be nothing left in the State pension to offset against REA if it were not for s. 59A(17). This allows REA to be reduced by the amount which the State earnings-related pension was reduced because of the guaranteed minimum. It states:

"Where the weekly rate of benefit is reduced under s. 29 of the Social Security Pensions Act 1975, there shall be subtracted from the amount which would otherwise fall to be deducted under sub-paragraph (14) or (15) above an amount equal to the reduction under that section."

Because of these various offsetting provisions REA will be reduced with each increase in the additional pension. For those in retirement whose allowance is frozen the eventual effect will be the loss of all entitlement to the allowance. This is the result of s. 59A(16) which states:

"Where a reduction falls to be made . . . , the person to whom it falls to be made shall be entitled to reduced earnings allowance only if there is a balance after the reduction and, if there is such a balance, of an amount equal to it."

8. REFORM

It is generally recognized that REA has been the feature of the industrial scheme which has caused most dissatisfaction. The Pearson Commission agreed that it required "radical rethinking", but recommended only that study be made of the European provisions for compensating partial incapacity. The DHSS did not do this. Instead, in its Discussion Document it put forward three broad options for reform. These were to abolish REA completely; to reduce its importance by returning to the original idea that it should compensate only if the wage loss were disproportionate to the loss of faculty; and finally, to retain the allowance as at present, but to make certain reforms which would meet the main criticisms. It was this last option which was adopted and led to the changes made in the SSA 1986.

The Discussion Document stated the blueprint for reform to be as follows:

"(i) The allowance should remain the subordinate means of compensation. Loss of faculty as the basis for the main benefit has been a success.

(ii) The starting point for the allowance needs to be the real loss to the claimant.

(iii) The person who has suffered a heavy loss of earnings because of his disability should receive compensation by way of an allowance which more nearly reflects that loss and conversely the person who has suffered only a small loss should get minimal compensation.

(iv) The allowance must take account of existing provisions within the social security scheme for invalidity."

These principles gave rise to the 1981 White Paper. Its proposals were largely followed in the 1985 Consultation Paper, although it was then suggested that, whereas certain changes could be implemented soon, others would have to be deferred until after a survey upon disablement becomes available, probably in 1988. The changes which could be made were implemented by the SSA 1986. Details of them have been examined at appropriate points earlier in this chapter. However, they are again outlined here in order for them to be related to the other reforms which are planned. Together they give a more complete picture of the immediate future of the allowance.

(1) The 1986 Act

The main changes to REA made by the SSA 1986 are:

(*a*) *Earnings are index-linked* in determining the probable standard of remuneration. This is discussed at p. 186. The change was widely supported, for it reduces the considerable administrative effort involved in establishing wage levels in order to compare the levels of earnings before and after the accident. It also makes it easier to raise the maximum allowance as considered in (2)(*a*) below. It was possible to justify the maximum by arguing that it prevented too detailed consideration of a claimant's position. However, there is now less need for the rate of REA to be kept low in order to ease the burden upon the DHSS. Instead it is index-linking which may prevent an individual's circumstances being considered in excessive detail.

(*b*) *The ceiling on the allowance is removed* by making it independent of disablement benefit. This is discussed at p. 195. The maximum allowance, when combined with disablement pension has been raised from 100 to 140 per cent of the maximum for a disablement pension alone. Only about 2 per cent of pensioners benefit from this change, although they are the more seriously injured who are assessed as at least 70 per cent disabled.

(*c*) *After retirement payment is frozen and offset against earnings-related pension.* This is discussed at p. 196. Instead of replacing REA with a small pension as originally proposed in the White Paper, the Act freezes the rate of the allowance on retirement. It also deducts from it any earnings-related additional pension so that gradually entitlement will be lost.

(2) Further changes planned

Three further proposals put forward in the White Paper were deferred by the Consultation Paper until the survey on disablement becomes available. They are:

(*a*) *The maximum allowance is to be raised* from its present rate, equivalent to a 40 per cent disablement pension, to that for 100 per cent. As with (1)(*b*) the general aim here is to increase the number of claimants who receive full reimbursement for their lost earnings. Only 10 per cent did so before the reform in (1)(*b*) and that figure will change little. The White Paper considered that, because of the costs involved in more than doubling the allowance, the change should be phased in over several years. The next proposal tries to avoid any increase in expenditure caused by raising the maximum.

(*b*) *Only half of any earnings loss is to be compensated.* This is put forward because, potentially, REA can lead to overcompensation. This may arise because entitlement to REA is not based upon a reduction in take-home pay, but upon the difference in gross earnings. Because REA is not taxed and national insurance contributions are not deducted, a claimant can receive more in benefit than the real wages lost. However, this rarely happens because there is a maximum amount of allowance that can be paid. This prevents the great majority of beneficiaries from being fully reimbursed for their actual losses. Few can make a profit. However, if the maximum is raised as suggested in 2(*a*), the White Paper considered that "genuine incentive problems" could arise. It therefore proposed that REA should replace only half of the earnings lost. In practice, this would mean that, because of the use of gross figures, around 80 per cent of the net wage loss would be replaced.

(*c*) *Payments for sickness and invalidity are to be taken into account.* This again reflects the concern of the White Paper to compensate only for the real loss of earnings, and to reduce any disincentive effects. It proposed that, if an industrial injury prevents a claimant from working, any sickness or invalidity benefit should be treated as post-accident earnings. Any actual earnings, such as employer's sick pay, should also be taken into account. In rare cases, where former low earners qualified for both REA and an invalidity pension, a particular restriction might have to be imposed to preserve incentives: the combined benefits should not exceed 85 per cent of the pre-accident earnings as revalued by index-linking.

CHAPTER 8

MAKING CLAIMS

A claim under the industrial scheme may be either for benefit, or for a declaration that an industrial accident has occurred. In both cases the first step is usually to report the accident to the employer, followed by giving notice of the claim to the DHSS. The claimant is then obliged to furnish relevant information and submit himself to medical examination and treatment. However, in practice the most important aspects of making a claim are the time limits involved, the excuses for not complying with them, and the extent to which benefit can be backdated.

1. REPORTING THE ACCIDENT TO THE EMPLOYER

One of the preliminary steps in making a claim is to report the accident to the employer.[1] If this is not done it can lead to disqualification from benefit as explained at p. 257. However, if there is "good cause" for not reporting the accident immediately the claimant will not be prejudiced. Thus claims succeeded in *R(I) 59/52* and in *R(I) 2/51* where the injuries were thought at first to be too trivial to be worth reporting, and only later proved to have serious consequences. It is good practice to report all accidents that occur, not only to prevent later disqualification from benefit, but also to ensure that a claim does not fail for lack of proof. By PD reg. 18 prescribed diseases need not be reported.

By SSA s. 88 and CP reg. 24 as soon as is practicable after the accident notice of it must be given either by the injured person, or by someone acting on his behalf. The notice can be written or oral and can be given to the employer, foreman or supervisor. One of the best ways of giving notice is to enter the details in the accident book. This book must be kept by employers of ten or more people working at the same premises, and by employers who occupy a mine, quarry or premises covered by the Factories Act 1961. The book must be made readily available to accident victims or their representatives and must be kept for three years after its last entry. It need not be kept on board a ship, for a special regulation deals with how an employee may then give notice and what are the obligations of an employer following an accident to a mariner.[2] In giving notice the following minimum details are required: the full name, address and occupation of the injured person; the date, time and place of the accident; the cause and nature of the injury; and particulars of the person giving notice.

---

[1] Willis p. 414 *et seq.*
[2] Reg. 6 of the Social Security (Industrial Injuries) (Mariners' Benefits) Regs. 1975 SI No. 470.

By CP reg. 25 employers have a corresponding duty to investigate an accident and if they find any discrepancy with the details notified to them they must record the circumstances. When a claim for benefit is made employers must complete form BI 76. This is sent by the DHSS in order to obtain information concerning the accident, and the nature of the claimant's job.

Employers are also under an obligation to give information in certain circumstances to the Health and Safety Executive. A duty to report is imposed by the Reporting of Injuries Diseases and Dangerous Occurrences Regulations 1985 (SI No. 2023) made under the Health and Safety at Work Act 1974. Employers must report not only fatalities, major injuries and dangerous occurrences, but also any accident which causes incapacity for work for more than three days. In addition these regulations introduce a basic system for reporting industrial disease. Most of the diseases presently prescribed under the industrial scheme must be notified. The most notable exceptions to this are occupational deafness, dermatitis, tenosynovitis and the various "beat" conditions. However, this new reporting system for diseases is still unlikely to produce a full picture of the extent illness is related to work. The duty to report lies only upon the current employer, and there is no requirement to notify diseases resulting from exposure during previous employment. The duty only arises if the employer has been given notice of the disease by a doctor, and for a variety of reasons it has been suggested that doctors frequently are not able to make a diagnosis connecting illness with employment in the specific manner required by the regulations. When these problems are combined with that of simply failing to report injuries which are notifiable, it is apparent that the regulations leave scope for the continued under-estimation of the extent that work can be damaging to health.

2. Claiming a Declaration that an Industrial Accident has Occurred

Although an accident may give rise to no immediate injury, its harmful effects may be revealed sometime in the future. Steps can be taken at the time of the accident to safeguard the right to benefit while the evidence is still fresh, and memories accurate. A claim for benefit need not be involved. By SSA s. 107(2)

> ". . . any person suffering personal injury by accident shall be entitled, if he claims the accident was an industrial accident, to have that question determined, and a declaration made and recorded accordingly, notwithstanding that no claim for benefit has been made in connection with which the question arise; . . ."

This right exists even if a claim for benefit is disallowed on other grounds. Despite its importance, there are few cases dealing with declarations However, one example is *CI 221/82* (unreported) where the claimant in the course of his work suddenly encountered a radio transmitting antenna and was exposed to a dose of radiation. Fearing the possibility of latent injury he successfully claimed a declaration that an industrial accident had occurred. Similarly a declaration may be sought where there is accidental exposure to asbestos. However, by Adj. reg. 41(1) declarations are not available for prescribed diseases.

The procedure gives statutory form to the practice which grew up under the Workmen's Compensation Acts of making a "declaration of liability" or "suspensory award".[3] Although the declaration is conclusive as to the question whether the accident arises out of and in the course of employment, according to SSA s. 117(3) it does not decide whether injury actually resulted, because that is a matter which can only be determined when a claim for benefit is made. This means that a declaration will be refused if proof of accident depends entirely upon proof of injury, as where the claim was in respect of a hernia in *R(I) 7/73*.

The right to a declaration is qualified by SSA s. 107(3) which gives power to the AO, SSAT or Commissioner, subject to appeal, to

"... refuse to determine the question ... if satisfied that it is unlikely that it will be necessary to determine the question for the purposes of any claim for benefit. ... ."

The power was exercised in *R(I) 1/82* where the Commissioner said:

"Many untoward accidents occur during the course of a person's employment without personal injury. If an employee's spectacles are damaged or broken, or he trips, falls, tears his clothing, slips or some other incident occurs without any suggestion of personal injury, in my opinion, a declaration of an industrial accident should depend upon the circumstances and not be as a matter of form."

3. ENTITLEMENT TO BENEFIT DEPENDENT UPON MAKING A CLAIM

Entitlement to benefit only arises if a claim is made, for the right to industrial injuries benefit cannot accrue as a matter of course. This was emphasized in *R(I) 6/62*(T) where a majority of Commissioners held that an award of REA from one period to another automatically terminated at the end of the set time, and a fresh claim had to be made if the allowance were to be renewed. If it were otherwise "a claimant could compel the statutory authorities to leave a claim in abeyance and could revive it many years afterwards when, owing to the lapse of time, there would be the utmost difficulty in investigating it". This position has now been affirmed by statute. SSA 1986 inserts s. 165A into the SSA 1975:

Except in such cases as may be prescribed, no person shall be entitled to any benefit unless, in addition to any other conditions relating to that benefit being satisfied — ...
(a) he makes a claim for it in the prescribed manner and within the prescribed time; or
(b) by virtue of regulations ... he is treated as making a claim for it."

In examining below the prescribed manner and time for claiming benefit it will be seen that there is a considerable degree of flexibility which allows, for example, claims to be backdated.

---

[3]   See Willis p. 335 *et seq.*

In examining below the prescribed manner and time for claiming benefit it will be seen that there is a considerable degree of flexibility which allows, for example, claims to be backdated.

4. CLAIMING BENEFIT ON THE APPROPRIATE FORMS

By CP reg. 4 claims for social security benefit must be in writing on a form approved by the Secretary of State or in some other manner which he accepts as sufficient. In practice a letter setting out the full facts may suffice, but it is better to use the claim forms available free of charge from any social security office. They are numbered as follows:

(1) For a declaration that an industrial accident has occurred — BI 95.
(2) For disablement benefit where entitlement is based on:-
    (a)   injury by accident — BI 100 A.
    (b)   most prescribed diseases — BI 100 B.
    (c)   occupational deafness — BI 100 (OD).
    (d)   pneumoconiosis and byssinosis — BI 100 (Pn).
(3) For constant attendance allowance — BI 104. (If the initial assessment of disablement is 100 per cent entitlement is considered automatically.)
Exceptionally severe disablement allowance is considered automatically with constant attendance allowance.
(4) For reduced earnings allowance — BI 103.

5. OBLIGATIONS ON MAKING A CLAIM

By CP reg. 7(1), made under SSA s. 88:

> "Every person who makes a claim for benefit shall furnish such certificates, documents, information and evidence for the purpose of determining the claim as may be required by the Secretary of State and, if reasonably so required, shall for that purpose attend at such office or place as the Secretary of State may direct."

In particular for industrial injury benefit CP reg. 26, made under SSA s. 89, requires that a claimant complies with all written notices from the Secretary of State requiring him either

> "(a) to submit himself to a medical examination by a medical authority for the purpose of determining the effect of the relevant accident or the treatment appropriate to the relevant injury or loss of faculty; or
> (b) to submit himself to such medical treatment for the said injury or loss of faculty as is considered appropriate in his case by the medical practitioner in charge of the case or by any medical authority to whose examination he has submitted himself . . . ."

Failure to comply with these obligations can lead to disqualification from benefit. This is considered in chapter 10 which deals, in particular, with the obligations to give information and to undergo medical treatment.

6. CLAIMING IN TIME

A claim for benefit can be made as soon as the claimant wishes, although by SSA s. 57(4) entitlement will only arise after 15 weeks have elapsed since the date of the accident, or onset of the disease. In order for the papers to be processed and benefit paid promptly, a claim should be made after about nine weeks.

Although there is no objection to making an early claim, there are disadvantages in leaving matters late. As noted above, SSA s. 165 A states that entitlement to any social security benefit only arises if a claim is made within the prescribed time. For industrial injury benefit the relevant limit is imposed by CP reg. 14 and sched. 1 made under SSA s. 82(1). A claim must be made within three months of "any day on which, apart from satisfying the condition of making the claim, the claimant is entitledto benefit.... ." Generally, therefore, a claim should be made at the latest within about six months of the accident, or onset of the disease. However, this does not mean that delay extinguishes the right to claim any benefit at all; it is not as if it were an action for common law damages which falls foul of the Limitation Acts. Instead the effect of delay is to make it possible to disqualify the claimant from benefit for any period more than three months before the date of the claim.

The three month time limit is not absolute for it is subject to the important exceptions examined below. Nor is it harsh by comparison to the limits imposed for other benefits, such as those for sickness or invalidity where claims must be made within three weeks. However, the limit still makes it important to claim benefit promptly. In particular, reduced earnings allowance should be sought as soon as the conditions of entitlement are satisfied even if, as yet, there is no current award of a disablement pension. It is often not appreciated that the allowance must be claimed separately and that entitlement is not considered automatically when disablement benefit is claimed. The three month time limit can then be the cause of the loss of a significant amount of benefit.

The number of claims for industrial benefit affected by the time limit is uncertain. In an IIAC report on time limits in 1952 (Cmd. 8511) it was noted that a survey had shown that "as many as 3 per cent of claimants for main disablement benefit suffered some forfeiture for delay in claiming". Following the report's recommendations the time limits were eased but with what effect is not known. The one book exclusively dealing with the subject, whilst unable to draw firm conclusions, considers that for benefits in general the limits "cause a significant amount of difficulty to claimants".[4] At the same time the study concludes that the reasons which have been put forward for the rules are not really justifiable in terms of the broad objectives of a social security system, and that the limits for all benefits should be extended to six months or a year.

In prescribing the three month limit for industrial injury benefit the regulations allow for two exceptions. The first of these is no longer of relevance following the ending of lump sum payments by the SSA 1986. This exception is that, although any pension including one lieu of a gratuity was affected, the disqualification did not apply to the claim for the gratuity itself. This was recognized as anomalous in *R(I) 14/74* but the position was

---

[4] M. Partington, *Claim in Time* (1978) p. 16.

affirmed in *R(I) 5/82*. The exception was given statutory force in 1986 when SI No. 903 amended the CP regs. to reflect these Commissioners' decisions.

By contrast the second exception is of current importance, and often enables the time limits to be avoided. It is that if there has been some continuous "good cause" for failing to make a claim in time the period can be extended to cover any earlier entitlement to benefit. If there is a good cause, as considered in the next section, the award can be backdated if necessary to years before the date of the claim, so that, for example, nine years benefit was obtained in *R(I) 10/74*. This means that, unlike other social security payments, industrial injuries benefit is not subject to the absolute limit imposed by SSA s. 82 which prevents benefit being obtained for more than a year before the claim even if good cause can be shown. According to the IIAC 1952 report the more generous treatment of injured workers is because disablement benefit, unlike other social security payments, includes a considerable element of compensation for the injury sustained. Despite this attempt at justifying the position, it appears anomalous, and it is difficult to defend the further advantage given to claimants under the industrial scheme.

However, if an award is backdated to a much earlier period in time, the rate to be paid is that applicable to the scale in force at that time. Thus in *R(I) 5/82* a gratuity was valued at the beginning of the period of assessment in 1969, and not at the date of the claim in 1977 when it would have been worth four times the sum. Similarly in *R(I) 1/86* a claimant, on review, obtained an increased assessment of his disablement which related back over 20 years. It was held that he was entitled only to the increase his pension based upon the rates in force at the earlier dates, even though the value of these payments had since been eroded by inflation. A reason for this denial of the real value of a claim was stated in *R(I) 5/82*: it would be wrong to allow a claimant to inflate the amount to which he would be entitled by making a long-delayed claim, even though he could have had interest on the money if he had claimed it earlier and invested it.

7. WHAT CONSTITUTES GOOD CAUSE JUSTIFYING A LATE CLAIM

Commissioners' interpretations of what amounts to a sufficient excuse to justify a late claim can vary considerably. In emphasizing the particular circumstances of the claimant, they make it difficult to apply clear general principles to decide whether there should be disqualification from benefit. Lord Macmillan's view of the workmen's compensation cases on the subject[5] in *Shotts Iron Co. Ltd. v. Fordyce* (1930) was that they

> "... furnish an unhappy instance of history teaching by examples, for the only lesson which they impart is that no one case can govern any other and that each case depends upon its own circumstances."

However, it is possible to recognize, as the Commissioners did in *R(I) 2/63*(T), that over the years the rules have been interpreted progressively in favour of claimants.

---

[5]   Willis p. 430 *et seq.*

Good cause was described in *CS 371/49* as meaning

> "some fact which, having regard to all the circumstances (including the claimant's state of health and the information which he had received and that which he might have obtained) would probably have caused a reasonable person of his age and experience to act (or fail to act) as the claimant did."

The many Commissioners' decisions cover a wide range of benefits. The following list of excuses, although dealing with the main general principles applicable throughout social security, concentrates upon the rules which are of special concern to the industrial scheme.

(1) Ignorance or misunderstanding of law

The most common excuse given by claimants for failing to apply for benefit in time is that they were unaware of any entitlement under the industrial scheme. Sometimes there is ignorance of the existence of disablement benefit but, more often, it is reduced earnings allowance which has caused problems. Many claimants would be surprised to be told, as in *R 7/84(II)*, that generally their ignorance does not justify delay. However, this rule is subject to such important exceptions as to appear at times to have been honoured more in the breach than the observance. The general rule was referred to in *R(S) 2/63:*

> "Ignorance of one's rights is not of itself good cause for delay in claiming. It is in general the duty of the claimant to find out what they are, and how and when they should be asserted. But an examination of numerous Commissioners' decisions shows that over the years there has been a gradual but appreciable relaxation of the strictness with which problems of good and reasonable cause have been approached."

Before examining any relaxation in the rule, its application can be illustrated by three cases. In *R(I) 16/53* the claimant believed that before he could claim he needed to establish with his own doctor that he had a good cause on medical grounds. His ignorance of the statutory procedures and of the existence of independent medical boards – was held to be no excuse, and benefit was lost. In *R(I) 79/54* the claimant's belief that her claim for sickness benefit would ensure that she would be awarded all the benefit to which she was entitled was also held to be no excuse for the delayed industrial injury claim.

Similarly, the claim failed in *R12/84(I)* despite the claimant being of low education, having little experience of forms, and reasonably relying upon the advice of a workmate.

Excuse

Apart from the claimant being subject to some personal disability, as considered in (3) below, there are three excuses which may enable a late claim to succeed if the claimant is unaware or had a mistaken view of his legal rights:

(a) *The claimant is unaware of any entitlement at all*

The distinction here is between the claimant who is unaware that a claim can be made, and one who is ignorant only of the application of the time limit rules. In *R 9/62(II)* the claimant was involved in a road accident but in circumstances which made him unaware that he was in the course of employment at the time. He failed to claim benefit for three years. Relying upon *R(S) 11/59,* the Commissioner allowed the late claim on the basis that:

> "... there is a fundamental distinction between failure to safeguard one's right in not making a claim within the time prescribed and failure to make a claim timeously, when there are reasonable grounds for being unaware that there are any rights which require to be safeguarded, or that the circumstances call for any inquiry as to possible rights."

Apart from the fact that many people do not appreciate that the industrial scheme can cover road accidents, it is difficult on the facts of this case to find any special reason for the claimant being generously treated in comparison to other less fortunate applicants who have fallen foul of the general rule as to ignorance of rights. However, the claimant also succeeded on a similar basis in *R(I) 43/55.* There it was held that he could not be expected to grasp the fine legal point that his psychoneurotic condition, resulting from a series of explosions at work, could be described as injury by accident.

(b) There has been a complex change in the law

In *CI 439/50*(T) the transitional provisions from workmen's compensation to the modern industrial injury scheme were held to be such that it was difficult for the claimant to decide how he should protect his rights, and this provided a good cause for the late claim. Given the frequency of legislative change, this argument could be of considerable importance, although *CG 125/50* suggests that ignorance of entitlement to new benefit cannot justify delay for a long period.

(c) The claimant relies upon inadequate advice

A claimant must take reasonable steps to find out about entitlement to benefit. If advice is sought and the claimant relies upon wrong information which causes him to fail to claim in time, he is likely to be able to establish a good cause. However, it remains unclear upon which sources the claimant may be taken to reasonably rely and what help should be expected from the DHSS. Cases have considered the following sources:

(i) DHSS FORMS AND LEAFLETS. Until recently many written sources of official information were drafted using the precise words of the relevant legislation. The result was that they were difficult to understand. Many of them still remain obscure, but that fact, of itself, will not enable a claimant to establish good cause for delay unless it can also be shown that the advice is misleading. This was the case in *R(I) 6/62*(T) where a leaflet on reduced earnings allowance wrongly implied that a further decision would be given automatically at the end of the period of the award, and that there was therefore no need for a further claim to be made. However, the allegation that a claim form was vague was rejected in *R 8/83(II).*

The DHSS failure to send out the proper forms was a factor in establishing good cause in *R(I) 25/61* and *R 4/64(II).* In its defence the department frequently relies upon having given notice of entitlement to other benefits in notes accompanying claim forms and leaflets. However, some reservation towards this attempted justification of the department's action was expressed by the Commissioner in *R 3/79(II).* He noted that

"... there are said to be at present approximately two million adults in the United Kingdom who are unable to read or have difficulty in reading. Doubtless there are many who, though able to read, are not well able to understand information contained in official documents. . . ."

For such people in the exceptional cases discussed below something more may be required than the distribution of a leaflet.

(ii) DHSS OFFICIALS. In *R(I) 10/74* affirmed in *R* v. *National Insurance Commissioner, ex p. Parkin* (1972), it was said that people should seek information from a local DHSS office where

"there is a clear duty on officials . . . to give proper advice and to be astute to ensure that a person understands the advice that is given".

The case involved a claimant who was correctly told by a clerk that on returning to his regular occupation he was not entitled to reduced earnings allowance. However, he later abandoned his old job and took lighter, less well paid work thus entitling him to the allowance. His disability became worse, and when he later successfully applied for a review to increase his assessment he also inquired whether he was entitled to other benefits. He was wrongly told that he was not. He was found to have good cause for failing to claim the allowance. The Commissioner relied upon *R(I) 28/59* where again the claimant "made it abundantly clear to the officials to whom he spoke that he was anxious to obtain every financial assistance. . . ". The difficulty here is what is to happen where claimants do not press their case quite so hard. To what extent will the DHSS be expected to take a more active role to ensure that claimants obtain the benefits to which they are entitled? It is clear that a burdensome review of the circumstances of all claimants, or the widespread distribution of unsolicited information on benefits, cannot be expected. Thus in *R 3/79(II)* it was agreed that the department did not have to review all cases of disablement benefit to discover whether there was also entitlement to reduced earnings allowance. However, on the facts of the case the Commissioner found special circumstances which led him to make the suggestion that, in similar cases, the DHSS should consider sending a claim form for reduced earnings allowance when it sends the claimant notice of entitlement to disablement benefit. The special circumstances of the case were that the DHSS had evidence not only that the claimant was clearly entitled to the allowance, but also that he was ill and of only limited education. Apart from such exhortations from Commissioners as to what ought to be done, a claimant may also rely upon common DHSS practice in order to establish that, in his particular case, there has been a failure of advice, or of proper procedure, and that good cause for delay therefore exists. The difficulty claimants then face is in discovering what constitutes DHSS common practice.

(iii) SOLICITORS. In *CSI 10/50* the claimant was advised by his solicitor that an industrial injury claim might prejudice his action for damages against his employer. He was advised instead to go to the Assistance Board where officials would "keep him right". Relying upon this advice he failed to claim industrial injury benefit in time, but he was found to have good cause for not doing so.

(iv) DOCTORS. In *R(I) 40/59* it was held that to act upon a doctor's advice as to the legal requirement of a claim was not good cause. However, on the facts of the case benefit was paid because the doctor had advised that the claim be delayed on the basis of his mistaken view that it was uncertain whether pneumoconiosis was present in addition to tuberculosis. Other cases of mistaken diagnosis are considered in (2) below.

(v) OTHER ADVISERS. Good cause may be established as in *R(U) 9/74* if reliance is placed upon advice from bodies such as citizens' advice bureaux, which specialise in giving information upon social security. However, advice from less expert sources such as fellow workmates as in *R12/84(II)*, friends, or family will generally not suffice. There is no authority on the position where advice is obtained from a trade union.

(2) Ignorance of medical condition

According to Willis the workmen's compensation rule was that:

> "When the effects of an injury are not apparent at the time, or when there is a well-grounded belief that the injury is trivial, the applicant will generally succeed in showing that his delay in giving notice of the accident or in making a claim was due to mistake or other reasonable cause."

This rule was applied in *CI 273/50* where the claimant injured his thumb at work, but reasonably believed the effects would not be serious and no loss of faculty would result. This belief was held to be reasonable in particular because the doctor had not indicated that the joint would become stiff. Five months after the accident it became clear that the injury was permanent, and benefit was successfully obtained for the backdated period. Similarly, later medical examinations revealed the true extent of the injury and successful claims were made in *R(I) 16/51* and *6/59(II)*.

A second ground for claiming good cause here is that, although a worker suffers from what may be a serious injury, he fails to connect it with his job and does not therefore seek benefit. This may happen because of a doctor's mistaken diagnosis. For example, the incapacity was thought to be due to bronchitis or tuberculosis and not pneumoconiosis in *R(I) 24/58* and *R(I) 40/59*. The mistake may also be made by the claimant himself. For example, in *R(I) 51/54* he failed to realize that an injury to a knee can also affect a tubercular hip joint.

A related third excuse for a late claim is that the claimant is entirely unaware of his injury. In *R(I) 6/54* the claimant thought that his shortness of breath and loss of strength was due to the onset of old age. Only following a routine check by a mass-radiography unit did he suspect that he had pneumoconiosis. Benefit was successfully obtained for a two year period before the date of claim. Reliance upon this case failed in *R 8/83(II)* where it was found that the claimant did in fact know that she might be suffering from byssinosis and yet failed to claim.

If any of these excuses are to succeed the claimant's belief must be reasonable and continuous up to the date of the claim. This means that if the claimant becomes aware that a doctor's diagnosis is mistaken and still fails to act promptly, benefit will be lost. This happened in *R(I) 16/53* where the claimant knew that his doctor's recommendation merely to apply a salve to his wrist was insufficient and that he was more severely handicapped than his doctor believed. However, he failed to inquire further and, in waiting to see whether his doctor's optimistic diagnosis was justified, he lost benefit. Similarly good cause was not established in *R(I) 82/53* where the claimant knew he was suffering from a disease related to work, but he did not know that it was one of the prescribed diseases until he contacted a dermatologist.

(3) Claimant's personal disability limits the capacity to claim

If a claimant is in some way less able to pursue his right to benefit than other injured workers there may be an excuse for failing to claim in time. The following factors have been taken into account:

(a) Intelligence or lack of education

Allowance was made for this in *R(P) 10/59*. The claimant's literacy may influence the decision whether the DHSS has communicated its views effectively, as in *R(I) 1/84* and as considered above in relation to *R 3/79(II)*. However, in *R(G) 1/75* illiteracy or language problems of themselves were considered insufficient to amount to good cause. In *1/51(II)* the fact that a claimant was a 15-year-old youth did not of itself justify a delayed claim.

(b) Physical disability

In so far as the claimant concentrates so much upon his injury that it prevents him thinking about making a claim, it may help him establish good cause for delay as in *R(I) 51/54*. The claimant's diabetes which required two injections a day was considered relevant in *R 3/79(II)*.

(c) Mental disability

In *R(I) 43/55* the mental state of the claimant was such that he could not be expected to grasp that he might have a claim for benefit. However, the claimant's fear of discovering that he really was suffering from pneumoconiosis in *R(I) 24/56* was no excuse for failing to seek benefit. This case contrasts with the "genuine phobia" about consulting a doctor in *R(S) 7/61*.

(4) Failure of those acting on the claimant's behalf

The regulations do not require that the claimant applies for benefit in person. It is sufficient that another does so on his behalf. Where the claimant has delegated responsibility in this way and there is delay in making the claim, good cause can be shown if the claimant has reasonably believed that the delegate would act for him. It is easier to show this if the delegate has been specifically told to make a particular claim, rather than simply being left to handle the claimant's affairs in general. Of a number of cases on the subject, only two deal with claims for industrial injury and in both of them the claimant was successful. In *R(I) 28/54* the agent was the employer, whilst in *R 3/72(II)* he was a solicitor. Although asked to deal with all claims arising out of an industrial accident the solicitor failed to claim reduced earnings allowance in time. The delegation provided the justification for the claimant obtaining an award backdated for three years. However, where a solicitor failed to appeal to a Commissioner in time in *CI 449/81* (unreported) it was suggested that "the claimant must be identified with the acts or omissions of his advisers and representatives". This case may be confined to time limits for appeals only, because in relation to claims for benefit the agency excuse is well recognized. Of particular interest to the industrial scheme is *CU 78/49* where delegation to a trade union official provided good cause for delay.

(5) Claimant awaits determination of other claim

In *R 4/64(II)* the claimant applied for a declaration that he had suffered an industrial accident. Although this application was successful the DHSS failed to send him notice of this, and whilst waiting for the result, the claimant was held to have a good excuse for failing to claim. The most important application of this general principle used to be in relation to reduced earnings allowance when, according to *R(I) 28/59* and *CI 322/82* (unreported) the claimant had good cause for delay in applying for the allowance if he awaited the outcome of the claim for disablement benefit. This excuse came to an end in 1984 when sched. 1 of the CP regs. was amended. Now, as further amended by reg. 5 of the Social Security (Industrial Injuries and Diseases) Miscellaneous Provisions Regulations 1986 (SI No. 1561), the CP regs. sched. 1 para. 10A provides that, for REA, the three month time limit runs

> "... from the first day on which the conditions, other than the making of the claim, for receipt of the allowance are satisfied."

This means that time continues to run in REA cases even if there is no current award of disablement benefit.

CHAPTER 9

ADJUDICATION UPON CLAIMS, APPEALS AND REVIEWS

1. INTRODUCTION

The system of adjudication in the case of an industrial injury is comprised of the four tiers indicated in the flow chart at p. 6: the initial decision on a claim is usually taken by an adjudication officer, and may be followed by successive appeals to a local tribunal or medical authority, a Social Security Commissioner and ultimately the High Court. Adjudication is more complicated than in other social security cases. In particular, industrial injury cases are more likely to give rise to medical questions and the scheme requires that these be resolved by expert bodies. In addition the complexity of the scheme has meant that more use has been made of the procedure for appeal and review than where other benefits have been involved. These factors partly account for the greater administrative cost of the scheme as discussed at p. 11. Although this chapter thus concentrates upon those features of adjudication which are peculiar to the industrial scheme and are of most concern to injured workers, it also describes the decision-making process for benefits as a whole. It therefore deals with matters covered in more general social security books.[1]

The relevant legislation has been revised in recent years. It is now largely contained within SSA sections 97-117 and the Social Security (Adjudication) Regulations 1984 (SI No. 451). In 1985 a 90-page booklet was published by HMSO entitled *Social Security Appeal Tribunals – A Guide to Procedure*. It has the approval of the President of SSATs and of the Regional Chairmen. However, further changes to the legislation have since been made by the SSA 1986. These are taken into account in this chapter, although they are not expected to be in force until April 1987.

An important feature of the adjudication is that it is largely achieved via a system of tribunals rather than through the more traditional court structure. The inter-war years saw growing dissatisfaction with adjudication of workmen's compensation by the courts. Private insurers were all too ready to resort to litigation in the event of a dispute and this threat was often a strong weapon in their hands. There was much criticism:

"In no time at all workmen's compensation descended from its lofty ideals of being a no-fault social service into a squalid legal battlefield between trade

---

[1] A. I. Ogus and E. M. Barendt, *The Law of Social Security* (2nd ed. 1982) chap. 15. For a critical analysis see J. Fulbrook, *Administrative Justice and the Unemployed* (1978) Part III. For a claimant's step by step guide see NACAB *Social Security Appeals* (1980).

unions and insurance companies, with lying, cheating and chicanery on all sides and astronomical expenditure on administrative, legal and medical costs."[2]

When industrial injuries were incorporated within the new system of national insurance in 1948 the courts were replaced by tribunals in an attempt to make the proceedings more informal and accessible to the public. The traditional court structure was abandoned together with its rules of evidence and procedure. In practice lawyers were almost entirely excluded from the system. The aim was to create a cheap, speedy, and informal system of justice. It was hoped that the new tribunals would soon develop special skills to make them into expert bodies processing claims efficiently and fairly. By comparison with the previous system these objectives have largely been met. Tribunals have proved so successful – not only in the field of social security – that there are now over 2,000 of them dealing with a wide spectrum of law. Their proliferation reflects two particular factors: firstly, that judges within the traditional court structure cannot be expected to have the expertize to deal with the many complex statutory schemes spawned by the welfare state especially in the last 40 years; and secondly, that it is inappropriate to resort to the paraphernalia of a court when many of the issues involved are factual. The result has been that the number of cases disposed of by tribunals are far higher than, for example, those decided by County Courts. They are so important that it has been said:

> "Social security tribunals should now be recognized for what in fact they are. For 90 per cent of the people 90 per cent of the time, tribunals are *the* courts and social security tribunals are the most important courts."[3]

2. THE ADJUDICATION OFFICER

The AO is a civil servant who works either in one of the 450 or so local DHSS offices spread throughout the country, or in one of the central DHSS offices. The AO makes the initial decision in almost all claims for benefit. Appointed for this adjudication function by the Secretary of State under SSA s. 97(1), the AO must act judicially, his sole allegiance being to the law, not the DHSS. However, few AOs spend all their time on adjudication because they also work for the DHSS by carrying out administration at the office where they are based. For example, they supervize clerical work and collect evidence on claims. According to the Chief Adjudication Officer's first annual report in 1985:

> ". . . most AOs are keen to produce a good standard of work but are frequently thwarted by the conflicting demands of their adjudicative and supervisory roles; by the working environment of the local office which is not conducive to considerate work; by insufficiency of training; and by the priorities of management, usually directed towards the speedy clearance of claims rather than to their accurate determination."

[2] Parsons (1974) 3 *Ind. Law J.* 129.
[3] Calvert, "Appeal Structures For the Future" in M. Adler and A. Bradley, *Justice, Discretion and Poverty* (1975) p. 201.

Although there are over 15,000 AOs only 2,500 have full powers enabling them to make decisions on a wide range of benefits including those for industrial injury. Those with this power can decide all the relevant issues concerning a claim for industrial benefit except for two questions which are reserved for others. These are, firstly, whether a claimant is an employed earner (this must be decided by the Secretary of State), and secondly, the "disablement questions" (these are reserved for the medical authorities).

Although as a rule personal contact between the AO and the claimant is discouraged, it may occasionally arise in industrial injury cases. This is because the complex questions involved may make the AO more prepared than in the case of other benefits to interview the claimant to sort matters out. However, even if this happens, the circumstances cannot be compared to an oral hearing before a tribunal. In the great majority of cases the AO makes a decision upon the basis of the papers alone, without contacting the claimant beforehand. The papers may contain evidence which the AO has sought from, for example, a medical authority as to the claimant's condition, or from an employer as to the circumstances of the injury or the nature of the claimant's work.

Acting on this information the AO is required by SSA s. 99 to dispose of a claim, in so far as it is practicable to do so, within 14 days of it being submitted. Disposal means making a finding either for or against the claimant, or referring a case to a tribunal for the initial decision. A referral to an adjudicating medical authority, as considered in chapter 4, is very common despite the AO having limited jurisdiction to make the initial decision. By comparison an AO rarely exercises his power to refer a non-medical case to a local tribunal. This happened only 22 times in 1985.[4] Having made his decision, the AO used to be obliged automatically to give his reasons in writing to the claimant. However, the SSA 1986 requires only that notification be given as prescribed in the regulations and these have not yet been made. However, it is expected that the rights of the claimant of industrial injuries benefit will be reduced: the Government intend to bring national insurance into line with supplementary benefit cases by requiring reasons to be given only if the claimant requests them.

If benefit is refused the AO's decision may be contested either by the claimant applying for it to be reviewed, as explained at p. 237, or by appealing to a SSAT under SSA s. 100. Leaflet NI. 246 offering guidance on how to appeal is available from the DHSS.

3. The Social Security Appeal Tribunal

An appeal or reference from an AO's decision is dealt with at an oral hearing by a SSAT. This tribunal is independent of the DHSS and consists of three people, its chairman being a lawyer. SSATs are the result of the merger in 1984 of national insurance local tribunals and supplementary benefit appeal tribunals and there are now over 330 of them distributed throughout the country. Of the 119,000 claims for disablement benefit made in 1985 about half were initially refused and, of these, about one in thirty

---

4 DHSS, *Social Security Statistics 1986* table 49.01B.

was appealed to a SSAT.[5] This rate of appeal is higher than in other benefit cases. This may be because entitlement is more complex and mistakes are more easily made. Another contributing factor is that claimants are encouraged to appeal by their trade unions which provide them with advice and representation. About 40 per cent of AO's decisions which are challenged on appeal are overturned in favour of claimants.[6] This success rate has remained constant since 1948. It is much higher than for other benefits. It rises even further if a claimant is represented by a trade union official when it has been found that over half of the appeals succeed.[7]

(1) Notice of appeal

By SSA s. 100(4) as amended by SSA 1986:

> "Regulations may make provision as to the manner in which, and the time within which, appeals are to be brought."

These regulations have not yet been made. It used to be that notice of an appeal had to be given to the local DHSS office within 28 days of the AO's decision. The Government have promised not to reduce this time limit. Previously it could be extended only by the SSAT chairman if good cause could be shown, as discussed at p. 226. The possibility of appealing against a chairman's refusal to allow a late appeal to be heard was very limited because in *R(I) 44/59* the Commissioner decided that he could only interfere in decisions of the tribunal, not those of its chairman alone. However, the chairman could reconsider his refusal in the light of further representations.

By SSA s. 100(5):

> "A notice of appeal . . . shall be in writing and shall contain a written statement of the grounds upon which the appeal is made."

An appeal may be made by completing either the simple DHSS form BF 39, or the relevant part of leaflet NI. 236 on how to appeal. However, claimants are not obliged to use either. Instead it is sufficient to send a simple letter, especially if delay in obtaining the form or leaflet might cause the claim to be filed out of time. The grounds of appeal only need to be outlined for, as *R(I) 15/53* points out, if more detail were required many claimants would be unfairly penalized. Even a DHSS counter clerk's written note of the claimant's simple wish to appeal has sufficed. The effect of this informality is that the written grounds of appeal, unlike High Court pleadings, cannot limit the scope of the tribunal hearing. Indeed, SSA s. 102 allows matters to be determined by the tribunal even if they have not been raised before the AO.

Although the law does not require the grounds of appeal to be drafted in detail, it may be to the claimant's advantage to present as full an account as possible. It could be argued that this approach at least counteracts the

---

[5] *Ibid.* In 1983 of 120,545 claims there were 1,783 appeals heard according to figures supplied to the author by the DHSS.

[6] DHSS, *Social Security Statistics 1986* table 21.20.

[7] Bell found a success rate of 54 per cent. See "National Insurance Local Tribunals – Part II" (1975) 4 *J. Social Policy* 1, 16.

AO's own submission to the appeal tribunal, and it may even encourage him to review his decision before the case goes that far. Against this it has been argued that tactically it may be better for the claimant to formulate only general grounds of appeal and wait until the AO's submission is received. The facts and law, including the statutory provisions and Commissioners' decisions relied upon by the DHSS official, can be checked in the reference books listed at p. 22. A full response can then be made before the case is heard. Whichever tactic the claimant employs he should give clear indication of the nature of his case because, if new matters are raised at the tribunal itself, the AO may ask for an adjournment for them to be considered. This can only delay further any payment of benefit.

(2) Administrative arrangement before the hearing

The DHSS forwards the notice of appeal to the AO. He either reviews the case in the claimant's favour, or prepares a submission for the tribunal as to why benefit should be refused. The submission is sent to the clerk of the SSAT, a junior DHSS officer. The clerk's duties include arranging the time and place of the hearing, dealing with all the correspondence and papers involved, and being present at the hearing to act as an usher and deal with administrative matters such as the payment of expenses. The claimant's representative should liaise with the clerk to be sure of receiving copies of the notices and papers which are sent to the claimant.

The clerk also arranges the date for hearing the case. This will be on the one or two days of the week when the tribunal usually sits. Adj. reg. 4 requires that, at least 10 days before the hearing, reasonable notice of its time and place be sent to the claimant and to anyone the chairman considers interested in the case. This could include the claimant's representative. If this has not been done the case cannot be heard without the consent of those who should have received such notice. In practice the average waiting period for a hearing is six months after the notice of appeal[7a], although this can vary according to the pressure of work upon the tribunal. The case may also be delayed if it is complex and, for example, requires medical or other evidence to be sought. If he wishes to postpone the hearing Adj. reg. 5(1) allows a claimant to apply in writing stating his reasons. The application may be granted by the chairman as he thinks fit. Even at the hearing itself the claimant may ask for the proceedings to be adjourned to a later date, and these applications under reg. 5(2) are usually granted. However, if the claimant fails to appear after being given proper notice of when his case is to be heard, reg. 4(3) allows the tribunal to proceed to make a decision which later can only be set aside on the limited grounds prescribed in Adj. reg. 10.

Before the hearing the clerk sends the claimant a copy of case papers. These include, on form AT 2, a summary of the facts and the AO's submission which refers to the relevant legislation and Commissioners' decisions. Adj. reg. 8 allows the chairman of the tribunal to exclude from these papers any medical evidence which would be harmful to the claimant's health. However, the confidential memorandum LT 1A for members of local tribunals notes that such evidence is normally disclosed

---

[7a]   DHSS, *Social Security Statistics 1986* table 49.02B.

to a representative, unless he is in a close personal relationship with the claimant.

The AO's submission can discourage many claimants especially if they are unassisted. They may decide even at this stage not to attend the hearing, when in fact they may have a good case for benefit. Some measure of perseverance is required. In fact the first report in 1985 of the Chief Adjudication Officer recognizes that the standard of written submissions by AOs leaves much to be desired:

> "Comments fell into 3 main areas. Firstly the submissions did not argue sufficiently closely specific issues involved, or included irrelevant matters; secondly, the facts of the case were not fully summarized; and thirdly, incorrect or insufficient statute or case law was quoted."

The facts and authorities relied upon by the AO should therefore be checked. The claimant may need to write a reply as discussed above. Arrangements must then be made for anyone who is willing to be called to be present at the hearing. However there is no power to require documents to be produced or to compel witnesses to attend. If witnesses are absent, a written statement of their evidence can be submitted. However, to encourage both the claimant and any witnesses to attend they can reclaim their travelling and out of pocket expenses including, on a fixed scale, any earnings lost. The clerk arranges for these to be paid. Tribunals meet in a variety of premises ranging from, most commonly, DHSS or other government offices, to community centres and town or church halls, with at least one tribunal meeting in the offices of a trade union.

(3) Participants in the hearing

The tribunal usually consists of three part-time members. By SSA s. 97(2E) the chairman must be a lawyer who has been qualified to practice for at least five years. At present there are about 640 such part-time chairmen. Although the requirement introduced in 1983 that a chairman be legally qualified has generally been welcomed, it does not guarantee that the chairman is an expert upon social security law. His previous legal experience is unlikely to have brought him into contact with this area of law and, until recently, there was little training or instruction to make up for this initial lack of knowledge of the social security system. Instead chairmen were expected to learn by simply doing the job. However, it is now the duty of the President of SSATs to train chairmen and keep them up to date. Despite this, chairmen have complained that they are still not aware of all recent developments, and especially of new Commissioners' decisions.

The two unpaid lay "wingmen" receive little training for their role. They sit less often than chairmen and therefore have less experience of hearing cases and of the law involved. They are drawn from a panel of people thought to be suitable by the President of SSATs. At present there are 6,154 people on this panel. According to SSA sched. 10 they must have "knowledge and experience of the conditions in the area" and be "representative of persons living or working" there. Despite the requirement that "if practicable, at least one of the members of the tribunal hearing a case shall be of the same sex as the claimant", women are still in the minority, constituting only 28 per cent of national insurance panels in 1983.[8] It is no longer necessary for one of the wingmen to be drawn from a panel representing employers and the other from one representing workpeople. However, the President has issued guidelines as to what constitutes a suitable balance of members for a tribunal. It is likely that SSATs will continue to be staffed by such people as middle range executives, particularly personnel managers, union officials and other nominees of Trades Councils, and by retired people. Many wingmen also serve on other tribunals or are magistrates or councillors. In criticism of them it has been said that they constitute a "local squirearchy",[9] and that "it is unfortunately true that, apart from shining exceptions, the intellectual acuity of many tribunal wingmen is not high."[10]

If a tribunal member has a previous connection with a claim which raises the possibility of bias, any decision reached is void as against natural justice. This was the result in *R(I) 25/54* where the wingmen had supplied information on the claim because he was the employer's personnel officer. However, in *R(I) 51/56* it did not matter that the wingman was a labour officer for British Coal in an area which included the pit where the claimant worked. Where there is only a remote interest it is necessary only for the member concerned to declare it at the opening of the hearing and ask if the claimant objects to him continuing to take part. The matter is one of degree. If a wingman fails to turn up for an appeal, Adj. reg. 18(2) allows the case to proceed only if the claimant agrees. In practice the claimant is asked for his written consent on form AT 3.

By Adj. reg. 18:

"(4) In such cases as the chairman of the appeal tribunal may determine, a medical practitioner may sit with that tribunal as an assessor.

(5) An assessor . . . shall not take any part in the determination or decision of that tribunal except in an advisory capacity."

According to *R(I) 14/51* and *R(I) 23/57* the assessor must not be regarded as a witness and has no judicial powers or duties. It is undesirable for the assessor to either ask or be asked questions. Although assessors are rare, they are more likely to be found in industrial injury cases than others. They advise, for example, as to whether a disease is due to employment. However, the assessor is not an expert on the relevant disease and "in practice the [DHSS] finds it difficult to attract even general practitioners to come in specially . . .".[11]

The DHSS case may be presented by the AO who has been dealing with the claim, but more often it is handled by another officer who regularly attends tribunal hearings. This officer may not be as familiar with the background details as the original AO. On rare occasions in the past a member of the DHSS Solicitor's Office has presented the case. However, it is more likely that the DHSS will not be represented at all for in one study it was shown that in one in thirty cases even the AO was absent.[12]

Studies have shown that a higher proportion of appeals are successful if

8   *Annual Report of the Council on Tribunals 1982-83* H.C. 129 (1983-84) para. 2.17.
9   Bell, *op.cit.* p. 315.
10   J. Fulbrook, *op. cit.* p. 229.
11   H. Street, *Justice in the Welfare State* (2nd ed. 1975) p. 20.
12   Bell, "National Insurance Local Tribunals – Part I" (1974) 3 *J. Social Policy* 289, 301.

the claimant attends the hearing and receives representation. Although claimants need not attend, 80 per cent of them do so in industrial injury cases compared to only 50 per cent in claims for other benefits.[13] Attendance is encouraged in industrial injury cases because trade unions provide representation for their members and the claimant is urged to be present.

About 60 per cent of claimants are represented.[14] There is no legal aid to cover the cost of a lawyer presenting the case, and most of the representatives are trade union officials. Usually a divisional or area officer is involved, although some unions use branch officers or, less commonly, a head office official. In complicated cases a union might instruct a solicitor. A tribunal may be influenced by whether there is a trade union support for a case because it is generally known that such assistance is given only to those appeals which have merit. However, smaller unions without a strong regional or district organization often are unable to represent members, and if they do so their representation may be relatively inexperienced. Adj. reg. 2(b) does not require the representative to hold any professional qualification. The claimant can be represented by anyone whether trade union official, advice bureau worker, relative, neighbour or friend. In the absence of the claimant a representative should be able to produce written authority to appear on his behalf, although this is not a statutory requirement and a chairman may be satisfied with less formal evidence.

By Adj. reg. 4(4) hearings must be held in public unless the claimant requests otherwise, or the chairman is satisfied that intimate personal or financial circumstances may be disclosed. However, even if the claimant fails to object and the hearing is held in public, often the only people present are the parties in the case. In particular, journalists never attend tribunals to file press reports of such hearings.

(4) Procedure at the hearing

By Adj. reg. 2(a) the procedure at the hearing is "such as the chairman shall determine" except where special provision is made. This means that the procedure can vary between tribunals but it must always comply with the rules of natural justice, as discussed at p. 234 in relation to MATs. The Franks Committee's *Report On Administrative Tribunals And Enquiries* in 1957 (Cmnd. 218) suggested that tribunals should aim to combine a formal procedure with an informal atmosphere.

> "On the one hand it means a manifestly sympathetic attitude on the part of the tribunal and the absence of the trappings of the Court, but on the other hand such prescription of procedure as makes the proceedings clear and orderly."

The absence of technical rules relating to the introduction of evidence and the examination of witnesses is one of the attractions of the tribunal system, especially when many claimants are unaided and do not appreciate the distinction between evidence and argument. No oaths are administered

---

[13] *Ibid*, and DHSS, *Social Security Statistics 1986* table 49.03B.
[14] *Ibid*. Lawrence, "Representation at National Insurance Tribunals: A Research Note" (1978) 5 *J. Law & Society* 246.

before evidence is given. However, if the chairman insists upon considerable formality as in *R(I) 36/61*, this alone may not provide a basis for challenging the tribunal decision.

In practice the chairman usually begins by introducing the tribunal members by name, emphasizing their independence from the DHSS and explaining procedure. One method of proceeding is for the AO to briefly outline the facts and then for the claimant, or his representative, to put his case and call evidence from witnesses. Any member of the tribunal may intervene to ask questions at any time, although in practice it is only the chairman who usually does so. In the guide to procedure, *Social Security Appeal Tribunals* (1985) the chairman is advised as follows:

> "He should let the claimant put any points he may wish to make in his own way and air any relevant real or imagined grievance, so that nobody can reasonably say that he did not have a fair hearing. The desire for informality should not, however, be allowed to defeat the primary objective of establishing the true facts so that the tribunal can come to a correct decision in accordance with the relevant statutory provisions. The chairman must therefore be prepared to intervene impartially, when necessary, in order to ensure that the proceedings are orderly or to curb lengthy speeches which are obviously irrelevant to the question at issue."

The AO is later invited to ask questions. In turn he then presents the DHSS case and may himself be questioned by the tribunal and claimant. In some cases an officer may even support the appeal if, for example, further evidence has come to light during or shortly before the hearing. The role of the AO was considered by Lord Denning in *R* v *National Insurance Commissioner, ex p. Viscusi* (1974):

> "The proceedings are not to be regarded as if they were a law suit between opposing parties. The injured person is not a plaintiff under a legal burden of proof. The proceedings are more in the nature of an inquiry before an investigating body charged with the task of finding out what happened and what are the consequences. . . . [The DHSS] are not there to oppose [the claimant]. . . . They are simply there to help the tribunal come to a correct decision."

This means that the AO is supposed to present an objective view of the case and bring out those points which are favourable to the claimant. However, according to the President of SSAT's letter to the Chief Adjudication Officer in February 1985, although the "better, more experienced Presenting Officers tend to act as *amicus curiae*, . . . those who are new or inexperienced tend to fight the AO's corner". Finally each side is invited to respond to the other's case and the chairman may summarize the salient points of evidence. The room is them cleared for the tribunal to make its decision.

(5) The decision

To arrive at its decision the tribunal must order everyone else to withdraw. This includes the AO, although the clerk may remain but take no part in the deliberations. Subject to the minor exceptions contained in Adj. reg. 2(2), if anyone else is present the decision is void. Within the precedent system, as explained at p. 26, the tribunal is bound by the law applied in previous Commissioners' decisions, but it is free to depart from the views expressed in other SSAT hearings, It can substitute its own view of the facts or the law for that of the AO. By SSA s. 102, if it thinks fit, the tribunal may proceed to determine a question within the AO's jurisdiction even if it was not considered by him. However, in *R 5/84(II)* the tribunal decision was overturned because, in exercizing this discretion to proceed to determine the new point, it placed the AO at a disadvantage.

The Adjudication regulations lay down the voting system involved and what must be recorded by the chairman. Reg. 19 states that

"(1) The decision of the majority of the appeal tribunal shall be the decision of the tribunal but, where the tribunal consists of an even number, the chairman shall have a casting vote.

(2) The chairman of an appeal tribunal shall –
   (a) record in writing all their decisions; and
   (b) include in the record of every decision a statement of the reasons for such decision and of their findings on questions of fact material thereto; and
   (c) if a decision is not unanimous, record a statement that one of the members dissented, and the reasons given by him for so dissenting."

In practice the chairman records this information by completing form AT 3 which also requires a note of the evidence to be taken. This should be done immediately after the hearing, with all tribunal members present. In cases such as *R(I) 81/51* and *R(I) 42/59* Commissioners have drawn attention to the importance of this record if the case is appealed further. The findings of fact must not be equivocal or simply record opposing contentions for the claimant must not be left guessing as to whether or not his evidence was accepted. According to *CI 409/82* (unreported):

". . . whenever a specific contention is made to a tribunal or there is detailed evidence on a particular point, the tribunal must in its decision deal with that contention or that evidence, and if it fails to do so altogether, then its decision is erroneous in law."

The reasons given must be adequate and the tribunal should identify precisely the legislation including the relevant sub-sections upon which reliance is placed.

Communication of decisions is dealt with by Adj. reg. 19(3):

"As soon as may be practicable after a case has been decided by an appeal tribunal, a copy of the report of their decision made in accordance with this regulation shall be sent to the claimant, to the adjudication officer and to any other person to whom notice of the hearing was given . . . and the claimant and any such other person shall be informed of the conditions governing appeals to a Commissioner."

In addition, although not bound to do so, at the end of the hearing the tribunal normally recalls the claimant and explains its decision orally. Payment of benefit following an appeal is considered at p. 260. A tribunal decision may be appealed to a Commissioner on a point of law alone, or review may be sought as considered at p. 237.

4. THE SOCIAL SECURITY COMMISSIONER

The Social Security Commissioners exercise considerable power over the benefit system. Not only do they sit alone, but in practice they almost always have the final word in a case because only a handful of their 75,000 decisions since 1948 have been appealed further. As explained at p. 26 their rulings must be followed by SSATs, MATs and AOs, although Commissioners themselves enjoy the freedom of not having to follow each other's decisions.

Commissioners are appointed by the Crown under SSA s. 97(3) from amongst the ranks of barristers and solicitors who have been qualified to practice for at least ten years. Their status is comparable with that of County Court judges. At present, apart from the Chief Commissioner, there are fourteen Commissioners in England (two being part-time), two in Scotland and three in Northern Ireland.[15] Their offices are in London, Edinburgh and Belfast (addresses in appendix C). There are now no Commissioners based in Wales, the Cardiff office having closed in 1986. Their work has been described by the former chief Commissioner, Sir Robert Micklethwaite in *The National Insurance Commissioners* (1976). They hear appeals from SSATs and MATs on points of law alone. Their jurisdiction to hear appeals against the facts found by a SSAT was brought to an end by the SSA 1986. Although they dispose of most cases on the basis of the papers alone, they can hold a hearing.

Compared to other benefits a higher proportion of claims for industrial injury are appealed to a Commissioner. This is not only because of the particular difficulties such cases cause, but also because of the readiness of trade unions to provide representation and take them to appeal. The number of appeals covering the industrial scheme which were decided by Commissioners rose from 319 in 1984 to 350 in 1985 at a time when the total number of cases disposed of by Commissioners fell from 3,553 to 3,166.[16] The scheme is therefore responsible for 11 per cent of the Commissioners' caseload. The success rate of claimants in industrial injury cases is around 30 per cent, which is half as much again as that for other benefits.

(1) The basis for appeal

An appeal to a Commissioner against either a MAT or SSAT decision may be made only on a point of law. In each case leave to appeal is required. SSA s. 112 allows an appeal to be made from an MAT decision, although until 1959 the only way such a decision could be challenged was by way of judicial review, as discussed at p. 228. It was much easier to appeal against SSAT decisions which could be challenged on a point of law or fact. However, SSA s. 101 now restricts such appeals to the law alone.

In *R(I) 14/75* The Commissioner referred to the following tests to be applied in deciding whether a decision is wrong in law:

---

[15] The details given in the *Annual Report of the Council on Tribunals 1984-85* H.C. 54 (1985-86) must now be revised.

[16] Figures supplied by the Chief Social Security Commissioner in a personal letter to the author May 1986.

(1) Has there been any breach of the rules of natural justice?
(2) Has there been a failure to comply with the requirement to state in writing the reasons and relevant findings of fact for the decision?
(3) Does the decision contain a false proposition of law *ex facie*?
(4) Is it supported by no evidence?
(5) Are the facts found such that no person acting judicially and properly instructed as to the relevant law could have come to the determination in question?

(2) Those who can appeal

Apart from the claimant, those who may appeal from a SSAT decision are listed by SSA s. 101, and from a MAT decision by SSA s. 112. Although an AO may appeal, in practice he would not do so unless an important point of law was involved which might have a wider effect upon the payment of benefits. A trade union or other "association which exists to promote the interests and welfare of its members" can appeal if the claimant either was a member at the time of the accident, or was a member both at the time of the appeal and immediately before the question at issue arose. This opportunity for a union to become directly involved in a case is important because it makes it possible to obtain an authoritative decision which can assist other workers. However, the value of the precedent system is limited because most cases remain unpublished, and a decision advantageous to claimants may remain hidden in the Commissioners' or union files.

(3) Leave to appeal

Appeals from SSATs have gradually been restricted. Following the SSA 1986 not only are they confined to points of law, but leave to appeal must be sought in all cases. Formerly leave was required only for those decisions which were unanimous and not if there was a dissenting tribunal member. The new requirements for leave, imposed by SSA s. 101, are as follows:

"(5A) No appeal lies under this section without the leave –
(a) of the person who was the chairman of the tribunal when the decision was given, or in a case prescribed by regulations, the leave of some other chairman of a social security appeal tribunal; or
(b) subject to and in accordance with regulations, of a Commissioner.
(5B) Regulations may make provision as to the manner in which, and the time within which, appeals are to be brought and applications made for leave to appeal."

Leave is also required for appealing from a decision of a MAT by SSA s. 112(3) and Adj. reg. 35.

The above subsections refer to regulations prescribing from whom and how leave may be sought. These regulations have not yet been made and the Adjudication regs. 1984 continue to govern this area. These allow leave to be obtained from the chairman or a Commissioner as follows:

(a) The chairman

The chairman can grant a request for leave to appeal and any refusal can be appealed to a Commissioner. No criteria for the chairman's decision are laid down and, according to *R(S) 4/82*(T), the discretion is unfettered. However, leave should be given where the proceedings are seriously questioned as opposed to where there is only general criticism without detailed objections being given. Permission can be sought either orally at the end of the hearing itself, or in writing afterwards. It must be obtained within six weeks of a SSAT decision or three months of a MAT decision, as considered at p. 237. By Adj. reg. 3(3) these time limits cannot be extended and any determination out of time will be held a nullity as in *R(I) 7/81*. Instead for late applications, or where leave is refused, application must be made to a Commissioner.

(b) A Commissioner

A Commissioner can grant the request under Adj. reg. 25(1) if either it is out of time for the tribunal chairman, or it has been refused by the chairman. Differing time limits are imposed as considered at p. 237. In *R(I) 2/82* the Commissioner was held to have the power to hold a hearing on the application and this is confirmed by Adj. reg. 26. That regulation also allows a Commissioner to refuse to give reasons for not granting leave to appeal. It is then extremely difficult to challenge his decision as is revealed by *R v Social Security Commissioner, ex p. Simon Connolly* (1985). In *R(I) 14/61*, *R(I) 3/64* and *R(I) 6/81* it was recognized that the Commissioner has a discretion to refuse leave to withdraw an appeal and this still exists even though many claimants now have a wider power to withdraw their appeal under Adj. reg. 6. By reg. 25(4) a Commissioner may treat the application for leave as an appeal. This means that he may use it as a short-cut to determine any question which arises as if it were the appeal itself.

The grounds for applying for leave to appeal on a point of law usually fall into one of the three main categories given in *Bland v Chief Supplementary Benefit Officer* (1983). These are that the tribunal misconstrued the relevant regulations, or that it failed to give sufficient reasons, or that it failed to make sufficient findings to enable the applicant or his advisers to know whether or not it had misconstrued the regulations.

(4) Notice of appeal

Although SSA s. 101(5B) authorizes regulations concerning how appeals are to be brought these have not yet been made. By the now repealed s. 101(5) notice of appeal had to be given to the local DHSS office within three months of the tribunal's decision. If leave was required the notice had to be sent within three months of the decision giving leave to appeal. Again the Commissioner could extend the time limit for special reasons. However, because the time limit was more generous here – being three times that for appealing to a SSAT from an AO's decision – extensions to it were granted less often. This was illustrated by *CI 449/81* (unreported). This case began by holding in favour of claimants. It decided that an application for an extension of time could be considered by one Commissioner even if it had already been refused by another. This was because such an application asked for the personal exercise of the Commissioner's discretion. This did not constitute a "decision" which could only be challenged on appeal or review, as was the case with the grant or refusal of leave to appeal. However, the case went on to restrict the likelihood of an extension time being granted. For the second application to succeed there had to be

> ". . . cogent evidence or new facts not reasonably available on the first application . . . which could on the second or subsequent application constitute 'special reasons'."

There were no such reasons on the facts of the case even though the first Commissioner was not aware that the claimant was ignorant of the failure to appeal. This did not matter because it was said that the claimant must be identified with the acts or omissions of his advisers and representatives.

Before SSA s. 101(5B) authorized regulations to be made to determine the details, it used to be that notice of an appeal had to be "in writing in a form approved by the Secretary of State stating the grounds of the appeal". This could be done by completing the simple form LT 43 available from the local DHSS office. The grounds of appeal did not have to be very specific. A former Chief Commissioner said that in practice appeals were construed "with the utmost liberality", and points were raised in favour of claimants although they were not in the grounds of appeal at all.[17] Nevertheless claimants are well advised to give full details of their argument because the appeal may be decided upon the basis of the papers alone. Specific reference should be made to the statutory provisions and the Commissioners' decisions upon which reliance is placed.

(5) Administrative arrangements

On receipt of the notice of appeal the local DHSS office notifies the Commissioners' office and forwards the appeal to the Chief AO's office in Southampton. This office takes over the case from the local AO. A new officer prepares a submission which forms part of the case papers. These also include the claimant's grounds of appeal in form AT 3 and any other evidence submitted. Enclosed with the copy of the case papers sent to the claimant is form LT 62 which allows him to make further observations in writing. At this stage it may be necessary to submit evidence in addition to that considered by the local tribunal. This may involve, for example, an up to date medical opinion being disclosed. However, it must be remembered that appeals are now only allowed on points of law, not fact. Although, as discussed below, Commissioners have been given new powers to admit evidence and make findings of fact, they can only do so if the appeal succeeds on a point of law. Because of this more limited ground for appeal, unions should abandon a tactic favoured by some of them in the past: in order to save expense occasionally a union would take its chance with limited evidence before a SSAT, and only obtain specialist advice or representation if the tribunal rejected the claim, and an appeal to a Commissioner proved necessary. Such a course is now ill-advised.

Although in practice the majority of cases are disposed of on the basis of papers alone, the parties may request an oral hearing. By Adj. reg. 26 the Commissioner must grant this request

> "unless, after considering the record of the case and the reasons put forward in the request for the hearing, he is satisfied that the application or appeal can properly be determined without a hearing. . . ."

17 R. Micklethwait, *The National Insurance Commissioners* (1976) p. 48.

In *Smith* v *Insurance Officer* (1985) the Court of Appeal interpreted this regulation as biased in favour of a hearing being held, and in the exceptional circumstances of the case an appeal against a refusal of a hearing was allowed. If a hearing is requested this can cause a considerable delay. Whether or not a hearing is requested one study revealed that in 1984 a case took on average a year and a half from the date of claim until it was finally decided by a Commissioner.[18] The longest case took 30 months. For an oral hearing the claimant and his representative are given reasonable notice of the hearing date as well as information about claiming expenses. Usually at least half a day is set aside for each case. Hearings are held in London, except for Scottish cases which are heard in Edinburgh. The separate Northern Ireland Commissioners' office is based in Belfast.

(6) Cases disposed of by a hearing

Hearings are held before a Commissioner sitting alone, except where under SSA s. 116 it appears to the Chief Commissioner that an appeal involves a question of law of special difficulty. He may then direct that the case be heard by a tribunal of three Commissioners. The clerk at the hearing is a lawyer who keeps a record of the evidence presented. By SSA s. 101 a Commissioner may refer any question for a doctor's report. He may also be assisted at the hearing by an assessor on questions of fact of special difficulty. His discretion whether or not to employ such help was recognized as very wide in *Fraser* v *Secretary of State for Social Services* (1986). However, there has been a decline in the use of medical assessors since their role was restricted by *R* v *Deputy Industrial Injuries Commissioner, ex p. Jones* (1962).

At the hearing the AO is normally represented by someone either from the DHSS Solicitor's Office, or from the Chief Adjudication Officer's Office. The claimant may either present his own case or be represented. In practice the great majority of claimants are represented even though there is no legal aid to pay for it. Although the hearing is more formal than that of a tribunal there are no wigs or gowns, and the atmosphere is not as intimidating as some may fear. The procedure is similar to that of a tribunal. It is not subject to the rules which confine a court. For example, even hearsay evidence can be admitted, although less weight is attached to it. However, one difference from a tribunal is that, by Adj. reg. 4(9), witnesses can only be called if the Commissioner agrees. A Commissioner must observe the principles of natural justice which are discussed below in relation to MATs. The importance of these principles was recognized in *R* v *Deputy Industrial Injuries Commissioner, ex p. Moore* (1965) where it was held that a Commissioner could rely upon medical evidence presented in previous cases provided that, if there is a hearing, the parties are given the opportunity to comment upon it.

(7) The decision

Although Commissioners may no longer hear appeals on questions of fact, they have been given new powers to admit evidence and make findings of fact having decided that there has been an error of law. SSA s. 101(5), as inserted by SSA 1986 sched. 5, states

---

[18] Villiers and Brewer, "Justice Delayed" (1985) *Legal Action*, July p. 12.

"Where the Commissioner holds that the decision was erroneous in point of law –
(a)   he shall have power –
   (i)   to give the decision which he considers the tribunal should have given, if he can do so without making fresh or further findings of fact; or
   (ii)   if he considers it expedient, to make such findings and to give such decision as he considers appropriate in the light of them; and
(b)   in any other case he shall refer the case to a tribunal with directions for its determination."

In addition a Commissioner is not bound by earlier findings of fact and by SSA s. 102 may determine questions which were not considered by the AO or local tribunal. Thus in *R 1/69(II)* the Commissioner was able to decide that the claimant had suffered an industrial accident, although previously the only issue had been whether a prescribed disease was involved. By Adj. reg. 26(4) the Commissioner must send the claimant a copy of his decision and the reasons for it "as soon as may be practicable". In practice where there is a hearing the claimant may be told the result at the end.

5. FURTHER APPEAL TO THE COURTS

Until 1980 a Commissioner's decision could only be challenged by a process known as judicial review. This was because no appeal was allowed on a point of law to the High Court. Judicial review involves applying to the High Court for the remedy of *certiorari* to overturn decisions which, for example, contain an obvious error of law, or which have been reached in breach of the principles of natural justice. However, the court has a discretion whether or not to grant this remedy and there is therefore an element of uncertainty in applying for judicial review. Partly because of this it has been rarely used in social security cases.

Courts seem to have been particularly reluctant to interfere with industrial injury cases. Judges have avoided doing so by narrowly defining the "law" found by Commissioners which would entitle them to intervene. Instead they have preferred to characterize decisions as based upon "fact". This general approach is apparent in the decision of Lord Denning in *R* v *National Insurance Commissioner, ex p. Michael* (1965). He justified it as follows:

"Where a real error of law is shown then this court will interfere, but it would in my opinion be wrong, by gradual erosion of the basic principle, to set up this court as in effect a court of appeal on fact from the decisions of the specialized tribunals . . ."

This reluctance contrasts with the readiness of the courts to intervene, for example, in tax cases. It has led to the criticisms that social security claimants have been unable to obtain authoritative decisions from the higher courts, and that tribunals in the past have been allowed an excessive degree of freedom.

In addition to judicial review an appeal on a point of law is now allowed by s. 14 of the Social Security Act 1980. The relevant grounds for appeals on points of law are considered at p. 224. Leave to appeal is required from a Commissioner, or if he refuses, from the Court of Appeal itself. Leave was refused by the appeal court because no question of law was involved in *Fraser* v *Secretary of State For Social Services* (1986). The Commissioner hearing the application for leave is usually the one who made the decision from which an appeal is sought, but by Adj. reg. 28 the Chief Commissioner can direct that the application be heard by another Commissioner.

6. THE DIVISION IN JURISDICTION BETWEEN THE MEDICAL AND STATUTORY AUTHORITIES

There are two sets of questions relating to industrial injuries benefit which are determined by the medical authorities: firstly, all "disablement" questions as defined at p. 137 must be referred to them; and secondly, the "diagnosis" and "recrudescence" questions relevant to a claim in respect of a prescribed disease and discussed in chapter 4 are usually determined by them. Although in certain circumstances an AO may make the initial decision on diagnosis or recrudescence, these questions are usually referred to an AMA as considered at p. 102. If they are not referred the AO's decision can be appealed to a medical authority within the 10-day limit noted at p. 237. The medical authorities can make no decisions other than those above, but when requested they may give advice to the AO on several matters. These include, for example, whether a prescribed disease is due to the nature of the claimant's occupation.

In the past there has been some confusion about the jurisdiction of the medical authorities and whether, in effect they can contradict an AO or SSAT's finding. Obviously they cannot question whether, for example, an accident has arisen in the course of employment. However, if an AO decides that personal injury has been caused by accident it is still open to the medical authority, in determining the disablement questions, to find that the accident causes no loss of faculty. They may then assess the disablement at nil and conclude, for example, that the cause of the claimant's trouble is entirely a condition which existed before the accident. If this happens it can appear that the respective authorities are in disagreement as to whether the claimant has suffered an accidental injury. The conflict was considered by the House of Lords in *Minister of Social Security* v *AEU (Re Dowling)* (1967) and in *Hudson and Jones* v *Secretary of State for Social Services* (1972). These decisions held that the finding of an AO or SSAT was final in that it could not later be questioned by the medical authorities. However, the cases were reversed by statute in 1972. SSA s. 117(2) states that

> ". . . any findings of fact or other determination embodied in or necessary to a decision, or on which it is based, [shall not be] conclusive for the purpose of any further decision."

This allows an AO's determination to be upset by a later finding of a medical authority that the loss of faculty does not result from the relevant accident.

The converse problem has also arisen: to what extent may a statutory authority depart from the finding of a medical authority? In determining incapacity for the purposes of REA *R* v *Industrial Injuries Commissioner, ex p. Ward* (1965) decided that the statutory authorities are not bound by all the views of the loss of faculty taken by the medical authority. The following paragraph from the Commissioner's decision in the case was approved:

> "It is for the medical authorities alone to decide whether the relevant accident has caused a loss of faculty and in what the loss of faculty consists. After that point there is a division of jurisdiction. The medical authorities make a forecast of the probable future effects of the relevant loss of faculty and it is on this forecast, or assessment, that disablement benefit is based. The statutory authorities however, have to decide what are the actual physical effects upon the beneficiary of the relevant loss of faculty at the time for which [REA] is claimed. In reaching this decision they are not bound by the forecast of the medical authorities though they would certainly regard that forecast as being of evidential value. They are at complete liberty, in my judgment, to admit and accept evidence tending to show that the disability expected by the medical authorities to continue has in fact ceased to exist."

This means, for example, as in *CI 14/85 (unreported)* that the statutory authorities can rely upon a consultant's report that a loss of faculty no longer exists even if there is a previous finding of a medical authority that the assessment would last for life. However, they cannot admit evidence to the effect that the original finding of the medical authority was wrong at the time it was made.

As held in *R(I) 4/84* emphasizes that the statutory authorities are not allowed to determine the loss of faculty itself, for that is a disablement question exclusively reserved for the medical authorities. In *R(I) 5/84*(T) this meant that the statutory authorities were not allowed to find that incapacity had arisen if it came about only because of a condition which itself arose out of the loss of faculty. On the facts of the case, although the medical authority had noted that a blow to the head had caused physical damage amounting to a loss of faculty, it made no mention of any psychological consequences. If this failure were to be remedied to enable the claimant to rely upon incapacity caused by his state of mind rather than his body, the proper course was to refer the matter back to the medical authority to fully explain the extent of the loss of faculty. The statutory authority could not itself call for a consultant's report and decide that the psychological consequences were part of the loss of faculty; it was not to determine what conditions constituted the loss of faculty, but only what were its effects. To enable this to be done the Commissioner stressed the importance of the medical authority stating unequivocally the full extent of the loss of faculty.

7. THE ADJUDICATING MEDICAL PRACTITIONER OR MEDICAL BOARD

Determination of medical questions in an industrial injuries claim is almost always made by an AMA. (Although the AO also has a limited jurisdiction in medical matters, it is rarely exercized). An AMA consists of either a single doctor drawn from a panel appointed for a particular area by the Secretary of State, or a board of two or more such doctors. The panel is usually composed of general practitioners. In 1984 there were 1,026 adjudicating medical practitioners making decisions at 104 medical adjudication centres throughout the country.[19] In the case of certain prescribed diseases special medical boards are required composed of specially qualified doctors and these are considered at p. 128. Apart from such cases an AMA usually consists of a single doctor, except where a board of two or more is required by Adj. reg. 32. A board may be called in three circumstances: firstly, where any prescribed disease is involved, except for those where a special medical board is required; secondly, where a case is reviewed by a medical authority; and thirdly, in any other case where the Secretary of State so decides. In 1985 AMAs or boards carried out 184,000 examinations for industrial injuries purposes.[20] The Pearson Commission estimated the outcome of a medical adjudication was in favour of a claimant in about 80 per cent of cases.

(1) The examination and the claimant's right to representation

By Adj. reg. 32(8) the claimant must be given reasonable notice of the time and place of the medical examination. If the claimant fails to appear the AMA cannot make any decisions unless the claimant consents. However, refusal to attend for examination can constitute a ground for disqualification from benefit as discussed at p. 257. If the claimant is too ill to attend, arrangements can be made for the examination to take place at the claimant's home. Although normally an AMA should carry out the examination, this may not be possible if the claimant lives outside the UK. A report may then be obtained from a doctor at the place where the claimant lives.

The AMA carries out its work in private, but must still comply with the rules of natural justice as discussed at p. 234. Its procedure is to meet with the claimant, informally ask questions and later carry out a medical examination. Witnesses are not normally heard, and if the claimant wants to present evidence this should be done in writing before the meeting takes place. If necessary the claimant should request the AMA to obtain the hospital notes or doctor's records relevant to the claim for this may not be done as a matter of course. The AMA establishes facts in a way quite different from a SSAT. There is no presentation of a case by a DHSS official nor does the claimant have a right to representation, although in practice assistance in presenting the facts is usually allowed. This is because of Adj. reg. 32(9) which provides that

". . . a sitting of an adjudicating medical authority is not an oral hearing, and no person shall be entitled to be present and be heard during the consideration of any question . . . other than the claimant and any other person whom the authority may, with the consent of the claimant, allow to be present as being a person who . . . is likely to assist . . . in the determination of that question."

Although the AMA can, if it wishes, refuse to admit any person other than the claimant, in practice another person is usually allowed to be present before the medical examination. At that stage the AMA asks questions

---

[19] Personal letter to the author from the DHSS, 29 March 1985.

[20] DHSS *Social Security Statistics 1986*, table 21.09. An additional 8,000 examinations were made in Northern Ireland according to table 14.3 of the DHSS *Northern Ireland Social Security Statistics* 1984.

about the nature of the claimant's accident, the symptoms, disabilities, previous treatment and medical and employment history. The claimant's representative may help to supply this information which is recorded in a statement prepared by the AMA. The claimant is asked to sign this to indicate that it is accurate.

The representative or friend is normally excluded from the medical examination which follows. However, the DHSS medical handbook suggests that exceptions may be made "where, for example, the claimant is a woman or is exceptionally nervous or suffers from some handicap such as a speech impediment or deafness, or has difficulty in understanding or using the English language".

(2) The decision

Where the board consists of two doctors Adj. reg. 32(5) requires that the decision be unanimous or the case will be referred to another board consisting this time of three members. By reg. 33 the AMA must record its findings of fact. To enable this to be done in practice there are forms to be completed. These differ, for example, according to whether a back or hand injury is involved. In giving its diagnosis the AMA is advised to refer to other doctors' reports where appropriate. Where injuries to limbs are involved it is instructed by the DHSS medical handbook to make findings about functional loss. For example, in the case of leg injuries

> ". . . it should be noted how far the claimant can walk, whether he uses a stick or crutches, whether he wears a surgical boot or appliance and, if so, whether it is satisfactory and whether he can ascend or descend stairs with either foot first etc."

The AMA should also record the relevance of all conditions found, showing the injuries which are wholly or partly due to the relevant accident. Finally, the AMA is asked to indicate how its assessment is calculated.

The decision must be sent to the claimant as soon as is practicable. It takes the form of a simple one-page summary on form BI 132F. However, a copy of the more detailed report form BI 118 may be requested from the local DHSS office. This report is sent automatically if there is to be an appeal. The DHSS medical handbook states that "it is important that the reports, in particular the medical terms, should be legibly written . . . and expressed in clear language with abbreviations kept to a minimum". This advice has not always been heeded in practice. An appeal may be made on fact or law to a MAT, or a review may be sought as explained at p. 237.

8. The Medical Appeal Tribunal

An AMA decision can be reconsidered by a MAT under SSA s. 109 and Adj. reg. 47 either as a result of an appeal by the claimant, or following a reference from the Secretary of State. A MAT is a more expert panel than an AMA. It consists of two doctors, usually of consultant status, and a legally qualified chairman. It makes its decision following an oral hearing. The claimant has a right to be represented here, and the procedure involved combines certain other features of a SSAT hearing with those of the medical examinations carried out by an AMA.

The rate of appeal from AMAs is relatively high. About 20 per cent of cases decided against claimants are reconsidered by one of the 24 regional MATs. These appeal tribunals are of tremendous importance to the industrial injuries scheme for they hear five times as many industrial injury cases as SSATs, although the questions referred to them are of narrower focus. The claimant is just as likely to be successful before a MAT as before a SSAT. In 1985 46 per cent of the 7,030 appeals on accidents and 50 per cent of the 320 appeals on disease were decided in favour of claimants. In addition claimants succeeded in 40 per cent of the 1,306 references to MATs by the Secretary of State.[21]

(1) The decision to appeal

Notice of appeal (or a decision by the Secretary of State to refer the case to a MAT) must be made within three months of the AMA's decision, as explained at p. 237. Although there is no particular DHSS form on which to appeal, Adj. reg. 3(1) requires the notice to be in writing. Occasionally the decision whether or not to appeal can be difficult because the MAT has power under SSA s. 109 to "confirm, reverse, or vary" the AMA's decision. The possibility of being made worse off caused the claimant to have second thoughts about his appeal in *R(I) 6/81*, but the MAT refused him leave to withdraw. This decision has since been reversed by Adj. reg. 6 which enables an appeal to be withdrawn at any time before it is determined. However, most claimants should not fear being worse off on appeal: almost half of them have their benefit increased, whilst for the great majority of others the previous decision is merely confirmed.

(2) Administrative arrangements

The administrative arrangements for the case are made by a clerk based at the DHSS regional office. The Secretary of State's representative is a specialist in presenting medical cases and also employed at the regional office. The case papers include the representative's submission and the AMA's report on form BI 118. Medical evidence may be withheld from these papers by Adj. reg. 8 if knowledge of it would harm the claimant's health. However, this does not prevent the MAT from taking it into account.

Having received the case papers the claimant may seek further medical evidence to answer the points raised. *R(I) 1/65* recognizes that it is for the claimant to place before the MAT any evidence not in the case papers for the burden of proof lies upon him. In particular, the claimant may need to ask the tribunal to obtain his hospital and other medical records. *R(I) 17/66* shows that the common belief amongst claimants that records will be obtained automatically is unfounded. The records cannot be released directly to the claimant. However, if they are relied upon by the AMA a

---

[21] These figures are all abstracted from DHSS *Social Security Statistics 1986*, table 21.21. In Northern Ireland in 1983 there were 205 appeals on accidents and 17 on diseases, as well as 15 references from the Secretary of State. See table 14.5 of the DHSS *Northern Ireland Social Security Statistics 1984*.

relevant précis appears in the case papers. Reasonable notice of the hearing must be given to the claimant, as discussed in relation to SSATs. The claimant must arrange for any witnesses to attend if he wishes to support his account of his reduced abilities as a result of the accident.

(3) The hearing and the rules of natural justice

The composition of a MAT is laid down by SSA sched. 12. It must consist of three members and its chairman must be a lawyer who has been qualified to practice for at least seven years. In Northern Ireland a Social Security Commissioner acts as chairman. The "wingmen" are medical practitioners appointed by the Secretary of State after consulting with academic medical bodies. In practice those appointed are usually consultants who are members of one of the Royal Colleges for either surgeons or physicians.

By Adj. reg. 36(1)

"A person shall not act as an adjudicating medical authority or as a member thereof or as a member of a medical appeal tribunal in any case if he –
(a) is or may be directly affected by the case;
(b) has taken any part in such a case as a medical assessor or as a medical practitioner who has regularly attended the claimant or to whom any question has been referred for report or as an employer or as a witness; or
(c) in the case only of a medical appeal tribunal, has acted as an adjudicating medical authority, or a member thereof, to whom the case was referred."

This regulation caused the decision to be quashed both in *R(I) 5/73*, where a member had supervised the claimant's treatment in hospital, and in *R(I) 28/61*(T) where the member had previously examined the claimant on behalf of insurers in connection with a claim for damages in respect of the same accident. However, in *R(I) 26/61* it was said that unless there was a real likelihood of bias it did not matter that a member had sat on other MATs which had rejected the claimant's previous applications.

Despite the informal nature of the hearing a tribunal must keep to the rules of natural justice. Although the precise limit of these rules is uncertain they enable scrutiny to be maintained over bodies exercizing some kind of judicial function. Basically they require that the procedure be fair and that the claimant sees all the evidence involved. He should be given both an opportunity to present his case in full and a chance to respond to the arguments made by the DHSS. According to *R(I) 6/69* the claimant has three particular rights. These are to be represented; to be provided with copies of relevant documents including all relevant specialists' reports as in *R(I) 35/61*; and finally, to be assisted in stating his case. The precise nature of this assistance has not been specified. Instead it has been held that it may vary depending upon the particular claimant, although a tribunal is expected to give more help to those who are unrepresented. Failure to invite such a claimant to address the tribunal constituted grounds for successful appeals in *R(I) 10/62* and *R(I) 29/61*(T). In the last case it was said that the claimant should have been brought back into the hearing room after the medical examination in order for him to comment upon any matters arising out of it. However, this was not considered to be a general rule in *R(I) 2/64* where it was emphasized that a decision cannot be challenged only because the claimant feels his case to have been presented poorly. Nor will a decision be quashed only because a tribunal fails to ask an unrepresented claimant whether there is further medical evidence and as a result the MAT makes its decision in ignorance of it. According to *R(I) 3/70*: "The requirements of natural justice must not be equated with those of sophisticated justice." The absence of an interpreter did not make the hearing in breach of natural justice in *R(I) 11/63*.

If some point not previously in issue arises during the course of a hearing *R(I) 29/61*(T) considered it desirable, although not always essential, that a claimant be given an opportunity to produce evidence in relation to it. This was supported by Lord Denning in *R v Deputy Industrial Injuries Commissioner, ex p. Howarth* (1968) and in *R(I) 4/71*. It meant in *R(I) 2/74*, for example, that the MAT could not reduce an assessment in order to take account of an earlier accident without giving the claimant the chance to discuss the extent to which he had been previously disabled. The rules of natural justice require that a MAT should not refuse a claimant's request for an adjournment in order to introduce expert evidence as in *R v MAT (Midland Region), ex p. Carrarini* (1966). Finally, after the end of a MAT or Commissioner's hearing it is not permissible for further evidence to be obtained, either by sending the clerk to ask the claimant more questions as in *R(I) 2/72*, or by obtaining further medical reports as in *R v Deputy Industrial Injuries Commissioner, ex p. Jones* (1962).

(4) The decision and record keeping

In *R v MAT, ex p. Hubble* (1958) a MAT was described as an expert investigating body entitled to use its own expertize to reach its own conclusions upon matters of medical fact and opinion. Unlike a court it is not therefore obliged to find according only to the evidence presented to it. By Adj. reg. 34 the decision may be reached by a majority vote. The tribunal reserves its decision and does not adopt the common practice of other tribunals of informing the claimant of the result immediately after the hearing, although as usual it must send notice as soon as is reasonably practicable thereafter. The claimant is sent a summary of the tribunal's written record. By reg. 34(4) this

"... shall include ... a statement of the reasons for their decision, including their findings on all questions of fact material to the decision."

Failure to record reasons and facts accurately has been the basis for an appeal to the Commissioner in a number of cases, although it may eventually produce only in a better explanation for the decision rather than a different result.[22] In *R(I) 18/61*(T) it was insufficient for the MAT to state only that they agreed with the medical board. In *R(I) 30/61* it was said that tribunals must make findings on specific submissions which go to the heart of the case, although they do not have to deal with every point raised by claimants. In both of these 1961 cases, as well as in others referred to below, Commissioners have been concerned not to impose too great a burden upon tribunals. It has been agreed that, depending on the case, the record can be very brief especially if, as recognized in *R(I) 22/63*, the

---

[22] *R(I) 23/61, R(I) 7/63*(T), *R(I) 8/63, R(I) 7/65, R(I) 3/66*(T), *R(I) 3/76, R(I) 1/79, R(I) 1/81*.

medical board's findings of fact are adopted. If the MAT finds that the disablement results from causes other than an industrial accident as in *R(I) 3/68*, it need not state what these causes are. Nor in *R(I) 14/75* did it have to discover the disease from which the claimant was suffering if it was not one of those prescribed. In *R v Industrial Injuries Commissioners, ex p. Viscusi* (1974) although the tribunal had to make all reasonable inquiries it did not have to follow up every suggestion and explore every avenue. Although Commissioners have emphasized the importance of giving reasons, *R(I) 1/73*, which was affirmed in *R v National Insurance Commissioner, ex p. Maiden* (1974) illustrates that the process should not be taken too far. Reasonable inferences may be drawn from the recorded reasons to prevent a decision being quashed on appeal. On the other hand in *CI 288/82* (unreported) the Commissioner reminded tribunals that:

> ". . . reasons and findings should be clear and capable of being understood by those unfamiliar with medical matters. When they are not, it is salutary to remit the case to the tribunal, even though there might not be a different result, because attention is thus drawn to the statutory requirement . . ."

(5) Appeal

It has always been possible to apply to the Divisional Court for judicial review of a MAT decision although, as discussed at p. 238, this jurisdiction has been rarely exercized.[23] It is more common for an appeal to be made to a Commissioner. However, this has only been allowed since 1959 and it is limited to a point of law alone. The grounds are discussed at p. 223. Leave and notice of the appeal are required as considered at p. 224. By Adj. reg. 38 a MAT may also refer a point of law to the Commissioner who, although able to determine the legal point, will not rule on medical matters. If the MAT decision is not confirmed the Commissioner in practice refers the case to a differently constituted tribunal. It is then reheard according to a procedure laid down in reg. 39. However, it is still open to the new tribunal to affirm the original decision unless it is precluded from doing so by the Commissioner's judgment. As an alternative to an appeal a review may be sought as discussed below.

9. THE SECRETARY OF STATE

There is now only one question concerning the industrial injuries scheme which is reserved for the determination of the Secretary of State. By SSA s. 93(1)(d) this is "whether a person is or was employed in employed earner's employment for the purpose . . ." of a claim for industrial injuries benefit. Which workers are covered by the scheme is discussed in chapter 2. The question can arise either by being referred by an adjudicating authority, or by a claimant applying for it to be determined. The procedural aspects are dealt with by Adj. regs. 12-17. The Secretary of State may appoint a person – in practice from the DHSS Solicitor's Office – to hold an inquiry and report on the question. The High Court can consider only points of law that may arise.

[23] But see *R v MAT, ex p. Burpitt* (1957), *R v MAT, ex p. Gilmore* (1957), *R v MAT, ex p. Griffiths* (1958) and *R v MAT, ex p. Hubble* (1958).

Whether a claimant is an employed earner is a question which must be satisfied in each claim and yet few cases are determined by the Secretary of State. This is because in the great majority of cases the answer is clear and is dealt with in passing by the AO. If there is doubt the matter should be referred to the Secretary of State and the AO should not rely upon any informal opinion from DHSS headquarters as in *R(I) 2/75*. The procedure to be applied if an AO makes a decision on facts which appear to him not to be in dispute, only for them later to be questioned and to require a determination from the Secretary of State, is considered by Adj. reg. 17.

Until the SSA 1986 the Secretary of State also decided whether there was entitlement to the allowances for constant attendance and exceptionally severe disablement which are considered in chapter 6. Although there was no fixed procedure, the decisions were usually taken on behalf of the Secretary of State by the DHSS regional office dealing with the claim. A medical board was often consulted. The Secretary of State could review the decision, but there was no provision for an appeal to the High Court unlike in the case of a determination of employed earner's employment. However, the Secretary of State's jurisdiction over these remaining supplements to disablement benefit was removed by the SSA 1986 which repealed SSA s. 95.

10. TIME LIMITS FOR MAKING APPEALS

Confusion can be caused by the various limits which have been placed upon making an application for leave to appeal on the one hand, and upon making the appeal or reference itself on the other. For convenience these limits are grouped together and set out in table form below. The limits are imposed by Adj. reg. 3 and sched. 2, except for 1 and 4(b) below which are imposed by SSA s. 100(4) and 101(5) respectively. All applications should be made to the local DHSS office except where leave is sought to appeal from a Commissioner's decision, in which case one of the Commissioners' offices should be contacted at the address given in appendix C.

Even if the relevant time limit has expired, Adj. reg. 3(3) allows it to be extended if there are "special reasons", except in the case of 6(a) and 7(a) below. These reasons which may justify a delayed appeal are based upon similar criteria to those which give rise to "good cause" for allowing a claim to be made late as considered at p. 206. For the refusal of an extension of time in an appeal to a Commissioner see *CI 449/81* (unreported) considered above at p. 225. There are no time limits restricting applications for review.

11. REVIEW

Review enables an adjudicating authority to have another look at a previous decision and if necessary revise it to take account, for example, of a mistake of law, or a mistake as to the true facts of the case. These facts previously may not have been fully presented to the authority, or there may have been a change in circumstances since the previous decision.

Appeals	Specified time
1. Appeal to a SSAT from an AO's decision. (SSA s.100(1))	This will be affected by regulations to be made under SSA s.101(4), as discussed at p.216. Formerly it was 28 days beginning with the date when the Secretary of State gave the claimant notice in writing of the decision.
2. Appeal to a medical board from an AO's determination of a diagnosis question or a recrudescence question. (Reg. 46)	10 days beginning with the date when notice of the decision was given to the appellant.
3. Appeal to a MAT from a decision of an adjudicating medical authority. (SSA s.109(2))	3 months beginning with the date when notice in writing of the decision was given to the appellant.
4. Appeal to a Commissioner –	
(a) from a decision of a MAT; (Reg.35(5))	(a) This will be affected by regulations to be made under SSA s.112(1)(b). At present the appeal has to be made within 3 months, beginning with the date when notice in writing of the decision giving leave to appeal was given to the appellant.
(b) from a decision of a SSAT. (SSA s.101(1))	(b) Again this will be affected by regulations. These will be made under SSA s.101(5B) as discussed at p.225. Formerly the appeal had to be made within 3 months, beginning with the date when the proper officer of the local tribunal gave the claimant notice in writing of the decision.

References	Specified time
5. Reference to a MAT at the instance of the Secretary of State. (SSA s.109(3))	3 months begining with the date of the decision of the medical board.

Applications for leave to appeal	Specified time
6. Applications for leave to appeal to a Commissioner from the decision of a SSAT –	This will be affected by regulations to be made under SSA s.101(5B) as discussed at p.224. The present limits are :–
(a) application to the chairman of the tribunal; (Reg.20(1))	6 weeks beginning with the date when a copy of the record of the decision was given to the applicant.
(b) application to a Commissioner, the chairman having refused leave on an application under (a) made within the specified time; (Reg.25(1))	(b) 6 weeks beginning with the date when notice in writing of the chairman's decision refusing leave was given to the applicant.
(c) application to a Commissioner, no application having been made to the chairman under (a) within the specified time. (Reg.25(1))	(c) 3 months beginning with the date when a copy of the record of the tribunal's decision against which he seeks leave to appeal was given to the applicant.
7. Application for leave to appeal to a Commissioner from the decision of a MAT	
(a) application to the chairman of the tribunal; (Reg.35(1))	(a) 3 months beginning with the date when a copy of the record of the decision was given to the applicant.
(b) application to a Commissioner, the chairman having refused leave on an application under (a) made within the specified time; (Reg.25(1))	(b) 28 days beginning with the date when notice in writing of the chairman's decision refusing leave was given to the applicant.
(c) application to a Commissioner, no application having been given to the chairman under (a) within the specified time. (Reg.25(1))	(c) Such time beyond that specified in respect of (a) as the Commissioner may for special reasons allow.
8. Application to a Commissioner for leave to appeal against a Commissioner's decision. (SSA 1980 s.14(2)(a))	3 months beginning with the date on which the Commissioner has given notice in writing of the decision to the appellant.

(1) Review compared to appeal

Sometimes it is difficult for a claimant to decide whether to ask for his case to be looked at again at all. This is because on both review and appeal the case can be considered entirely afresh and there is power to alter the previous findings for better or worse. This means, for example, that although a claimant only wants the percentage of disablement to be reassessed, it is possible for matters of causation to be raised. Then his disability could be found unrelated to any industrial accident and he would lose all his benefit. However, in practice this would be an unusual result for a review rarely makes the claimant worse off.

If the claimant wants his case to be looked at again he is faced with another difficult decision: should he apply for appeal or review? Any mistakes of law made by other than an AO or AMA can only be dealt with on appeal. Again appeal is more appropriate if there is dissatisfaction only with the facts found or inferences drawn on the basis of the evidence presented, and there are no facts, whether new or old, which the authority failed to take into account. However, if there are such facts it is better to apply for review. When there are grounds for a review it may be preferred to an appeal because no hearing is necessary and it is usually the easier, quicker and more informal way of challenging a decision. It is certainly better than waiting, for example, for up to a year for a Commissioner to hear an appeal. Another advantage of review is that it is not restricted by the time limits which confine applications for appeal, although if it is really an appeal which should be brought an application to be heard out of time is often successful. A final advantage of review is that it confers a wider discretion to backdate benefit than is in the case of an appeal: by Adj. reg. 83 on a review a disablement pension can be revised to as early a date as is reasonable in the circumstances, whereas on an appeal a three month time limit is imposed. However, as discussed at p. 206 in relation to *R(I) 1/86*, the amount to be paid following either a successful appeal or review is only the rate appropriate to the period of assessment, not that at the time when the arrears are paid.

(2) The review procedure and its legislative basis

A decision can be reviewed not only if the claimant applies for it, but also upon the initiative of the AO or Secretary of State. The latter acts, in effect, on behalf of the DHSS. In many cases the AO or DHSS may seek to reduce or withdraw benefit. The attempt to do so in *R(I) 1/71* failed because the onus of proof in a review is upon those seeking to overturn the previous decision and, on the facts of that case therefore, the DHSS. However, the AO or Secretary of State can also intervene on behalf of claimants to secure new or increased payments of benefit. Review enables a decision against a claimant be reversed without the DHSS having to wait for an appeal to be decided. Often appeals are not made when they should be, and a review therefore can benefit those claimants who, for whatever reason, fail to take the initiative themselves to ask for their case to be re-examined. Another reason which may prompt an AO to review a case in favour of a claimant is that he has filed notice of his intention to appeal to a SSAT.

Review involves the two stage process indicated in *R(I) 11/62*(T): firstly, the authority must consider whether the conditions for review are established, and secondly it must go on "to make a substantive decision on the merits of the case in the light of all the evidence now available" as in *R(I) 47/59*. This means that, once the grounds for review are established, the case can be considered afresh. The authority may then take into account not only any new facts or change of circumstances, but also other facts, opinions and arguments which were not put before the first authority when it made its original decision. However, the result of this may be only that, although the determining authority finds good grounds for review, there is no justification for changing the decision. This is because the right conclusion has been reached, albeit for the wrong reasons as in *R(I) 4/54*.

SSA s. 104 establishes the grounds upon which either an AO or, if an AO refers the case, a SSAT may review decisions of an AO, SSAT or Commissioner. All such decisions may be reviewed by the AO except for those on diagnosis and recrudescence, as defined in chapter 4. By Adj. reg. 50 these questions can only be reviewed by the medical authorities. The latter also have the exclusive power to review, on grounds specified by SSA s. 110, the disablement questions as defined at p. 137. Under SSA s. 96 The Secretary of State may review his decision as to whether the claimant is an employed earner according to a procedure governed by Adj. reg. 15.

Until SSA 1986 a claimant could not obtain review of one particular type of decision if it went against him. SSA s. 107(6)(*b*) used to prevent review of a finding that an accident was not an industrial accident. This section was interpreted in *R(I) 11/62*(T) and *R(I) 9/85*. In the first case it was decided that it did not prevent review of a decision that there had been no accident. However, in the second case it was recognized that there could be no review if the decision was that there had been an accident, but that it did not arise out of and in the course of employment. This has now been changed and s. 107(6)(b) has been repealed. However, the authorities, for their part, can still find it difficult to review a similar decision if it goes in the claimant's favour. This is because by SSA s. 107(6)(*a*) if a claimant obtains a declaration that there has been an industrial accident, the AO or SSAT cannot review the decision unless

". . . the decision . . . was given in consequence of any wilfun non-disclosure or misrepresentation of a material fact."

Two reasons for the restriction on review were noted in the AO's submission in *R(I) 9/85*:

"The decision whether an accident was an industrial accident is that on which all other decisions rest; it is also a decision which turns mainly on the facts. It was therefore felt that a degree of certainty in this field was necessary, with a final decision being given at an early stage whilst the facts were fresh. Thus the right to review has been strictly limited. . . ."

(3) Grounds for review by an AO or SSAT

By SSA s. 104(2) a claimant must apply for review by writing to the AO stating his grounds for wanting the case to be examined again. In fact in cases such as *R(I) 50/56* a claim for benefit has been treated as an application for review in order to prevent a good claim being defeated by a technicality. Applications for review must be dealt with by the AO in much the same way as claims for benefit in so far as the time taken for their disposal and notification of their result is concerned. Decisions on review can be appealed as if they were original decisions.

An AO's decision can be reviewed on one of four grounds, three of which also apply to SSAT and Commissioners' decisions. They are laid down by SSA s. 104 and are as follows:

(*a*) *Mistake of fact*

By SSA s. 104(1)(a) this ground is that

"... the officer or tribunal is satisfied that the decision was given in ignorance of, or was based on a mistake as to, some material fact."

The mistake must be that of the determining authority and not that of the claimant. It must have existed at the time the decision was given so that later changes, for example in the claimant's physical condition, do not justify a review on this ground. The mistake must be one of fact not law. Thus in *CI 345/83* (unreported) it was said that

"... it will not suffice simply to assert that the decision reviewed appears to be an unjustifiable inference from the totality of the facts. That, if anything, is a matter for appeal, not review. To justify a review there must be clearly shown some specific fact, as to which the tribunal was either ignorant or mistaken."

The materiality of the mistake was considered in *R(I) 3/75* where it was held that a review could not take place only because an AO believed an earlier inference to be mistaken. Instead it had to be shown that the inference might not have been drawn at all, or that a different inference would have been drawn had the new fact been known.

R(I) 3/73 is one of several cases which have imposed restrictions upon reviewing awards of REA. In that case new advice from a medical authority was held insufficient to justify a decision on review that payment should be stopped. Further restrictions were imposed by *CI 31/82* (unreported). Relying upon *R(I) 4/54* and *R(I) 73/53* the Commissioner noted that although certain elements of the original decision related to issues of hard fact, others required estimates of probability, such as where future earnings had to be forecast. If later events proved such estimates to be wrong a review based on mistake of fact was not justified. Nor was a review for a change of circumstance appropriate on the facts of the case because the AO had foreseen the very type of employment which the claimant later obtained. However, review on this ground was allowed in *R 1/72(II)*. The general reluctance to allow review to succeed has a policy basis: it is usual and administratively convenient for an award of REA to be made for a year at a time and therefore, as stated in one case, "there are sound reasons for inhibiting too frequent a review".

Other cases on mistake of fact are considered below in relation to review by the medical authorities. They deal with the meaning of "fresh evidence" which used to be required to review a Commissioner's decision. The SSA 1986 removed this requirement, but also authorized regulations to define when fresh evidence would be required for review on this ground. As discussed at p. 244 these regulations have not yet been made. They may still make it important to note that, for example, further evidence given by a medical expert in a later trial for common law damages did not constitute fresh evidence in *R(I) 11/59*(T) because it could have been produced at the original hearing for social security benefit.

(b) *Change of circumstances*

By SSA s. 104(1)(b) this ground is that

". . . there has been a relevant change of circumstances since the decision was given."

This ground is the same as that under the Workmen's Compensation Acts where it was given a wide meaning.[24] However, a restrictive interpretation was applied in *R(I) 11/59*(T). The tribunal of Commissioners held that a decision that an accident had not been suffered would not be reopened only because the High Court had found – in a tort case which awarded damages to the claimant – that an accident had in fact occurred. Whilst this different finding of fact in other proceedings may not justify a review, a subsequent change in the law may do so as in *R(I) 25/63*. Such a change may result from either new legislation or a later court or Commissioner's decision.

Although later medical reports may justify a review, Commissioners have been loathe to accept the exercize of this power in relation to REA. The reason for restricting review in such cases has been referred to above in relation to *R(I) 3/73* and mistake of fact. In *R(I) 1/71* the AO reviewed an award on the ground of change of circumstances because he had received advice from a medical board that the claimant's incapacity was not the result of an industrial accident but of arthritis which had developed afterwards. This advice did not force the AO to find that there had been a change of circumstance, but it did provide him with good evidence from which he could draw such a conclusion. However, his ability to do so was limited by rules as to the burden of proof, and because of this his decision to stop the allowance was overturned on appeal. The medical evidence was open to different interpretations and, given that the burden of proving the relevant change of circumstance was upon the AO, he could not show that his interpretation of the evidence was that which should be accepted. For similar reasons the AO's decision was overturned in *R 1/73(II)*.

These last two cases, when combined with those on mistake of fact, make it appear that it is very difficult to revise any payment of REA during the usual one year currency of an award. However, there are two cases where such a review was successful. In *R 1/72(II)* the claimant's increase in wages, even though temporary, was held a sufficient change of circumstance to justify a review, and in *CI 10/81* (unreported) a review was also allowed because the claimant had left the country on an indefinite basis.

(c) *Revised determination by other authorities*

By SSA s. 104(1)(c) a decision can be reviewed if it is

". . . based on a decision of a question which . . . falls to be determined otherwise than by an adjudication officer and the decision of that question is revised."

---

[24] *Willis* pp. 369-72.

Thus a decision can be reviewed if a medical authority revises its determination of one or more of the "disablement questions" considered in chapter 5.

(*d*) Error of law

By SSA s. 104(1A)

> "Any decision of an adjudication officer may be reviewed, upon the ground that it was erroneous in point of law, by an adjudication officer or, on a reference from an adjudication officer, by a social security appeal tribunal."

This ground was first introduced in 1983 but applies only to decisions of an AO and not to those of the other determining authorities. Whether a decision is wrong in law is considered at p. 223. By Adj. reg. 89(2) the power cannot be used

> ". . . so as to make benefit payable or not payable, or to alter the rate or amount of benefit payable, in respect of any period . . . more than 52 weeks before the date of application for review. . . ."

(4) Grounds for review by the medical authorities

The claimant is not required to apply for a review of a medical decision in any particular way, but the local DHSS office will supply a relevant form on request. By Adj. reg. 50 a review of a MAT decision on diagnosis or recrudescence can only be made with the leave of that tribunal. Leave is also required if an assessment made by a MAT is to be reopened on the ground of unforeseen aggravation.

There are three grounds for review laid down by SSA s. 110 as follows:

(*a*) *Mistake of fact*

By SSA s. 110(1) this ground is that the medical authority is

> ". . . satisfied that the decision was given in ignorance of a material fact or was based on a mistake as to material fact."

Mistakes may be revealed by later medical reports, although these cannot be conclusive as to the facts and are only evidence which may be taken into account by the medical authority in arriving at its own decision. The reports may suggest, for example, that there is a fracture not identified by earlier X-rays, or that, following blood tests, a previously unidentified condition can now be diagnosed. However, as recognized in *CI 442/81* (unreported) such evidence must relate to fact. It is not enough to rely upon a new opinion of the same known medical facts for otherwise there might be no end to the number of applications for review.

Fresh evidence

It used to be that the evidence as to fact had to be "fresh" and this further limited the claimant's ability to obtain a review. Although the SSA 1986 removed this requirement, it also authorized regulations to define circumstances where fresh evidence would be required for a review. In committee the Minister stated:

"Everyone supported the removal of the fresh evidence rule except the commissioners and the Council on Tribunals, who were anxious that it might lead to an over-hasty overturning, by lower level adjudicating authorities of high-level commissioners' decisions. We thought we should at least have the power to be able to do something about it if the anxiety proved to be real. This is the reason for the regulation-making power being in the Bill. The Government have no commitment to reinstate the fresh evidence rule. Our approach is to abolish it."[25]

The following account of the fresh evidence rule is therefore only of importance for cases arising before the relevant section of the 1986 Act is brought into force, and for the interpretation of any new regulations which may be made.

According to *R(I) 16/57* fresh evidence was confined to that "which the claimant was unable to produce before the decision was given or which he could not be expected to have produced in the circumstances of the case". Although this interpretation was supported in *R v MAT, ex p. Hubble* (1958) the Divisional Court added further limits to the meaning of fresh evidence. The evidence had to

". . . relate to something which has happened since the former hearing or trial, or it must be evidence which has come to the knowledge of the party applying since the hearing or trial, and which could not by reasonable means have come to his knowledge before that time."

Unlike *R(I) 16/57* this prevented a review on the ground that a claimant reasonably did not produce evidence at the original hearing even though he had knowledge of it at that time. However, *R(I) 17/66* allowed a review to take place despite such knowledge and its "wider and more benevolent" interpretation of *ex p. Hubble* was supported in *R v National Insurance Commissioner, ex p. Viscusi* (1974) where it was said that "fresh evidence" should be interpreted liberally.

In *CI 422/81* (unreported) the Commissioner referred to *Ladd v Marshall* (1954) where three principles were applied to justify the reception of fresh evidence. According to Denning LJ, these were that

"first it must be shown that the evidence could not have been obtained with reasonable diligence for use at the trial; secondly, the evidence must be such that, if given, it would probably have an important influence on the result of the case, though it need not be decisive; thirdly, the evidence must be such as is presumably to be believed, or in other words, it must be apparently credible, though it need not be incontrovertible."

These principles were applied by the House of Lords in *Langdale v Danby* (1982).

One reason for requiring the evidence to be fresh was that according to *R(I) 11/59*(T) it prevented a party from not calling evidence at the hearing only to make successive applications based upon it later. The rule meant that a review was not allowed if the claimant, or his advisers, failed to do one of two things: firstly, they failed to obtain the relevant evidence although they had the opportunity to do so, as in *R(I) 16/57* and *R(I) 27/61*;

---

[25] H. C. Deb., Standing Committee B, col. 1351, 22 April 1986.

and secondly, they failed to present the evidence at the hearing as in *R(I) 11/59*(T) and *R(I) 47/59*. A review was more likely to be refused if the claimant's attention had been drawn to the need for the evidence and he had been given a sufficient opportunity to produce it.

In establishing that they had no reasonable opportunity to present evidence earlier, claimants relied upon two particular sets of circumstances. These were, first, that the evidence could not be given at the original hearing because witnesses were unavailable. On this basis the absence of a workmate from the hearing and his later reappearance justified a review in *R(I) 47/52*. The second circumstance was that the claimant could not reasonably be expected to obtain the evidence because he was handicapped in some way in presenting his case. In *R(I) 43/52* the handicap was the claimant's "limited education and experience of affairs", whilst in *R(I) 17/66* the MAT took into account that the claimant was unrepresented and deaf. The other circumstances which could be relevant were uncertain.

(b) Unforeseen aggravation

By SSA s. 110(2) this ground is that the medical authority is

> ". . . satisfied that since the making of the assessment there has been an unforeseen aggravation of the results of the injury."

Even where there is no current assessment a review can be made, so that it may take place even if the medical authorities have previously found that there was no loss of faculty at all, or where the period covered by a final assessment of disablement has expired.

Review on this ground is sometimes sought where the claimant is dissatisfied with the assessment of disablement by the medical authority. However, an application for review should not be made if an appeal would be more appropriate. This is because firstly, the grounds for review are narrower than those for an appeal, and secondly, wider issues may be raised on an appeal and a rehearing can take place. Unlike the other grounds for review there is no advantage here compared to an appeal with regard to the backdating of benefit. A limit is imposed by Adj. reg. 86 so that a revised assessment for unforeseen aggravation can only take into account the three month period before the application is made.

There are restrictions upon applying for a review which are particular to this ground. By SSA s. 110(5) and Adj. reg. 37 a MAT assessment can only be reopened with the leave of that tribunal. Where leave was refused in *R(I) 15/68* the Commissioner considered that he had no jurisdiction to overturn the decision. In cases of occupational deafness PD regs. 30 and 31 limit applications for review, although for that disease appeals are also severely curtailed.

According to *R(I) 18/61*(T) to establish this ground for review three questions must be considered:

    (i)   whether there was in fact any worsening of the claimant's condition since the decision was given;

    (ii) whether that worsening was an aggravation of the results of the relevant injury, or whether it was due to constitutional or other factors; and

    (iii) if it was such an aggravation, whether the aggravation was foreseen and was sufficiently allowed for in the assessment, or was unforeseen and merited a higher assessment.

In practice it is easier to obtain revision of a nil assessment than others for if the condition becomes only a little worse it is easier to show that the assessment should be changed. Review on this ground is especially appropriate to deal with sequelae. As explained at p.101, these are conditions which result from the industrial injury and because they may take some time to develop, they may not be included in the original assessment. Thus in *R(I) 12/65* the claim was in respect of a hernia in the groin which was said to be an aggravation of a foot injury suffered two years previously. It is not necessary that there should be a worsening of the industrial injury itself for a case may be reopened if there is a greater disability due to the interaction of the industrial injury with the worsening of a congenital defect, disease or non-industrial injury. It is suspected that there are many accident victims who are attributing their greater disabilities to old age and are failing to appreciate that their accident is having an increased effect upon them. Their cases could be reopened and higher benefit obtained. However, for all of them the usual causation rules apply. As in *R(I) 18/62* these require that the industrial injury be the effective cause of the increased disability, even if that disability is not brought about by the worsening of the industrial injury itself, but by its connection with some other condition.

If an assessment is final it has been suggested that there should be no power to reopen a case to reduce benefit because of an improvement in the claimant's condition. Otherwise it would be a deterrent to recovery and the claimant's rehabilitation might be hindered. It is for this reason that medical decisions cannot be reviewed on the basis of a change of circumstance. This may also suggest that review for unforeseen aggravation can only lead, if anything, to an increase and never a reduction of benefit. However, this may not always be the result. It is true that such a review cannot directly reduce benefit for it can only take place if initially the condition is made worse. However, on the review SSA s. 110(6) allows the medical authority to substitute a provisional assessment for a final one, and this may happen where, for example, the effects of the worsening condition can only be fully established at a later date. At the end of that provisional assessment period the medical authority has power to make any decision it considers appropriate so that it could decide that the claimant's condition will improve and that there should be a reduction in the assessment. Although this may be an unusual case it actually happened in *R(I) 7/65* where the claimant ended up with less benefit than he had been awarded before the review for aggravation.

(c) *Error of law*

This ground was introduced by the SSA 1986 which inserted a new s. 110(1A) into the SSA 1975.

> "Any decision of an adjudicating medical practitioner may be reviewed at any time by such a practitioner if he is satisfied that the decision was erroneous in point of law."

Whether a decision is wrong in law is considered at p. 223.

CHAPTER 10

PAYMENTS OF BENEFIT

1. BENEFIT RATES

This section considers the rates of payment for industrial injuries benefit. The figures given are for the year beginning 6 April 1987. Although they will be out of date in a year, the figures are used here not only to give an idea of the relative values of different benefits, but also to illustrate how the benefits are calculated. The current rates are contained in the annual Social Security Benefits Up-Rating Order which is laid before Parliament, and publicised in DHSS leaflet NI 196.

Each year the Secretary of State is required by SSA 1986 s. 63 to review benefits. Generally, he must uprate them in line with the rise in prices. To coincide with the beginning of the new tax year payments are to be increased from 1987 in April each year instead of November.

(1) Disablement pension

The rate of pension depends upon two factors. The first, and most important of these, is the percentage of disablement as assessed by the medical authorities and discussed in chapter 5. There is provision for rounding up or down the exact percentage in order to treat it as a multiple of 10. By this means any assessment of 14 per cent or more can be made to correspond with the table of rates for payment which is contained in SSA sched. 4 and is given below. This table also reveals that the second factor affecting the rate of pension is the age of the claimant: a higher rate is paid to beneficiaries over the age of 18, that is, the vast majority of beneficiaries.

Assessment of disablement (percentage)	Rates as from 6th April 1987	
	Higher £ p	Lower £ p
100	64.50	39.50
90	58.05	35.55
80	51.60	31.60
70	45.15	27.65
60	38.70	23.70
50	32.25	19.75
40	25.80	15.80
30	19.35	11.85
20	12.90	7.90

(2) Reduced earnings allowance

REA is paid at a rate which represents the difference between the earnings in the claimant's former regular occupation, and the lower amount, if any, which he can now probably earn in work which is suitable for him. The details of how this difference is calculated are given in chapter 7. In particular at p. 194 it is noted that REA must not exceed either of the following limits:

(a) REA alone must not exceed a rate which traditionally has been equivalent to a 40 per cent disablement pension. From 6 April 1987 this is £25.80.

(b) When added to a disablement pension (but ignoring any allowance for constant attendance and severe disablement), REA must not exceed 140 per cent of the maximum for a disablement pension alone, being £90.30. This limit was raised from 100 per cent by the SSA 1986 and will take effect from when sched. 3 para. 5 comes into force, probably in April 1987.

(3) Constant attendance allowance

The effect of Benefit reg. 19 is to require this allowance to be paid at one of four rates. These depend upon two factors: firstly, whether the attendance is needed on a full-time or only a part-time basis; and secondly, upon the severity of the disablement. The number of beneficiaries receiving each rate is given in the table on p.5.

(a) For full-time attendance

There are two rates. The higher applies where

". . . the beneficiary is so exceptionally severely disabled as to be entirely, or almost entirely dependent on such attendance for the necessities of life and is likely to remain so dependent for a prolonged period and the attendance so required is whole time. . . ."

The lower rate applies where

". . . the beneficiary. . . is to a substantial extent dependent on such attendance for the necessities of life and is likely to remain dependent for a prolonged period. . . ."

For the year beginning 6 April 1987 these rates are:
Higher rate (known as the "exceptional" rate) – £51.60.
Lower rate (known as the "normal maximum" rate) – £25.80.

(b) For part-time attendance

Again there are two rates. The higher applies where the claimant would have qualified for the higher rate in (a) above, except that only part-time attendance is needed. The maximum for this rate is one and a half times the lower rate in (a).

The lower rate is paid where the claimant would have qualified for the lower rate in (a) except that only part-time attendance is needed. Here a claimant may be better off receiving an attendance allowance under the main scheme. The rates are:

Higher rate (known as the "intermediate" rate) – is not to exceed £38.70.

Lower rate – is "such sum as may be reasonable in the circumstances".

(4) Exceptionally severe disablement allowance

For the year beginning 6 April 1987 this is paid at a weekly rate of £25.80.

2. RATES FOR LUMP SUMS OR PENSIONS IN LIEU, AVAILABLE BEFORE SSA 1986

(1) A lump sum gratuity

Before the SSA 1986 the degree of disablement made a difference to the form that payment could take. For lower assessments a lump sum was usually paid, whereas for the more seriously disabled, payment always took the form of a pension. The crucial dividing line was at 20 per cent disablement. Assessments below that figure would be paid only by means of a lump sum except in the limited circumstances, described under the next heading, where a pension could be taken in lieu. The 1986 Act has changed this, and in effect, abolished all lump sum payments. As from October 1986 there has been no entitlement to disablement benefit for assessments below 14 per cent unless certain diseases are involved; and a pension has been paid at the 20 per cent rate for assessments of 14 to 19 per cent. However, for old claims, or on an appeal or review, it might still be important to understand how the lump sum was calculated.

By Benefit reg. 14(1) the amount depended upon two factors: firstly, the percentage of disablement assessed, and secondly the period for that assessment. If this period was for life, or for a definite period of at least seven years, the full amount in the table below was payable. However, if the assessment was for less than seven years, only a proportion of the full amount was payable. For example, for an assessment for a two year period, two-sevenths of the full amount would be paid. The rates in the third column of the below table were in force from 28 July 1986 until 6 April 1987. Benefit regs. sched. 3 specifies the proportions which appear in the second column of the table. SSA sched. 4 specifies the maximum lump sum payment, that is, for a 19 per cent assessment. From that payment the other sums for lesser disablement can be calculated.

By Benefit reg. 18(2) a lump sum was assessed on the scale applicable on the first day covered by the claim for benefit. The amount was not increased if the period of assessment included a later period for which, because of uprating, higher amounts were payable. This was recognized as diminishing the value of a late claim for a lump sum in *R(I) 5/82*.

Assessment of disablement (percentage)	Proportion of maximum payment (percentage)	Lump sum for assessment for life or at least 7 years (Rates from July 1986 to April 1987) £
1	10	420
2	15	630
3	20	840
4	25	1050
5	30	1260
6	35	1470
7	40	1680
8	45	1890
9	50	2100
10	55	2310
11	60	2520
12	65	2730
13	70	2940
14	75	3150
15	80	3360
16	85	3570
17	90	3780
18	95	3990
19	100	4200

(2) A pension in lieu of a lump sum

Where this can be obtained, the amount is calculated by applying the following table. The first two columns of this table are derived from Benefit reg. sched. 4, and the rates are those applicable for the year beginning 6 April 1987.

Assessment of disablement (percentage)	Proportion of 20 per cent pension (percentage)	Weekly rate as from 6 April 1987 £ p
16–19	100	12.90
11–15	75	9.68
6–10	50	6.45
1-5	25	3.23

A pension in lieu of a lump sum could be obtained in the three circumstances listed below. The first and third of these remain of importance even after the SSA 1986.

(a) Where there is also entitlement to reduced earnings allowance

If special hardship allowance (now called reduced earnings allowance) could be claimed as well as a lump sum, a claimant could opt, under Benefit reg. 18(2), for a pension in lieu of a gratuity. Those entitled to such a pension before 1 October 1986 can continue to receive it at least for a short while. This is because of reg. 7 of the Social Security (Industrial Injuries and Diseases) Miscellaneous Provisions Regulations 1986 (SI No. 1561). However, the regulation also states that the pension in lieu must end when either the period of assessment expires, or the assessment is reviewed, or when REA ceases to be payable, whichever is the earlier. If an award is revised on review and disablement is assessed for a further period a pension in lieu cannot be claimed.

Having elected for a pension in lieu, a claimant could not later change his mind. A request for the balance of the lump sum was therefore refused in *R(I) 77/53* and *R(I) 14/54*. The only way in which a pension could be reconverted was if entitlement to the allowance for reduced earning capacity were lost. Then the claimant could receive a lump sum, subject to a deduction for the amount of pension he had received in lieu. Often this meant that nothing further was payable, as in *R(I) 30/56*.

(b) Where there were successive accidents

Benefit reg.38 allowed a pension to be taken in lieu of a lump sum in the following situation. If the claimant were entitled to a disablement pension for life (this could include pension in lieu according to *R(I) 2/84*, disagreeing with *R(I) 30/56*) and, because of another accident, the claimant then became entitled to an award for which a lump sum was normally paid, he could choose to receive a pension instead of the gratuity for the increased disablement.

(c) Where certain diseases are involved

Where the claim was in respect of pneumoconiosis, byssinosis or diffuse mesothelioma a lump sum was never paid. Instead for these progressive, but slowly developing diseases a pension in lieu had to be taken. These three diseases comprise the exceptional cases where compensation continues to be available after the SSA 1986 no matter what the level of disablement. They are therefore not subject to the 14 per cent disablement threshold for benefit required in other claims. A pension continues to be paid in these cases even if there is a low assessment, provided that it is for at least 1 per cent disablement. This is the result of PD reg. 20(1) as substituted by reg. 3(3) of SI 1986 No. 1561. The latter also adds PD reg. 20(1A) which prescribes the first two columns of the below table governing the rate for the pension. In practice this is the same as that previously payable for a pension in lieu of a lump sum.

Assessment of disablement (percentage)	Rate of pension	Weekly rate as from 6 April 1987 £ p
1–10	¹⁄₁₀ of 100 per cent rate	6.50
11–19	20 per cent	12.90

3. REFORM OF BENEFIT RATES

(1) Freezing the disablement pension

Although the DHSS Discussion Document considered that the level of benefits was "mainly a matter for political judgment", it went on to suggest that industrial injuries payments "are very generous when compared with the sums available to those whose injuries have a non-industrial cause". It therefore considered the possibility of freezing the value of the disablement pension. Although it recognized that this was a radical step, it concluded that

">. . . the level of preferential benefits is now so high that it must be kept continuously under review so as to ensure that the extent of the preference afforded to the favoured groups does not increase beyond the point of acceptability; some might argue that this point has already been reached."

The possibility of freezing benefit attracted much criticism, especially since there had been no investigation of the standard of living of industrial injury pensioners. In so far as the IIAC supported the removal of the industrial preference, it opposed any levelling down of benefit. In the White Paper there was no mention of the general level of benefits, and the Government continued to uprate industrial injury benefit alongside other social security payments. However, it also commissioned a study of the number and needs of disabled people, and this is expected to be published in 1988.

(2) Reallocation in favour of the more seriously disabled

The White Paper proposed that more of the available resources should be directed towards the more seriously disabled. One way of achieving this would be to revise the scale which relates assessment of disablement to the amount of the weekly pension. The White Paper criticized the strictly mathematical scale used at present. This makes payments for assessments of less than 100 per cent in direct proportion to the 100 per cent pension rate, so that an assessment of 20 per cent attracts one fifth of the maximum disablement pension. According to the White Paper this

">. . . does not allow the scheme to recognize fully the strain which severe disablement (even falling short of 100 per cent) may place upon an injured person, as compared with his less disabled counterpart. The Government sees advantage in amending the scale so that *more* than twice the compensation is available for a 40 per cent assessment than one of 20 per cent, and more than twice again where an 80 per cent assessment is given."

It therefore proposed to revise the scale as follows:

Percentage assessment	Percentage of 100 per cent pension payable
20	15
30	25
40	35
50	50
60	65
70	75
80	85
90	95
100	100

The changes would improve the pension of for those assessed at 60–90 per cent disabled, at the expense of those assessed at 20-40 per cent. However, because many more beneficiaries are assessed at the lower levels, the effect of this proposal would be to reduce the resources spent on the scheme unless benefit were improved in other ways. Based on appendix A, table 2, it can be estimated that about 13,000 of the more severely disabled pensioners would benefit, but 135,000 others would be adversely affected. The Consultation Paper defers consideration of this proposal until the survey of disablement becomes available in 1988.

4. THE DELIVERY OF PAYMENT

By CP reg. 16(8)

"Weekly sums on account of any industrial injuries benefit . . . shall be payable on Wednesdays."

If entitlement begins or ends on some other day, it will not effectively do so until the following Wednesday.

CP reg. 16(2) requires that industrial injuries benefit

". . . shall be paid weekly in advance by means of benefit orders payable in each case to the beneficiary at such place as the Secretary of State, after inquiry of the beneficiary, may from time to time specify."

In practice, payment is made by means of an order book, containing a number of individual foils which cover a 52-week period. The book is produced by the DHSS North Fylde office. It is sent to the local DHSS office, who post it to the beneficiary. Payment can only be made at the post office nominated by the beneficiary and specified in the book.

In 1979 the DHSS scrutiny committee noted that the cost of paying disablement benefit, including REA, to 200,000 beneficiaries was £10 million a year (Appendix to the Report of the Social Services Committee 1980, Cmnd. 8106). In recent years there have been several reviews of the arrangements for delivering social security benefit. Greater efficiency has been achieved especially by paying some benefit at less frequent intervals. In addition, for certain benefits claimants are encouraged to accept automated credit transfers. These involve the DHSS making payments directly into a bank or other account. As part of this change banks would prefer payments to be made only at four week intervals. Although the DHSS scrutiny committee in 1979 thought that this was an appropriate interval for the payment of industrial injuries benefit, as yet no change has been made to the weekly order book system. The way in which benefit will be paid in the future depends upon, amongst other factors, the progress of computerisation at the DHSS.

5. OBTAINING PAYMENT IN TIME TO PREVENT EXTINGUISHMENT OF A RIGHT

CP reg. 22 authorizes the extinguishment of the right to be paid benefit if payment is not obtained within a year of it being treated as having arisen. Usually the right to payment arises at the date of issue of an order made payable to the claimant. However, extinguishment may also occur if, instead of the claimant being sent an order for payment, he is given a notice that a sum is available for collection. A claimant may avoid extinguishment by using a similar excuse to that which prevents disqualification from entitlement to benefit because of failure to claim in time. This excuse is that the claimant has "good cause" for his failure to obtain payment, and it is discussed at p. 206.

Even if no order or notice is issued the right to payment can still be extinguished if a year has elapsed since a date, determined by the Secretary of State, upon which the right to payment is deemed to arise. This procedure is rarely used. In its 1952 report (Cmd. 8511) the IIAC recommended that it be replaced and that the statutory authorities should determine the date according to a prescribed code. However, this proposal was not implemented. The procedure has been considered only in one case. In *R(I) 1/84* the claimant, entitled to a disablement pension, moved to Bangladesh. Over a period of time he failed to reply to some DHSS letters, but he was never sent any notice that money could be collected. Although the Secretary of State attempted to determine that the right to payment had arisen in respect of a certain period, he failed to specify a particular pay day. This procedural error enabled the claimant to appeal successfully against the extinguishing of his right to payment. He also succeeded in showing, in any event, that he had good cause for delay in requesting payment because of language, postal and other difficulties.

6. DISQUALIFICATION FROM, OR SUSPENSION OF, BENEFIT

There are six circumstances which can result in disqualification, suspension or reduction of benefit under the industrial scheme. Most of the relevant regulations are made under SSA s. 82.

(1) Failure to claim in time

A late application can lead to disqualification from benefit in respect of any period more than three months before the date of the claim. This is fully considered in chapter 8.

(2) Failure to give information

Benefit reg. 40(2) authorizes disqualification from benefit if, without good cause, the claimant fails to give information in the two circumstances noted below. The AO, SSAT or Commissioner may disqualify the claimant in respect of the period of his failure to give the information and, by reg. 40(4), may decide to suspend for a time proceedings on the claim or payment. The excuse that the claimant has "good cause" for his failure is examined in relation to the failure to claim benefit in time at p. 206.

(a) Information relating to the claim

By reg. 40(2)(a) disqualification may occur if a claimant, without good cause,

> ". . . fails to furnish to the prescribed person any information required for the determination of the claim or of any question arising in connection therewith."

The extent of this obligation has already been examined. It involves giving notice to the employer, as required by CP reg. 24 and described at p. 201.

Information must also be given to the DHSS via the Secretary of State, as required by CP reg. 7 and described at p. 204.

(*b*) *Notice of any change of circumstance*

By reg.40(2)(*b*) disqualification is also authorized if the beneficiary, without good cause,

> ". . . fails to give notice to the prescribed person of any change of circumstances affecting the continuance of the right to benefit or to the receipt thereof. . . ."

Information must therefore be given not only on making a claim, but also when obtaining payment. By CP reg. 23(1) "certificates and other documents and such information . . . as the Secretary of State may require" must be given. In particular the beneficiary must

> ". . . notify the Secretary of State in writing of any change of circumstances which he might reasonably be expected to know might affect the right to benefit, or to its receipt, as soon as reasonably practicable after the occurrence thereof."

In practice, a claimant is informed of what changes in circumstances are relevant by a notice which appears in the back of the pension order book. Failure to comply can lead not only to disqualification from benefit, but also to the DHSS demanding repayment and even instituting a criminal prosecution. These possibilities are considered at the end of this chapter.

(3) Refusal of, or misconduct in relation to, medical treatment

Benefit reg. 40(2)(*c*) authorizes disqualification if, without good cause, a claimant fails to comply with CP reg. 26. As set out at p. 204, this regulation requires a claimant to submit to medical examination and treatment as required by the Secretary of State. It was applied in *CI 244/50*.

Benefit reg. 40(3) made under SSA s. 90(2) makes further provision for disqualification. It applies if a claimant

> ". . . wilfully obstructs, or is guilty of other misconduct in connection with any examination or treatment to which he is required under [CP reg.26] to submit himself. . . ."

Benefit reg. 40 places two restrictions upon the extent to which there can be disqualification based upon either of the above grounds. Firstly, the period of disablement can be for no longer than six weeks. This period gives the claimant time to consider his actions, and if necessary, a further period of disqualification can be imposed if the claimant continues to fail to comply. Secondly, by reg. 40(6):

> "No person shall be disqualified from receiving any benefit for refusal to undergo a surgical operation not being one of a minor character."

(4) Absence from the country

By SSA s. 82(5)(*a*) a claimant is disqualified from benefit for any period of absence from this country, except where the regulations provide otherwise. However, these regulations provide for very wide exceptions and in most cases, allow industrial injury benefit to continue to be paid. Those who go to an EEC country, or one with which Britain has a reciprocal agreement, are especially favourably treated. However, the general rules for absences are contained in the Social Security (Persons Abroad) Regs. 1975 (SI No. 563). (Entitlement for an injury occurring abroad is distinct from later disqualification because of absence, and is considered in chapter 2.)

(*a*) The Persons Abroad regulations

Although these regulations prevent anyone being disqualified from a disablement pension because of absence, the two supplements to the pension can be stopped unless the exception contained in reg. 9(4) applies. This prevents the claimant being disqualified from the allowances for constant attendance and severe disablement

> ". . . by reason of being temporarily absent from Great Britain during the period of six months from the date on which such absence commences or during such longer period as the Secretary of State may, having regard to the purpose of the absence and any other factors which appear to him to be relevant, allow."

Similarly REA can be stopped when the exception contained in reg. 9(5) applies. In effect there can be disqualification from REA if the absence is not temporary or is for more than three months, unless, again, the Secretary of State allows an extension, or the absence is for the purpose of work, or is not covered by the period of the award. A claimant living in India could not show that his absence was temporary and was therefore disqualified from REA in *CI 10/81* (unreported). Airmen and mariners can avoid disqualification by relying upon reg. 4 of the Social Security (Industrial Injuries) (Airmen's Benefits) Regulations 1975 (SI No. 469), and reg. 5 of the similarly titled Mariners' Benefits Regulations 1975 (SI No. 470).

(*b*) Countries with which there are reciprocal agreements

The limited provisions for disqualifying from benefit under the Persons Abroad regulations are further reduced if a claimant goes to a country which has entered into a reciprocal social security agreement with Britain. These agreements are noted at p. 35, and claims are dealt with by the DHSS Overseas Branch, Newcastle.

(*c*) EEC countries

A final restriction on disqualification applies if the claimant goes to an EEC country. As discussed at p. 35, EEC regulations aim to co-ordinate the national systems of social security in order to promote unity and encourage the free exchange of labour. The regulations therefore try to remove restrictions on the payment of benefit which depend upon the claimant's nationality, or upon territorial limits. Thus, by article 10 of EEC reg. 1408/71, industrial injury payments, amongst others,

". . . shall not be subject to any reduction, modification, suspension, withdrawal or confiscation by reason of the fact that the recipient resides in the territory of a Member State other than that in which the institution responsible for payment is situated."

Articles 52, 54 and 55 of this regulation specifically deal with the protection of benefit for industrial injury. Claims for benefit where this protection could be relevant are again dealt with centrally by the DHSS Overseas Branch, Newcastle.

(5) Imprisonment or detention in legal custody

SSA s. 82(5)(*b*) authorizes disqualification from benefit for those "undergoing imprisonment or detention in legal custody". Unlike absence abroad, the exceptions here are narrow. Throughout his period of detention a claimant is disqualified from REA and the allowances for constant attendance and severe disablement. Although Benefit reg. 2(6) allows a disablement pension to continue to be paid, it can last for no more than a year. By reg. 3 even this payment can be suspended until the claimant is released from prison.

However, there are two circumstances in which, despite being detained, the claimant cannot be disqualified from any industrial injuries benefit. The first of these is where the claimant is held in custody pending the conclusion of criminal proceedings against him. By Benefit reg. 2(2) he can only be disqualified if, at the end of these proceedings, he is sentenced to a period of imprisonment or detention. The second circumstance is where the claimant is detained in a mental hospital, again as a result of criminal proceedings against him. However, Benefit reg. 2(3) only protects the right to benefit of those who are sent directly to hospital, not those who are transferred there after a spell in prison. Claimants relying upon this exception to prevent loss of benefit may nevertheless find that constant attendance allowance is not paid because of the rules which affect all those spending time in hospital for whatever reason. These are considered next.

(6) Going into hospital

By SSA s. 82(6):

"Regulations may provide –
(b) for suspending payment of benefit to a person during any period in which he is undergoing medical or other treatment as an in-patient in a hospital or other institution."

The main regulations made under this section are the Social Security (Hospital In-Patients) Regulations 1975 (SI No. 555). However, they do not stop any of the present industrial injury benefits being paid during a stay in hospital. Instead it is Benefit reg. 21 which ends entitlement to constant attendance allowance for the remaining period in hospital after the claimant has received free in-patient treatment for four weeks. All other industrial injury benefits can continue to be paid.

7. Payment Following an Appeal

A claimant who is successful in an appeal may not be able to obtain immediate payment of the new award of, or increase in, benefit. Benefit reg. 41 allows the DHSS to delay payment for up to 28 days following an appeal. Within that time if the AO gives notice of, or applies for, leave to appeal, the award can be delayed until the appeal is decided, unless the Secretary of State directs otherwise.

If a decision in favour of a claimant is reversed on an appeal, or an award is reduced, it is unlikely that the benefit which has been paid in the meantime will have to be repaid. However, as explained under the next heading, this can be required if the claimant has misrepresented or failed to disclose some material fact.

8. Repayment of Benefit Following a Misrepresentation or Non-Disclosure

Benefit can sometimes be paid only for it to be discovered that there was no entitlement to it. If overpayment is the result of a misrepresentation or non-disclosure of the true position, repayment of the excess can be required from the person who misrepresented the facts. The power to reclaim the money is given to the DHSS, via the Secretary of State, by SSA 1986 s. 53. Although it can only be exercized if the earlier decision favourable to the claimant is reversed or varied on appeal, or is revised on a review, the power can be applied against innocent as well as guilty parties. The section catches not only the perpetrator of a fraud, but also the morally blameless, passive recipient of payments, who is not aware that a change of circumstance has reduced his entitlement to benefit. This is because s. 53(1) states:

> "Where it is determined that, whether fraudulently or otherwise, any person has misrepresented, or failed to disclose, any material fact and in consequence of the misrepresentation or failure –
> (a) a payment has been made in respect of a benefit to which this section applies; or
> (b) any sum recoverable by or on behalf of the Secretary of State in connection with any such payment has not been recovered,
> the Secretary of State shall be entitled to recover the amount of any payment which he would not have made or any sum which he would have received but for the misrepresentation or failure to disclose."

This section is expected to be in force by April 1987. Under the previous legislation repayment was not required if the determining authorities were satisfied that, throughout the relevant period, the beneficiary had taken "due care and diligence" to avoid overpayment. However, this subjective excuse is no longer available, and it now does not matter that the claimant is honest and has taken all reasonable steps to avoid overpayment.

9. Criminal Offences in Obtaining Benefit

Anyone obtaining money by deception may be guilty of a criminal offence under the Theft Acts, and a serious penalty may be imposed. However, specific provision for an offence in relation to social security benefit is made by SSA 1986 s. 55. An offence is committed under s. 55(1) if a person for the purpose of obtaining benefit

> "(a) makes a statement or representation which he knows to be false; or
> (b) produces or furnishes, or knowingly causes or knowingly allows to be produced or furnished, any document or information which he knows to be false in a material particular. . . ."

On summary conviction a fine can be imposed, or the offender sentenced for up to three months imprisonment. The offence may be committed if deception takes place either in order to obtain an award, or when receiving payment. False statements which may be made in connection with industrial injuries benefit include, for example, attributing non-work injuries to employment, exaggerating the effects of injury and misrepresenting potential earning capacity in order to obtain REA.

CHAPTER 11

OTHER SOURCES OF COMPENSATION

1. UNDER THE INDUSTRIAL INJURIES SCHEME

(1) Old cases of workmen's compensation

The industrial injuries scheme only applies to accidents or diseases which develop after 4 July 1948. Claims relating to an earlier period are still governed by the Workmen's Compensation Acts. There is only a very remote chance of any new claim arising under these Acts, for even the most latent and insidious form of disease is now likely to have shown its effects. However, rights under the earlier legislation are still important. This is because the value of workmen's compensation has been increased in order to bring the benefits more into line with those of the present industrial injuries scheme. For this to be done no further contributions have been required from the employers or private insurers who originally paid for workmen's compensation. Instead, extra funds have been made available by the State to provide either a supplement to existing benefit, or an entirely new benefit. The supplement increases the value of the workmen's compensation payments still being received by the claimant. By contrast the new benefit is available to those other workers who, although once entitled to workmen's compensation, no longer receive payments because, for example, their employer went bankrupt. These benefits can be claimed under the Industrial Injuries (Old Cases) Act 1975 and, in particular, under its regulations which provide the framework for the two relevant schemes. As considered below these are the Workmen's Compensation (Supplementation) Scheme 1982 (SI No. 1489) and, for particular diseases, the Pneumoconiosis, Byssinosis and Miscellaneous Diseases Scheme 1983 (SI No. 136).

All claims are dealt with by the DHSS North Fylde office. According to the first report in 1985 of the Chief Adjudication Officer, in the previous year there were 373 decisions upon claims relating to employment before 1948. They were dealt with by only one specialist AO with the assistance at times of another. The weaknesses in adjudication were found to be with regard to interpreting two particular provisions. These were, firstly, late claims (art. 18 of the 1982 scheme and art. 17 of the 1983 scheme), and secondly, prescription in mesothelioma claims (art. 2 of the 1982 scheme), where evidence must be obtained in respect of employment which took place at least almost 40 years ago.

(a) The Workmen's Compensation (Supplementation) Scheme

An outline of this scheme is contained in DHSS leaflet WS. 1. The following allowances may be paid:

(i) A basic allowance – can be claimed by those suffering an industrial accident or disease before 1924 if, as a result, they are totally or partially incapacitated for work. Claimants must also have had a right after 20 March 1951 to weekly payments under the Workmen's Compensation Acts, or under any contracting out schemes run by their employers. The small pool of beneficiaries continues to decline: in 1983 there were only 160 supplementary allowances in payment, this number also including the allowances in (ii) and (iii) below for pre-1924 injuries.[1] The basic allowance has a very small value. It cannot exceed £2 a week. However, a right to the allowance can help establish entitlement to the much more valuable major incapacity allowance.

(ii) A major incapacity allowance – is available to those who have been entitled to weekly payments of workmen's compensation (which may include the basic allowance) at some time since 5 July 1956. Claimants must also show that their industrial accident or disease has made them totally incapable of work and that they are likely to remain so for a considerable period. The scheme thus draws a distinction between total and partial incapacity. Where a worker who had suffered an accident was totally incapacitated but the accident produced only part of this incapacity, *R(I) 6/80* decided that a major incapacity allowance was not payable, although a claim for a lesser incapacity allowance could be made.

By s. 2(6)(*b*) of the Industrial Injuries and Diseases (Old Cases) Act 1975 the amount of the allowance

"shall be the corresponding disablement pension rate less the amount of the recipient's workmen's compensation and less the amount of his basic allowance if any."

The allowance can therefore increase the weekly compensation to the same rate as that for 100 per cent disablement under the current scheme. In 1984 there were 514 beneficiaries receiving this allowance.

(iii) A lesser incapacity allowance – is available to a worker not entitled to (*ii*) but who has been partially or totally incapacitated, and has been entitled since 1 March 1966 to weekly payments of workmen's compensation for loss of earnings. There is no entitlement if, before that date, the right to payments ended because, for example, the claimant accepted a lump sum settlement. The rate of the allowance is based upon a proportion of the individual claimant's loss of earnings, up to a maximum amount. For the year beginning 6 April 1987 this maximum amount is £23-75 based on loss of earnings of over £30-95. In 1984 there were 2,358 beneficiaries receiving such payments.

(iv) Certain industrial injury scheme supplements – are available to those entitled to workmen's compensation who are incapable of work and likely to remain so permanently. These additions can increase the value of a major incapacity allowance so as to place recipients on an almost equal footing with those receiving disablement benefit. By Benefit regs. 42 and 43 both the allowances for constant attendance and exceptionally severe disablement can be claimed by those injured before 5 July 1948.

[1]   *Social Security Statistics 1985*, table 23.30.

(*b*) *The Pneumoconiosis, Byssinosis and Miscellaneous Diseases Benefit Scheme*

The scheme contained in SI 1983 No. 136 is described in DHSS leaflet PN. 1. It provides benefits for death and disablement caused by one of the diseases listed, if the following three conditions are met:

    (i) the disease must arise out of employment before 5 July 1948.

    (ii) nothing must be payable under the Workmen's Compensation Acts or industrial injuries provisions of the SSA.

    (iii) no damages must have been received as a result of a common law claim in respect of the disease.

The scheme's schedule lists eight other diseases in addition to those in its title which are covered in respect of particular occupations. These other diseases almost all involve various forms of cancer where long latency periods are common. However, over 90 per cent of the awards actually made relate to pneumoconiosis. The benefits are similar to those listed in the supplementation scheme in (*a*) above, except that in the event of death a lump sum of up to £300 is provided for dependants. In 1985 there were 131 allowances in payment for total incapacity and 874 for partial incapacity.[2] There were 48 new awards made that year. On average, in the past few years the scheme has given rise to about 20 cases a year before local tribunals and one appeal to a Commissioner.

(2) Supplementary scheme for colliery workers

Until 1980 the Secretary of State had power under SSA s. 158 to approve supplementary schemes to provide additional payments for those receiving industrial injury benefit. Only one such scheme was ever registered, although there have been many employers and friendly societies who have provided supplementation. Examples of these additional payments are the private arrangements made in cases of disease which are considered later in this chapter. The one scheme which was approved and registered still exists. It is contained in the National Insurance (Industrial Injuries) (Colliery Workers' Supplementary Scheme) Amendment and Consolidation Order 1970 (SI No. 376). The scheme provides extra payments for those who were entitled to a disablement pension before 30 March 1970 because they suffered a colliery accident or developed a colliery disease. At first the scheme was paid for by the contributions of workers alone. However, later, British Coal lent financial assistance and now it fully funds and administers the scheme. In 1965 the benefits were equal to a third of the disablement pension, but since that time they have been frozen. In 1985 there were 650 people receiving benefits under the scheme, whilst 95 others decided that year to take a once and for all lump sum, thus ending their entitlement. The total payments for the fiscal year 1984-85 amounted to £50,000. A British Coal director based at the Pensions and Insurance Centre in Sheffield has pointed to other possible beneficiaries:[3]

"We have records of over 7000 men who, on the face of it, could be entitled to a lump sum benefit if they were to make a claim, but, of course these records

---

[2]   DHSS, *Social Security Statistics 1986*, tables 24.30, 24.31 and 50.04.
[3]   Personal letter to the author, May 1985.

are sometimes years old and it is quite possible that many of the people concerned have died."

2. STATE PROVISION UNDER THE PNEUMOCONIOSIS ETC. (WORKERS' COMPENSATION) ACT 1979

This Act was passed to compensate those employees suffering from certain dust diseases who, although entitled to disablement benefit, can neither sue for damages, nor agree any private no-fault scheme of compensation with their employer. The reason for this is that their employer is no longer in business. The Welsh Nationalist MPs who pressed for this legislation were particularly concerned about the victims of slate quarrying. However, advantage of the Act can also be taken by, for example, those who worked with asbestos, or in mining iron ore, or in the china clay industry including pottery making. Receipt of the tax-free lump sum available under the Act has no effect upon a claim under the industrial injury scheme.

At first the Act required claimants to be sufferers from either pneumoconiosis (defined at p. 120 to include silicosis, asbestosis and kaolinosis), byssinosis (see appendix E, disease D2), or diffuse mesothelioma (see appendix E, disease D3). However, by SSA 1985 s. 24 the Secretary of State was given power to specify additional diseases which qualify for payment, and by SI 1985 No. 2034 a claim can now be made in respect of:

> "(a) Primary carcinoma of the lung where there is accompanying evidence of one or both of the following:
>   (i) asbestosis
>   (ii) bilaterial diffuse pleural thickening;
> (b) bilateral diffuse pleural thickening."

These are discussed in appendix E in relation to diseases D8 and D9 of the schedule of prescribed diseases.

The conditions which a worker must satisfy are laid down by s. 2 of the Act. As modified by SSA 1986 these are:

> "(a) that disablement benefit is payable to him in respect of the disease or,. . . would be payable to him in respect of it but for his disablement amounting to less than the appropriate percentage;
> (b) that every relevant employer of his has ceased to carry on business; and
> (c) that he has not brought any action, or compromised any claim for damages, in respect of the disablement."

However, an action which has been withdrawn, or dismissed, without the merits of the case being heard will not affect entitlement. Dependants of a worker who died may also be entitled to benefit under the Act.

The amount of the lump sum depends upon the degree of disablement assessed by a special medical board, the period covered by the assessment and the claimant's age at the time of assessment. Amounts vary between £1,100 and £15,000 as prescribed by the Pneumoconiosis etc. (Workers' Compensation) (Payment of Claims) Regulations 1985 (SI No. 2035) which is uprated each year.

Under the Pneumoconiosis etc. (Workers' Compensation) (Determination of Claims) Regulations 1979 (SI. No. 727) a claim must be made within 12 months of the date on which disablement benefit was awarded. For a dependant the claim must be made within 12 months of the death. However, the regulations give the Secretary of State a discretion to accept a later claim if he considers it appropriate to do so in the circumstances of the case. Further details are contained in leaflet PL 640 which is available, together with application forms, from the Department of Employment, Branch HSL Level 2, Caxton House, Tothill Street, London SW1.

3. PRIVATE ARRANGEMENTS WITH EMPLOYERS OR THEIR INSURERS

(1) Introduction

Private no-fault compensation schemes for some work injuries can benefit those employed in certain industries. The schemes have been agreed between unions on the one hand, and employers and, at times, their insurers on the other. Injured workers may claim benefit without having to resort to the courts in order to prove negligence. For example, in 1985 certain road transport employers agreed to a scheme of compensation for bus drivers and conductors who were assaulted in the course of their duties. Other schemes involve claims for disease rather than accidents, and these sometimes offer benefits only as a substitute and not as an addition to common law damages. Money is then paid on the condition that the worker gives up any right of action alleging that the employer was at fault. However, even this type of scheme has no effect upon a claimant's right to industrial injury benefit. Details of no-fault schemes for disease are given below in order to emphasize that, for some workers, the private arrangements are important alternative or additional sources of compensation to that provided by the State or at common law.

The advantage of a no-fault scheme over a claim for common law damages is that it can provide a relatively informal method of obtaining speedy benefits; it can avoid the delay, expense and uncertainty involved in what has been called the "forensic lottery" of the common law. Private schemes have been devised in recent years especially to deal with claims of industrial disease. The reasons for this are considered in relation to the individual schemes examined below.[4] They include the difficulty of determining the cause of a disease rather than an accident. Establishing the work connection can be particularly complicated if the disease has a long latency period. Often evidence of both the claimant's medical and work history over a period of many years must be examined, and matched against the standard of care to be expected of the employer at the time of exposure to the hazard. The costs of both bringing and defending such an action can be high. Unions have been particularly concerned about the delays that can result where, following recent evidence of a connection between work and a particular disease, they are faced with having to process a large number of common law claims all on an individual basis. For their part, employers have been equally concerned to avoid the costs of repeated litigation. In some cases they have been able to settle claims at a level lower than that of common law damages. However, at least some of those workers who have received compensation under the schemes listed below would have received only social security payments had it not been for the no-fault agreements.

---

[4] See J. Stapleton, *Disease and the Compensation Debate* (1986) pp. 17-87.

(2) British Coal's pneumoconiosis compensation scheme

This scheme was introduce in 1974 having been prompted by *Pickles* v *NCB* (1968). In that test case a miner successfully brought a common law action for the damage caused to his lungs by coal dust. Other cases were waiting in the wings, but to avoid the protracted and costly litigation potentially involved, management and unions agreed to a no-fault compensation scheme. This provides lump sums of up to £10,000 as well as allowances for loss of earnings, and benefits for dependants in fatal cases. Claimants must be employees of British Coal who are certified for DHSS disablement benefit purposes as entitled to a pension for pneumoconiosis. Although the scheme makes use of special medical boards' assessments to determine its own level of compensation, in other respects it is entirely independent of the industrial injuries scheme. In particular the no-fault benefits are paid in addition to disablement benefit. However, no overlap is allowed with common law damages for, if benefits are accepted under the scheme, workers must agree not to sue. There is a strong incentive for common law rights to be relinquished because the unions have agreed not to support any member who seeks damages instead of accepting the benefits under the scheme they have negotiated.

Settlements under the scheme up to 21 February 1985 were as follows:[5]

		Cases	£
(1)	Pre 1974 certifications	64,376	125,327,675
(2)	Post 1974 certifications	4,336	3,095,880
(3)	Supplementary payments	9,880	3,154,825
(4)	Commutation cases	2,7121	1,632,600
	TOTAL	81,313	133,210,980

(Commutation cases involve those miners or their widows who have been paid a once and for all lump sum in lieu of weekly payments under the Workmen's Compensation Acts.)

(3) Occupational deafness compensation schemes

Only in recent years has it been recognized that exposure to noise at work can cause loss of hearing which deserves compensation. It can be a serious injury affecting a large number of workers. However, in individual cases it can be very difficult to establish the cause of deafness and, as chapter 4 points out, this has resulted in strict limits being imposed upon the extent of coverage under the industrial scheme. If an action for damages at common law is brought the plaintiff must not only satisfy the requirement of proving that work was the cause, but also must show that the employer was at fault. Even if both cause and fault can be shown the employer may be able to claim that because of the general lack of knowledge in the past about the dangers of noise, a failure to take precautions should only be found in relation to the work done in recent years. The employer may then claim that the plaintiff's hearing had already

---

[5]   Figures supplied in a personal letter to the author from British Coal, Pensions and Insurance Centre, Sheffield.

deteriorated before the date from which he could be considered negligent. This argument resulted in the payment of only a small amount of damages to older workers who had been subject to noise over a long period in *Thompson* v *Smith Shiprepairers* (1984). The limit imposed in this and other cases upon the ability of workers to claim damages has encouraged unions to look towards no-fault compensation schemes as an alternative means of obtaining benefit. The following schemes have been negotiated:

(a) Ministry of Defence civilian employees scheme

This was negotiated by the Boilermakers union and the Transport and General Workers on behalf of their members who worked in the Royal Dockyards. The scheme came into operation in the late 1970s and in its first year over 1,100 cases were settled. The agreement ended in 1982 but it is still operating informally on a local basis.

(b) British Rail employees scheme

An informal agreement with unions exists to provide compensation according to the degree of hearing loss. Both this scheme and that in (c) take account of the effects of tinnitus. Unlike (c) however, receipt of monies under this scheme does not prevent later resort to a common law action.

(c) The Iron Trades Insurers scheme

In 1979 these insurers agreed with several unions, principally the AUEW and GMBTU, to compensate on a no-fault basis those employees of firms which they insure against liability at common law. The 1986 agreement with the Boilermakers covered hearing damage of at least 10 dB caused by exposure to noise for a year or more between 1963 and 1978. These two dates represent respectively the "date of knowledge" before which employers (in shipbuilding and heavy engineering at least) have been judged in the courts not liable for the consequences of over exposure to noise; and the date after which employers claim that, in general, protection was being provided so that negligence for any later period can be denied.

The scheme contains a procedure for agreeing medical reports. There is a fixed scale of lump sum compensation according to the degree of hearing loss, but it does not take account of tinnitus which may be compensated separately. For a hearing loss of 96 dB or more the maximum award of £6,900 is payable. Provision can be made for widows or dependants. It has been estimated that the scheme has paid out over £14 million. The firm of solicitors handling most of the union claims were dealing with over 20,000 cases at the beginning of the settlement process. In return for the compensation each claimant must waive any right to damages at common law for their hearing loss. As their part of the agreement trade unions have conceded that they will not instruct solicitors to litigate any common law claim on behalf of members covered by the scheme. Another agreement between the same parties covers vibration white finger.

(4) Other schemes for disease

In 1984 the TUC published a booklet *Compensation Schemes For Occupational Diseases*. It refers to the other no-fault schemes listed below. Whereas (a)-(c) are substitutes for a common law claim, (d)-(f) are additional remedies which provide compensation, in particular, for loss of earnings and resettlement costs resulting from an enforced change or loss of job. (The prescribed disease number refers to the relevant industrial injury provision as tabled in appendix E.)

(*a*) *Certain conditions due to vinyl chloride monomer* (prescribed disease C24)

Both British Petroleum and ICI offer compensation for liver damage caused by VCM. Although the ICI scheme has not been negotiated with the unions, it is open to voluntary adoption by eligible employees. Since 1975 it has provided a yearly lump sum plus an allowance for lost wages. A pension is available after retirement age. The scheme extends to widows and children in fatal cases.

(*b*) *Bladder cancer* (prescribed disease C23)

An ICI scheme provides for benefits similar to those in (*a*). However, the decision of the Company Medical Officer as to the cause of the disease is final. Dunlop Ltd. also have a scheme, but it does not prejudice common law rights.

(*c*) *Radiation induced diseases* (prescribed diseases A1 and A2)

Prompted by the success in 1977 of a widow in claiming common law damages, British Nuclear Fuels negotiated a no-fault scheme with the GMBTU ad the Institute of Professional Civil Servants to provide compensation for the death of workers caused by radiation. The scheme was agreed in 1982, and in its first four years 11 awards of compensation were made. Payments have been as high as £75,000 to widows and dependants.

(*d*) *Effects of toluene di-isocyanate* (prescribed disease C7)

Unions have agreed with several packaging companies that compensation will be paid for loss of earnings to sensitized workers.

(*e*) *Occupational allergies*

The TGWU has agree with Beechams Pharmaceuticals a list of allergy cases for which there are lump sum resettlement grants for workers who are forced to leave their job.

(*f*) *Vibration white finger* (prescribed disease A11)

An agreement made between the GMBTU and the Iron Trades insurance companies offers compensation to those who have worked on any vibrating machinery for more than two years between 1976 and March 1985, provided that they have been employed by one of the companies protected by one of the relevant insurers for the period in question. The agreement has several of the features of that agreed between the same parties in respect of occupational deafness. In particular the union agrees not to support a member who seeks damages for such an injury at common law. A condition of receiving any money under the scheme is that payments are made in full and final settlement of any claim, including that at common law, which might otherwise have been brought against the company. Payments are made on a graded scale according to the severity of the disease. Unlike the deafness agreement there is provision for a sum to be negotiated to compensate for any past or future loss of earnings. Any promotion prospects which may be lost because of the sufferer being forced to avoid vibrating machinery can also be taken into account.

4. SUING FOR DAMAGES AT COMMON LAW

A claim for common law damages in respect of a work injury is the subject of specialist books on the law of tort. It is therefore considered only briefly here. However, space is given to one aspect which raises directly the relationship of tort to the industrial injuries scheme. This is the extent to which industrial injuries benefit is taken into account when calculating the claimant's financial loss in order to assess any damages to which he may be entitled. Before this is considered, the section begins with a brief general introduction to the action in tort, and a comparison is made with the industrial scheme. Further details of this comparison are given in chapter 1.

(1) Nature and extent of claims

To succeed in a common law claim a worker must usually show that the injury or disease was caused by the negligence of either the employer himself, or someone acting for or on his behalf. For example, the employer himself may have been at fault in failing to provide a safe system of work, or the negligent act may have been done by another employee for whom the employer is vicariously liable. Another related basis for a claim is that the accident has been caused by the employer failing to meet the standards laid down in certain statutes which deal, for example, with safety in factories. Any damages awarded in tort are paid in a lump sum. These may be reduced if the worker was at fault himself and helped to bring about his own injuries. By contrast, entitlement to industrial injury benefit does not depend upon proving that someone was at fault; payment can only take the form of a pension, not a lump sum; and it is made irrespective of the claimant's lack of skill or competence at his job. Although in extreme cases a claimant's wrongdoing can take him outside of his course of employment, and therefore outside of the scheme, there is no provision, as there is in tort, for his compensation to be reduced in proportion to his degree of fault.

For a variety of reasons only a minority of accident victims obtain any damages at common law, and it can be argued that, for workers, the industrial scheme has provided a more important source of compensation. The Pearson Commission found that although work accidents comprised 46 per cent of all tort claims,[6] only one in ten of those injured at work – about 90,000 people – obtained any damages at all.[7] By contrast at the same time the industrial scheme was compensating three times as many

---

[6] Pearson vol. 2, p. 19 table 11.
[7] *Ibid.*, p. 50 and p. 22 table 14 which is based upon injuries causing four days incapacity for work. Another survey looked at more serious injuries – those causing incapacity for at least two weeks. It found that the number of workers compensated doubled but it was still only one in five of all those injured. See D. Harris *et al.*, *Compensation and Support for Illness and Injury* (1984) p. 51 table 2.2.

workers, most of them continuing to receive a pension in respect of an injury which had occurred years previously. The annual expenditure on the industrial scheme continues to be twice the amount of damages paid in tort for injuries at work. Indeed the benefits paid out are more than the total compensation given by the common law for all injuries whether caused at work or elsewhere.

Contrary to the expectations of many lawyers the tort system therefore may be seen as only a secondary source of compensation for those injured at work. In addition, the way that it provides compensation has attracted much criticism. Two of the main reservations about the tort system may be noted here. First, it is expensive to administer. The Pearson Commission estimated that its costs were 45 per cent of the combined total of compensation and operating costs, whereas the comparative figure for the industrial injury scheme is only 12 per cent.[8] Secondly, damages are often only paid after much delay. Although 99 per cent of cases are settled out of court, and payment is made in 80 per cent of these within two years of the claim,[9] there are much longer delays in cases involving more serious injury and in cases of industrial disease. If a case goes to court, on average, it is not heard until three years after the injury.[10] Costs and delay are two of the reasons which account for the conclusion of the leading commentator on accident compensation that:

> "It is hard to believe that anyone could make a dispassionate review of the tort system and the industrial injury system without coming to the firm conclusion that on almost every count the latter is the superior and more up to date model of a compensation system."[11]

(2) Effect of disablement benefit upon damages

(a) Deduction under the 1948 Act

Whether a court should take into account a plaintiff's entitlement to social security benefits by deducting them from its assessment of the damages a defendant must pay at common law has been a controversial issue. Much depends upon the nature and purpose of the benefit involved when considered against the various aims of the damages award. On the one hand it has been argued that the plaintiff should not be overcompensated and have his needs met twice because of the different sources of support. On the other hand it has been suggested that the defendant ought not to be relieved of part of his liability only because of the existence of the welfare state. When this matter was considered by the Monckton committee in 1946 (Cmd. 6860) it led to a division of opinion and a minority report: one side favoured full deduction, the other none at all. Eventually a compromise solution was adopted by the Law Reform (Personal Injuries) Act 1948 which deducts certain benefits, but only by half of their value and for only a limited period. With the rise in value of social security payments there has been increasing criticism of the failure of damages to take into account the full amount of the monies received. Despite this criticism the 1948 compromise continues in force. As amended s. 2 of the Act states:

[8]   Pearson vol. 1 para. 261.
[9]   *Ibid.*, vol. 2 p. 24 table 17.
[10] *Ibid.*, vol. 2 p. 173 table 129.
[11] P. S. Atiyah, *Accidents, Compensation and the Law* (3rd ed. 1980) p. 407.

"(1) In any action for damages for personal injuries. . ., there shall in assessing those damages be taken into account, against any loss of earnings or profits which has accrued or probably will accrue to the injured person from the injuries one half of the value of any rights which have accrued or probably will accrue to him therefrom in respect of . . . [certain social security benefits including] disablement benefit, for the five years beginning with the time when the cause of action accrued . . .

(2) In determining the value of the said rights there shall be disregarded any increase of an industrial disablement pension in respect of the need for constant attendance."

(b) Benefits which are deducted

The section applies to not only disablement benefit, but also reduced earning allowance. However, constant attendance allowance and exceptionally severe disablement allowance are left out of account by s. 2(2). There are special rules for taking a gratuity into account as noted in (d) below. Other benefits included by s. 2(1) are those for sickness and invalidity. Attendance allowance and mobility allowance are not mentioned in the Act but *Bowker* v *Rose* (1978) decides that they should be ignored. The Act also says nothing about what should be done with regard to benefits accruing after the five year period, but *Denman* v *Essex Area Health Authority* (1984) decides that they should not be deducted.

The deduction can only be made against the damages awarded for loss of earnings or profits. For this purpose loss of earnings includes loss of earning capacity according to *Foster* v *Tyne and Wear County Council* (1986). There can be no offset against the compensation paid for pain and suffering. Nor can benefit be deducted from the compensation obtained for the expenses resulting from the accident, as where damaged clothing needs to be replaced or private medical treatment sought. The result of these rules is that if an industrial injury victim returns to work soon after the accident, but is left with a residual disability entitling him to benefit under the industrial scheme, there is only a limited opportunity to reduce any damages awarded. This is because there may be little lost earning against which entitlement to a disablement pension can be offset.

It is only benefit which is received or which the plaintiff can still claim that can be offset; no deduction is made in respect of benefit to which the plaintiff is no longer entitled because of lapse of time. This was decided in *Eley* v *Bedford* (1971) where the plaintiff came to court having been refused disablement benefit because she had presented her claim too late. In assessing her common law damages the judge refused to deduct the amount of disablement pension and reduced earnings allowance which she could have obtained had she been aware of her rights and made her claim at the appropriate time. Whether a claim for disablement benefit will fail because of delay is considered at p. 206. In particular it should be noted that if there is good cause for a late claim it is possible for disablement benefit to be backdated for an unlimited time before the date of the claim. It is not subject to the limit of one year which applies in the case of other benefits.

(c) Practical problems

In order to obtain the required information as to the amount of benefit that has been paid a letter can be sent to the DHSS specifying that the information is required for the purposes of the 1948 Act. Although there is no specific statutory authority for releasing the information, in practice it will be supplied, often after some delay. However, the DHSS statement may not be enough to enable the full deduction to be calculated because it will only deal with the benefit actually received and will not estimate future entitlement. The deduction requires account to be taken of benefit which would accrue up to the end of the five year period following the injury. This calculation can be difficult to make for it may require the value of disablement benefit to be assessed for some years into the future. This can be a considerable problem during a period of high inflation. However, it has been suggested that s. 2(1) does not require a precise calculation to be made. Upjohn LJ in *Hultquist* v *Universal Pattern and Precision Engineering Ltd.* (1960) suggested that figures can be determined by a judge exercising his own discretion and common sense.

(d) Deduction for a gratuity

Gratuities used to be awarded to claimants assessed at less than 20 per cent disabled. They have now been abolished by the Social Security Act 1986. However, their relationship to the tort system may be of importance for some time yet, for claims at common law may continue to be brought for accidents occurring even years ago. Gratuities are dealt with by s. 2(6) of the 1948 Act:

> "For the purposes of this section disablement gratuity is to be treated as benefit for the period taken into account by the assessment of the extent of disablement in respect of which it is payable."

In *Hultquist* v *Universal Pattern and Precision Engineering Ltd.* (1960) the Court of Appeal held that the amount to be taken into account is one half of that proportion of the gratuity which relates to the five year period immediately following the accident. In so far as the gratuity relates to a period of assessment beyond the five years after the cause of action accrues, it should be left out of account. On the facts of the case the claimant had been awarded a gratuity of £210 which at that time represented a 14 per cent assessment for life. In his action for damages his expectation of life was assessed at 35 years. The calculation was therefore:

$$\frac{1}{2}\left(\frac{210 \times 5}{35}\right) = \text{£15 deduction}$$

Upjohn LJ also stated that

> "If . . . a gratuity is assessed for life but there is no evidence before the judge as to the beneficiary's expectation of life, he will, no doubt, make some rough and ready assessment of the proper proportion of the gratuity to be taken into account. . . ."

(e) Effect of contributory negligence
By s. 2(3) of the 1948 Act:

> "The reference . . . to assessing the damages for personal injuries shall, in cases where the damages otherwise recoverable are subject to a reduction under the law relating to contributory negligence . . . , be taken as referring

to the total damages which have been recoverable apart from the reduction or limitation."

This means that the deduction to take account of disablement benefit must be made from the total damage before any further deduction is made from that net figure for contributory negligence.

(f) Reform

Although the Pearson Commission recognized that the 1948 Act may have been a reasonable compromise at a time when the social security system was in its infancy, it considered that there was now no justification for the overlap between damages and benefits if the compensation sought to achieve the same objective. This conclusion was supported by the weight of evidence received by the Commission. For example, the TUC were not opposed to social security benefits being deducted in full, provided that some improvement was made to the industrial injuries scheme. The Commission's method of making the deduction was based upon dividing into three categories both the various social security benefits and the several parts of a damages award. Each category depended upon the purpose for awarding the compensation involved. Only those benefits listed in a particular group were to be deducted from the corresponding category of the damages award so that there was to be no overlap between the categories. The overall effect would be to reduce awards of damages by around £38 million (19 per cent) at 1977 prices. The divisions were to be as follows:

	Loss of Income	Expenses	Non-pecuniary Loss
Industrial Injuries Benefits	Reduced earnings allowance *Unemployability supplement*	Constant attendance allowance Exceptionally severe disablement allowance	Disablement benefit *Hospital treatment allowance*
Other Relevant Benefits	*Industrial death benefit* Sickness benefit Invalidity benefit	Attendance allowance Mobility allowance	

Italics indicate withdrawal by SSA 1986

An alternative to these offsetting proposals is to allow the DHSS to recover the relevant payments of benefit directly from either the plaintiff or the court. This would not lessen the liability of negligent employers and it could enable improvements to be made in Social Security benefits. However, in its White Paper the Government rejected this idea as impractical because it would involve a disproportionate increase in staff numbers, and there would be particular difficulty in obtaining recovery where cases were settled out of court. Instead the Government accepted the Pearson Commission proposals and announced its intention to amend the 1948 Act. However, there have been no further developments since 1981 and the subject is not mentioned in the 1985 Consultation Paper.

5. Social Security Benefits not Confined to Work Injuries

(1) Outline of relevant benefits

If injury or illness causes the claimant to become incapable of the kind of work which he could reasonably be expected to do entitlement may arise to the benefits listed in (*a*) – (*c*) below. Benefits relevant to specific circumstances caused by disablement and which also may be noted here are considered in (*d*) – (*f*) below. DHSS leaflets HB 1 and FB 18 deal with the general help available to handicapped people and include an outline of the range of relevant benefits.

(*a*) *Statutory sick pay (SSP)*

Most employees are entitled to receive SSP from their employers for the first 28 weeks in a tax year in which they are absent from work because of sickness or disablement. After exhausting that entitlement period claimants may be transferred to invalidity benefit, considered in (*c*) below. The employer can reclaim the cost of SSP by deducting payments made from the monthly national insurance bill. The administration of the scheme has been left largely in the hands of employers so that, subject to certain guidelines, it is for them to decide, for example, how employees are to give notice of their claim and what proof of incapacity they must provide. After deducting tax and the employee's national insurance contributions the employer pays SSP at one of two rates, depending upon the employee's normal weekly earnings. DHSS leaflets on the scheme include the employer's guide NI 227 and for employees NI. 244. Many employees will be entitled to more generous sick pay arrangements under their occupational pension schemes. However, these payments are usually adjusted to take account of the right to SSP.

(*b*) *Sickness benefit*

For those employees not entitled to SSP there remains the possibility of obtaining sickness benefit from the DHSS for the first 28 weeks of incapacity for work. By SSA s. 50A anyone incapable of work as a result of injury in the course of employment will be taken to have satisfied the contribution conditions for this benefit.

(*c*) *Invalidity benefit*

After receiving SSP or sickness benefit those still incapable of work after 28 weeks will be transferred to invalidity benefit. If necessary this benefit can continue until retirement. It has two components: firstly, invalidity pension which is flat rated, although it may be increased if there are dependants, and a small addition may also be made depending upon the claimant's earnings since 1978; and secondly, invalidity allowance which is paid as a flat rate addition to the pension to those who became unfit for work five years or more before retirement age. See DHSS leaflet NI. 16A. Both invalidity allowance and the earnings related addition to the pension may be set off against entitlement to reduced earnings alllowance under the industrial scheme, as discussed at p. 197.

(*d*) *Mobility allowance*

This benefit is intended to help with the extra cost of getting about. It is payable to those under 66 who are unable or virtually unable to walk unaided. The claimant must also show that the disablement is expected to last for at least a year, and that he is in a position to benefit from increased mobility so that he is not, for example, too ill to be moved. The tax free flat rate benefit must end when the claimant reaches 75. See DHSS leaflet NI. 211.

(e) Attendance allowance

This benefit is payable to a claimant who has been so disabled for the past six months as to require throughout the day either "frequent attention . . . in connection with his bodily functions" or "continual supervision . . . in order to avoid substantial danger to himself or others". The tax free payment is made at one of two rates, the higher being paid if supervision is required at night. The allowance may be important to those who are unable to meet the conditions for constant attendance allowance, paid as an increase of industrial disablement benefit as discussed at p. 159. Attendance allowance is considered in DHSS leaflet NI. 205.

(f) Invalid care allowance

This benefit is not actually for the disabled person but for the relation or friend who cares for him or her and is unable to work as a result. There are no contribution conditions and the allowance is not means tested. It is paid to those who "regularly and substantially" care – this must be for at least 35 hours a week – for a severely disabled person who is entitled to an attendance allowance. Until 1986 the allowance could not be claimed by the most likely carers: neither a married woman nor one who lives with a man as if she were his wife were entitled. This discrimination was held to be contrary to the EEC directive on equal treatment and the law was changed. The remaining exclusions from benefit affect people of pensionable age and those whose earnings from work are in excess of a limited sum per week. The flat rate benefit can be increased to take account of dependants. See DHSS leaflet NI. 212.

(2) Effect of Industrial injuries benefit upon other social security payments

SSA s. 85 and the Social Security (Overlapping Benefits) Regs. 1979 (SI No. 597) provide for adjusting benefit if certain other social security allowances are also payable. The general aim is to prevent double compensation in respect of the same risk. However, receipt of industrial injury scheme payments causes but few other benefits to be reduced as a result. The legislation treats neither the disablement pension, nor exceptionally severe disablement allowance as overlapping with other social security benefits; each may be claimed in addition to the others. However, the earnings related element of both a retirement pension and invalidity benefit may be offset against reduced earnings allowance, as discussed at p. 197. In addition constant attendance allowance is deducted from attendance allowance under the main scheme. Receipt of benefits under the industrial scheme is taken into account to reduce entitlement to supplementary benefit. A pension is treated as income, whilst money which was paid as an industrial injuries gratuity is considered a capital resource by regs. 3(2)(a) and 11(2)a) of the Supplementary Benefit (Resources) Regs. 1981 (SI No. 1527).

APPENDIX A

TABLES BASED UPON DHSS SOCIAL SECURITY STATISTICS 1986

(Together with additional information supplied to the author by the DHSS statistics and research branch, Newcastle.)

Other tables and charts included in the text are:

TABLE 1: (DHSS TABLE 21.32)

Pensions, or pensions in lieu of gratuities, current at 30 September 1983(a): analysed by age

Thousands

	All ages	Age at 30 September 1983								
		Under 25	25–34	35–44	45–49	50–54	55–59	60–64	65–69	70 and over
All assessments:										
All causes	186(b)	1	8	20	16	20	26	29	24	41
Accidents	150	1	8	20	15	18	21	22	17	28
Pneumoconiosis	23	–	–	–	–	1	3	4	5	11
Occupational deafness	7	–	–	–	–	1	2	2	1	1
Other prescribed diseases	6	–	–	–	–	1	1	1	1	2
Life assessments:										
All causes	148	1	6	17	14	17	21	23	18	32

Source: 10 per cent sample of claimants.

Notes: (a) Including awards made up to 18 March 1984.

(b) 166,000 males and 20,000 females.

(c) The DHSS *Northern Ireland Social Security Statistics 1984* table 14.7 reveals that in the Province there were an additional 4,000 pensions for accidents and 1,000 for prescribed diseases current in 1983.

TABLE 2: (DHSS TABLE 21.34)

Pensions, or pensions in lieu of gratuities, current at 30 September 1983(a): analysed by percentage assessment

Thousands

	All assess-ments	Percentage assessment								
		1 to 10	*11 to 19*	*20 to 24*	*25 to 34*	*35 to 44*	*45 to 54*	*55 to 64*	*65 to 84*	*85 to 100*
All causes	186	21	3	67	46	22	11	6	6	4
Accidents	150	10	3	58	40	18	9	5	4	4
Pneumoconiosis	23	9(c)	. (d)	6	3	2	1	1	1	1
Byssinosis	3	1(c)	. (d)	1	–	1	–	–	–	–
Occupational deafness	7	.	.	1	2	1	1	1	1	–
Other prescribed diseases	4	1	–	1	1	–	–	–	–	–

Source: 10 per cent sample of claimants.

Notes: (a) Including awards made up to 18 March 1984.
      (b) 166,000 males and 20,000 females.
      (c) Paid at 10 per cent rate.
      (d) Paid at 20 per cent rate.

TABLE 3: (DHSS TABLE 21.36)

Pensions, or pensions in lieu of gratuities, current at 30 September 1983(a): analysed by year of first pension assessment

Thousands

	All Years	Year of first pension assessment								
		1948 to 1962	1963 to 1967	1968 to 1972	1973 to 1978	1979	1980	1981	1982	1983
All assessments:										
All causes	186	75	27	27	30	5	6	5	5	7
Accidents	150	59	24	24	23	4	4	3	4	6
Pneumoconiosis	23	13	2	2	3	–	1	1	1	–
Occupational deafness(c)	7	.	.	.	3	1	1	1	–	–
Other prescribed diseases	6	3	1	1	1	–	–	–	–	–
Life assessments:										
All causes	148	63	24	24	25	4	3	2	1	1
Accidents	139	59	24	23	22	4	3	2	1	1
Pneumoconiosis	3	2	–	–	–	–	–	–	–	–
Occupational deafness(c)	4	.	.	.	2	–	–	–	–	–
Other prescribed diseases	3	2	–	–	1	–	–	–	–	–

Source: 10 per cent sample of claimants.

Notes: (a)   Including awards made up to 18 March 1984.

           (b)   166,000 males and 20,000 females.

           (c)   Occupational deafness was first prescribed on 28 October 1974.

TABLE 4:

Examinations for Pneumoconiosis and Byssinosis made by Special Medical Boards in 1984 and analysed by industry (calculated on the basis of figures supplied to the author by the DHSS statistics branch).

	Disease not previously diagnosed			Reassessments
	Diagnosis Accepted	*Diagnosis Refused*	*Total Examinations*	
A. BYSSINOSIS				
Cotton	53	352	405	1,191
Flax	3	4	7	9
B. PNEUMOCONIOSIS				
Mining:				
(1) Coal	330	797	1,127	7,193
(2) Slate (including				
splitting)	8	47	55	148
(3) Other mining	0	0	0	33
Foundry workers:				
(1) Iron	13	9	21	183
(2) Steel	0	9	9	40
(3) Non-ferrous	1	1	2	10
Sandstone	3	3	6	33
Steel dressers	3	5	8	50
Pottery				
manufacture	9	19	28	336
Refractories	5	6	11	66
Asbestos	186	364	550	763
Other scheduled				
occupations	18	17	35	150
Unscheduled				
occupations	2	32	64	38
TOTALS	633	1,696	2,329	10,243

Total examinations for all industries including reassessments 12,572.

TABLE 5:

Industrial Chest Diseases Newly Diagnosed (calculated on the basis of table 25.03 of the DHSS Social Security Statistics 1986)

List No.	*Prescribed Disease*	*Diagnosed in 1985 by:*		*Diagnosed in 1984 by:*	
		Special Medical Board	*Medical Appeal Tribunal*	*Special Medical Board*	*Medical Appeal Tribunal*
D1	Pneumoconiosis				
	coal mining	364	21	330	
	other mining and quarrying	4	–	15	30
	pottery	14	–	9	
	other industries	47	–	37	
	asbestos	273	28	186	14
	sub total	702	49	577	44
D2	Byssinosis	37	–	56	7
D3	Diffuse mesothelioma	–	5	–	–
D7	Occupational asthma	166	4	137	6
D8	Lung cancer	8	–	–	–
D9	Bilaterial diffuse pleural thickening	61	2	–	–
C15	Poisoning by oxides of nitrogen	–	2	1	–
C17	Beryllium poisoning	–	–	–	–
C18	Cadmium poisoning	2	–	4	–
C22(b)	Cancer in certain nickel workers	2	–	5	–
B6	Extrinsic allergic alveolitis (including farmers lung)	8	–	4	–
	Totals	986	62	775	57

TABLE 6: (DHSS TABLE 21.50 (PART 2))

Initial assessments commencing in year ended 30 September analysed by attributable Industry and Type (a)

		Number	
Order		*1983*	
Number		*Accident*	*PD(b)*
	All industries	53360	1430
0	Agriculture, Forestry and Fishing	520	10
1	Energy and water supply	11670	390
2	Extraction of Minerals, Ores other than fuels:	4110	130
	Manufacture of Metals, Mineral products and Chemicals		
3	Metal Goods, Engineering and Vehicles	9570	420
4	Other Manufacturing Industries	5270	260
5	Construction	4150	30
6	Distribution, Hotels and Catering, Repairs	4480	20
7	Transport and Communication	3730	10
8	Banking, Finance, Insurance, Business Services and Leasing	1120	10
9	Other Services	8440	150
	Others	6830(c)	1470(c)

Source: 100 per cent sample of claimants

Note: (a) According to the Standard Industrial Classification (revised 1980)

        (b) Prescribed diseases (PD) includes Pneumoconiosis

        (c) Late awards not analysed by Industry Code

TABLE 7: (DHSS TABLE 21.42)

Reduced earnings allowances (then known as special hardship allowances), and supplements current at 30 September 1983(a).

Thousands

	All cases	*Percentage assessment*								
		1 to 10(b)	11 to 19(b)	20–24	25–34	35–44	45–44	55–64	65–84	85 & Over
1. Reduced earnings allowances:										
—Allowances payable with pensions(c):										
All causes	70(d)	15	3	19	14	8	5	3	3	–
Accidents	54	9	3	15	12	6	4	3	3	–
Pneumoconiosis	12	4(e)	. (f)	3	2	1	1	1	–	–
Other prescribed diseases	4	2	–	1	–	–	–	–	–	–
—Allowances payable following gratuities:										
All causes	75(g)	43	31	.	.	.	.	.	.	.
Accidents	68	37	31	.						
Prescribed diseases	7	6	1	.						
2. Hospital treatment allowances	0.1	.								
3. Unemployability Supplement	0.3(h)	.								
4. Constant attendance allowance	2.2(h)	.								
5. Exceptionally severe disablement allowance	0.7(h)	.								

Source: 10 per cent sample of claimants.

Notes:
(a) Including awards made up to 18 March 1984.
(b) Gratuities percentage assessment groups are 1–9 per cent and 10–19 per cent.
(c) Including 13,000 pensions in lieu of gratuities.
(d) 61,000 males and 9,000 females.
(e) Pensions paid at 10 per cent rate.
(f) Pensions paid at 20 per cent rate.
(g) 62,000 males and 13,000 females.
(h) Including cases paid under the Pneumoconiosis, Byssinosis and Miscellaneous Diseases Benefit Scheme, and the Workman's Compensation Supplementation Scheme.
(i) The DHSS *Northern Ireland Social Security Statistics 1984* table 14.11 reveals that in the Province there were an additional 3,270 awards of reduced earnings allowance current in 1983, and 66 constant attendance allowances, 18 of these also attracting an exceptionally severe disablement allowance.

TABLE 8: (DHSS TABLE 21.10)

Assessments commencing in year ended 30 September: analysed by type

Thousands

	1966	1971	1976	1978	1979	1980	1981	1982(a)	1983
1. *Gratuities*:									
Accidents:									
All assessments	247	203	168	170	163	151	136	130	118
Initial assessments	127	100	86	86	81	73	65	65	56
Re-assessments from gratuity	101	89	70	73	72	68	61	56	53
Re-assessments from pension and other assessments(b)	18	14	11	12	10	10	10	9	9
Prescribed diseases:									
All assessments	9	9	6	6	6	5	5	4	4
2. *Pensions*(c):									
Accidents:									
All assessments(d)	29	21	16	15	14	12	10	9	10
Initial assessments	23	16	11	10	9	7	7	6	7
Re-assessments from gratuity and other assessments(b)(d)	6	6	5	5	5	5	4	3	2
Prescribed diseases:									
All assessments(d)	2	2	3	2	2	3	2	1	2

Source: 20 per cent sample of claimants up to 1968/69: 10 per cent samle from 1969/70.

Notes: (a) Provisional figures, no late awards processes 1982.
       (b) Including transfers from Northern Ireland; cases reviewed after final payment has been made or following nil assessment, etc.
       (c) Including pensions in lieu of gratuities.
       (d) Excluding re-assessments from pensions.
       (e) According to the DHSS *Northern Ireland Social Security Statistics 1984*, table 14.4 there were 4,895 gratuities commencing in 1983 and 525 pensions.

APPENDIX B

PUBLISHED REPORTS OF THE
INDUSTRIAL INJURIES ADVISORY COUNCIL

It was accepted in *R(I) 2/85* that these reports can be examined in order to assist in the interpretation of the industrial injuries legislation.

Cmd 8093	November 1950	TUBERCULOSIS – Report on the question whether Tuberculosis and other Communicable Diseases should be prescribed under the Act in relation to Nurses and other Health Workers.
Cmd 8511	April 1952	TIME LIMITS – Report on the Time Limits for claiming and obtaining Payment of Benefits under the Act.
Cmd 8866	July 1953	PNEUMOCONIOSIS – Report on the method of prescribing Pneumoconiosis under the Act.
Cmd 9347	December 1954	RAYNAUD'S PHENOMENON – Report on the question whether Raynaud's phenomenon should be prescribed under the Act.
Cmd 9673	January 1956	BYSSINOSIS – Report on the provision made for byssinosis under the Act.
Cmd 9674	January 1956	CADMIUM POISONING – Report on the question whether cadmium poisoning should be prescribed under the Act.
Cmd 9827	August 1956	PAIRED ORGANS – Report on the rules governing assessment of disablement in cases involving damage to an organ which, in a normal person is one of a pair.
Cmnd 416	April 1958	PRESCRIBED DISEASES – Report on the question whether any adjustments should be made in the terms of prescription of Prescribed Diseases other than Pneumoconiosis and Byssinosis.
Cmnd 1095	July 1960	BYSSINOSIS – Report of the occupational cover in respect of byssinosis within the cotton industry.
Cmnd 2403	July 1964	FARMER'S LUNG – Report on the question whether Farmer's Lung should be prescribed under the Act.
Cmnd 2730	July 1965	BYSSINOSIS – Report on the question whether there exists a respiratory condition analogous to byssinosis which should be treated as a prescribed disease under the Act in relation to workers in the flax and hemp industry.
Cmnd 3114	October 1966	EROSION OF THE TEETH – Report on the question whether erosion of the teeth due to acid should be prescribed under the Act.
Cmnd 4145	August 1969	INDUSTRIAL NOISE AND ITS EFFECT ON HEARING – Appraisal of the final report of the

research made into noise in industry and its effect on hearing.

Cmnd 4430 July 1970 VIBRATION SYNDROME – Interim report on the question whether diseases of bones, joints, muscles, blood-vessels or nerves of the hand, arm or shoulder (including Raynaud's phenomenon) caused by vibrating machines should be prescribed under the Act.

Cmnd 4971 May 1972 BRUCELLOSIS – Report on whether brucellosis should be prescribed under the Act.

Cmnd 5443 October 1973 PNEUMOCONIOSIS AND BYSSINOSIS – Report on a review of the provisions for pneumoconiosis and byssinosis under the Act.

Cmnd 5461 October 1973 OCCUPATIONAL DEAFNESS – Report on the question whether there are degrees of hearing loss due to occupational noise, which should be prescribed under the Act.

Cmnd 5965 March 1975 VIBRATION SYNDROME – Final report on the question whether diseases of bones, joints, muscles, blood-vessels or nerves of the hand, arm or shoulder (including Raynaud's phenomenon) caused by vibrating machines should be prescribed under the Act. (Contains full copy of the interim report – Cmnd 4430 – in the Appendix).

Cmnd 6257 October 1975 VIRAL HEPATITIS – Report on the question whether viral hepatitis should be prescribed under the Act and if so, for what occupations.

Cmnd 6620 October 1976 VINYL CHLORIDE MONOMER – Report on the question whether there is any condition resulting from exposure to vinyl chloride monomer which should be prescribed under the Act and if so, for what occupations.

Cmnd 7266 July 1978 OCCUPATIONAL DEAFNESS – Report on the operation of the provisions for occupational deafness and on other processes with severe noise levels.

Cmnd 8121 January 1981 OCCUPATIONAL ASTHMA – Report on the question whether there is any condition resulting from exposure to industrial asthma-inducing agents which should be prescribed under the Act.

Cmnd 8350 September 1981 VIBRATION WHITE FINGER – Report on the question whether, having regard to those sections of Council's 1975 report on Vibration Syndrome relating to Vibration White Finger and to the new evidence on that condition which has since come forward, Vibration White Finger should be prescribed under the Act.

Cmnd 8393 October 1981 INDUSTRIAL DISEASES: A REVIEW OF THE SCHEDULE AND THE QUESTION OF INDIVIDUAL PROOF – Report on the question whether adjustments should be made in the terms of prescription of the diseases prescribed in Part I of Schedule 1 to the Social Security (Industrial Injuries) (Prescribed Diseases) Regulations 1980 and whether compensation should be extended to any individual claimant who can show that his disease is occupational in origin and a particular risk of his occupation.

Cmnd 8749　November 1982　OCCUPATIONAL DEAFNESS – Report on the operation of the provisions for occupational deafness and on whether these should be extended.

Cmnd 8750　November 1982　ASBESTOS-RELATED DISEASES WITHOUT ASBESTOSIS – Report on the question whether asbestos-related diseases without asbestosis should be prescribed under the Act.

Cmnd 8959　July 1983　NEOPLASM OF THE BLADDER – Report on the question whether the description of the prescribed disease should be extended to include other forms of neoplasm of the bladder and whether the nature of occupation should be extended to include exposure to any other substances.

Cmnd 9147　February 1984　VIRAL HEPATITIS – Report on the question whether the terms of prescription for viral hepatitis should be amended to cover other occupational groups.

Cmnd 9184　March 1984　ASBESTOS-RELATED DISEASES WITHOUT ASBESTOSIS – Supplement to the report (Cmnd 8750) on the question whether asbestos-related diseases without asbestosis should be prescribed under the Act.

Cmnd 9413　December 1984　DISEASES INDUCED BY IONISING RADIATION – Interim report as to whether the terms of prescription for such diseases should be amended to cover a wider range of conditions.

Cmnd 9717　January 1986　OCCUPATIONAL ASTHMA – Report recommending that benefit should be payable for asthma caused by any one of seven sensitising agents at work.

Cm 37　December 1986　OCCUPATIONAL LUNG CANCER – Report recommending that prescription be extended in favour of tin miners, and those exposed to certain chemicals.

Appendix C

ADDRESSES OF RELEVANT ORGANISATIONS
AND SOURCES OF HELP

1. *Department of Health and Social Security*

For the local DHSS office see under "Health and Social Security, Department of" in the telephone directory except where it is listed in Scotland under "Social Security", and in Northern Ireland under "Government of Northern Ireland, Department of Health and Social Services".

DHSS National Headquarters
Alexander Fleming House
Elephant and Castle
London SE1
Tel: 01-407-5522

DHSS
North Fylde Central Office
Norcross
Blackpool
Lancashire
Tel: 0253-856123
(Deals with claims in respect of pneumoconiosis and allied diseases and old cases of workmens compensation. It also provides statistics and information on medical matters relating to the industrial scheme)

DHSS
Leaflets Division
P.O. Box 21
Stanmore
Middlesex

DHSS
Northern Ireland Headquarters
Dundonald House
Upper Newtonards Road
Belfast

DHSS
Statistics and Research Branch
Headquarters Division SR8
Central Office Longbenton
Newcastle upon Tyne

DHSS
Overseas Branch
Newcastle upon Tyne
(Provides information and administers benefit for those working abroad)

2. *Administration and Adjudication*

(i) *Social Security Commissioners*

For England and Wales:
6 Grosvenor Gardens
London SW1
Tel: 01-730-9236

For Scotland:
23 Melville Street
Edinburgh EH3
Tel: 031-225-2201

For Northern Ireland:
Yorkshire House
Linenhell Street
Belfast
Tel: 0232-235111

(ii) *President of SSATs and MATs*
(The President's duties include arranging for the appointment and training of chairmen)

President of SSATs and MATs

Judge J. Byrt
Almack House
26/28 King Street
London SW1
Tel: 01-839-1621

In Northern Ireland:

Mr. C. G. MacLynn
7th floor
Clarendon House
Adelaide Street
Belfast BT2
Tel: 0232-249577

(iii) *Regional Chairmen of SSATs*
(These assist the President in discharging his duties)

North Eastern:

J. W. Tinnion
York House
York Place
Leeds
Tel: 0532-451246

Wales and South Western:

C. B. Stephens
Oxford House
The Hayes
Cardiff
Tel: 0222-378071

Midlands:

I. G. Harrison
Room D21, Block 6
Government Buildings
Chalfont Drive
Nottingham
Tel: 0602-291111

North Western:

R. S. Sim
The Triad
Stanley Road
Bootle
Merseyside
Tel: 051-9226767

London North:

J. R. Martyn
Whittington House
19-30 Alfred Place
London WC1
Tel: 01-580-3941

Scotland:

R. W. Deans
28-38 Thistle Street
Edinburgh
Tel: 031-2259313

London South:

R. P. Huggins
Room 219
Sutherland House
29-37 Brighton Road
Sutton
Surrey
Tel: 01-642-6022

(iv) *Others*

Industrial Injuries Advisory Council
(IIAC)
Friars House
157-168 Blackfriars Road
London SE1
Tel: 01-703-6380

Office of the Chief Adjudication Officer
Mr. Michael Platt
15-17 Cumberland Place
Southampton
Tel: 0703-34541
(Duty to advise AOs and report to the Secretary of State on the standard of adjudication. Receives complaints about adjudication. Prepares cases which are appealed to a Commissioner)

3. *Advice on Bringing a Claim*

Citizens Advice Bureau
(Check the telephone directory for the local advice centre – there are over 900 nationwide.) Otherwise contact the National Association of Citizen Advice Bureaux – Middleton House
115/123 Pentonville Road
London N1
Tel: 01-833-2181

Child Poverty Action Group
1-5 Bath Street
London EC1
Tel: 01-242-9149/4913
(Offers claimants advice and contact with an appropriate Citizens Advice Bureau or Law Centre via its Citizens' Rights Office)

The Disability Alliance
25 Denmark Street
London WC2
Tel: 01-240-0806

Disablement Income Group
Attlee House
28 Commercial Street
London E1
or
32 Howden Street
Edinburgh EH8

National Federation of Claimants'
   Unions
For list of local branches contact
Dame Colette House
Ben Johnson Road
London E1
Tel: 01-790-9070

Solicitors
Advice can be obtained under the "green form" legal advice scheme, but this does not cover the cost of representation at a hearing. A list of legal aid solicitors is available at local libraries, or from the Law Society, Chancery Lane, London WC2

4. *Analytic Services and Consultants on Occupational Health*

The following list is partly based upon a longer one given by the Health and Safety Commission (address below) in their guide *Asbestos-Measurement and Monitoring of Asbestos in Air*. Referral to an appropriate service may also be made following an inquiry, without charge to unions, to either the TUC Medical Advisor (at the TUC address below) or, via a union headquarters to:-

The TUC Institute of Occupational Health
London School of Hygiene and Tropical Medicine
Keppel Street
London WC1
Tel: 01-580-2386

(i) *University Centres*

Department of Occupational Health
   and Safety
The University of Aston in Birmingham
Gosta Green
Birmingham

Department of Occupational Health
University of Manchester
Stopford Building
Oxford Road
Manchester

Robens Institute of Industrial and
   Environmental Health and Safety
University of Surrey
Guildford
Surrey

Institute of Occupational Health
University of Birmingham
PO Box 363
Birmingham

Wolfson Institute of Occupational
  Health
University of Dundee
Environmental Health Service
Medical School
Ninewells
Dundee
Tel: 0382-644625

Occupational Medicine Section
Department of Community Medicine
Welsh National School of Medicine
Heath Park
Cardiff
Tel: 0222-755944

(ii)   *For Particular Injuries*

Noise

Institute of Sound and Vibration
  Research
University of Southampton
University Road
Highfield
Southampton
Tel: 0703-559122

Radiation

Atomic Research Establishment
Environment and Medical Services
  Division
Harwell
Oxfordshire
Tel: 0235-24141

(iii)   *Other Centres*

Institute of Occupational Medicine
Roxburgh Place
Edinburgh
Tel: 031-667-5131

The National Occupational Hygiene
  Service Ltd
12 Brook Road
Fallowfield
Manchester
Tel: 061-224-2332/3

West Midlands Industrial Health
  Service Ltd
83 Birmingham Road
West Bromwich
West Midlands
Tel: 021-553-7116

North of England Industrial Health
  Service
Occupational Health Department
20 Claremont Place
Newcastle upon Tyne

5.   *Other Addresses*

British Society for Social
  Responsibility in Science (BSSRS)
9 Poland Street
London W1
Tel: 01-437-2728
(Offers its scientific skills to workers to
help fight pollution and health hazards.
Publishes the Hazards Bulletin)

Society for the Prevention of Asbestosis
  and Industrial Diseases (SPAID)
Secretary Mrs. Tait
38 Drapers Road
Enfield
Middlesex
Tel: 01-366-1640
(Registered charity to promote the
prevention of Industrial disease,
encourage research, and provide a
source of information on the subject)

Health and Safety Commission/
  Executive Headquarters
Baynards House
1 Chepstow Place
London W2
Tel: 01-229-3456

Trade Union Congress
Congress House
Great Russell Street
London WC1
Tel: 01-636-4030

International Labour Office
87-91 New Bond Street
London W1
Tel: 01-499-2084
(Office of the international organisation
based in Geneva. Draws up standards
for the protection of workers and offers
advice and publications on occupational
health)

Her Majesty's Stationery Office
   (HMSO)
Bookshops can be found in London,
Edinburgh, Birmingham, Manchester,
Bristol, and Belfast.
Orders by post should be sent to:-
HMSO
PO Box 276
London SW8
Tel: 01-622-3316

Appendix D

FORMS USED IN CLAIMS, APPEALS AND ADJUDICATIONS

The following forms are reproduced with the permission of the Controller of Her Majesty's Stationery Office and copyright in them vests in the Crown:

Claim forms

1. BI 100A   – for disablement benefit for injury by accident.
2. BI 100(Pn) – for disablement benefit for pneumoconiosis and byssinosis.
3. BI 103   – for special hardship allowance, now known as reduced earnings allowance.
4. BI 104   – for constant attendance allowance and exceptionally severe disablement allowance.

SSAT forms

5. AT 2   – appeal or reference to a tribunal (the "case papers").
6. AT 6   – form accompanying AT 2 concerning hearing date etc.
7. AT 3   – report and decision of SSAT.

Medical adjudication forms

8. BI 118   – AMA report form for an accident.
9. BI 140   – Medical board report form on diagnosis of a prescribed disease.

Claim Disablement Benefit on this form
if you have had an accident at work

Only use this form if you have had an accident at work. Do not use this form if you are suffering from a disease which you think was caused by your work. Ask your local Social Security office for the claim form for the disease you think you are suffering from.

You may want some help with filling in this form. You can ask a friend to help you, or you can ask us at the Social Security office.

Send the form back to us as soon as you can. If you delay, you could lose benefit.

1 About you
Please write clearly

a Surname

b Mr Mrs Miss Ms

c Other names

d Address and postcode

Postcode

e Phone number where we can ring you during the day

f Date of birth /   /

g NI (National Insurance) number, if you know it

Letters Numbers Letter

h What was the name and address of your employer at the time of the accident?

Name

Address

Postcode

i What was your job?

j What was your works or clock number?

2 About the accident

a What was the date of the accident? /   /

If you are not sure of the exact date, what was the approximate date?

b What was the time of day when the accident happened?

am **or** pm

If you are not sure of the exact time, what was the approximate time?

c Where did the accident happen?

Please turn to the next page

d How did the accident happen?

e What injury did the accident cause? Please be precise eg injury to **left** arm.

f In what way are you now disabled as a result of the accident?

g Have you been in hospital, or have you been a hospital out-patient because of the accident?

No Yes
☐ ☐ Please tell us about all the hospitals you have been in or been to because of the accident.

Name and address of hospital	The date the treatment started and ended	Hospital reference or admission number	The type of patient you were	Were any X-rays taken?
	started ....../....../............. ended ....../....../.............		in-patient ☐ out-patient ☐	Yes ☐ No ☐
	started ....../....../............. ended ....../....../.............		in-patient ☐ out-patient ☐	Yes ☐ No ☐

h Are you fit enough to travel for a medical examination?

No Yes
☐ ☐

We will send you details of the travel expenses you can claim when we write to you about the examination.

i What is the name and address of your doctor?

Doctor's name

Address...

....

Postcode

j May we ask your doctor or the hospital for information to do with this claim?

No Yes
☐ ☐

k The Medical Authorities may need to see your medical records. Do you agree to let them see your records to help with your claim?

No Yes
☐ ☐

Please go to the top of the next page

3 Your benefit

a If Disablement Benefit is awarded, what is the name and address of the Post Office you would like to be paid at?

If you are not sure about the address, ask the Post Office to stamp the form in the box on the right.

b Are you getting a pension from any Government Department because of disablement?

No Yes
☐   ☐   Which Department is paying you the pension?

What is your pension number?

c Have you received any money as a gratuity from a Government Department because of disablement?

No Yes
☐   ☐   Which Department paid you the money?

What was the reference number, if you know it?

d Are you getting Supplementary Benefit?

No Yes
☐   ☐   What is your reference number, if you know it?

e Are you waiting to hear the result of a claim for Supplementary Benefit?

No Yes
☐   ☐

4 Declaration

Read the declaration and then sign and date the form.

I understand that if I give information that is incorrect or incomplete, action may be taken against me.

I declare that the information I have given on this form is correct and complete, to the best of my knowledge and belief.

This is my claim for Disablement Benefit.

Signature   Date
                                   /   /

Please turn to the next page

5 What to do now

Make sure that you have filled in all the parts of the form, and that you have signed and dated it at the end.

Send this form to your local Social Security office as soon as you can. You can get an envelope that does not need a stamp from your nearest Post Office. The address is in the phone book under 'HEALTH AND SOCIAL SECURITY, Dept of' ('Social Security' in Scotland).

6 Help and advice

You can make free phone calls for general advice on Social Security and National Insurance. Just dial 100 and ask for Freefone DHSS.

7 What happens next

If your accident is **not** accepted as an accident at work we will tell you. If your accident is accepted as an accident at work, you will need to have a medical examination.

If you are not fit to travel, the doctor may examine you at home. If you are in hospital, the examination may take place in hospital.

You will get a letter shortly before the examination to tell you where and when the examination will take place. You can give the doctor any extra information that you think will help with your claim.

We will write to you about 3 weeks after the examination to tell you the result of your claim.

8 Extra money you could get on top of Disablement Benefit

You may be able to get extra money if, **as a result of the accident,** any of these 5 points apply to you.

a **You cannot earn as much money as you earned before the accident**
If you cannot go back to your normal job, and you cannot do another job with similar pay, you may be able to get Special Hardship Allowance.

b **You are permanently unable to work**
You may be able to get Unemployability Supplement.

c **You have to have someone to look after you all the time**
You may be able to get Constant Attendance Allowance if your disablement has been assessed at 100 per cent. You must also need help with everyday things like getting out of bed, getting dressed and going to the toilet and be likely to need this help for a long time.

This allowance will usually be considered at the time of your examination for Disablement Benefit. You do not normally have to make a separate claim for it.

d **You are exceptionally handicapped**
You may be able to get Exceptionally Severe Disablement Allowance. This will be considered at the same time as Constant Attendance Allowance. You do not have to make a separate claim for it.

e **You have to go into hospital for treatment for your injury**
You can claim Hospital Treatment Allowance while you are in hospital. This allowance will bring your Disablement Benefit up to 100 per cent.

Where to find out more

You can find out more about these extra benefits, and about Disablement Benefit generally, in leaflet NI 6, 'Disablement Benefit and Increases'. You can get a copy of this leaflet from any Social Security office.

If you would like us to send you a copy, please tick here ☐

Form BI 100A

Printed in the UK for HMSO Dd8972280 60000 7/86 26781

DEPARTMENT OF HEALTH AND SOCIAL SECURITY

Social Security Act Industrial Injuries Provisions

Claim for Industrial Disablement Benefit for Pneumoconiosis (including Silicosis and Asbestosis) or Byssinosis

FOR OFFICE USE

Please note the following

Full information about Industrial Disablement Benefit and who can claim it is given in leaflet NI 3 which you are advised to read before completing this form.

If you need advice or help in filling up this form the Department's local office will be glad to help you.

Date of Issue

If your National Insurance number is not shown here, please write it in:

Letters	Figures	Letter

1. Full name *Mr./Mrs./Miss* ....
   (BLOCK CAPITALS)

2. Address (including postcode) ....
   (BLOCK CAPITALS)

   ....

   ....

3. Date of birth .... *(day)*...............................*(month)* ....*(year)*

4. Please put a cross in the appropriate box against the disease for which you are claiming

   pneumoconiosis   ☐

   byssinosis   ☐

5. From what date do you claim to have been suffering from the disease...

6. (a) Are you incapable of work as a result of the disease? (YES or NO) ....

   (b) Are you fit to travel for medical examination? (YES or NO)...

   (c) Please state the name ....
       and address
       of your doctor ....

       ....

       ....

Form BI 100 (Pn)   **Please turn over**

7. Please enter in the spaces below details of all your employments since leaving school finishing with your present or last occupation.

Industry	Precise Occupation	Name and address of employer	Place of employment and check number (if any)	Period of employment	
				From	To

(If necessary, continue on a separate sheet of paper)

8. Have you ever been awarded or paid workmen's compensation under the Workmen's Compensation Acts for the disease (or a similar disease)? (YES or NO) ....

(*Note: This question does not refer to previous benefit from a Department of Health and Social Security Office*)

If YES please give date...

and give particulars ....

including details of any lump sum settlement ....

....

9. Have you ever been examined or X-rayed by a Silicosis, Pneumoconiosis or Byssinosis Medical Board under the Workmen's Compensation Acts or the Industrial Injuries Provisions of the Social Security Act? (YES or NO) ....

If YES, please give date...

and place of last examination or X-ray ....

and result ....

10. Have you been X-rayed by the National Coal Board Chest X-ray Unit? (YES or NO) ....
If YES please answer the following questions—

When were you last examined by the Unit?...

Did the NCB advise you to make a claim? (YES or NO)...

(*Note: If you were advised to make a claim as a result of the NCB X-ray scheme, please send the letter of advice with this form. It will be returned to you.*)

If the NCB did not advise you to claim, were you advised by your own doctor, a hospital, chest clinic or other medical authority? (If you were, state which)...

11. Have you attended a hospital or clinic for chest X-ray or treatment for a chest condition? (YES or NO)...

If YES

(1) Please complete the following:—

Names and addresses of hospitals or clinics	Whether in-patient or out-patient	Period of treatment		Hospital reference or admission number	Name of Department/ Clinic if out-patient or ward if in-patient and name of Specialist, if known
		From	To		

(2) Do you agree to your hospital and medical records being obtained by a Medical Officer of the Department of Health and Social Security for the assistance of the Medical Board or Medical Appeal Tribunal in their consideration and assessment of your claim? (YES or NO)...

If you wish to submit any additional medical evidence, please attach a separate note giving details.

Please turn over

12. Are you receiving a pension or have you ever received a gratuity for disablement from any Government Department? (YES or NO).....................

If YES, please state the Department

....

and your pension number (if any) ....

13. State the official name and address of the Post Office at which you wish to draw disablement benefit, if awarded. (USE BLOCK CAPITALS)

....

....

....

If in doubt about this ask the Post Office clerk to impress the office date stamp here

---

DECLARATION

(WARNING: TO GIVE FALSE INFORMATION MAY RESULT IN PROSECUTION)

I DECLARE that, to the best of my knowledge and belief, the information given is true and complete. I claim Industrial Disablement Benefit accordingly.

Signature .... *Date* ....

INCREASES OF DISABLEMENT BENEFIT

The increases shown below may be paid in addition to disablement benefit. The conditions for each allowance are explained more fully in leaflet NI 6 which may be obtained from any local Social Security office. If you do not have a copy of this leaflet and you wish one to be sent to you, please put a cross in this box

SPECIAL HARDSHIP ALLOWANCE
You may be entitled to this allowance if, as a result of the disease, you are unable to go back to your regular occupation or to do other work of an equivalent standard.

UNEMPLOYABILITY SUPPLEMENT
You may be entitled to this supplement if you are likely to be permanently incapable of work as a result of the disease.

CONSTANT ATTENDANCE ALLOWANCE
You may be entitled to this allowance if as a result of the disease, you are dependent on attendance for the necessities of life, are likely to remain so for a prolonged period and your disablement is assessed at 100 per cent. This allowance will normally be considered by the Medical Board without an application being made when they examine you for your disablement benefit.

EXCEPTIONALLY SEVERE DISABLEMENT ALLOWANCE
You may be entitled to this allowance if your disablement renders you exceptionally handicapped. This allowance will be considered together with Constant Attendance Allowance and no application is necessary.

HOSPITAL TREATMENT ALLOWANCE
You can claim this allowance, which will bring your benefit up to the 100 per cent rate, if you go into hospital for treatment of the disease.

Printed in the U.K. for H.M.S.O.   Dd 8810897 36M 2/84 G035

DEPARTMENT OF HEALTH AND SOCIAL SECURITY

Special Hardship Allowance

Please note the following

Full information about special hardship allowance and who can claim it is given in leaflet NI 6 which you are advised to read before completing this form.

If you need advice or help in filling up this form this local office of the Department of Health and Social Security will be glad to help you.

Please return the completed form to this office.

Delay in claiming may lead to loss of benefit.

PART 1. – PARTICULARS OF CLAIMANT (To be completed by the local office)

1. Name...
   (Surname and initials)

2. National Insurance Number

3. Date of accident..

   or

   Name of prescribed disease..

Form BI 103

G8759 Gp3643 Dd530063. 35M. 9/77 Swift Ptrs.

PART 2. – DETAILS OF REGULAR OCCUPATION (To be completed by the claimant)

NOTE: Your regular occupation is the occupation which you *normally* followed at the time of the accident or onset of the prescribed disease. If at that time you were temporarily engaged in a different occupation, but intended to return to your normal work, then your *normal* occupation is your regular occupation. If just before the accident or onset of the prescribed disease you had taken up a new occupation which you intended to follow permanently, the new occupation is your regular occupation.

4. What was your occupation at the time of the accident or development of the disease?
(See date at item 3 overleaf) ....

....

5. Was the occupation shown at item 4 overleaf
your regular occupation? (Yes or No)..

    If "NO",

    Please state what you regard as your regular occupation

    ....

    Please give name and address of employer for whom you last worked in that occupation

    ....

    ....

    Clock or Check No..

6. Were you following any other employment in addition
to any occupation shown above? (Yes or No)..

7. Please describe the nature of the duties performed in your regular occupation
(See note 7 below)

....

....

....

....

....

    NOTE 7. Indicate any special physical effort that is involved—for example, much kneeling, bending, lifting, climbing, etc—and any unusual conditions under which the work is performed—for example, underground, in confined spaces or at heights, exposure to heat, liquids, etc. Details of weights lifted should be given where appropriate.

8. In what way do you consider that your injury or disease is likely to prevent you from following your regular occupation? (See note 8 below)

....

....

....

....

....

....

....

....

....

....

....

NOTE 8. In stating this please indicate which part of your regular occupation you would be unable to perform either temporarily or permanently and give reasons.

9. What were your average weekly earnings? £..

NOTE 9. You should state your gross salary or wages, etc, ie before deductions for income tax, national insurance, etc. Any additions such as the provision of living accommodation, free fuel, light, etc should be stated also with their value, if known.

If, in the normal course, persons employed in your regular occupation have prospects of advancement to better paid work and you consider that the injury or disease has caused you to lose such advancement, or the prospects of it, please tell this office.

DECLARATION

(WARNING: TO GIVE FALSE INFORMATION MAY RESULT IN PROSECUTION)

I declare that to the best of my knowledge and belief the information given is true and complete. I claim special hardship allowance.

Signature... Date..

DEPARTMENT OF HEALTH AND SOCIAL SECURITY

(Address Stamp)

Application for

Constant Attendance Allowance

under the Industrial Injuries Provisions

Please note the following:—

Full information about constant attendance allowance and who can apply for it is given in leaflet NI6 which you are advised to read before completing this form.

If you need advice or help in filling up this form any local office of the Department of Health and Social Security will be glad to help you. Delay in applying may lead to loss of benefit.

Particulars of Applicant

Surname ....Mr/Mrs/Miss

Other names ....

Address ....
(Including postcode)

....

Your National Insurance number   Letters   Figures   Letter

Form BI 104   *Please turn over*

Details of attendance required

What are you unable to do for yourself because of your disablement?

....

....

What does your attendant do for you? ....

....

....

Is attendance required daily? *(Write Yes or No)* ....

For how many hours is attendance required each day? ....

For how long have you been in need of constant attendance? ....

DECLARATION

(WARNING: TO GIVE FALSE INFORMATION MAY RESULT IN PROSECUTION)

I declare that the information given is true and complete.

I apply for Constant Attendance Allowance accordingly.

Signature... Date..

6010 0588585 52-0-0 15M 6/78 V.P.Co.

SOCIAL SECURITY APPEAL TRIBUNAL

For hearing on
Appeal Register Number
Sheet   Line

IN CONFIDENCE   **Appeal or Reference to Appeal Tribunal**

Benefit .... Tribunal ....

FULL NAMES OF PERSONS CONCERNED		National Insurance Number
(Surname)	(Other names)	

Name of claimant
*(Mr/Mrs/Ms/Miss) ....

Address ....

....

Benefit reference number

1

*Reference dated .... for **decision** whether

*Appeal received on .... against the following decision of the Adjudication

Officer (Code no(s) ....) which was issued on ....

Adjudication Officer's Decision

2 Provisions in Acts and Regulations considered by the Adjudication Officer to be relevant

3 Reported decisions of the Commissioner considered by the Adjudication Officer to be relevant

Form AT 2   *Delete as necessary*   OVER

Person(s) concerned ....

---

4 | **Claimant's grounds of appeal dated**
(Appeal cases only)

(continue on separate sheet if necessary)

Originals of any documents which are copied in whole or in part will be available at the hearing.

Printed in the UK for HMSO Dd 8931870 1/86 (31862)

SOCIAL SECURITY APPEAL TRIBUNAL

Office
Address

Telephone   Extension

_____

_____   19

_____

_____

Dear

ABOUT YOUR APPEAL

I am writing to let you know that your appeal will be heard by the appeal tribunal

at ....

on .... day 19   , at...............am/pm

WHAT TO DO

Please read the enclosed papers which are copies of the papers that the tribunal will look at. Then answer the questions on pages 3 and 4 of this form and return them to me as quickly as possible. I have enclosed an envelope which needs no stamp. You will want to keep page 2 which tells you what expenses you may claim.

IF YOU WANT TO KNOW MORE

You can find out about how the tribunal works by getting a copy of Leaflet NI 246 from your local social security office. If you want to know more about either the hearing itself or expenses please telephone me.

WOULD YOU LIKE HELP WITH THIS APPEAL?
WOULD YOU LIKE SOMEONE TO SPEAK FOR YOU AT THE TRIBUNAL?

If so contact your local Citizens' Advice Bureau, independent advice centre, or Law Centre. They can give you free advice and sometimes they will go along with you to the tribunal. You can get their addresses from the phone book, or the library, or from your local council.

Yours sincerely

Clerk to the Tribunal

Form AT6   Page 1

NOTES ON TRAVELLING EXPENSES, SUBSISTENCE ALLOWANCE, COMPENSATION FOR LOSS OF EARNINGS AND CHILD MINDING EXPENSES

1. Travelling Expenses

We can only refund fares which you had to pay because of your attendance. You should buy return tickets or other cheap bookings if this saves money. If we gave you a travel warrant or if you have a concessionary pass or season ticket you may claim any extra fares which you paid.

We can refund taxi fares only if the Department's doctor or the tribunal chairman is satisfied that you could not travel by any other method because, for example of poor health or lacking public transport. You must produce a receipt when you claim.

If you travel by your own private motor vehicle you can claim expenses at the current mileage rate. You can claim an extra allowance per mile if an approved passenger travels with you. Ask the clerk about this.

If we are satisfied that you have to use a private car, for example because a doctor has recommended it, you may get a higher rate. Ask the clerk about this. You cannot get the higher rate if you drive a disabled person's vehicle issued by the Department of Health and Social Security.

2. Subsistence

To get this allowance you must be away from home (or work) for at least 2½ hours. If you have to spend a night away from home, you can claim night subsistence allowance unless bed and board are provided at public expense, for example in hospital. The clerk will tell you the 2 different rates. You cannot claim night subsistence if you are able to travel to and from the tribunal on the same day.

3. Compensation for loss of earnings

If you lose earnings by attending you may claim for earnings lost on the day of attendance. We cannot however pay compensation for a full day if you could reasonably have worked before or after attending. In your own interest, therefore, you should make arrangements with your employer so that you lose as little working time as possible. In any case, we cannot pay you more than the daily maximum amount, nor can we pay for more than 3 consecutive days in any one week. The clerk will tell you what this amount is. If you intend to claim, you should ask your employer for a certificate to support your claim. The certificate which should have your employer's official stamp on it, should show details of how much you expect to lose and your hourly rate of pay. If you cannot get a certificate before you attend, you can get one when you return to work and send the claim in then.

If you are self-employed you do not need a certificate. Instead, write "self-employed" after your occupation and work out the amount you have lost (if any) by attending.

4. Child Minding Expenses

We can pay an allowance subject to a maximum amount to cover the cost of employing a person to look after your children while you attend the hearing. Where we are satisfied that it is necessary for you to employ a child minder, an allowance will be paid on production of a receipt or a letter from the child minder showing the amount you have had to pay.

5. If someone comes with you

If someone comes with you, for example an escort needed for medical reasons, or a witness or representative, that person may also be entitled to expenses. Please ask the clerk for details.

PLEASE COMPLETE THIS SECTION

Tear
here

Where 'Yes' and 'No' Boxes are provided please enter a tick (✔) in the appropriate box.

Date of hearing ....

Reference ....

Name ....

The Tribunal hope that you will come to the hearing because they want to hear what you have to say.

1. Will you be coming to the hearing?

   Tick one box   Yes ☐   No ☐

   If you have ticked 'Yes' proceed to Question 4, if 'No' proceed to Question 2.

If you do not come to the hearing the Tribunal may hear the case in your absence depending on why you are not there.

2. If you have ticked 'No' to Question 1 please give your reasons ....

   ....

   ....

   ....

3. If you could come on a different day, which dates would be suitable?

   I could come on ....

You can ask another person to come to the hearing on your behalf, whether you come or not.

4. Will someone be coming to speak on your behalf? Tick one box

   Yes ☐   No ☐

   If 'Yes', please write their name and address below

   ....

   ....

   ....

SPECIMEN

Tribunal hearings are open to the public unless you ask for a private hearing.

5. Do you wish your case to be heard in private?

Tick one box Yes ☐   No ☐

If you have ticked 'Yes' please give your reasons

....

....

....

....

A full tribunal consists of a chairman and two members. If one member cannot come the hearing must be adjourned unless you consent to a two-person Tribunal. If you consent and the two participants agree their decision, it is counted as a normal unanimous decision. If they disagree, the chairman makes the final decision, which is counted as a majority decision.

6. Are you willing to have your appeal heard if the Tribunal is incomplete?

Tick one box Yes ☐   No ☐

Once you have read the appeal papers, you may wish to comment on what they say, or submit further evidence. If so, send it on a separate sheet of paper.

7. Do you have any further comments or evidence for the Tribunal?

Tick one box Yes ☐   No ☐

A person who has lodged an appeal may decide at any time to withdraw it.

8. Now that you have seen the appeal papers, do you wish to withdraw your appeal?

Tick one box Yes ☐   No ☐

Travelling expenses will be refunded after the hearing. If the return fare is more than £2.00 and you cannot wait until after the hearing for a refund, you can claim fares in advance.

9. Do you wish to claim fares in advance?

Tick one box Yes ☐   No ☐

If 'Yes' please state how you will be travelling and what the return fare will be.

....

....

....

....

Sign Here   Signed ....

               Date ....

IN CONFIDENCE

Record of proceedings of................ .... Social Security Appeal Tribunal held on....../......./ 19

Full name of Appellant	(Surname)	(Other names)	Case List No. /
Local office			Tribunal Reg No. /

Constitution of tribunal	Names of others present (write "None" where appropriate)
*Full/Chairman and one member	Appellant's representative (state organisation if any)
Names of Tribunal Chairman and Members	
	Witness(es)

Appellant notified of hearing on ..../..................19	Appellant Present*/not present	Others (state capacity)
		Adjudication officer

Consent to hearing by less than full Tribunal

*Appellant's consent given on tear-off portion of form AT6.
I consent to this case being proceeded with in the absence of a member of the Tribunal other than the Chairman.
I understand the Chairman will have a casting vote if required.

Appellant's signature ....

1 | Chairman's note of evidence *(ie concise details of all oral and written evidence put before the Tribunal)*

SPECIMEN

APPELLANT ....

---

2 | **Findings of Tribunal on questions of fact material to decision** *(ie the relevant facts accepted from the evidence available)*

---

3 | **Full text of *unanimous/*majority decision on the *Appeal/*Reference** *(including amounts and effective date(s) as appropriate)*

***Reasons for dissent if Tribunal not unanimous**

---

4 | **Reasons for decision** *(ie an explanation of why, when applying the facts to the statutory provisions and case-law, a particular conclusion has been reached. And why, if it is not clear from box 2, certain evidence has been accepted or rejected).*

Date .... Chairman's Signature...

For Clerk's use only   **Form AT 22 noted**

SSAT decision notified to

interested parties on ....19...... Initials...................Date.....................................19......

Delete as necessary   Printed in the UK for HMSO Dd 8826201 3 84 (28966)

(3)

PART IV. CAUSATION AND RECRUDESCENCE NOTE FOR MEDICAL BOARD. QUESTIONS 17-19 SHOULD BE COMPLETED ONLY IF YOU DIAGNOSE A PRESCRIBED DISEASE AT ITEM 16

17. (a)   Do you consider the attack of the disease dealt with at item 16
           to be due to the nature of the claimant's employment?   (Yes or No) ....

     (b)   If "Yes", what employment? (For the employment claimed to be the cause, see items 8-10 on first page)

           ....

18. In your opinion -
     (a)   Does the claimant's incapacity for work result from disease diagnosed at item 16?   (Yes or No) ....

     (b)   Can it reasonably be assumed to have done so from the date mentioned in item 7?   (Yes or No) ....

           If not, from what date?..

19. Do you, having regard to the information at item 11 or 12, decide that the claimant's
     disease diagnosed at item 16 is :-
     (a)   a recrudescence, ie, predominantly a sequel of an earlier attack of the same disease? ....
     OR
     (b)   a fresh contraction, ie, predominantly due to further exposure to risk of the disease at work since the earlier attack?

           ....

PART V.   STATEMENT OF THE BOARD'S FINDINGS ON ALL QUESTIONS OF FACT MATERIAL TO THEIR DECISION(S)
(For example, particular features affecting the decision: diagnosis (if any) of condition found, if not a prescribed disease; etc)

20.

(Regulations require that a summary of these findings shall be notified to the claimant with the Board's decision)

21. DOCUMENTS BEFORE THE BOARD (These should be returned with the form. If the claimant produces further written evidence direct to the Board, it should be attached, a separate note being made if he has asked for it to be returned to him).

     Report(s) of examining medical practitioner and list of prescribed diseases (form BI 91) dated ....

     Other reports or statements :- ....

     ....

     (Appeal cases)   Copy of statement(s) submitted by or on behalf of the claimant, dated ....

Place of examination ....   Signatures ....Chairman

Date of examination..   .... Member

Date of completion ....

PART VI INSURANCE OFFICER'S DECISIONS (Entries should NOT be made in this part by the Medical Board)

NOTE: Reference to an Insurance Officer is not necessary where the effect of the Medical Board's decision is (a) to reject an appeal against a decision already given by the Insurance Officer, or (b) to refuse to revise a decision already given by the Insurance Officer or by another Medical Board.

22. Referred to Insurance Officer for decision :-
    *(a) Whether in view of the Medical Board's decision on the diagnosis question, the claim(s)

    for .... Benefit may be disallowed from and including .... (date)
    *(b) Whether the disease is to be treated as having been contracted afresh or as a recrudescence of the attack for which Injury/

    Disablement Benefit was awarded from and including .... (date)
    *(c) Whether the disease is to be treated as a recrudescence of the disease in respect of which compensation under the Workmen's Compensation Acts, or any contracting out scheme duly certified thereunder, has been awarded or paid, and not as having developed on or after 5th July 1948.
    *(d) As to the date of development of the disease for the purposes of the claim.

    *(e) Whether prescribed disease Number .... is prescribed in relation to the claimant.
    *(f) Whether the disease is due to the nature of insurable employment.

    Refer the appropriate question to the Insurance Officer as follows :-
    Question (a) : If the Medical Board have decided that the claimant is not (and has not been during the period in question) suffering from the prescribed disease. If Question (a) is referred delete Questions (b)-(f).
    Questions (b) and (c) : Only if the questions arise on the claim in question.
    Questions (d)-(f) : Except where the Medical Board have decided that the claimant is not (and has not been during the period in question) suffering from the prescribed disease.

    Note of any special points to which the Insurance Officer's attention is drawn :-

    The following documents are submitted in connection with the above reference(s) :-

23. Insurance Officer's decision :-
    NOTE: If the Medical Board have reversed (either on appeal or as the result of an application for review) a previous decision on a "diagnosis" or "recrudescence" question, the Insurance Officer should, in addition to completing this form, note any previous decisions based on the previous decision on the "diagnosis" or "recrudescence" question, "Appeal/Review: see form BI 140 dated.."

    †(a) ....Benefit is not payable for the period .... to ....(both dates included) because the Medical Board have decided that the claimant has not been suffering from the prescribed disease.

    Number .... (known as...
    ....
    or from any condition resulting therefrom.
    †(b) Decision on Form BF 10/LT 54 attached.
    †(c) Decision on Form BF 10/LT 54 attached.
    (d) For the purpose of the claim the date of development of the disease is .... (date)

    †(e) (i) Prescribed Disease Number .... is prescribed in relation to the claimant.
        (ii) The disease is NOT prescribed in relation to the claimant (decision on Form BI 77 attached).
        (iii) Refer question to Local Tribunal.
    †(f) (i) The disease is due to the nature of insurable employment.

        (ii) .... Benefit is not payable because the disease is not due to the nature of the claimant's insurable employment.
        (iii) Refer question to Local Tribunal.

        †*Delete as follows :-*
        Decision (a) : Delete Decision (a) unless Question (a) has been put. If Decision (a) applies delete Decisions (b)-(f).
        Decision (b) : Delete Decision (b) unless Question (b) has been put. If a Decision on Question (b) is such that the claim is disallowed, delete Decisions (c)-(f).
        Decision (c) : Delete Decision (c) unless Question (c) has been put. If a Decision on Question (c) is such that the claim is disallowed, delete Decisions (d)-(f).
        Decision (e) : Delete two of the alternatives (i), (ii) and (iii). If a Decision on Question (e) is such that the claim is disallowed, delete Decision (f).
        Decision (f) : Delete two of the alternatives (i), (ii) and (iii).

Supervisor's signature -   Insurance Officer's signature -
....
Date ....   Date ....

Dd8011171 46m 4/79 J.I.H. Ltd.,

Part IV: – Decision on loss of faculty

4. (a) Specify what injury resulted from the accident ....

....

(b) The first date on which disablement benefit may become payable, ie the date following the last day of the period of 90 days (excluding Sundays). The earliest date may be a Sunday.

At any time from that date has the accident resulted in a loss of physical or mental faculty? enter yes or no

(If 'no' specify the unconnected conditions at Part V and then go to Part IX).

(c) Specify the relevant loss of faculty ....

....

Part V: – Disabilities (numbered serially)

5. (a) Specify the disability which results from the relevant loss of faculty stated at 4(c). If the disability results solely from the relevant loss of faculty, mark 'F'. If there is another effective cause, mark 'P'.

Serial No	Description of Disability	F or P

(b) If 'P' is entered at 5(a) above specify which condition, having regard to the clinical findings at Part III 3(a) and other evidence at Part III 3(b), is the other effective cause. Conditions which pre-existed the accident should be marked 'O (Pre)'. Those arising after the accident should be marked 'O (Post)'.

Serial No	Defect, injury or disease constituting the other effective cause	O (Pre) or O (Post)

(c) Any condition listed at Part III which, through interaction, has the effect of increasing the disability arising from the relevant loss of faculty (shown at 5(a)), but which is **not** itself the other effective cause of that disability, should be specified and marked 'C'.

Serial No	Defect, injury or disease giving rise to greater disablement	C

(d) **Unconnected injuries, diseases etc.**
Enter below all other abnormalities described in Part III which have no effect upon the disablement resulting from the disability marked 'F' or 'P' at 5(a).

....

Part VI: – Disablement – effect of relevant loss of faculty

6. Describe the way in which the disability shown at 5(a) above, as affected by those conditions shown at 5(b) and 5(c) handicap the claimant in the ordinary activities of life (eg, walking, gripping, bending, etc).

Part VII: – Calculation of assessment (Serial numbers to correspond with those shown in Part V)

Disability shown in Part V, Item 5(a). Entries under 'Gross assessment' and 'Offset' required only where an O (Pre) condition has been identified at Part V, Item 5(b).

7. Any O (Pre) condition (Part V 5(b)) should be offset only to the extent to which disablement would have resulted from it during the period under consideration even if the accident had not occurred. The residual net assessment therefore includes any addition for the resultant greater disablement and no addition should be made at box 8 below.

   Any disablement arising from the presence of an O (Post) condition should be entirely ignored. Assess only the disablement appropriate for the accident had the O (Post) condition not occurred. The assessment should be recorded only as **net** at box 7.

Serial No	Gross assessment	Offset (give percentage and condition)	Net assessment

8. Any 'C' condition (Part V Item 5(c)) should **not** itself be assessed. Any interaction between the 'C' condition and the 'F' or 'P' disability which has the effect of increasing disablement during the period under consideration should be considered. This element of greater disablement should be quantified and an appropriate assessment entered at box 8.

   Any O (Pre) condition (Part V 5(b)) requires no further action, **no** addition should be made at box 8.

   Any O (Post) condition: **no** addition should be made if the total net assessment (boxes 7 and 8) is less than 11 per cent. If the total net assessment is 11 per cent or more, assess the extent to which the 'P' disability is worsened by the presence, during the period, of the O (Post) condition. Enter the appropriate additional assessment for this worsening at box 8. **No** addition should be made for the O (Post) condition itself.

Serial No	Additional assessment

Part VIII: – Decision on assessment

9. At what degree does the Adjudicating Medical Authority assess the disablement resulting from the relevant loss of faculty (total of net assessments at boxes 7 and 8 above).

   per cent: figures [ ]   words [ ]   per cent [ ]

10. On what day does the assessment begin? (It should be the date at Part IV, Item 4(b) or later).

    [/ /]   enter date or **Life**

11. To what date is the assessment to continue?

    [/ /]

12. Is the assessment provisional or final?

    [ ]

Part IX: – Remarks

13.

Note: If appropriate complete form(s) BI 118D (Constant Attendance Allowance), BI 138 (industrial rehabilitation) or form MX 43 (letter to GP) – see II Handbook, Part 3 and Appendix 3.

Date of examination	[/ /]	name of member	[ ]
Place of examination	[ ]	signature	[ ]
Date of completion	[/ /]	name of chairman	[ ]
		signature	[ ]

Printed in the UK for HMSO Dd8936661 115M 12/85 A G Ltd 7596

Social Security Act (Industrial Injuries Provisions)

REPORT OF MEDICAL BOARD ON DIAGNOSIS
PRESCRIBED DISEASE CLAIM

RO Stamp

PART 1. PARTICULARS OF CLAIMANT, ETC

1. Surname .... Other Names ....
   (BLOCK CAPITALS)   (Mr, Mrs or Miss)

2. Address ....
   ....

           D   M   Y

3. Date of Birth   4.   National Insurance Number

5. *The above named has claimed benefit for prescribed disease No ....

   *The above named has claimed benefit for a condition which may be prescribed disease No ....
   ....

6. Benefit claimed.   *Injury/Disablement Benefit.   *(If Disablement Benefit, delete item 18 from page 3)*

7. Date from which benefit is claimed ....(See Notes (a) and (d) below)

8. Employment said to have caused the disease ....

9. Period of such employment : From ....19.......to ....19...............

10. Name and place of business of last employer in such employment...
    ....

11. Previous benefit awarded for the prescribed disease at item 5 above, with dates :-
    ....
    .... (See Notes (b) and (e) below)

12. Previous Workmen's Compensation for the same disease as at item 5 above, with dates :-
    ....
    .... (See Notes (c) and (e) below)

13. Reason for reference to Medical Board :-

    *Reference by Insurance Officer (otherwise than as a result of an appeal).

    *Appeal by claimant against decision of Insurance Officer that claimant is not suffering from a prescribed disease.

    *Appeal by claimant against decision of Insurance Officer that disease has, in fact, not been contracted afresh.

    *Appeal by claimant against decision of Insurance Officer that disease has, in fact, been contracted afresh.

    *Application for review - see Form BI 140(R) attached.

NOTES ON THE PREPARATION OF THIS FORM

(a) Item 7.   Actual date from which benefit is claimed (contrast with item 16(b)).

(b) Item 11.   Entry to be made ONLY if an IB Period or an award of Disablement Benefit was CURRENT AT DATE SHOWN AT ITEM 16(b) Otherwise delete and see Note (e).

(c) Item 12.   Entry to be made ONLY if the claimant had received a lump sum settlement or AT THE DATE SHOWN AT ITEM 16(b) was receiving, or was entitled to receive, weekly payments of Workmen's Compensation. Otherwise delete and see Note (e).

(d) Item 16(b).   The date to be inserted is the date from which benefit is claimed, ie, the date shown at item 7 above, or the date from which benefit would commence if later. This question and item 16(c) should be deleted before the form is sent to the Medical Board where, exceptionally, the diagnosis question is being raised afresh on an injury benefit claim and the Insurance Officer has referred the question to the Board.

(e) Item 19.   If both item 11 and item 12 are blank, or if the diagnosis question before the Board has been raised afresh, delete item 19.

(f) Item 21.   ALL documents to be put before the Board in connection with the Diagnosis or Recrudescence Questions are to be listed. If the printed references to form BI 91 or claimant's appeal are inapplicable they should be deleted.

Form BI 140   * *Delete as necessary*

(2)

PART II. CLAIMANT'S STATEMENT TO THE MEDICAL BOARD

(The statement should record, as nearly as possible in the claimant's own words, what he has to say about his industrial and medical history, and should be read to him for agreement and signature below)
14.

I agree that the above is a correct record of my statement.

Signature .... Date ....

PART III. DIAGNOSIS (To be completed by the Medical Board)

NOTES: (1) The Medical Board are asked to consider whether the claimant is suffering or has suffered from any of the *prescribed diseases.

      (2) Cases of disagreement. Where a two-doctor Board are unable to reach a unanimous decision on a question referred to them (at item 16 or 19), they should leave the answers uncompleted and return the form with a note explaining the position. When a Board consists of three doctors, their decision on any question referred to them will be the decision of the majority of the members, but a statement that one of the members dissented, and the reason given by him for dissenting, should be recorded at item 20.

      (3) When this form is accompanied by form BI 118 "Disablement Benefit: Initial Medical Board Report", relating to the same claim, the Board are asked:-

         (a) To complete form BI 118 if they have diagnosed a prescribed disease at item 16.

         (b) NOT to complete form BI 118 if they have NOT diagnosed a prescribed disease.

15.   Symptoms and signs

16. (a) Is the claimant now suffering from a *prescribed disease
        or from a sequela of a *prescribed disease?   (Yes or No) ....

    (b) Has the claimant suffered from such a condition at any time since ....?   (Yes or No) ....

    (c) If so, during what period? ....

    (d) If an answer "Yes" has been given above, which prescribed disease is diagnosed?   Number..

* *Except pneumoconiosis, byssinosis and prescribed diseases No 17, 36, 37(b), 40, 43, 44 and 48*

Disablement Benefit: Social Security Act (Industrial Injuries Provisions)
Initial Report by Adjudicating Medical Authority (Accident)

Part I: – Particulars of Claimant

Mr/Mrs/Miss/Ms

Date of birth

Surname (use block capitals)

National Insurance Number

Other names

Date of accident (as shown in box 8 of form BI8)

Part II: – Claimant's statement to Adjudicating Medical Authority

(This statement should be as nearly as possible in claimant's own words and should be read to him for agreement and signature below)

SPECIMEN

I agree that the above is a correct record of my statement

Signature

Date

Form BI 118 (Accident)

Part III: – Findings of Adjudicating Medical Authority

1. Are you satisfied that the person before you is the person referred to at Part I overleaf?

   [ ] enter yes or no

2. Describe the claimant's general state of health, recording the exact nature of any physical or mental abnormality whether resulting from the accident or not.

   (a)   i weight [ ]

                ii height [ ]

   (b) blood pressure [ ]

   (c) urine   i albumen [ ]

                ii sugar [ ]

   (d) If nothing abnormal is detected in any of these systems enter NAD

   Respiratory [ ]

   Alimentary [ ]

   Circulatory [ ]

   Nervous [ ]

3. (a) Details of Clinical findings:

SPECIMEN

   (b) Other evidence before the Authority (eg medical reports and any relevant history emerging from examination). An extract of relevant information from hospital case notes and X-ray reports should be made in chronological order on form BI 127A.

   [   ]

THE SCHEDULE OF PRESCRIBED DISEASES

Diseases which are prescribed are listed in part I of schedule I of the PD regs. This schedule appears in roman type in the first two columns of this appendix. The information in italics is not part of the legislation, but is the author's annotation. This falls into four sections: in the first column the annotations indicate the more common or shorthand descriptions of the disease; in the second column, the sort of occupations from which the diseases may result; in the third column, the relevant symptoms to which the diseases may give rise; and in the fourth column, any interpretation of the schedule by Commissioners and others.

Prescribed disease or injury	Type of occupation	Symptoms	Notes
A. CONDITIONS DUE TO PHYSICAL AGENTS (*physical cause*)	Any occupation involving		
A1. Inflammation, ulceration or malignant disease of the skin or subcutaneous tissues or of the bones, or blood dyscrasia, or cataract, due to electro-magnetic radiations (other than radiant heat), or to ionising particles. *Radiation diseases. e.g. certain kinds of leukaemia due to exposure to radiation at work.*	Exposure to electro-magnetic radiations (other than radiant heat) or to ionising particles. *e.g. workers exposed to radiation in the nuclear fuel and power industry, hospital X-ray departments.*		*"Due to electro-magnetic radiations" in effect requires a worker to establish causation before he can show that he has a prescribed disease. The presumption under PD reg. 4 that the prescribed disease is due to the employment does not help a worker establish the causation element required by the description of the condition prescribed.* *In its 1981 report on the schedule (Cmnd. 8393) the IIAC recommended that radiation induced diseases be fully reviewed. In particular their investigations are examining whether diseases A1 and A2 should be amalgamated to provide cover for conditions arising from ultra-violet light, lasers and micro-waves. There is also increasing evidence of the more widespread effects of radiation than is indicated in the schedule. For example, soft tissues and individual organs such as the pancreas might be directly affected, and some changes are needed to ensure that diseases, including cancers, caused by ionising radiation are covered. An interim report on this subject was issued in 1984 (Cmnd. 9413)* *If the claimant is exposed by accident to a dose of radiation a declaration may be obtained as discussed at p.202.*

A2. Heat cataract. *Disease of the eye.*	Frequent or prolonged exposure to rays from molten or red-hot material. *e.g. glass and metal workers, stokers.*	Progressive increasing dimness of vision.	*The stoker's claim succeeded in CI288/50. Exposure to metal not verging on melting occurred every quarter of an hour.*
A3. Dysbarism, including decompression sickness, barotrauma and osteonecrosis. *e.g. The Bends*	Subjection to compressed or rarefied air or other respirable gases or gaseous mixtures. *e.g. underwater, high altitude or tunnel workers.*	*Pains in the limbs, itching, vertigo, nausea, breathlessness. Sometimes partial paralysis. Symptoms similar to severe arthritis in the joints later.*	
A4. Cramp of the hand or forearm due to repetitive movements. *e.g. Writer's cramp.*	Prolonged periods of handwriting, typing or other repetitive movements of the fingers, hand or arm. *e.g. typists, clerks and routine assemblers.*	*Spasms, trembling and pain in the hand or forearm.*	
A5. Subcutaneous cellulitis of the hand. (Beat hand).	Manual labour causing severe or prolonged friction or pressure on the hand. *e.g. miners and road workers using picks and shovels.*	*Redness, swelling and pain in the palm of the hand.*	*"Manual labour" – see A7*
A6. Bursitis or subcutaneous cellulitis arising at or about the knee due to severe or prolonged external friction or pressure at or about the knee (Beat knee). *e.g. Housemaid's knee.*	Manual labour causing severe or prolonged external friction or pressure at or about the knee. *e.g. workers who kneel a lot especially in wet conditions. Gas, water and electric workers and carpet layers.*	*Redness, swelling and pain in and around the knee.*	*"Manual labour" – see A7*

Prescribed disease or injury	Type of occupation Any occupation involving	Symptoms	Notes
A7. Bursitis or subcutaneous cellulitis arising at or about the elbow due to severe or prolonged external friction or pressure at or about the elbow. (Beat elbow.)	Manual labour causing severe or prolonged external friction or pressure at or about the elbow. *e.g. jobs involving continuous rubbing or pressure on the elbow.*	Redness, swelling and pain starting at the point of the elbow and passing down the forearm.	"Manual labour" does not necessarily mean some laborious activity calling for much physical strength or muscular effort. It merely means physical or bodily work and may include occupations which are essentially sedentary or clerical or non-manual but which incidentally involve manual labour as something subservient to the main object. This definition enabled a successful claim to be made by the operator of a manual switchboard at a telephone exchange dealing with 2000 calls a day in R(I)60/51, but in R(I)78/54 benefit was refused because the operator's duties involved only 100 calls a day and did not cause "severe or prolonged" friction at the elbow.
A8. Traumatic inflammation of the tendons of the hand or forearm, or of the associated tendon sheaths. *Tenosynovitis.*	Manual labour, or frequent or repeated movements of the hand or wrist. *e.g. routine assembly workers, rubber working.*	Pain and swelling spreading up the forearm with some loss of strength. Moving the arm may cause a cracking noise.	"Manual labour," see A7
A9. Miner's nystagmus. *Jerky movements of the eyeballs.*	Work in or about a mine.	Constant and uncontrollable movement of the eyeball in any direction.	
A10. Occupational deafness.	(See p.112 above)		See p.108 et seq.

A11. Episodic blanching, occurring throughout the year, affecting the middle or proximal phalanges, or in the case of a thumb the proximal phalanx, of:–

(a) in the case of a person with 5 fingers (including thumb) on one hand, any 3 of those fingers or

(b) in the case of a person with only 4 such fingers, any 2 of those fingers, or

(c) in the case of a person with less than 4 such fingers, any one of those fingers or, as the case may be, the one remaining finger.

(Vibration white finger also known as Raynaud's phenomenon).

(a) The use of hand-held chain saws in forestry; or

(b) the use of hand-held rotary tools in grinding or in the sanding or polishing of metal, or the holding of material being ground, or metal being sanded or polished, by rotary tools; or

(c) the use of hand-held percussive metal-working tools, or the holding of metal being worked upon by percussive tools, in riveting, caulking, chipping, hammering, fettling or swaging; or

(d) the use of hand-held powered percussive drills or hand-held powered percussive hammers in mining, quarrying, demolition, or on roads or footpaths, including road construction; or

(e) the holding of material being worked upon by pounding machines in shoe manufacture.

Fingers go white and numb particularly in cold weather. Loss of muscular control in the fingers and a reduced sensitivity to heat and cold.

The IIAC did not recommend prescription of this disease until its fourth report on the subject in 1981 (Cmnd. 8350). Previous reports had found insufficient evidence in 1954 (Cmnd. 9347), 1970 (Cmnd. 4430) and 1975 (Cmnd. 5965). Following the 1981 report it took a further four years before the disease was added to the schedule. There are three categories of severity of the disease. The mild form is common in up to ten per cent of the working population, although it normally occurs only in the presence of cold. However, only the most severe form of the disease has been prescribed. It requires that three or more fingers must be affected throughout the year and this is comparatively rare unless there is an occupational cause. Diagnosis is made by a special medical board. PD reg. 7 relating to recrudescence does not apply to this disease. As yet there is no standard method by which vibration is measured, and the disease has therefore been prescribed only in relation to the use of specified tools. The IIAC is keeping the disease under review so that, if justified by further evidence, the terms of prescription can be extended.

According to the DHSS Chief Medical Officer's report for 1985, about a third of the few claims then decided had failed to satisfy the diagnostic criteria, whilst 86% of workers who received some compensation were assessed at less than 6% disabled. Following the SSA 1986 a minimum assessment of 14% is required for entitlement to disablement benefit.

Prescribed disease or injury	Type of occupation Any occupation involving	Symptoms	Notes
B. CONDITIONS DUE TO BIOLOGICAL AGENTS *(caused by animal, plant or other living organism)*			
B1. Anthrax.	Contact with animals infected with anthrax or the handling (including the loading or unloading or transport) of animal products or residues. *e.g. glue and shaving brush makers, handling bonemeal.*	*Headache, shivering, joint pains and nausea. It usually starts with inflammation spreading from a pimple, but may start with congestion of the lungs or diarrhoea and vomiting, depending on the site of infection.*	*The reference to loading and transport was added as from 30 October 1983.*
B2. Glanders.	Contact with equine animals or their carcasses. *e.g. farm and slaughter house workers and grooms handling horses.*	*Headache, nausea and joint pains followed by swollen glands and swelling and ulceration at the point of infection. It later affects the liver and spleen. There is also a chronic form (Farcy) lasting years marked by widespread swellings and ulcerations.*	
B3. Infection by leptospira. *e.g. swamp fever, swineherd's disease, and Weil's disease.*	(a) Work in places which are, or are liable to be, infested by rats, field mice or voles, or other small mammals; or (b) work at dog kennels or the care or handling of dogs; or (c) contact with bovine animals or their meat products or pigs or their meat products. *e.g. farm, veterinary, sewerage and slaughter house workers coming into contact with urine or being bitten.*	*High fever with headaches. The eyes may be seriously affected. It sometimes leads to jaundice and discolouration of the urine.*	*"Infested" indicates the presence of rats either persistently or in large numbers. The presence of an occasional rat is not enough. The Commissioner awarded benefit to a colliery surface worker in R(I)92/53 and to a building site labourer in R(I)20/52.*

B4.	Ankylostomiasis Hookworm disease.	Work in or about a mine.	Pallor, lethargy, joint pains, digestive disturbances.	
B5.	Tuberculosis. TB.	Contact with a source of tuberculous infection. e.g. doctors, nurses, ambulance crews, pathology technicians and social workers.	Feeling generally unwell, slight fever, coughing. Often only discovered by X-ray.	The disease was the first upon which the IIAC reported. See the 1950 report (Cmnd. 8093). The terms of prescription were extended as from 3 October 1983 and no longer only benefit those in medicine having a close and frequent contact with the infection. Because the disease is now prescribed in the widest possible terms it is no longer necessary or possible to claim that the infection amounts to an accident as in CI. 65/52. The claimant need not identify the exact source of infection if it results from working where undisclosed cases of the disease frequently occur as in R(I)70/52(T) cf. R(I)31/54.
B6.	Extrinsic allergic alveolitis (including Farmer's lung). Includes mushroom pickers' lung, pigeon or budgerigar fanciers' lung etc.	Exposure to moulds or fungal spores or heterologous proteins by reasons of employment in:- (a) agriculture, horticulture, forestry, cultivation of edible fungi or maltworking; or (b) loading or unloading or handling in storage mouldy vegetable matter or edible fungi; or (c) caring for or handling birds; or (d) handling bagasse.	Breathlessness, coughing, fever with chills and sweating. In severe cases coming on suddenly there may also be blueness of the face, crackling noises in breathing and coughing blood.	Farmer's lung was the subject of an IIAC report in 1964 (Cmnd. 2403). The terms of prescription were extended as from 3 October 1983. Determination of medical questions is made by a special medical board, and 11 cases were newly diagnosed in 1983.

Prescribed disease or injury	Type of occupation Any occupation involving	Symptoms	Notes
B7. Infection by organisms of the genus brucella. *Brucellosis.*	Contact with:- (a) animals infected by brucella, or their carcasses or parts thereof, or their untreated products; or (b) laboratory specimens or vaccines of, or containing, brucella. *e.g. farm, veterinary, slaughter house, animal laboratory workers.*	Fever with fluctuating temperature, coughing, pains in the back and limbs. There may be a long period of depression, fatigue and headaches with or without a previous acute attack.	An IIAC report was issued in 1972 (Cmnd. 4971) and the terms of prescription were extended as from 3 October 1983. A policeman whose duties included attending auctions and visiting farms obtained benefit in R(I)6/69.
B8. Viral hepatitis. *An infection of the liver by a virus.*	Contact with:- (a) human blood or human blood products; or (b) a source of viral hepatitis infection. *e.g. medical and hospital workers, residential social workers, ancillary staff in schools.*	Tiredness, headaches, chills, loss of appetite and stomach pains followed after days or weeks by jaundice.	First listed in 1976 following an IIAC report in 1975 (Cmnd. 6257), the terms of prescription for this disease were extended as from 3 December 1984, following an IIAC report in 1984 (Cmnd. 9147). Close and frequent contact is no longer required nor need claims be confined to particular occupations connected with medicine or human blood products.
B9. Infection by streptococcus suis. *A very rare form of meningitis from exposure to infected pigs or pork products.*	Contact with pigs infected by streptococcus suis, or with the carcasses, products or residues of pigs so infected. *e.g. pork butchers, pig breeders, slaughter house workers.*	Fever and headaches.	Disease added as from 5 October 1983.

C. CONDITIONS DUE TO CHEMICAL AGENTS
(chemical cause)

C1. Poisoning by lead or a compound of lead.	The use of, or exposure to the fumes, dust or vapour of, lead or a compound of lead, or a substance containing lead. *e.g. plumbers, painters, enamellers, pottery glazing workers, demolition workers, smelters and car workers.*	*Rather varied. Most common are tiredness, pains in the head, muscles and joints, loss of appetite and weakness in the wrists and feet leading to paralysis. The appearance of a blue line round the teeth is now a rare symptom. Sudden high exposure may cause stomach pains, nausea, etc.*	*A painter failed in his claim in the medical decision R(I)40/54.*
C2. Poisoning by manganese or a compound of manganese.	The use or handling of, or exposure to the fumes, dust or vapour of, manganese, or a substance containing manganese. *e.g. dry battery, pottery glazing and soap workers.*	*Sleepiness, loss of facial expression, termors altered gait.*	
C3. Poisoning by phosphorus or an inorganic compound of phosphorus or poisoning due to the anti-cholinesterase or pseudo anti-cholinesterase action of organic phosphorus compounds.	The use or handling of, or exposure to the fumes, dust or vapour of, phosphorus, or a compound of phosphorus, or a substance containing phosphorus. *e.g. pest control, agricultural workers, workers on incendiary devices, match makers.*	*Inflammation and irritation of the gums affecting the jaw bone. From the gas, lung troubles, including bleeding. From insecticides, stomach trouble and fatigue followed by convulsions and paralysis.*	

Prescribed disease or injury	Type of occupation Any occupation involving	Symptoms	Notes
C4. Poisoning by arsenic or a compound of arsenic	The use or handling of, or exposure to the fumes, dust or vapour of, arsenic or a compound of arsenic, or a substance containing arsenic. *e.g. leather, agricultural and metal pickling workers.*	*From the gas, headaches, giddiness, pallor, stomach trouble followed by jaundice, sometimes red urine. From the dust, stomach trouble, inflammation of the skin, nose, throat and eyes, browning of the skin. Lung cancer is an accepted sequela.*	
C5. Poisoning by mercury or a compound of mercury.	The use or handling of, or exposure to the fumes, dust or vapour of, mercury or a compound of mercury, or a substance containing mercury. *e.g. mirror/thermometer makers, market gardeners in contact with seed dressings, explosives workers and paper makers.*	*Trouble with teeth and gums, tremors, anxiety and depression. Irritation of the skin and membranes leading to ulceration.*	
C6. Poisoning by carbon bisulphide.	The use or handling of, or exposure to the fumes or vapour of, carbon bisulphide or a compound of carbon bisulphide or a substance containing carbon bisulphide. *e.g. artificial silk and cellophane makers, rubber vulcanisers.*	*Jaundice, and trouble with the skin, stomach and bladder may occur.*	
C7. Poisoning by benzene or a homologue of benzene. *Benzol/benzole, toluene/toluol, xylene/xylol.*	The use or handling of, or exposure to the fumes of, or vapour containing, benzene or any of its homologues. *e.g. paint, dye, rubber goods and artificial leather workers.*	*Tiredness, pallor, muscular weakness, bleeding at the mouth and other mucous membranes. In women there may be menstrual disturbances.*	

C8. Poisoning by a nitro- or amino- or chloro-derivative of benzene or of a homologue or benzene, or poisoning by nitrochlor-benzene. *e.g. Tri-nitro-toluene (TNT).*	The use or handling of, or exposure to the fumes of, or vapour containing, a nitro- or amino- or chloro-derivative of benzene or of a homologue of benzene, or nitrochlor-benzene. *e.g. dyeing and chemical workers, solvents, disinfectants and wood preservative makers and users.*	*Stomach troubles and mental disturbance, tremors leading to partial paralysis. Heart attacks.*	*Not prescribed in relation to the claimant engaged in the distillation of beta naphthylaimine in CI. 195/50.*
C9. Poisoning by dinitrophenol or a homologue of dinitrophenol or by substituted dinitrophenols or by the salts of such substances. *Di-nitro-ortho-cresol (DNOC).*	The use or handling of, or exposure to the fumes of, or vapour containing, dinitrophenol or a homologue or substituted dinitrophenols or the salts of such substances. *e.g. dye and wood preservative makers and users, agricultural workers.*	*Stomach upsets. In severe cases, breathlessness, rapid pulse, fever, weight loss, occasional yellow staining of skin.*	
C10. Posioning by tetrachloroethane.	The use or handling of, or exposure to the fumes of, or vapour containing, tetrachloroethane. *e.g. photographic film, wax polish, adhesives, safety glass workers.*	*Headaches, stomach troubles, jaundice. Numbness and twitching of the hands and face, eventual paralysis of the hands and feet.*	
C11. Poisoning by diethylene dioxide (dioxan). *Not dioxin (2 4 5 T)*	The use or handling of, or exposure to the fumes of, or vapour containing, diethylene dioxide (dioxan). *e.g. polishing compounds, cosmetics and paint stripper makers.*	*Cold-like symptoms, followed by headaches, vertigo and stomach trouble.*	

Prescribed disease or injury	Type of occupation Any occupation involving	Symptoms	Notes
C12. Poisoining by methyl bromide.	The use or handling of, or exposure to the fumes of, or vapour containing, methyl bromide. *e.g. pest controllers, makers and users of fire extinguishers.*	*Smarting of the eyes and nausea followed by blurred vision and symptoms of drunkness. Skin burns and blisters. Later loss of memory and mood changes.*	
C13. Poisoning by chlorinated naphthalene.	The use or handling of, or exposure to the fumes of, or dust or vapour containing, chlorinated naphthalene. *e.g. synthetic wax and insulated wire makers.*	*Acne, jaundice.*	
C14. Poisoning by nickel carbonyl.	Exposure to nickel carbonyl gas. *e.g. oxyacetylene welders, nickel refinery workers.*	*Mild cases: dull persistent headaches, severe cases: giddiness and nausea, followed by breathlessness and coughing.*	
C15. Poisoning by oxides of nitrogen.	Exposure to oxides of nitrogen. *e.g. explosives and nitric acid workers.*	*Sudden severe exposure causes coughing followed after some hours by severe lung troubles resembling pneumonia, with the skin turning blue. The effects of gradual exposure are uncertain.*	*Determination of medical questions is made by a special medical board. In its 1981 report on the schedule (Cmnd. 8393) the IIAC agreed to investigate low grade exposure which, for example, may cause chronic lung damage without giving rise to an acute episode.*
C16. Poisoning by gonioma kamassi. (African boxwood).	The manipulation of gonioma kamassi or any process in or incidental to the manufacture of articles therefrom. *e.g. weaving shuttle makers.*	*Loss of mental and physical energy symptoms of asthma or hay fever.*	

C17. Poisoning by beryllium or a compound of beryllium.	The use or handling of, or exposure to the fumes, dust or vapour of, beryllium or a compound of beryllium, or a substance containing beryllium. *Beryllium (or glucinum) is found in the manufacture of: fluorescent lights, neon signs, metallic alloys, atomic energy, radio-valves, crucibles and electric porcelain.*	*Slowly progressive shortness of breath, irritating cough, weight loss. Sometimes lumps from particles penetrating the skin.*	*Determination of medical questions is made by a special medical board. For cases diagnosed see appendix A, Table 5.*
C18. Poisoning by cadmium.	Exposure to cadmium dust or fumes. *e.g. alkaline battery, jewellery and fluorescent light makers. Nuclear reactor workers. Electroplating and rustproofing workers.*	*Urinary problems, loss of sense of smell, yellow staining of teeth, occasionally breathlessness.*	*This disease was first prescribed following an IIAC report in 1956 (Cmd. 9674). Determination of medical questions is made by a special medical board. For cases newly diagnosed see appendix A, table 5.*
C19. Poisoning by acrylamide monomer.	The use or handling of, or exposure to, acrylamide monomer. *e.g. paper, adhesive, dye, artificial leather, photographic emulsion makers.*	*Weakness of the limbs, unsteadiness, slurred speech, numb finger tips. Fatigue. Red peeling skin on the hands.*	

Prescribed disease or injury	Type of occupation Any occupation involving	Symptoms	Notes
C20. Dystrophy of the cornea (including ulceration of the corneal surface) of the eye. *Wasting and ulceration of the corneal surface of the eye.*	(a) The use or handling of, or exposure to, arsenic, tar, pitch, bitumen, mineral oil (including paraffin), soot or any compound, product or residue of any of these substances except quinone or hydroquinone) or (b) exposure to quinone or hydroquinone during their manufacture. *e.g. photographic emulsion manufacture.*		
C21. (a) Localised new growth of the skin, papillomatous or keratotic; *Warts and scaliness.* (b) Squamous-celled carcinoma of the skin. *A form of skin cancer/chimney sweep's cancer.*	The use or handling of, or exposure to, arsenic, tar, pitch, bitumen, mineral oil (including paraffin), soot or any compound, product or residue of any of these substances except quinone or hydroquinone. *e.g. bituminous shale workers, optical lens makers, cotton mule spinners, workers exposed to tarry fumes.*	*Warts and ulcers which will not heal, often preceded by general inflammation of the skin (dermatitis). The genitals are often affected if they have been in contact with oils etc.*	*Para (b) was the earliest form of cancer to be prescribed, being first listed 1921.*
C22. (a) Carcinoma of the mucous membrane of the nose or associated air sinuses; *Cancer of the lining of the nose or air sinuses.* (b) Primary carcinoma of a bronchus or of a lung. *Cancer of the lung or bronchus.*	Work in a factory where nickel is produced by decomposition of a gaseous nickel compound which necessitates working in or about a building or buildings where that process or any other industrial process ancillary or incidental thereto is carried on.	*(a) Pain, obstruction of the nose, internal and external bleeding.* *(b) Coughing and hoarseness, followed by weight loss. Chest pain.*	*First prescribed in 1949 the disease was held not to be prescribed in relation to a claimant in R(I)5/57 who was involved on a nickel plating process for it did not involve the production of nickel. "Process" is considered in relation to C23 below. Determination of medical questions for (b) is made by a special medical board and for cases newly diagnosed see appendix A, table 5.*

C23. Primary neoplasm (including papilloma, carcinoma-in-situ and invasive carcinoma) of the epithelial lining of the urinary tract (renal pelvis, ureter, bladder and urethra). *Includes a form of cancer of the lining of the bladder or urinary tract.*	(a) Work in a building in which any of the following substances is produced for commercial purposes:– (i) alpha-naphthylamine or beta-naphthylamine or methylene-bis-orthochloroaniline; (ii) diphenyl substituted by at least one nitro or primary amino group or by at least one nitro and primary amino group (including benzidine); (iii) any of the substances mentioned in sub-paragraph (ii) above if further ring substituted by halogeno, methyl or methoxy groups, but not by other groups; (iv) the salts of any of the substances mentioned in sub-paragraphs (i) to (iii) above; (v) auramine or magenta; or	*Bleeding, with or without pain, in urinating.*	*First listed in 1953 the terms of prescription were extended as from 3 October 1983 following a report from the IIAC in 1983 (Cmnd. 8959). The use of the most notorious chemical, beta-naphthylamine, has been banned since 1967.*

In 1986 the IIAC reported on the links between lung cancer and other occupations (Cm. 37). It recommended that the prescription of lung cancer be extended in favour of tin miners, those exposed to the chronetes of certain chemicals and those exposed to BCME. The Government accepted these recommendations and intends to make the relevant regulations in 1987.

Paras. (a) and (b) were considered in R(I)2/77 where it was accepted that the use or liberation of even very small quantities of a relevant substance is sufficient. The claim failed under para. (a) because although the substance was contained in truck tyres which were being produced in the building, the substance was not being "produced for commercial purposes." But the claim succeeded under para. (b). Although the claimant did not handle the substance himself (he only handled a formula containing the substance), he did work in "a process in which . . . such substance is used" by others. "Process" was broadly defined so as to fit the whole business of producing truck tyres even though it could have been divided up into a

Prescribed disease or injury	Type of occupation Any occupation involving	Symptoms	Notes
	(b) the use or handing of any of the substances mentioned in sub-paragraph (a) (i) to (iv), or work in a process in which any such substance is used, handled or liberated; or (c) the maintenance or cleaning of any plant or machinery used in any such process as is mentioned in sub-paragraph (b), or the cleaning of clothing used in any such building as is mentioned in sub-paragraph (a) if such clothing is cleaned within the works of which the building forms a part or in a laundry maintained and used solely in connection with such works. *e.g. gas retort workers, workers in the synthetic dye, rubber, cable and chemical industries.*		*number of subsidiary processes. Thus the tyre builder worked in the "process" of producing tyres even though he had nothing to do with producing tyre treads where the relevant substance was used. "Magenta" was held not to include Durindone magenta in R(I)16/59.*
C24. (a) Angiosarcoma of the liver; *A form of liver cancer.* (b) Osteolysis of the terminal phalanges of the fingers; *A condition of the bones of the finger-tips.* (c) Non-cirrhotic portal fibrosis. *A form of liver damage.*	(a) Work in or about machinery or apparatus used for the polymerization of vinyl chloride monomer, a process which, for the purposes of this provision, comprises all operations up to and including the drying of the slurry produced by the polymerization and the packaging of the dried product; or	*For (a) & (c) there may be no symptoms in the early stages. Gradual onset of jaundice, enlarged liver or spleen and bleeding in the gullet. For (b) The end of the finger becomes limp and floppy. If it heals it will be shorter and clubbed. Whitening and numbness of the fingers is also very common.*	*First listed in 1977 following an IIAC report in 1976 (Cmnd. 6620) the terms of prescription were extended by the addition of para. (c) from 3 October 1983. "Process" is considered in relation to C23 above. In their 1981 report on the schedule the IIAC agreed to keep other effects of VCM exposure under review, giving particular attention to any evidence of lung function defects. The Council is presently conducting a broad review and has requested evidence in relation to other diseases including malignancies of the*

	(b) work in a building or structure in which any part of that process takes place. *e.g. PVC makers.*		*brain and central nervous system, Reynaud's phenomenon and osteolysis of bones other than fingers.*
C25. Occupational vitiligo. *White patches on the skin.*	The use or handling of, or exposure to, para-tertiary-butylphenol, para-tertiary-butylcatechol, para-amylphenol, hydroquinone or the monobenzyl or monobutyl ether of hydroquinone. *e.g. car, shoe and chemical workers.*		*Added as from 15 December 1980.*
D. MISCELLANEOUS CONDITIONS NOT INCLUDED ELSEWHERE IN THE LIST			
D1. Pneumoconiosis. *Includes silicosis and asbestosis.*			*See pp.120–131.*
D2. Byssinosis. *A respiratory condition.*	See p.123. Work in any room where any process up to and including the weaving process is performed in a factory in which the spinning or manipulation of raw or waste cotton or flax, or the weaving of cotton or flax, is carried on. *Cotton or flax workers.*	*No symptoms until well advanced, then various kinds of breathing difficulty. It tends to make the symptoms of other lung conditions worse. Coughing and breathlessness. Tightness in the chest, particularly on the first day at work after a holiday or weekend.*	*First prescribed in 1940, this disease has been the subject of reports by the IAAC in 1956 (Cmd. 9673), 1960 (Cmnd. 1095), 1965 (Cmnd. 2230) and 1973 (Cmnd. 5443). It also forms part of the investigation announced in November 1985 into chest diseases in textile workers. The Council is considering whether, following improvements in working conditions, it may now be appropriate to consider occupational lung disease in cotton and flax workers as a type of occupational asthma, disease D7.*

Prescribed disease or injury	Type of occupation	Symptoms	Notes

	Any occupation involving		*Of the 36,000 pensions current in 1983 for prescribed diseases byssinosis accounted for 3,000. Byssinosis is therefore the most important disease after pneumoconiosis and occupational deafness. However, a third of the pensions are in respect of disablement of 10 per cent or less and these might have been affected by the changes introduced by SSA 1986 which removed the right to payment for disablement assessed at less than 14 per cent. However, the Minister of Social Security stated that because it is a progressive disease, byssinosis will continue to be compensated at all levels. This is now the result of PD reg. 20(1) as substituted by SI 1986 No. 1561. For the calculation of payment see p.253. With the decline in the cotton industry relatively few new pensions are awarded. In 1984 only 56 new cases were diagnosed, although there were 412 initial examinations. However, there were 1,200 re-assessments that year. Almost all cases relate to cotton rather than flax (see appendix A, table 4).*
			
			   By Adj. reg. 32(2) determination of medical questions is made by a special medical board. The restriction which prevented an appeal to a MAT within two years of a previous one was lifted by SI 1986 No. 1374. By PD reg. 35 the period of assessment must be for at least a year.
			
			   With regard to causation it could not be shown that flax dust had caused the disease and contributed to the death in R9/84 (II).

"Room" according to R(I)26/58 means an interior portion of a building divided by walls or a partition. It does not include an area imperfectly separated from another.
"Process" is considered in relation to disease C23 above.
"Manipulation" was held to include flax scrutching in R(I)1/66 (II).

D3. Diffuse mesothelioma (primary neoplasm of the mesothelium of the pleura or of the pericardium or of the peritoneum). *A cancer starting in the covering of the lungs or the lining of the abdomen.*	(a) the working or handling of asbestos or any admixture of asbestos; or (b) the manufacture or repair of asbestos textiles or other articles containing or composed of asbestos; or (c) the cleaning of any machinery or plant used in any of the foregoing operations and of any chambers, fixtures and appliances for the collection of asbestos dust; or (d) substantial exposure to the dust arising from any of the foregoing operations.	*Shortness of breath, chest pains, pain and/or swelling in the stomach area.*

First listed in 1969 the terms of prescription were extended to include primary neoplasm of the pericardium as from 3 October 1983. There is a long latency period usually of between 20 and 50 years between first exposure to the dust and the appearance of the tumor. Determination of medical questions is made by a special medical board.

Concern has been expressed especially by the Society for the Prevention of Asbestosis and Industrial Diseases that special medical boards are failing to diagnose asbestos-related diseases. (Criticism of the work of boards in relation to pneumoconiosis is noted at p. 128.) A further problem, as the DHSS have admitted, is that in the past it has taken too long to process asbestos-related claims. The training of specialist officers at regional offices to deal with such claims is being considered. The Under-Secretary of State for Social Security wrote in reply to SPAID in 1985 that revised procedures are also being considered as a matter of urgency to ensure that such claims "are given priority at the outset both in the arrangements for medical adjudication

Prescribed disease or injury	Type of occupation Any occupation involving	Symptoms	Notes
			and in the confirmation of employment conditions. In addition, a much improved monitoring system is to be devised to monitor claims from the date they are first received". Although the SSA 1986 removed the right to disablement benefit for assessments below 14 per cent, this is one of three progressive diseases which continue to attract compensation at all levels of disablement. This is the result of PD reg. 20(1) as substituted by SI 1986 No. 1561. For the calculation of payment see p. 253. "Exposure to dust" is considered at p. 122.
D4. Inflammation or ulceration of the mucous membrane of the upper respiratory passages or mouth produced by dust, liquid or vapour. Inflammation of the nose, mouth and throat.	Exposure to dust, liquid or vapour.	*Any kind of inflammation or ulceration of the membranes. The "septum" which separates the nostrils is most commonly affected and may be perforated. Ulcers are not always painful, but may bleed.*	*The presumption created by PD reg. 4(1) that the disease is due to the nature of the employment does not apply to this disease, but in practice the disease does not usually pose problems in establishing a causal connection. "Exposure to dust" was considered in detail in R(I)1/85 where "dust" was defined as earth or other solid matter reduced to minute particles so as to be easily raised and carried in a cloud by the wind. It does not include all solid matter capable of becoming airborne, such as pollen. The degree of "exposure" is examined at p.122.*

Prescribed disease or injury	Type of occupation Any occupation involving	Symptoms	Notes
D5. Non-infective dermatitis of external origin (including chrome ulceration of the skin but excluding dermatitis due to ionising particles or electro-magnetic radiations other than radiant heat). *Skin rash, dermatitis.*	Exposure to dust, liquid or vapour or any other external agent capable of irritating the skin (including friction or heat but excluding ionising particles or electro-magnetic radiations other than radiant heat).		*This disease accounts for more short term absences from work than all the other prescribed diseases put together. Infective dermatitis is accepted as a resulting condition, or sequela, of non-infective dermatitis. The presumption created by PD reg. 4(1) that the disease is due to the nature of the employment does not apply here, but despite this the claim succeeded in R(I)10/53(T), CI.102/49, R(I)30/51, and R(I)17/53 but failed in R(I)87/53 and R(I)98/53.*
D6. Carcinoma of the nasal cavity or associated air sinuses (nasal carcinoma). *Cancer of the nose.*	(a) Attendance for work in or about a building where wooden goods are manufactured or repaired; or (b) attendance for work in a building used for the manufacture of footwear or components of footwear made wholly or partly of leather or fibre board; or (c) attendance for work at a place used wholly or mainly for the repair of footwear made wholly or partly of leather or fibre board.	*Pain, obstruction of the nose, internal and external bleeding.*	*Para. (a) was first listed in 1969 and its terms were extended in 1983. Paras. (b) and (c) were added in 1979.*

Prescribed disease or injury	Type of occupation Any occupation involving	Symptoms	Notes
D7. Asthma which is due to exposure to any of the following agents:- (a) isocyanates; *used in making e.g. plastic foam, synthetic inks, paints and adhesives.* (b) platinum salts; *affects e.g. laboratory and platinum refining workers.* (c) fumes or dusts arising from the manufacture, transport or use of hardening agents (including epoxy resin curing agents) based on phthalic anhydride, tetrachlorophthalic anhydride, trimellitic anhydride or triethylenetetramine; *used in a wide variety of industries e.g. adhesives, plastics, moulding resins and surface coatings.* (d) fumes arising from the use of resin as a soldering flux; *e.g. electronics industry.* (e) proteolytic enzymes; *used in the manufacture of "biological" washing powders, and in baking, fish, silk and leather industries.*	Exposure to any agents set out in column one of this paragraph.	*Wheezing, breathlessness, tightness of the chest, coughing. Attacks may be delayed for several hours after an exposure at work. There is a preliminary period of symptomless exposure, ranging from days to years, before symptoms of sensitisation appear. Once developed sensation may be permanent. Further attacks may occur not only in response to the sensitising agent but also to general irritants such as tobacco smoke or extremes of temperature.*	*First prescribed in 1982 this disease was the subject of reports by the IIAC in 1981 (Cmnd. 8121) and 1986 (Cmnd. 9717), each resulting in the listing of 7 sensitising agents. The Council keeps the disease under constant review, receiving periodic reports from its working group monitoring research. The conditions of entitlement are outlined in DHSS leaflet NI.237, and leaflet NI.238 provides clinical notes which examine the sensitising agents, aetiology and diagnosis of the disease. By PD reg. 48(1) a claim must be made within 10 years of the claimant last working in a listed occupation. Determination of medical questions is made by a special medical board.* *The agents (a) to (f) were listed from 29 March 1982 and agents (h) to (n) were added, and (f) revised, from 1 September 1986. Of the 538 cases which were newly diagnosed in the two and a half years 1983–85, the main agents according to the DHSS Chief Medical Officer were isocyanates (198 cases), dusts from flour and grain (145 cases) and soldering flux (89 cases). Exposure to sensitising agents other than those listed can amount to injury by accident.* *The IIAC report of 1986 refused to recommend that formaldehyde and rosin fumes, other than those arising in soldering, be listed as agents. However, it is keeping*

(f) Animals including insects and other arthropods used for the purposes of research or education in laboratories.

(g) dusts arising from the sowing, cultivation, harvesting, drying, handling, milling, transport or storage of barley, oats, rye, wheat or maize, or the handling, milling, transport or storage of meal or flour made therefrom.

(h) antibiotics;

(i) cimetidine;
used in making a drug for peptic ulcer treatment.

(j) wood dust;

(k) ispaghula;
an ingredient in laxatives.

(l) caster bean dust;
the beans are grown abroad but can affect e.g. merchant seamen, laboratory workers and felt makers.

(m) ipecacuanha;
used in preparing emetic tablets.

(n) azodicarbonamide;
used in the manufacture of expanded foam plastics for wall and floor covering and in packaging and insulation.

both under review. The Council also considered whether open prescription should be adopted, that is, the omission of all references to sensitising agents. On balance it rejected the idea for the present.

The claimant succeeded in showing that he had worked in a prescribed occupation in CI.270/80 (unreported). It was then for the AO to prove that the asthma was not due to the claimant being exposed to proteolytic enzymes in the tannery process.

Prescribed disease or injury	Type of occupation Any occupation involving	Symptoms	Notes
D8. Primary carcinoma of the lung where there is accompanying evidence of one or both of the following:– (a) asbestosis; (b) bilateral diffuse pleural thickening.	(a) The working or handling of asbestos or any admixture of asbestos; or (b) the manufacture or repair of asbestos textiles or other articles containing or composed of asbestos; or (c) the cleaning of any machinery or plant used in any of the foregoing operations and of any chambers, fixtures and appliances for the collection of asbestos dust; or (d) substantial exposure to the dust arising from any of the foregoing operations.	Shortness of breath, chest pain.	*Following an IIAC report in 1982 (Cmnd. 8750) this disease was added to the schedule as from April 1985. It is considered in DHSS booklet NI.226. Lung cancer was already an accepted sequela of asbestosis which is prescribed as disease D1. Mesothelioma was also prescribed for asbestos workers as disease D3. However, these diseases did not cover changes occurring in the pleura – the membrane covering the surface of the lung and anatomically separate from it. This was one of the reasons for the refusal of benefit by special medical boards who rejected up to two-thirds of claims in asbestosis cases. Claimants may now be able to bring their case under disease D8 or D9.* *At first the IIAC proposed to define a minimum level of pleural thickness as part of the terms of prescription. However, in its supplementary report in 1984 (Cmnd. 8750) it recommended that any thickening would suffice. The occupational exposure is the same as that defined for disease D3.*

| D9. Bilateral diffuse pleural thickening. | (a) The working or handling of asbestos or any admixture of asbestos; or
(b) the manufacture or repair of asbestos textiles or other articles containing or composed of asbestos; or
(c) the cleaning of any machinery or plant used in any of the foregoing operations and of any chambers, fixtures and appliances for the collection of asbestos dust; or
(d) substantial exposure to the dust arising from any of the foregoing operations. | *May cause breathlessness, or tightness and pain in the chest.*

See note on D8. |

INDEX